COLORADO MOUNTAIN COLLEGE S.V.
1 03 0001099752

W9-DHG-358

# The Hereditary Bondsman

# THE HEREDITARY BONDSMAN

## Daniel O'Connell

*1775–1829*

*Oliver MacDonagh*

ST. MARTIN'S PRESS
NEW YORK

*For Carmel, again*



First published in the United States of America in 1988

Printed in Great Britain

ISBN 0–312–01616–6

**Library of Congress Cataloging-in-Publication Data**

MacDonagh, Oliver
The hereditary bondsman : Daniel O'Connell, 1775–1829 / Oliver MacDonagh.
p. cm.
Bibliography: p.
Includes index.
ISBN 0–312–01616–6 : $3.00 (est.)
1. O'Connell, Daniel, 1775–1847. 2. Nationalists—Ireland–
–Biography. 3. Politicians—Ireland—Biography. 4. Ireland–
–Politics and government—19th century. I. Title.
DA950.22.M23 1988
941.5081'092'4—dc19
[B] 87–27770
CIP

# Contents

# Illustrations



All except number 10 are reproduced with the permission of the Commissioners of Public Works, Ireland. Number 10 is reproduced with the permission of Shannonside Tourist Office, Ennis, co. Clare.

# Preface

Belloc once suggested that a preface would be more properly entitled 'In praise of this book'. He lived in sturdy days. Now 'In defence of this book' would usually be more appropriate. I shall however attempt neither variation, but merely observe that I have tried to write a biography of O'Connell to 1829, which is also a study of the early formation of modern Irish culture and nationalism. My biography is not a 'life and times', or a 'portrait', or a psycho-history, and my study of cultural formation is implicit rather than specific. But these are not, I trust, things which, intrinsically, either secure merit or require excuse. The book ends at 1829 because this completes (as I see it) the first part of a sharply divided life. I intend however shortly to supplement it by another study of O'Connell, covering the years 1830–47.

References are provided for all direct quotations, and more general attributions may be found in the Bibliographical Note accompanying the Select Bibliography. Biographical Notes are also supplied to help the reader who seeks more information than the text itself has to offer.

For the rest, the only necessary preliminary is perhaps to indicate that my title derives from the couplet by Byron which O'Connell used more often in his speeches than any other lines:

> *Hereditary bondsmen! know ye not,*
> *Who would be free themselves must strike the blow?*

It would not have been possible to write a book like this at all without the publication from 1972 onwards of the magisterial new collection of the O'Connell correspondence edited by Professor M. R. O'Connell with the assistance of Mr Gerard J. Lyne. My debt to Professor O'Connell, however, far exceeds the opportunity to use this fundamental source. He made the letters not yet in print available to me in transcript or proof form; in addition I had, of course, his own important writings on O'Connell to draw on.

Secondly, I am much indebted to colleagues who read – and improved – drafts of chapters or part chapters. Drs Patricia Jalland, Iain McCalman and F. B. Smith and Professor K. S. Inglis of the Department of History in the Research School of Social Sciences at the Australian National University, and Dr Tom Dunne of University College, Cork, are my foremost, but far from my only, creditors on this account. Equally, I am most grateful to Mrs Pamela Crichton, and to Mrs Beverly Gallina and all the other members of the secretarial staff of the Department of History, Research School of Social Sciences, for going far beyond the calls of duty in preparing the typescript for press. The mere expression of gratitude, however warm, seems a very inadequate return for their labours and, still more important, their solicitude.

Most kindly, Mr B. MacDermot gave me access to the Scully papers in his possession, together with generous hospitality while I consulted them.

It gives me a special pleasure to be able to thank as well the Master and Fellows of my old College, St Catharine's, Cambridge, for electing me to a Fellow Commonership for the Michaelmas Term, 1986, which enabled me to complete the book.

Last, and most, and always, I thank my wife.

*December, 1986* O. MacD.

# Mise-en-Scène

Most of the old biographies of O'Connell began by depicting 'the O'Connell country'. This more or less coincided with the baronies of Iveragh and South Dunkerron (generally spoken of simply as 'Iveragh' by the O'Connells), the western portion of the main peninsula of Kerry, which runs south-west to the Atlantic from the Kenmare-Killorglin line. There was good reason for such an opening. Iveragh is matchless for its strange variety of weather, seascape, headland, bay, mountain, rock, torrent, lake and valley. O'Connell himself once struggled bravely to convey its 'awful beauty' through the swathes of contemporary prose. In 1838 he wrote to W. S. Landor,

> Would that I had you here . . . I could show you at noontide – when the stern south-wester had blown long and rudely – the mountain waves coming in from the illimitable ocean in majestic succession, expending their gigantic force, and throwing up stupendous masses of foam, against the more gigantic mountain cliffs that fence . . . my native spot . . . or, were you with me amidst the Alpine scenery that surrounds my humble abode, listening to the eternal roar of mountain torrent as it bounds through rocky defiles, I would venture to tell you how I was born within the sound of the everlasting waves . . .
>
> Perhaps, if I could show you the calm and exquisite beauty of these capacious bays and mountain promontories, softened in the pale moonlight which shines this lovely evening, when all which during the day was grand and terrific has become calm and serene in the silent tranquillity of the night – perhaps you would admit that the man who has been so often called a ferocious demagogue, is, in truth, a gentle lover of Nature . . .[1]

It was standard form to present Iveragh as symbolic of O'Connell himself. The storms and calms, thunder and quiet, steep falls and level sands of south-west Kerry were taken to epitomize not only his popular oratory but also the range and changeability of his disposition. Even for his oratory, the symbolism was not especially apt. The equally hackneyed metaphor of O'Connell playing on an audience as on an instrument was closer to the truth. At least, it

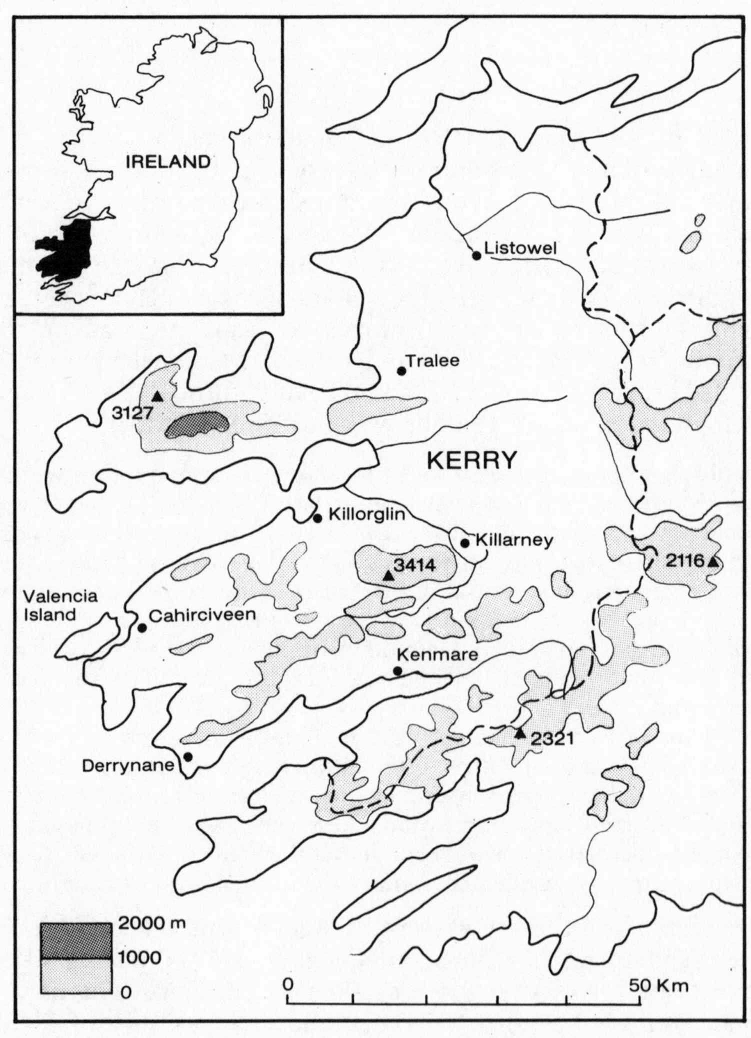


Map 1. County Kerry

allowed for the orator selecting his own pitch and for the interaction between demagogue and crowd. But to categorize O'Connell as volatile, or swinging between extremes of mood and conduct – and the image of Iveragh was meant to convey just this – was quite misleading. He was an extraordinarily resilient being, but steadfast in his resilience; and his life was singularly purposive and patterned.

None the less Iveragh stamped O'Connell deeply. As he played upon his audience, so it played upon him. This is not to imply that he was an *extraordinarily* impressionable person. Quite an ordinary share of sensitivity was enough. For Iveragh is one of the more memorable settings of the world. Apart from the dreamlike succession of dramatic terrain and ocean vista, it is hauntingly beautiful in light and sound. Cloud, massive, shredded or scattered puffball; skies, low and leaden, washed blue, patching cobalt or milky pale; land, grey, green, dun and chocolate, broken by heather and yellow furze – the shades deepening and lightening almost momentarily – paint the mind. Seas breaking riotously or metronomically, streams in tumult or steady glide, rain stealthy or imperative, and wind and the calls of gulls or solitary curlews provide accompaniment. O'Connell was deeply responsive to this incomparable physical, chromatic and aural whole. His vacations in Iveragh, after he grew to manhood, were literally recreative: they restored his harmony. It was not merely a matter of being in tune again with an extraordinary environment, or of the revivification of a sense of ownership of such natural beauty, but also a sort of ratification of his own identity.

O'Connell himself specifically explained his life of political agitation as a response to his native countryside: 'the loveliness as well as the dreariness of the ocean and Alpine scenes' engendered in him, he claimed, 'a greater ardour to promote the good of man, in his overwhelming admiration of the mighty works of God.'[2] This was far-fetched, even if some wandering connexion between feelings of reverence and feelings of altruism may seem plausible enough.

But there was nothing vague or shallow about O'Connell's rooting himself, psychologically, in Iveragh. In all senses it provided the ground for his absolute assurance about his own identity. The point is important. The romantic type of nationalism which was to challenge O'Connell's formulation – that stemming from the Young Ireland movement of the 1840s – centred upon the question, 'Who am I?' For O'Connell this was never a question; if it were, the answer would have been quite self-evident. Being Irish was merely being himself; and totally assured and at ease in his national identity, he could extend this identity large-heartedly to all the inhabitants of his island. Various elements went into the making of such poise. But first and perhaps even foremost was his sense of fitting into his own land and in particular into his own wild square of Kerry.

O'Connell's intense sense of location was more than topographical. The O'Connells had been a minor but persistent force in their part of Kerry for at least two centuries. As wardens for the MacCarthy Mórs they had enjoyed the hereditary custodianship of a castle. Even after the Cromwellian and Williamite débâcles, they – rarely among Catholic proprietors – retained possession of some land. Aptly enough in the light of O'Connell's career to come, the law's quirks had favoured them in this. They also maintained a profitable French connexion, a trade in priests and soldiers as well as brandy, silks and other luxurious contraband, throughout the eighteenth century. All of this, all their capacity to survive and even to advance as small gentry, depended more or less upon their geography. No part of Ireland was less accessible or freer of state surveillance than mountainous, roadless Iveragh. No strip of coast was more contorted or indented, richer in small coves and beaches, safer from customs and naval vigilance than the run from Kenmare to Carragh (now Waterville). No peninsula in the land was better placed for a traffic with Brittany.

The O'Connells had never been pressed down into mere peasantry because they had recognized and exploited the natural advantages of their environment. 'We have peace in these glens,' said O'Connell's uncle, Maurice (generally known as Hunting Cap), to an antiquarian, Charles Smyth, seeking information on Kerry in 1753, 'and amid their seclusion enjoy a respite from persecution: we can still in these solitudes profess the beloved faith of our fathers . . . but if you make mention of me or mine, these seaside solitudes will no longer yield us an asylum. The *Sassenagh* will scale the mountains of Darrynane, and we too shall be driven out upon the world without house or home.'[3] Isolation was not, however, in itself enough to guarantee security. Even the poor-lands of West Kerry attracted a scatter of planters in the Cromwellian settlement; and this petty Ascendancy was gradually reinforced by conforming Catholics. The eighteenth-century O'Connells (epitomized by Hunting Cap) accommodated themselves effectively to the superior caste. As thoroughly organized and business-like smugglers, they supplied the local Anglican gentry regularly with contraband. This rendered them extremely useful. It even purchased them practical immunity from the law. Moreover, Kerry was too wild and broken a terrain to be easily amenable to anglicization. Something of the old clan system survived, and families like the O'Connells retained considerable power over their immediate followers and dependants. Thus they could participate, even if only upon a Lilliputian scale, in a form of 'indirect rule' which was extremely helpful to the authorities. The order and quiescence which they could instil in their own territory was a tacit *quid pro quo* for their freedom from religious persecution. Finally, both the paucity of the Kerry upper class and their intermarriages led to a strong sense of local solidarity which, to some extent, transcended even the religious boundaries. Prudential conversions to the established church helped to blur the distinction. They could also help more directly. A conforming cousin of Hunting Cap's, Hugh Falvey, saved some of the O'Connell property on several occasions by fictitious or collusive legal actions.

Of course, good relations with the immediate controllers of their destinies had to be paid for by a subservient mien and some political pandering. Maurice O'Connell's reply to the antiquarian Smyth reveals the characteristic Catholic cringe, the characteristic shrinking from the master's eye, of the penal era. To some extent, this was deceptive. As with the speeches of Thady Quirk, the 'faithful steward' in Edgeworth's *Castle Rackrent*, sly self-parody and a not-entirely-concealed resentment may be read into Hunting Cap's words. Irony has always been a defence of the colonized. Certainly, Hunting Cap would never countenance opposition to the Irish Administration. Certainly, he would curry favour with Dublin Castle when he could. But there is abundant evidence of his hidden anger at the systematic abasement of Irish Catholics. He was fully sensitive to the contempt and injustice of the Ascendancy. It was not to Irish Protestants that he looked for relief from his legal disabilities but to British cabinets. He was unquestionably a loyalist but it was to the British, rather than to the Irish, Crown that he was loyal.

Yet covert hostility was only one facet of a complex attitude to the Ascendancy; and down to the 1780s at least, it was of small practical importance. Normally, the Catholic well-to-do of the peninsula lived in a tolerably comfortable little system of limited mutual support, civil relations and cross-favours with their Protestant counterparts. Sectarian suspicion and dislike, and the vaunting of superiority or resentment of inferiority, were generally subordinated to the business of ordinary living. It is important to remember that the locale which produced this special type of relationship cradled O'Connell no less than his uncle, Hunting Cap. O'Connell was reared in much the same

Iveragh as Maurice – but not quite the same, for their boyhoods were separated by almost fifty years, and this made a certain difference. All the traditional elements of the Kerry Catholic's bearing towards the privileged are to be found in O'Connell, too. But their relative weight and emphasis had changed significantly over the half century.

The O'Connells were, then, decidedly favoured by their location at the end of a poor and remote peninsula. The comparative strength, numbers and wealth of better-off Catholics in Iveragh derived largely from the isolation and lack of 'development' of the region. No family did better out of these conditions than the O'Connells. Their survival and even slow advance, economically and socially, after 1700 is testimony of their extraordinary capacity to turn their geographical advantages to good account. The same forces tended to produce in them a curious historical cast of mind. On the one hand, the very fact of survival in their ancient territories engendered a sense of continuity, even of immemorial possession. This naturally reinforced the feeling that they were in their proper or ordained situation in the world. On the other hand, their furtive and precarious hold upon their hereditary lands gave them a degenerative view of history. Inevitably they looked back resentfully to the supposed golden era in which they had been masters in their own place. Moreover, the tenacious O'Connells could remember that they had lost one branch, expelled across the Shannon to co. Clare, and that their collateral, Maurice O'Connell of Caher-barnagh, had died on the roadside on his journey northwards. But the sense of continuity, which stretched back in family annals at least to the Hugh O'Connell commissioned by Edward III in 1337 to reduce his neighbourhood to order, and the sense of discontinuity, located in the cataclysms of 1649 and 1691, could join hands. Each induced the bitterest resentment of the fallen state of the native aristocracy. When at the Clare election of 1828 the tory candidate, Vesey Fitzgerald, spoke *de haut en bas*, though kindly, about his opponent, O'Connell rounded upon him fiercely with 'this man, in my native land – the land of my ancestors – where my forefathers were for centuries the Chieftains of the land, and the friends of her people, makes it a species of kindness that he honours me with his patronage. I treat with disdain and contempt the condescension of such patronage.'[4] This epitomized the O'Connell image of the past. The ferocity sprang from a consciousness of degradation in one's native spot.

*CHAPTER 1*

# Growing Up

## *1775–93*

### I

To specify place and time, Daniel O'Connell was born in a cottage close to Carhen, near Cahirciveen, on 6 August 1775. Carhen was a farmhouse, moderate in size and abutted by small farm buildings. But its location, on the banks of an estuary, and facing low mountains upon the opposite shore, was open, spacious and dramatic. Carhen and the surrounding land was one of several pieces of O'Connell property which the family was able to retain by virtue of leases pre-dating 1691; and as such, it had passed to Morgan, Daniel's father, one of the older of the twenty-two children of Donal Mór and Máire Duibh O'Connell. Morgan, like his eldest brother, Hunting Cap, combined the occupations of grazier, merchant and smuggler. But his operations were on a much smaller scale, and indeed he often acted as Hunting Cap's agent or junior partner. Nor did he acquire extensive new land or set up in manufactures, such as tanning or salt-making, after Hunting Cap's fashion. Like Hunting Cap, he married into a Catholic family, of similar rank, fate and fortune to his own. His wife, Catherine O'Mullane, belonged to a small landowning family in north-west Cork. But whereas Hunting Cap was childless, Morgan and Catherine had ten children; and Daniel was the first of the long line, as well as the eldest boy, of the next generation of O'Connells. This conjunction was to be crucial in O'Connell's career.

Partly because it was customary in Gaelic society but perhaps also because of the pressure upon space in a modest middle-class home where servants and followers were numerous and children arrived with almost annual regularity, O'Connell was fostered-out in infancy and did not return to Carhen until he was four years old. His surrogate mother was the wife of a herdsman on Morgan's own land. The home of his infancy was meagre, an ill-ventilated mud cabin; his earliest experience that of a poor country child; his only tongue the Irish language. The herdsman and his wife were, in his eyes, his parents. When, on a visit to Carhen, his father asked him (in Irish, of course) if he had ever eaten mutton before, O'Connell answered, 'Yes . . . My Dad brought in one of Morgan O'Connell's sheep and killed it.'[1] Yet there is no suggestion that such an early childhood had the traumatic consequences which the present century would predict. O'Connell became deeply attached to his true mother and father. The bond with his foster-parents – to be rewarded, according to the conventions of the day, by subsequent favours and support – remained strong; but this implied no division of loyalty or psychological confusion. So far from resenting his own early exile, O'Connell subjected his two eldest sons, Maurice and Morgan, and some at least of his younger children, to the same experience. It was after all the social norm, from which no one anticipated – and perhaps therefore everyone escaped – injurious results. Nor were such familial devices confined to remote Irish peninsulas or the 1770s or 1800s. Readers of Trollope's *Dr Thorne* will recall that in that most English of counties, Barsetshire, Frank Gresham was fostered out to Mrs Scatchard, and in effect 'bonded' to her, in the 1830s.

It scarcely needs saying that fostering-out in the form and for the length of time that O'Connell experienced gave him a profound knowledge of Irish peasant attitudes, needs, aspirations and forms of thought. It was a later commonplace that he could enter into and play masterfully upon the minds of ordinary Irish people, and especially country people. The social system in which he grew up in Iveragh, and the shared experience of inferiority of all the Catholic classes, would have promoted such powers of divination in any case. But to first realize the world in a herdsman's dwelling, and to see it through the eyes of the herdsman and his family, laid bare the secret life of even the very poor. It was, in many ways, the perfect opening lesson for a demagogue.

When O'Connell returned to Carhen, and still more when he later removed to his uncle's home at Derrynane, he left, to some degree, the Gaelic world. Both Hunting Cap and Morgan had dropped the patronymic 'O'. They called themselves 'Connell'. This was a standard mid-eighteenth-century precaution against easy identification as Catholics. But it was of course only in English that the name was, or ever could be, changed. As the alteration indicates, the male O'Connells had become bi-cultural. Irish was their working language with servants, labourers and tenants. But among themselves they spoke, and wrote, in English only. The contrast with their parents and in particular with their mother, Máire Duibh, was striking. Throughout Kerry she was celebrated as a Gaelic poet and rhetorician; she never moved from the old ways of life. The sea-change between her and her children's generation was beautifully epitomized by a scene at the death-bed of one of her many sons. She was outraged when her daughter-in-law knelt down to pray in silence by the bedside. Instantly, she broke into a torrent of poetic lamentation in Irish. The women all about took up the funeral keening, in counterpoint, as she extemporized with magnificant abandon.

The process of de-Gaelicization was far from complete in Hunting Cap's generation. He himself exercised the traditional sway over his tenants and followers, even to the romantic detail of a crooked-handled knife, *sgian na coise cuime*, as the symbol of his authortity. When, in 1782, contraband was captured at Derrynane,

> Hunting Cap knew the peasants were furious at the capture, and dreaded mischief, so he besought the officer to let him send with him one of his nephews (the O'Sullivans of Couliagh), as otherwise he could not answer for the people. In Captain Butler's presence he handed the crooked knife to his nephew, bidding him escort the officer to the river-bank at Waterville.
>
> Thus singularly guarded, the representative of law and order set out. In passing through the hamlet of Cahirdaniel they noticed lowering looks and hostile gestures, but a sight of the crooked knife caused the peasants to make way. Some distance beyond the village, Captain Butler begged young O'Sullivan to go back, and struck across the high mountain for his home . . . a mob of angry peasants had skirted the other brow from Cahirdaniel. They fell on the officer, routed his men, and beat him to within an inch of his life.[2]

This glimpse of the ancient Celtic world of spells and tribal fealty is matched by Morgan O'Connell's struggles with the Crelaghs, a band of local cattle thieves. They raided his herds; he and his followers assailed them in the mountains; they in turn attacked and almost killed him in revenge. It could have been a story from the Red Branch cycle before the embellishments of folklore.

Moreover, several of the women of Hunting Cap's generation remained totally unanglicized. As late as 1795, his sister Alice mourned her husband in an outburst of Irish poetry as passionate yet formalized as that of Máire Duibh herself. Indeed the greatest of all such laments in Irish literature was composed by another of Hunting Cap's sisters, Eileen O'Leary, in 1773. Five years before, Hunting Cap had greeted the news of her elopement with the wild Art O'Leary, who was soon to be outlawed and shot, with: 'I am sorry to Learn that our

Sister Nelly has taken a step contrary to the Will of her Parents, but Love will not know or hear reason.'[3] As Gerard Murphy describes the sequel,

> That document [Hunting Cap's letter] is preserved, for it belongs to the Anglo-Irish side of O'Connell tradition. Nelly's own Gaelic version of the incident would have been lost, however, to history, were it not for the retentive memory of Irish-speaking farmers and cottiers in Cork and Kerry. *Mo ghrá go daingean tu*, she said, as in May 1773, some five years after the elopement, she stood beside her outlawed husband's bloodstained corpse,
>
> *Mo ghrá go daingean tu!*
> *Lá dá bhfeaca thu,*
> *Ag ceann tí 'n mharagaidh,*
> *Thug mo shúil aire dhoit,*
> *Thug mo chroí taitneamh doit,*
> *D'éaluíos om anthir leat,*
> *I bhfad ó bhaile leat:*
> *Is dom nárbh atuirseach!**
>
> Already in reading those opening lines do we not feel ourselves transported into a different world? – a world in which Nelly is no longer Anglo-Irish Nelly, but Gaelic Eibhlín Dubh, and in which her husband is no longer 'poor Arthur Leary', whose 'violence and ungovernable temper' were disapproved of by his brother-in-law, but Art, son of Conchúr, son of Céatach, son of Luíseach Ó Laoghaire . . . and terror of the Sasanaigh who killed him . . .[4]

O'Connell grew up, then, in a sort of double dualism. Carhen and Derrynane were islands in a still largely Gaelic sea; and for the most part his elders were either bound by practical necessity or committed instinctively to the traditional culture. This had, however, remarkably little effect upon himself. On 7 December 1796 he wrote in his private journal apropos the *Ossian* controversy, which had happened to engage his attention then, 'the names of Ossian's heroes were familiar to my infancy, and long before I had heard of Macpherson or his translation the characters of the poem[s] were mostly known to me.'[5] It was equally characteristic of O'Connell, first, that he should have known the Ossianic legends from his childhood, secondly, that he should have taken them for granted as one might do nursery rhymes, and thirdly that he should have been led to notice them again only through a British literary dispute. O'Connell was ever at ease with, not

* You are my beloved for ever! One day that I saw you, At the market-house gable, My eye perceived you, My heart loved you, I eloped from my father with you, Far from home with you: I never repented it.

to say casual about, his Gaelic heritage. He entered smoothly into not only the language but also the thought-forms and private codes of the Iveragh peasantry whenever he was 'home' in later life. But in the larger matters it was Hunting Cap whom he followed, and not his aunts. In fact, O'Connell represented the next stage on in Gaelic disintegration. He needed to employ Irish less than his father or uncles. The old order was weakening in Kerry, even in his adolescence; and his adult life was to be spent in work and places where English was universal. He was, moreover, a deliberate utilitarian about the native language, where Hunting Cap was simply bent upon the common courses of self-security and advancement. When asked in 1833 whether the use of Irish 'was diminishing among our peasantry', O'Connell answered,

> Yes, and I am sufficiently utilitarian not to regret its gradual abandonment. A diversity of tongues is no benefit; it was first imposed on mankind as a curse, at the building of Babel. It would be of vast advantage to mankind if all the inhabitants of the earth spoke the same language. Therefore, although the Irish language is connected with many recollections that twine around the hearts of Irishmen, yet the superior utility of the English tongue, as the medium of all modern communication, is so great, that I can witness without a sigh the gradual disuse of Irish.[6]

Perhaps this credo is not in itself decisive on O'Connell's attitude to Irish. It was, after all, but a single conversational response. But it certainly matched his general approach in manhood. He did speak in Irish occasionally from the platform, though reports of such speeches are few and far between. But even these excursions were 'sufficiently utilitarian'. He spoke in Irish only where he had to do so in order to be understood. The rarity of such performances in a period when there were still extensive monolingual Irish-speaking regions in itself indicates that the prime sources of his support lay elsewhere. Nor did O'Connell ever show interest in the preservation or revival of the Gaelic language or culture, although enthusiasts, both singly and collectively, were already beginning to promote these causes. The work of Peter O'Connell of Clare on an Irish-English dictionary was shown to O'Connell by Peter's nephew in 1824 'expecting that he would call public attention to it'; O'Connell who (according to Eugene O'Curry) 'had no taste for matters of this kind . . . suddenly dismissed his namesake, telling him that his uncle was an old fool to have spent so much of his life on so useless a work.'[7]

This is not to say that O'Connell had no romantic attachments to the past. But his Golden Age lay not in Ossianic Ireland, or in the pre-

Norman or pre-Tudor Gaelic world, but in the early Christian era, and in particular in the sixth and seventh centuries A.D. It was the Island of Saints and Scholars which inflamed his imagination – according to his own account – from very early days: 'my dreamy boyhood dwelt upon imaginary intercourse with those who are dead of yore, and fed its fond fancies upon the ancient and long-faded glories of that land which preserved literature and Christianity when the rest of now civilized Europe was shrouded in the darkness of godless ignorance.'[8] In 1827 he spoke of pre-invasion Ireland as 'a nation famous for its love of learning, its piety, its heroism',[9] and two years later told Bishop James Doyle, 'Ireland seems to me to be the most proper nursery for missionary priests . . . in my day-dreams I revise the brighter period of Irish history when Erin was the hotbed of saints and Science.'[10] All this was a far cry from the Golden Ages of the Irish Revival movements of later in the nineteenth century, which glorified either the pagan Celts or the traditional peasant culture. O'Connell's vision was in fact outward-looking or even imperialistic, at least in the spiritual sense. It was Irish domination, in terms of monasteries and bishoprics, from Lindisfarne to Malmsbury, from Ghent to Angoulême, as far east as Mecklenburg and Vienna and as far south as Lucca and Taranto, which fired his imagination. It was an empire of high and formal, instead of popular and mythic, learning, and positively Christian, not to say positively Catholic, in purpose.

How are we to explain O'Connell's virtual abandonment of his Gaelic 'birthright'? The basic reason for the decline of Irish and the advance of the English language – the two processes are effectively if not necessarily linked – was the desire to survive in the modern world, or better still to improve one's lot. This is why the proportion of monolingual Gaelic speakers in the Irish population declined from 50 per cent to 0.5 per cent in the course of the nineteenth century. It is also why the Catholic *avant garde*, the gentry, merchants and professional men of whom the O'Connells were archetypal, had led the way in this cultural surrender. In mid- and late-eighteenth-century Ireland, social advancement, and even the emergence from a helot condition, depended largely upon the acquisition and use of English. This was generally the case, but it applied with special force to the upper Catholic classes. Not only had they to traffic constantly in the Anglo-Irish polity, but also their striving for some measure of social parity with the local squirarchy and other elites impelled them to enter, if they could, the Anglo-Irish culture. Class instinct reinforced the instinct for survival. For English was, practically speaking, the sole language of administration, law, politics, commerce, money-making and the towns. It was also, almost universally, the language of literacy and letters.

By 1750 the old connexion between Gaelic culture and the aristocratic way of life had been completely broken. The sophisticated court poet had given way to the peasant poet, and the development of Gaelic as a literary language or as a medium of learning had long since been arrested. Side by side with this interchange and petering out, the Irish language had come to be associated more and more with ignorance, indigence, struggle and distress. Hunting Cap and his brothers were merely anticipating by sixty or seventy years, and at a much higher social level, the nineteenth-century drive of the Catholic masses to rid their children of the language of poverty and subordination and replace it by one more materially advantageous.

It may be significant that in O'Connell's family it was women who preserved the Gaelic tradition longest. At least, there are striking instances of its survival among them for a generation after it had been rejected by the men, who had to deal first and most with the greater world. The women still lived largely in their domestic circles; and they had little or no social intercourse with Protestants. In O'Connell's generation, however, even these vestigial remains of Gaelicism seem to have disappeared. His own sisters appear to have been thoroughly anglicized. Nor is there anything to indicate that his wife, Mary, was even capable of speaking Irish. She lived all her life before marriage in a middle-sized town, Tralee, and though the chances may have been against it, a child could certainly have grown up monolingually English-speaking in such a place in the last two decades of the eighteenth century.

Very broadly, then, O'Connell may be said to have belonged to the third anglicized generation upon the male side and to the second such generation upon the female. Yet, equally important, the process of de-Gaelicization was not complete in him: indeed the first language learnt by his two eldest sons was still Irish. He had no doubts – whatever about sentimental regrets – that Irish would and should disappear as a working language. From boyhood his ambitions were projected into political and professional arenas where it could scarcely have a place. On the other hand, he had been thoroughly immersed in infancy in Gaelic milieux. In certain senses, and to a considerable degree, we might even speak of him as their product. It was not merely a matter of spoken language, of folkloric inheritance and of the web of customary life – important though all three were – but also of idiosyncratic thought patterns and modes of understanding and communication. Yeats once described William Carleton as 'the great novelist of Ireland by right of the most Celtic eyes that ever gazed from under the brow of a storyteller'. How much more truly could the equivalent be said of O'Connell in terms of public affairs. No other Irish politician of the first rank stands on a par with him in intuitive sympathy with the native heart and mind; nor can any match him in being totally and unselfconsciously bi-cultural. Even de Valera's self-vaunted insight into 'the aspirations of the Irish people' was often at odds with more than half of the Irish population, while his Gaelicism could never be more than a conscientious artefact. This is not of course to claim any inherent personal superiority for O'Connell. It was the chances of time and place which rendered him, in the fullest sense, a man of two worlds, moving effortlessly about both Gaelic and post-Gaelic Ireland. But it was of crucial importance that this should have been the case. It gave him ease and security in his Irishness, and presented him with a key to mastery of the masses.

## II

While still very young – in which year we do not know but possibly as early as 1780 – O'Connell was, in effect, adopted by his uncle, Hunting Cap. Derrynane Abbey then became his home. It was a real break with Carhen. Although Derrynane was scarcely a dozen miles away according to a straight line drawn upon the map, the journey was very difficult across rugged and mountainous terrain.

Derrynane lay, like Carhen, upon the shore of an estuary. But its water prospect was much grander, its opposing mountains much more distant and its inland surroundings much more enclosed. As if to escape attention, not merely was it hidden by high trees and a steep rise of ground upon the landward side but it also 'resolutely turned its back on sea and sunshine, and looked into a walled courtyard'.[11] The air of secretiveness and even gloom which encompassed Derrynane was apt, for the building had been begun by O'Connell's grandfather in the nadir of Irish Catholic fortunes, the 1720s. But this was accompanied by an air of substance and solidity. Derrynane was not a Big House, after the usual eighteenth-century fashion; it was much too small and undesigned for that. None the less it was remarkable in its own neighbourhood as easily the largest and best finished residence, far superior in scale and pretension to such a farmhouse as Carhen. Moreover, no inwardness of aspect or agglomerative ugliness could substract from the magnificence of the southern vista, embracing verdant strip, bone-clean sands, the ruined monastery of the Canons Regular on a spit, a lacework of tiny coves, bays and promontories, the great sweep of the Kenmare river and the wall of the Slieve Miskish mountains far away. This was to be the main home of O'Connell's boyhood. He had passed rapidly from the lowest to the highest level of Kerry Catholic society, with only a brief interval at Carhen.

When O'Connell moved to Derrynane, Hunting Cap was a childless widower in his early fifties and already a landed and commercial magnate, in a modest way. He was also strongly patriarchal and dynastical in temperament, as well as something of a clan chieftain in the old sense. As eldest son himself, he accepted unquestioningly responsibility for the younger members of his family, and not least for the increasingly numerous children of his brother Morgan. He was probably urged in the same direction by another of his brothers, Daniel, then a colonel in the French Army, who was particularly solicitous for the future of his nephews. All this helps to explain Hunting Cap's evident intention that Morgan's eldest son, Daniel, should be his successor. We do not know the exact terms on which he received the boy into his house. But there seems to have been at least a tacit understanding that O'Connell was Hunting Cap's heir-presumptive – the presumption being, in this case, that he would prove himself grave, prudent, industrious and ambitious enough to be worthy of such a destiny. At any rate, it is clear that O'Connell spent his boyhood proper in his uncle's house and under the shadow of great expectations.

The 'adoption' placed an immense burden upon the boy, even if it also spread great possibilities before him. He was, permanently, on trial; he was totally dependent on a patron; his own easy-going father had been replaced by a hard and implacable foster-parent. He grew up in fear and awe; and the spell of Hunting Cap upon him was not altogether broken for over forty years. Hunting Cap was always dominant and often domineering. But it would be wrong to cast him as a tyrant, still less as an ogre, however much this might be suggested by the subservience and even servility which he commanded. For Hunting Cap's authority was innate, as much the product of strength and depth of character as the consequence of wealth and station. In 1794, his brother Daniel (by now forty-nine years old, a count of France and in rank a major-general) whom he had given, out of simple generosity, 300 guineas in the preceding year, wrote to him in these very deferential terms:

> I shall not attempt justifying my having spent so large a sum as 150 guineas in the course of one year, but merely by stating that the accomplishing the object I had in view required I should live in the best company and make a decent, tho' modest, appearance. On that line I have walked those twelve months, and trust you will approve of it. Sincerity, that the greatest comfort of my life will always be to merit your approbation. The part you have ever acted towards me being that of a kind Parent, I consider myself as much bound from duty as I am led from inclination to lay my heart and actions before you on every occasion.[12]

This should place what might seem the nervous obsequiousness of O'Connell's later dealings with Hunting Cap in fair perspective. It also reveals the paradoxical willingness of one who was rightly notorious as a tight-fisted – in fact, positively grasping – accumulator, to part with money. We should never forget that, however sourly, Hunting Cap eventually did meet every account during the long years of O'Connell's education. This expenditure alone cost him well over £1,000.

Hunting Cap determined that O'Connell's education should begin early, and he apparently arranged for him to be tutored locally. According to his own account, O'Connell proved to be both precocious and competitive. At the age of four (he told W. J. O'Neill Daunt much later), 'I learned the alphabet in an hour. I was, in childhood, remarkably quick and persevering. My childish propensity to idleness was overcome by the fear of disgrace: I desired to excel, and could not brook the idea of being inferior to others.'[13] Three stories of his early boyhood are suggestive. Two relate to 1784, when he was nine years old. First, at a dinner-table discussion of current Irish politics Charlemont was generally denounced and Flood generally lauded, but the company was hotly divided on Grattan's recent conduct. O'Connell, naturally silent among the contesting adults, seemed also quite abstracted; but when one of the women asked him suddenly, 'What ails you, Dan? – what are you thinking of?' 'I'll make a stir in the world yet', he answered. Secondly, it was in 1784 that he was given what became the favourite book of his boyhood, Cook's *Voyages*. Much later he recalled the hours spent half-hidden in one of the recessed window seats which flanked the main door of Derrynane, poring over the *Voyages* and tracing their successive references with his finger on the map. 'I used to run away and take my book to the window, . . . there I used to sit with my legs crossed, tailor-like, devouring the adventures of Cook.'[14] He had chosen his reading-place to escape the other children and their calls to play. The third – undated

– glimpse of the small boy at Derrynane reports his fascination with the *Dublin Magazine*'s portraits of contemporary celebrities, most of them the leading Irish politicians of the time. One day, O'Connell told his elders, his picture would appear in the illustrious succession. As it happened, he was right: the *Magazine* published his portrait in 1810.

One can build little upon a handful of random recollections. But, for what it is worth, they indicate solitary, autodidactic and escapist strains scarcely discernible in the later O'Connell. They also hint at elements much more familiar in the customary accounts: ambition, the passion for mastery and the prizing of political, and in particular parliamentary, achievement. For this last trait, the early 1780s were extraordinarily exciting. Ireland was in an unprecedented ferment, and this was popularly presented in a simplistic form, in which an imaginative boy could readily participate. The cult of personality and the romanticization of issues had been unleashed. It was an epoch of apparent heroes and villains in Irish politics, and of apparently noble causes and ignoble resistance to national reform. O'Connell's lifelong glorification of the Patriot 'victory' of 1782 and praise of its 'architect', Henry Grattan, may have had their roots in the consequent childish idealization and choice of sides.

But Derrynane must also have taught him something of the practicalities of Irish politics. Hunting Cap would not have taken 1782 or the Patriots at their face value. His primary objective was Catholic liberation, and the slackening of Britain's control over the Irish Parliament might not prove at all conducive to this end. On the other hand, prudence dictated that one stay on terms with the Ascendancy. O'Connell was seven years of age when in 1782 the family's greatest crisis of the century brought this home to all. When Captain Butler was savagely assaulted after the capture of contraband at Derrynane, a warrant was prepared for the arrest of Hunting Cap, of O'Connell's father, Morgan, and of their cousin, Daniel O'Connell of Tarmons, for having instigated the attack. The repentant Butler himself secretly alerted Hunting Cap to what was afoot; and immediately the enlistment of Kerry Protestant friends and connexions to ward off the danger got under way. The real peril was that the defendants would be refused bail. If this happened, the trial would almost certainly take place in Dublin, with the chance of a conviction there upon a capital charge. But by pulling every string to hand and by engaging as leading counsel the brother-in-law of the powerful John Fitzgibbon, Hunting Cap managed to exercise sufficient influence upon the lord chief justice (whose decision it was) to be granted bail, and with it a hearing at the Tralee assizes. Here, with a grand jury composed largely of O'Connell customers, the bills were immediately dismissed and the charged men triumphantly acquitted. But the crisis had lasted many weeks; and even as a child of seven, O'Connell must have sensed the family's alarm and come to understand something of the tactics necessary for Catholic survival in a still dangerous world. Whatever else, the episode certainly made clear the importance of mutuality in Irish life. This was to become – and remain – central in O'Connell's politics.

O'Connell left Derrynane for boarding school in the summer of 1790, when he was little short of fifteen years of age. Catholic schools had only recently been rendered legal; and the one to which O'Connell went at Reddington (or Ballybrassil) on the Great Island in Cork Harbour may even have been the first such post-penal establishment. It was very small, conducted singlehandedly by the Rev. James Harrington, a Jesuit who had been secularized when the order was suppressed. Although the building was a mere converted farmhouse, Reddington gave O'Connell a new experience of beauty in landscape. The house looked south across an immense harbour to the headlands at its mouth. To the right lay other islands and the roadsteads, often thronged with sails. To the left the harbour crept about until the water was lost to sight between the near and far-off woods. Though each looked out upon the trapped Atlantic, its prospect was very different from Derrynane's; level planes of slate-grey, blue or turquoise sea prevailed, and the innumerable slopes and declivities in distant view were green and gentle. But it was just as heart-stirring and haunting in its way.

Much later O'Connell claimed to have been an assiduous and fearful pupil:

> I was the only boy who wasn't beaten at Harrington's school; I owed this to my attention . . . One day I was idle, and my teacher finding me imperfect in my lesson, threatened to beat me. But I shrank from the indignity, exclaiming, 'Oh, don't beat me for one half hour! If I haven't my lesson by that time, beat me *then*!' The teacher granted me the reprieve, and a lesson, rather a difficult one, was thoroughly learned.[15]

But in 1848 James Roche, who knew several of O'Connell's classmates, remarked that 'if not beaten by the master, he was by the scholars for his unsociability, apparent shyness and preference of study or secluded reflection, to play.' O'Connell's schoolfellows, Roche added, had assured him that he was not 'particularly distinguished amongst them for superior capacity, at that early period'.[16] This tends to confirm the fragments of self-portrait which paint O'Connell as a solitary, reading boy, living in a world of models for emulation. But if he really failed to stand out among the handful of pupils at Harrington's, either the remainder were extraordinarily able boys or he was to leap forward suddenly in his fifteenth year. For when he left the Academy for school in France, he was immediately recognized there as a boy of quite exceptional talent, whose grounding in classics was remarkable.

## III

Despite the establishment of regular Catholic schools in Ireland in the 1780s, O'Connell was always destined to finish his secondary education in France. For decades this had been the pattern for boys of his class, and his own uncle, General O'Connell, had long been a prime arranger of the French education of boys from Cork and Kerry. Although Harrington himself was an unusually able man, his single-handed Academy, with a mere dozen pupils, could not compare in quality with the great English Catholic schools upon the Continent.

Evidently it had been decided that O'Connell's brother, Maurice, a year younger than himself, should accompany him to school in France. This would explain why Hunting Cap did not apply to the General to arrange for the boys' education until 21 May 1789, when Daniel was already almost fourteen years of age – the normal age of commencement was thirteen. Four weeks later, the General replied recommending St Omer as the most suitable college but also proposing that the boys enter in the autumn of 1790 rather than 1789. 'Maurice [O'Connell] of Tarmons', he wrote, 'proposes, I believe, to spend next Summer in Ireland, and you can charge him with the care of the two Boys as far as St Omers, where I shall previously make it my business to ensure their admittance.'[17] Hunting Cap concurred, and the boys continued at Harrington's for the period 1789–90.

The General had expressed no concern about the state of France when he wrote in June 1789. Seven months later, however, he was thoroughly alarmed, and advised Hunting Cap strongly not to send the boys abroad 'until tranquillity be more solidly established': not merely did disorder threaten France, but her troubles were likely to spill over into the Austrian Netherlands, where the other major English Catholic colleges were located. 'I shall let you know', the General continued, 'in the month of April or May [1791] my fixed sentiment in the Matter, and if things shu'd not bear a prospect of peace, I would be very much at a loss to point out a proper place to send them to . . . You see, Dear Brother, that it's no easy matter to determine a proper place to send two Children without a Governor.'[18] Again Hunting Cap acquiesced, and the boys remained at Harrington's for yet another year, 1790–1. In fact, the General did not wait until the spring of 1791 to make his final determination but wrote again on 2 September 1790, this time so despairing of what had once been 'the finest country in Europe' as to tell his brother that all plans for a Continental education should be abandoned. 'I think you must lay aside all thoughts of sending our young Nephews over. I know no place either in France or the Low Countries where you can safely send 'em.'[19]

But Hunting Cap was not to be deflected from his purpose. Despite the General's decisive advice, despite the rapidly growing instability of France and its neighbours, despite the disruption of the Irish network of mutual assistance on the Continent, he dispatched the boys at last to the English College at Liège in August 1791. Apparently, the decision was a sudden one. Certainly, the rector at Liège was not forewarned nor was the general (whose position as a French royalist officer close to the Court was in any event becoming desperate) involved in the arrangements. Why was Liège abruptly substituted for St Omer? Possibly because Hunting Cap hoped that, located as it was in an independent and neutral prince-bishopric, the College might escape the coming conflict. It is hard to find any reason beyond his own iron determination for Hunting Cap's decision to send the boys abroad at all at such a stage. But O'Connell was now sixteen years of age: it would soon be too late – if it were not too late already – for him to enter any secondary school.

In fact, O'Connell and his brother *were* rejected as beyond the age for entry when they presented themselves at Liège; and the rector posted them on to Holy Trinity in Louvain (a preparatory college for Louvain University). There they awaited orders from Derrynane to tell them what they should do next. The boys' letters to Hunting Cap never mentioned – let alone complained of – either their difficulties or their fears. He was not the sort of man to whom one confessed weakness. But their experience must have been frightening. Daniel, just sixteen years of age, had been packed off, probably in a hurry and without much funds to spare, to an unknown country, whose language he could not have spoken well, to hosts who had no forewarning of his arrival, and with a younger and still more ignorant boy in tow. At a time when even moderately prudent foreigners were streaming out of France and the Low Countries, the young O'Connells had been pitched there for a two- or three-year sojourn. Only two casual recollections of the journey survive. Forty years later, O'Connell told his son John that his first experience of England was a ducking in the surf as he disembarked from the Irish brig at Dover, and that his first national challenge – by a Frenchman who abused him for England's iniquities on the diligence from Ostend to Liège – was met with this reply, 'Sir, England is not my country. Censure her as much as you please, you cannot offend me. I am an Irishman, and my countrymen have as little reason to love England as yours have – perhaps less.'[20] No anxieties or trepidation were recalled. But boys upon such an adventure at such a time could not possibly have escaped them.

Although the boys had to wait six weeks in Louvain before Hunting Cap's answer reached them, they were fortunate in their enforced staging post. Louvain was an ancient university city, with innumerable Irish connexions. Maurice later told his uncle that they had been received with much kindness at the houses of both the Irish Franciscans and the Irish Dominicans. They did not study at Holy Trinity, where the courses were too advanced, but (again according to Maurice) 'attended the University schools . . . and had recourse to the library of the Dominicans'.[21] We may take this with several grains of salt. Hunting Cap would have been enraged at the thought of their enjoying weeks of idleness on the Continent at his expense. But in fact there was little that they could or would feel inclined to do but sightsee and lark about. On 19 October 1791, Hunting Cap's orders arrived at last. They were to go immediately to St Omer. Thus all the delays and diversions ended with their entering more than two years late the college for which they had been originally intended.

St Omer, founded in the late sixteenth century by the great English Jesuit, Robert Parsons, but since 1762 in the hands of the English secular clergy, epitomized three traditions – Counter-Reformation Catholicism, Renaissance educational theory, and aristocratic and gentry recusancy. Neither O'Connell nor his brother ever adverted to the first in their correspondence: piety was not the sort of subject one discussed with Hunting Cap. For that matter, neither ever wrote a word about people, whether masters, boys, servants or St Omerians, or about the place in which they lived, the college with its three heroic centuries, the charming town or the tamed countryside of Artois.

The second tradition, that of Renaissance pedagogy, was a different

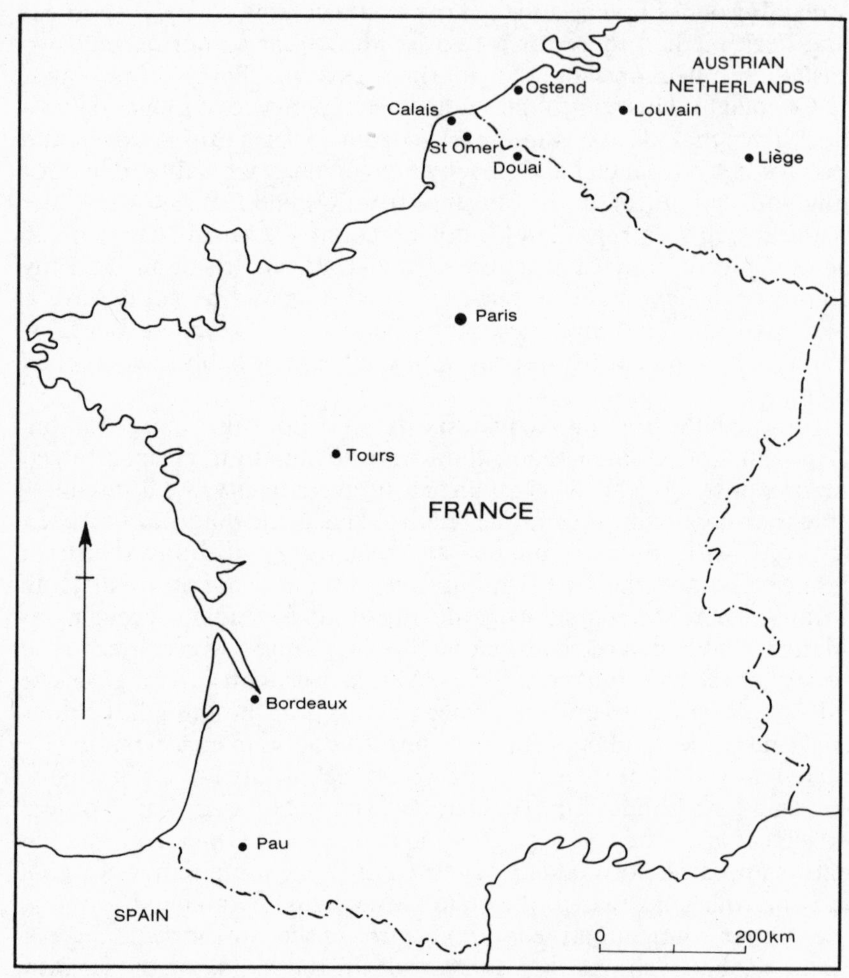


Map 2. O'Connell's continental locations

story. As a school, St Omer remained faithful to its sixteenth-century origin. The basic curriculum consisted primarily of Greek and Latin, and secondarily of English and French (which the boys were obliged to speak); arithmetic and geography were the minor subjects. The gentlemanly accomplishments, which embraced dancing, fencing, music and drawing but also included 'mathematics', were optional.

The aim of such an educational system might not be immediately apparent today. It was – following Cicero's and Quintilian's texts on oratory – designed to produce the complete public man, whose eloquence was based on sound learning and a thorough grasp of the techniques of exposition and persuasion. In practice, the syllabus included declamation, dialectic and dramatic performance; and its climax was the regular study of rhetoric and philosophy. All in all, it was well-tailored for O'Connell's subsequent careers of lawyer, demagogue and tribune. Whether or not St Omer did much to train him directly for these trades, it certainly provided him with a vision and defence of the ideal, and a body of supporting metaphors and images.

O'Connell succeeded at once at St Omer. Three months after his arrival, he reported to Hunting Cap,

> In this college are taught the Latin and Greek authors, French, English and geography, besides lessons given during recreation hours in music, dancing, fencing and drawing. I have not yet inquired about rhetoric but will do it (please God) as soon as I receive an answer from my uncle [General O'Connell]. We have composed for the second time since I came here. I got second in Latin, Greek and English, and eleventh in French; before the places are read out there is a scene or two of play acted on a small stage, which is in the college, by one of the first four schools (each in its turn); these they call orations, and of them there are eight in the year. Of consequence we compose eight times; there is a whole play acted in the month of August.[22]

He soon advanced to work in which the oratorical element was still more to the front, 'Mignot's harangues, Cicero and Caesar . . . Caesar is given us chiefly to turn into Greek; our Greek authors are Demosthenes, Homer and Xenophon's Anabasis; our French one is Dagaso's speeches.'[23] But well before this elevation, the president of St Omer had marked him out as an extraordinary boy. Soon after the O'Connells reached the college, Hunting Cap had asked the president, Dr Stapylton, for a candid opinion of his nephews, apparently adding the observation that such candour was not ordinarily to be had from headmasters. Stapylton, an English gentleman, administered a delicate rebuke to the rough inquirer, before going on to make a most remarkable prediction.

> You desire to have my candid opinion respecting your nephews and you very properly remark that no habit can be worse than that of the instructors of youth who seek to gratify the parents of those under their care by ascribing to them talents and qualities which they do not really

> possess. You add that, being only the uncle of these young men, you can afford to hear the real truth respecting their abilities and deficiencies. It is not my habit to disguise the precise truth in reply to such inquiries as yours; you shall therefore have my opinion with perfect candour.
>
> I begin with the younger, Maurice. His manner and demeanour are quite satisfactory. He is gentlemanly in his conduct and much loved by his fellow-students. He is not deficient in abilities, but he is idle and fond of amusement. I do not think he will answer for any laborious profession, but I will answer for it, he will never be guilty of anything discreditable – at least, such is my firm belief.
>
> With respect to the elder, Daniel, I have but one sentence to write about him, and that is, that I never was so much mistaken in my life as I shall be unless he be destined to make a remarkable figure in society.[24]

Though based upon less than three months' acquaintance, Stapylton's analysis of Maurice's character was masterly. Yet he says nothing of Daniel's except possibly by implication. We can, I think, infer that he thought O'Connell to be ambitious, able and assiduous. We cannot fairly infer that he thought him lacking in Maurice's more attractive qualities, such as gaiety and being 'much loved by his fellow-students'. But the president's 'one sentence' does seem to carry something of that air.

It is difficult to gain any impression of O'Connell's own reactions to St Omer: his letters to Hunting Cap are altogether formal and even stylized. But one wistful observation, 'I had no place to retire to from whence I might write to you',[25] may reflect a boarding-school boy's hopeless longing for solitude. Again, each of O'Connell's letters from St Omer, even the first, dated 3 February 1792, pointed out that the college did not provide the highest range of studies: rhetoric, logic and philosophy. This does not necessarily mean that he himself was pressing to be sent where they might be pursued, for his uncle, the General, had long been an advocate of these subjects for the boys. None the less, O'Connell's persistency seems to provide some *prima facie* evidence of his determination to excel. At any rate, it carried the day. Soon after O'Connell wrote for a second time to Hunting Cap about 'the college of Douai' where the higher syllabus could be followed, although 'French is paid no great attention to there, nay almost totally neglected',[26] an instruction arrived from Derrynane that the boys were to remove there immediately from St Omer.

The departure for Douai, some seventy-five miles inland from St Omer, was as uncomfortably precipitate as each of the boys' earlier journeyings. Leaving St Omer at 5 a.m. on the morning of 20 August 1792, they reached Douai on the same evening: it was no light affair to travel such a distance by diligence. Hunting Cap had simply given the boys their marching orders, leaving them to solve their many difficulties for themselves. They had to borrow their coach money from Stapylton, and further monies from the rector of Douai and from an Irish pupil there, as soon as they reached their destination. For Douai, an ecclesiastical seminary as well as a secondary school, was much more austere than St Omer. 'At St Omer's', wrote O'Connell on 14 September 1792, 'everything was done for the boys, here the boys are obliged to do everything themselves.'[27] Not until they arrived did the O'Connells discover that the pupils were obliged to supply their own furniture. Their first night was spent in a room containing only beds, and they had to borrow several guineas next day to buy mirrors, candlesticks, basins, chairs, desks, cupboards, powdering-tables, knives and forks and similar equipment. Meanwhile, his first stark night at Douai had left O'Connell with 'fits of ague',[28] and he soon departed for the infirmary. Another unpleasant surprise was the meagre servings at dinner. Most boys – those on scholarships excepted – received additional helpings, called 'seconds', at a cost of £3–4 per annum. In this case, O'Connell plucked up enough courage to ask Hunting Cap to pay the extra fee. 'We would be much obliged to you for leave to get them [seconds], but this as you please. I hope, my dear Uncle, that you will not think me troublesome in saying so much on those heads.'[29]

Moreover, Hunting Cap had failed to consider the rhythm of the school year. At Douai the rhetoric and philosophy courses began at Whitsuntide, so that O'Connell had almost a term's leeway to make up. We have no idea how he fared: in fact, all that we can discover about his career at Douai derives from the school account which tells us little more than that he bought a violin, took violin lessons and much frequented the school infirmary. Everything was overshadowed, anyhow, by the growing political crisis. The September massacres of 1792 rightly plunged the college into fear soon after the boys' arrival; and the move to Douai had brought them almost to the war-zone as the Austrians advanced into northern France. The battle of Jemappes was fought so close to Douai on 6 November 1792 that the boys could hear the distant roar of the cannon; and soon afterwards, when they were on a school walk, a waggoner of Dumouriez's army so frightened them by shouting, 'Voilà les jeunes jesuites, les capucins, les récolets!', that they ran headlong back all the way to the college.

It was soon clear that Douai's status as 'the English College' would not preserve it much longer from revolutionary depredation; by the beginning of 1793, those boys who had their parents' permission were being allowed to go home. The O'Connells were in their usual predicament of needing Hunting Cap's sanction for every action, with a six- to eight-week interval between the dispatch of a letter and the receipt of a reply. On 4 January 1793 Maurice sent a panic-stricken appeal to Derrynane. Already, he wrote, they were in danger of being cut off in Douai, where the local revolutionaries were increasingly menacing. 'From above 206 [pupils] . . . there are now not 90, and these decreasing every day.' If Daniel and he should be forced to leave suddenly, 'we will go to London, write immediately, and having been supplied with money by the procurator or Mr Kirwan, will wait until we hear from you.'[30] Their uncle, the General, who had fled France in September 1792, was in London already.

For once the boys had to act on their own initiative, or possibly they were driven to act by the college president. On 21 January 1793, they left by coach for Calais – a two-day journey – in such haste that most of their clothing, to say nothing of their other belongings, was abandoned, to the ultimate benefit of the French Republic. The journey from Douai to Calais was dangerous enough. Louis XVI was guillotined in Paris on the day they left, the war with Great Britain only ten days off. The O'Connells were certainly treated as if they were English, as well as clericalist and reactionary. The carriage was surrounded by republicans and butted by soldiers' rifles in the towns, and the passengers denounced as 'young priests' and 'little aristocrats',[31] despite the tricolour cockades the boys wore in their hats as protective colouring. When they were safe at last upon the packet boat at Calais, they threw the cockades defiantly into the water, to the fury of French fishermen alongside.

> Then two Irishmen joined them on board, full of excitement, as they were just come from Paris. They had even been present at the execution, and they soon produced a handkerchief, horribly stained with red, which they had bribed one of the National Guard to steep for them in the blood of Louis XVI. A passenger asked them how they could have brought themselves to face such a revolting scene. 'For the love of the cause,' was their reply. The two Irishmen were the brothers Sheares . . . afterwards to be executed for complicity in organising the rebellion of 1798.[32]

The whole scene was deeply symbolic. The Sheares and O'Connell stood for opposite Irish reactions to insurrectionary violence. O'Connell was always to separate himself from bloodshed, revolutionary disorder and conspiracy. The experiences of his last months in France had even driven him temporarily onto the right wing.

## IV

O'Connell has left us with few contemporary and still less later impressions of his seventeen months in the Austrian Netherlands and France. We can certainly list much that he experienced. The landscape of Brabant, Flanders and Artois, flat, mild, tidily pieced and untouched by oceans, contrasted altogether with his boyhood world. He who had never lived in towns was placed in turn in Liège, Louvain, St Omer and Douai. Each was an ancient provincial centre, redolent of the sixteenth century, with intricately patterned forms of urban and ecclesiastical life. He spent his time abroad in large, regimented institutions, cheek by jowl with many other boys, and speaking an unfamiliar language on most occasions; all this was new. We cannot tell what he made of these strange surroundings and circumstances, apart from one hint that he sighed for solitude and another, that his happiest days on the Continent were the few spent at a country house owned by the college near St Omer.

We are still more in the dark about O'Connell's religious formation. This is curious. After all, his seventeen continental months were spent in great bastions of the English – and in the case of Louvain, also the Irish – Counter-Reformation. Each had its roll of honour, scholars and martyrs. Each had a special ethos of piety, developed over many generations. Yet O'Connell recorded nothing whatever under either head. We cannot assume from his silence that they left no stamp upon him. Eighteenth-century schoolboys rarely wrote about such things, and Hunting Cap himself would have expected a decent reticence. Still, there is nothing in O'Connell's later life to suggest that he was marked significantly by his exposure to the traditions of seminarian gallantry or the simple, severe spirituality of the English colleges. For that matter there is nothing to suggest that he made even one English friend at either St Omer or Douai.

But there is some evidence on O'Connell's reaction to the political turmoil by which he was surrounded in 1791–3. What a chance, to have seen one critical phase of the Revolution at close range! He had reached Ostend soon after Louis XVI's abortive flight to Varennes; he left Calais two days after his execution. In between, O'Connell had breathed the air and felt the interior life of the ancien regime, even while it was being steadily weakened, and crushed in parts, by the revolutionaries. In between, France had gone to war, and Catholicism become aligned with the opposition to the new order. Moreover, in the five months of O'Connell's sojourn at Douai, Anglo-French relations had worsened rapidly. His surroundings, teaching and companions all impelled him towards the counter-revolutionary camp. It is true that O'Connell's mildly Francophile upbringing, and his boyish espousal of 'Grattanism' in Irish politics, told a little the other way. But this was easily outweighed by the grim realities of violence, social upheaval, republicanism and irreligion which pressed upon him in the Netherlands and France – especially as these were mediated by the reactions of the communities in which he lived, and the alarms of his royalist uncle, the General. He said later that when he left France in 1793 he was 'half a Tory'.[33] This was probably a considerable underestimation: 'three-quarters of a reactionary' might have been closer to the mark.

O'Connell was soon to undergo a political sea-change. By 1795 he might fairly be described as radical. Yet his experiences at St Omer and Douai had placed permanent limits upon his radicalism. He had discovered what it meant to be deeply frightened, both as a person and as a member of a group. He had learnt that revolutions can quickly gather an irresistible momentum, and slip beyond rational control and predictable direction. He had come to loathe mob rule and the unleashing of the irrational in politics. Above all, in his last six months in France he had heard almost daily of great carnage, by the guillotine and in war, and this left him with a lasting hatred of bloodshed, as almost the ultimate evil in affairs. It also left him with a lasting dislike of France and a lasting suspicion of French models. All these legacies of his continental schooldays certainly circumscribed and gave peculiar directions to his radicalism.

Yet the most important single effect of O'Connell's French education may well have been the reinforcement of his ambition to be a public man. As we have seen, the educational programme of St Omer and Douai was specifically designed to produce leaders, statesmen and orators – polished men of action, but of constitutional action only. The fundamental metaphor employed by the ancients, from whom this concept of education derived, was that of the vestibule. There the young, by mimic contention and disputation, prepared themselves for the real theatre, the great auditorium of affairs. There, as Cato put it, 'those who are preparing for what is done in the forum, as in the field of battle, may alike learn and previously try their power, by practising in sport.' To this end, boys should also be trained as easy-mannered and accomplished gentlemen. Thus when Stapylton predicted that O'Connell would cut 'a remarkable figure in society' he had a particular type of success in mind – the political. That O'Connell himself was deeply impressed by this teaching is evident from several of his later reflections. An excellent example is the self-programme which he outlined for Hunting Cap's benefit nearly three years after he had fled from Douai.

> I have now two objects to pursue. The one, the attainment of knowledge; the other, the acquisition of all those qualities which constitute the polite gentleman. I am convinced that the former, besides the immediate pleasure which it yields, is calculated to raise me to honours, rank, and fortune: and I know that the latter serves as a general passport or first recommendation. And as for the motives of ambition which you suggest, I assure you no man can possess more of it than I do. I have indeed a glowing and (if I may use the expression) an enthusiastic ambition which converts every toil into a pleasure and every study into an amusement . . . Indeed as for my knowledge in the professional line that cannot be discovered for some years to come. But I have time in the interim to prepare myself to appear with greater *éclat* on the grand theatre of the world.[34]

O'Connell's sixteen months in the English Colleges, dedicated to the ideals of Renaissance education, may have only confirmed and explicated his innate tendencies and boyish dreams. But this they certainly did, in providing him with an elaborated programme and a justificatory philosophy for what he proposed to do. By chance, the opportunity for an Irish Catholic boy to become in time 'a public figure' had suddenly opened up while he was still 'composing' for his 'orations' at St Omer. On 18 April 1792 Sir Hercules Langrishe's Act (32 Geo. III c. 21) enabling Catholics to practise as lawyers, and even as junior counsel at the Irish Bar, had received the royal assent.

## CHAPTER 2

# London

## *1793–6*

### I

So far as was practicable, O'Connell and his brother Maurice took up again in England the life of Douai from which they were forced to flee. They had not expected to stay in London. At first, they were meant to return to Kerry with cousins who were also refugees from France. But their uncle, the General, who had now fixed himself in London as the most promising place for finding new military employment, intervened and persuaded Hunting Cap that the boys should continue their education there under his own eye. A fellow Hiberno-French emigré, Chevalier Fagan, accepted them into his 'academy', a sort of crammer's school which was run from Fagan's house in the Strand. The boys saw him periodically for the supervision of their work and the allotment of new tasks and reading; and O'Connell later boarded with him for a time. Their syllabus was little changed by the translation from Douai. On 3 June 1793 O'Connell reported to Hunting Cap,

> We study at present Rhetoric and logic. For the Rhetoric we read and get by heart Cicero's orations, Orationes Collectae, Bossuet's funeral orations and Boileau's art of poetry. The two last are French authors. In Logic we get by heart the Douai College dictates, not being able to find any other book on that subject in this town, I mean any valuable work for there are treatises on logic in English but none with theses, at least, that we could find. Besides, the Douai College dictates are good. We write themes very often . . .[1]

Fagan also groomed the boys in the gentlemanly arts, setting them, as O'Connell wrote, 'a kind of exercise to go through every day for about 20 minutes or half an hour' to improve their 'carriage'.[2]

O'Connell and Maurice had left France so precipitately as to carry with them little more than the clothes in which they stood up: 'we had every single article of wearing apparel to buy.'[3] Probably it was the

General who first doled out Hunting Cap's money to them; but by July 1793 Fagan was acting as their banker. They overspent and were soon in Hunting Cap's black books for some unauthorized expenditure. Having already twice apologized profusely for their foolish and ungrateful conduct, O'Connell abased himself yet again in writing to Hunting Cap on 1 July:

> You have seen by it [a second letter of apology] only a part of that sorrow which I was not able to express as I wished. No one can be more convinced than I am of the justice of your anger against us. You have done everything for us, and we have shown no advantage from it. I shall not, my dear Uncle, take up your time in making promises. That would be childish. I shall only beg of you to be assured of my regret and to reckon on the future.[4]

Maurice fell into much worse trouble later in the year. There are no clues as to the nature of the scrape, but it was serious enough for Hunting Cap to bring his education to a close and recall him to Kerry to put him to some lowly occupation. O'Connell courageously protested, telling Hunting Cap that Maurice had been reared 'with the idea that he should never be necessitated to earn his own bread', and that being forced into 'business, I mean [a] mechanic one' would probably drive him to despair and thence to ruin.[5] Maurice was spared eventually – at least to the extent of his being purchased a commission in the army. It was doubtless the General's pleas rather than O'Connell's which carried the day with Hunting Cap. But it was true testimony of fraternal love that O'Connell, at the age of eighteen, should have braved Hunting Cap's anger for his brother's sake. It was also an augury of his future at the bar, for his long letter was a skilful piece of advocacy, down to its emotional peroration. 'But what do I say? No, I hope he will never be guilty of such a complicated piece of ingratitude as to offend again. Do then, my dear Uncle, forgive this once more. Add this to the many favours you have hitherto loaded us with.'[6] Meanwhile O'Connell's own schooldays were coming to an end. Fagan closed his academy suddenly in October 1793. Costs had risen and the number of pupils had fallen off: O'Connell was one of only two 'constant boarders' by that stage. But, as Fagan told him, he suffered very little from the closure. He was practically at the end of his course in logic – rhetoric had presumably been completed earlier in the year – so that the only substantial change in his circumstances was the welcome one of removing from Fagan's to other lodgings.

Hunting Cap had decided some time before (possibly when Langrishe's Act was passed) that O'Connell should read for the bar. He now determined that he should be entered at the Temple in time for the next law term. But after more than two years abroad the boy was homesick, as well as faced with the imminent loss of his brother Maurice who had been his companion during all his exile. This drove him to present an elaborate plea to Hunting Cap to be allowed to read law instead at the newly constituted King's Inns in Dublin. Again, the artistry of his argument was striking. Having distanced himself from those to whom London offered advantages, 'giddy and thoughtless young men who come there to spend money, not to study', and taken the precaution of securing both Fagan's and the General's 'approbation' (for what is not clear), O'Connell proceeded to draw up a balance sheet showing how much less he could live on in Dublin than in London. He could not deny that the common law of England and Ireland was essentially the same; but he made the most of the solitary significant difference in the respective legal systems, the laws of place. He also attempted to turn his own youth to account and to play effectively upon his uncle's *amour propre*.

> As for the other class how am I to discern the honest man from the designing villain? The experiment would be dangerous in the highest degree for my youth and inexperience. But in Dublin your known credit and character would be the means of introducing me into the acquaintance of some of the most eminent lawyers in the Kingdom; who would not only assist me in forming the plan of my studies, but likewise be of service to me when engaged in the profession.[7]

Hunting Cap was unmoved. But although O'Connell had probably spent several days in composing his petition, it was not altogether wasted time. He had made another remarkable trial in advocacy.

On 19 January 1794 O'Connell enrolled at Lincoln's Inn: he had had to change his allegiance when it had turned out that the Temple was still closed to Catholics by its requirement that members take the sacrament. So began a lonely year in London. Neither lectures nor examinations were available to, let alone mandatory for, bar students. Eating thirty-six dinners in one's Inn and occasional attendance at the court of King's Bench during term constituted the entire formal education of a barrister. The best contemporary apprenticeship for the bar was to devil with a celebrated counsel. But this, at a cost of at least £100 per annum, was beyond O'Connell's reach. All that remained was the steady, untutored reading of textbooks in his dingy lodging room off the Strand, scraping acquaintance with fellow-students if he could, and joining a circulation library. Professional reading began, inevitably, with the four volumes of Blackstone's *Commentaries*: this headed a long list of legal works which he compiled in the hope that his uncle would purchase them for him in Cork. But from the 30,000 volumes of the circulating library which he joined, he set out to 'relax' his mind 'with the study of History and the Belles Lettres, objects absolutely necessary for every person who has occasion to speak in public, as they enlarge the ideas, and afford that strength and solidity of speech which are requisite for every public speaker.'[8]

He appears to have had few if any London friends, at any rate during 1794. The two or three acquaintances whom he mentions in this year were Irish youths. He was poor. There is no reason to doubt his statement of 11 March 1794, 'I have not gone to one single place of entertainment since I came to London', nor the truth of his wistful observation, 'I am perhaps the only law student in London without a Watch.'[9] Three months later he had to try to justify to Hunting Cap an appeal to his own father for some money. He pleaded that, through inexperience and inattention, he had failed to anticipate fully his daily needs. Meanwhile his health was poor. A 'weakness of nerves' from which he suffered in the spring of 1794 suggests perhaps some psycho-somatic disorder or adolescent crisis. In summer he fell seriously ill of 'ague' and 'slow nervous fever'. After he had recovered – despite the heroic remedies of 'a bottle of port per day during the first ten or twelve days of my sickness' and 'a blister applied to my side' which rendered him unconscious from pain – he told Hunting Cap, 'I was attended by a country man of ours, a Dr Pendergast who having already made a fortune by his profession, behaved very genteely to me as he gave me the four last visits without a fee. Notwithstanding this you may be convinced my illness has cost a round sum of money . . . your former kindness induces me to hope that you will be good enough to make it up in my next half-term's allowance.'[10] The General warmly backed O'Connell's plea. The malady, he told Hunting Cap on 21 August 1794, had inevitably proved expensive, the cost of medical fees and drugs in England being 'enormous': 'It is, however, a great Comfort that he [Daniel] is perfectly recovered, having been severely attacked.'[11] This was a characteristic intervention. The General invariably supported O'Connell's requests for more money during his London years. Early in 1794 he had assured his brother that O'Connell could not possibly live in even 'the most modest gentility' in London under £120 per annum.[12] A year later he revised this to £130–140 at the very least. 'Every article has risen in price very considerably, and in the line he lives in a certain appearance must be kept up. You know as well as I do that professional Abilities, however transcendant, require to be supported by genteel Manners and gentlemanly Education. Mixing in good company is the only way of acquiring them.'[13] Equally important, his London uncle vouched for O'Connell's rectitude and gratitude to his Derrynane uncle: he 'will show himself worthy of your unequalled favours, which he entertains the deepest sence[sic] of'.[14] Hard as O'Connell's path as a student may have been, it would have been much stonier without an indefatigable and respected intercessor.

## II

Before the close of 1794, O'Connell's political and religious opinions had begun to change direction. Almost certainly, a crucial event was the trial of Thomas Hardy for high treason, which O'Connell attended between 28 October and 5 November 1794. Hardy, secretary of the London Corresponding Society, was a foremost radical of the day, and from the beginning his prosecution was a trial of strength between the forces of repression and libertarianism, conducted amid great publicity and excitement and charged with political passion. The defence, led by Erskine, called upon leading liberals like R. B. Sheridan and Philip Francis as witnesses to such good effect that the case proved an immense triumph for the reformers. When the jury returned a verdict of 'not guilty', Hardy was drawn through the streets of central London by the crowd; and later the whig Earl Stanhope presided over a grand celebratory dinner. Not only had the contest been protracted and dramatic, but it had also taken the shapes of David against Goliath and of freedom against suppression. It was not likely that a twenty-year-old student would have hesitated long in choosing sides. Moreover, some time in 1794 O'Connell had joined the Cogers, a London debating club of artisans, journalists and self-improvers, in which radicals and freethinkers predominated. If he had become a member early in the year, some of the ground for the political turnabout which followed his attendance at the Hardy trial had probably been tilled already.

We do not know how rapidly O'Connell's radicalism developed. It had certainly gone far by the close of 1795 when he began to compose his journal. Two items entered under 30 December of that year record his uncle Daniel's railing at him for his 'folly in being a democrat',[15] and an American girl's gibe that 'in fifty years I [O'Connell] would doubt whether I was a man or a cabbage-stump, so much was I inclined to scepticism'.[16] This democratic and philosophical 'conversion' may have been only recently completed. Certainly, O'Connell had undergone two significant radicalizing experiences in the three weeks or so preceding these entries. First, he had read William Godwin's *Political Justice*: probably no other book affected him so profoundly. Secondly, he had moved his lodgings from a cul-de-sac off Coventry St to Mrs Rigby's *pension* at Chiswick, a nest of the avant garde and *esprits forts*.

O'Connell had failed to win Hunting Cap's permission to return to Kerry for the long vacation in either 1793 or 1794, but he at last succeeded in 1795: it was by then almost four years since he had seen his family or homeland. When he returned to London in October 1795 he found that his rent had been raised to a guinea and a half per week ('so much has the price of provisions increased'[17]), and accordingly he was ordered by Hunting Cap to find a cheaper place out of town, at any rate for vacations. This explains his move to Chiswick at the end of the Michaelmas law term of 1795; and doubtless Mrs Rigby's establishment was chosen because his solitary friend among law students, R. N. Bennett, stayed there. On 10 December 1795 he described his translation to Hunting Cap with his customary guile:

> The society in the house is mixed – I mean composed of men and women all of whom are people of rank and knowledge of the world; so that their conversation and manners are perfectly well adapted to rub off the rust of scholastic education. Nor is there any danger of riot or dissipation as they are all advanced in life; another student of law and I being the only young persons in the house. This young man is my most intimate acquaintance . . . His name is Bennett. He is an Irish young man of good family, connections and fortune. He is prudent and strictly economical. He has good sense, ability and application. I knew him before my journey to Ireland. It was before that period our friendship commenced. So that on the whole I spend my time here not only very pleasantly but I hope very usefully.[18]

No doubt Hunting Cap was not completely taken in. But he would surely have been astonished had he read O'Connell's private 'sketch' of his new landlady. Mrs Rigby, O'Connell noted in his journal, was endowed with 'a strong mind, a clear comprehension, and a tenacious memory', fluency in French and Italian, a fair knowledge of Latin and excellent knowledge of history, literature, heraldry, drama and the stage.[19] She was

> a most violent and inveterate democrat, as well as a deist. Her own misfortunes make [her] peevish on these subjects. But, with all her information, she has not a grain of common prudence. The servants neglect

> their business, plunder and cheat her . . . while she should be exerting herself to procure another house she is talking of Beaumont and Fletcher's plays, descanting on Paine's *Age of Reason*, or arguing on the politics of the day . . . In her attachment for cats she becomes foolish and absurd. But she has a greater failing than any yet mentioned. It is a fondness for liquor. She gets drunk sometimes and would in all probability do it oftener were she unrestrained by the fear of her lodgers forsaking the house. She is at all times familiar, but when heated with drinking she is rude in her familiarities.[20]

Such was the mistress of the raffish, bohemian and free-thinking household in which O'Connell was to spend his remaining year and five months in London.

O'Connell's new home was in a tranquil setting. The large house fronted the Thames, with Barnes to be seen on one side of the opposite shore and the Margrave of Ansbach's mansion upon the other. Chiswick Eyot, replete with the reeds and osiers so lovingly described in many a Victorian idyll of the suburban Thames, lay directly across from the hall door. The lodgers' rooms, O'Connell noted, were spacious and isolated apartments, as if each were living in a separate house.

His life at Chiswick, however, by no means mirrored the Arcadian surroundings. Even before he went to live at Mrs Rigby's, he and other young men had been involved in a semi-drunken fracas there in which a servant had been struck and a constable called to separate the combatants. In his first month or so at Mrs Rigby's, he was served with a writ for non-payment of debt, and all but took the disastrous step of signing a *post obit* for £1,200 for a man whom he thought might become a bankrupt. He also attracted the amorous attentions of a young married woman; he was by now a tall, splendidly proportioned youth, strikingly handsome in the blue-eyed, black-haired Kerry style. This 'fine young woman . . . seemed to be partial to me, and I endeavoured to improve this partiality. She is a most debauched woman. She pretended before we parted to have taken a great liking to me. Nay, she acted the part of an *inamorata*.'[21] He was moreover bound over to keep the peace in consequence of a dispute with Douglas Thompson, the son of a local porter brewer, over the favours of another young woman. When O'Connell had called on Thompson to issue a challenge for a duel, Thompson struck him repeatedly with a stick: 'I seized him, and though I had a heavy cane in my hand I did not return the blow.'[22] When O'Connell later sent his friend Bennett with a more formal challenge, Thompson's father had him arrested. The upshot was O'Connell being hauled before a magistrate with his uncle Daniel having to act as his bondsman. The General gave O'Connell a rare dressing down, abusing his new politics equally with his behaviour. He 'railed at me for not having returned the blow', O'Connell wrote resentfully, but would have been angrier still had O'Connell been so ungentlemanlike as to fight 'with cudgels like common porters, etc., etc.'.[23] Despite the berating, Uncle Daniel had treated O'Connell with his usual generosity, for not a word of this or of the earlier scrape was passed on to Derrynane.

None of these were perhaps very wild oats for a nineteen-year-old boy, loose in London for almost two years already, to have sown. But they were considerably wilder for O'Connell than they would have been for others of his age. The shadow of Hunting Cap lay always across his path. This was partially counteracted by his great good fortune in having the General's unwavering support, in advocacy as well as silence, according to occasion. When, for example, Hunting Cap was enraged at what he took to be O'Connell's negligence in arranging for being entered on the books of King's Inns, Dublin, it was his London uncle who pleaded, 'Dan's Letter to Mr Franks came to Dublin at a time when he was absent, therefore the Disappointment, or rather the Delay, cannot be imputed to our Dan, because he could not forsee the circumstance. I hope you have before now received his letter, which I forwarded you from here, and I beseech you to relieve him from the anxiety he feels least [sic] he might have incurred your displeasure.'[24] But there was also a strong streak of caution in O'Connell himself even in his 'wildest' day. He reproached himself deeply for falling into debt and almost falling into ruin by signing another's *post-obit*. 'I remark a great deal of neglect, or at least a certain dilatoriness of disposition, which seems a constitutional failing of mine',[25] he wrote of the first. As to the second, 'the chance of this [the *post-obit*] transaction coming to my uncle's knowledge would (had I been concerned in it) be a source of continual anxiety and apprehension.'[26] He was far from sure that he would have responded to the young wife's advances had there been an opportunity for the affair to develop. Indeed he speaks of marriage at this time with deep respect as the event which constitutes the source of 'unmixed sorrow' or of 'pure happiness'.[27] Even the frustrated duel was a matter of moralizing and self-analysis. He had not returned Thompson's blow (O'Connell decided) because Thompson was smaller and weaker, because O'Connell might have killed him, and because he remembered his earlier fisticuffs and 'its consequent expenses, troubles and inconveniences . . . having no witnesses, I was afraid of the law'. On the credit side, he was delighted to discover that he had courage enough to challenge another to a duel, although this left him with a new fear of 'precipitation in plunging myself in future quarrels'. Again, while duelling was a vice, 'yet there is a certain charm in the independence which it bestows on a man'. Interestingly, in the light of events a quarter of a century away, O'Connell wound up his laborious examen with the announcement of his decision never to fight a duel again 'from the time I become *independent* of the world'.[28]

Whatever about duelling, there is a certain charm in O'Connell's youthful sententiousness. True, no gleam of wit or gaiety relieves the leaden periods of his journal – here the contrast with Wolfe Tone's sparkling self-notes could not be more complete. Not only did O'Connell sometimes sink to the owlishness of a solemn schoolboy, but also he was as bent on self-improvement as Samuel Smiles. In fact, his prime reason for keeping a journal was to eradicate his 'faults', the most obdurate of which continued for years to be over-sleeping in the mornings! None the less, O'Connell's earnest, pedantic wrestling with experience should touch the heart of anyone who can recapture the frets and fears of adolescence. The struggle to impose order upon his matters for decision, and even the laborious moral balance-sheets and numbered pros and cons for actions done, are in the end impressive. No less, if rather less pleasantly, so are the shrewdness and calculated self-interest underlying certain of his decisions. Towards the end of 1795, for instance, he noted, 'I have entirely lost this day owing to my being in town. I believe it will be better for me [to] attend the Society [of Cogers] no longer. It is true I there acquire a great fluency of speech, but the loss of time and money which my attendance occasions makes me conceive it preferable to go there no more.'[29] O'Connell certainly took seriously the furnishing of his mind according to the Ciceronian specifications he had received at Douai. When at home at Chiswick he read and noted his reading 'almost continually'. Characteristic was his entry for 19 January 1796:

> I read this day 110 pages of Gibbon [*Decline and Fall*], Vol.4, thirty-two pages of Godwin, and thirty-three pages of Para [*Physique Experimentale*]. I read likewise part of the treatise on aerology in Hall's *Encyclopaedia*.
>
> I read but five pages of 'E.N.P.' [Espinasse's *Nisi Prius*].[30]

As this indicates, apart from his legal work (normally a much larger portion of the whole than on 19 January), O'Connell read extensively in history, political philosophy and natural sciences. His fluency in

French much increased of course his potential range. But he also read poetry spasmodically (eighty-five pages of 'Ossian's *Poems*' and two hundred and thirty-four of Pindar's in one evening) as well as belles-lettres, Shakespeare and the Bible. Johnson, Blair, Voltaire and Rousseau were among the crop of one short season. He worried repeatedly about the poverty of his style, his failure to arrange 'a united train of ideas', and his incapacity to express himself aright or say exactly what he meant. 'This defect has, I believe, two sources, the one an inherent shallowness of conception, the other frequent interruption. The first can be remedied one [*sic*] by the attainment of a more enlarged stock of ideas; the latter, being only a bad custom, may be laid aside with the assistance of care.'[31] He devoted much time to Gibbon's *Decline and Fall* not only for its intrinsic excellence as history, but also as the supreme stylistic model.

O'Connell, then, saw himself as both an apprentice studying the work of masters and an accumulator of a store of reference and allusion against his eventual appearance on the world's stage. But he was not always on parade. He confessed to reading novels and 'trifling productions of the day unworthy of my notice'.[32] These he generally regarded as lost time, to record which would be merely to waste more time still. But he made two exceptions: Mackenzie's *The Man of Feeling* and Godwin's *Caleb Williams* were discussed at length. The choice is significant. Each novel was foremost in its genre in the late eighteenth century. They glorified, respectively, the cults of sensibility and rational improvement. As always in such cases, it is difficult to say whether the deep impression which these two novels made upon O'Connell derived from his own predisposition. But certainly he carried their doctrines forward into his future, as, say, his courtships and his dauntless advocacy of humane causes will richly testify. Perhaps the hero of his own projected novel (which may have been begun as early as February 1796) would have attempted to intertwine the strains. According to his sketched plot, an illegitimate son of George III was to have been taken as a child from his mother, Hannah Lightfoot, sent to school at Douai, and thence taken to the West Indies. 'He was to be a soldier of fortune – to take a part in the American war – and to come back finally to England, imbued with republican principles.'[33] It is difficult to guess at the intended fate of O'Connell's hero, for nothing of the novel has survived. But he was surely fulfilling many of his creator's day-dreams – parentage, presumably, apart!

But the staple, if not always the bulk, of O'Connell's reading at

Chiswick was law. He had to determine for himself even which books to buy and study, with no further outside assistance than the occasional offhand advice from Irish barristers whom Hunting Cap had importuned for help. It was a dreary and often repellent grind. Of Coke's *Institutes*, for instance, O'Connell wrote that 'were it not for the happy absurdities with which they abound, the pedantry of style, the obscurity of matter, and the loathsome tediousness of trifling would create unsurmountable disgust.'[34] Blackstone's *Commentaries* alone were endurable, Blackstone being both clear in style and attractive in exposition. Espinasse's *Nisi Prius* (a collection of recent judgments) was, conversely, the most odious of all. O'Connell found the 'artificial' distinctions of the judiciary sickening and 'the iniquity of punishing ignorance' a shock. Doubly was ignorance punished in the courts. To the inevitable unfamiliarity with law which brought down many of its lay victims was to be added the still more appalling lack of knowledge of many of the special pleaders. 'The omission of a word in a declaration is sufficient to set aside the best-founded judgment. And this case is peculiarly cruel, as the individual who suffers is innocent of the mistake or neglect which proved fatal to his interests.'[35]

Perhaps the most striking expression of O'Connell's hostility at this time to the operating principles of the profession for which he was preparing followed an attendance at the Old Bailey on 14 January 1796.

> Two highwaymen were tried and found guilty. Now, if these unfortunate individuals are hanged, will one more virtue be infused into the bosom of any individual? Will one crime less be committed than would be had they escaped? Certainly not. The experience of ages has shown the inefficacy of punishment. The reasoning of the speculatist shows its immorality. Yet men continue to inflict punishment on their fellow-beings. Driven to despair by the wants of nature and the contempt of his acquaintance, the man whose most strenuous efforts are insufficient to procure him subsistence takes the road and forcibly deprives the luxurious or the unfeeling of a portion of their superfluities. The sacred rights of property, thus violated, devote the head of the *unwilling* spoliator to destruction. And this is what we are thought to call justice. O, Justice, what horrors are committed in thy name![36]

Doubtless this was written under the influence of reading Godwin, who was opposed to all punishment – with a final flourish perhaps from Mme Roland. But it also accorded with O'Connell's earlier, as well as his later, disposition. For although he was to become a finished lawyer, in every technical respect, he remained strangely at odds with his calling in certain of its fundamental contemporary assumptions. One was the punitive system of the day, in either its vengeful or its deterrent aspect. It was fortunate for him that on the criminal side he was almost invariably a defending counsel. Not only by nature but also by abiding inclination was he cast in the role of a Bayard of the courts.

Until the publication of his journal more than a century after its composition, the accepted picture of O'Connell's tertiary study was that of a sedulous, uncritical reader of legal texts, and of nothing else beyond Gibbon and the Bible. This as we have seen was quite mistaken. In fact he tried systematically to garner knowledge, taste and modes of judgment from every field within his touch. At the same time, he set about mastering law as if it were the language of the enemy.

## III

Perhaps the most important elements in O'Connell's intellectual development in London, which lay hidden before the publication of his journal, were the sources of his political ideas and his lengthy period of religious scepticism. Fortunately the two months in which he kept up his journal at Chiswick appear to coincide with the critical stage in each of these unfoldings.

Godwin's *Political Justice* was O'Connell's crucial piece of reading at this time. Its essential theme was human perfectibility. By means of reason, man is bound eventually to attain intellectual amd moral perfection and complete control of both his own nature and the external world: in the end all government and every external restraint would fall away as otiose. Meanwhile, many existing institutions should be abolished: marriage, organized religion, private property, contract, monarchy, the peerage and various other apparent immutabilities. All this was little more than the outer limits of one form of contemporary radicalism. Where Godwin really struck home with O'Connell was, first, in his total opposition to violence and revolution as bound to hold back the long march of rational progress – 'Revolutions . . . suspend the wholsome [*sic*] advancement of science, and confound the process of nature and reason'[37] – and secondly, his conviction that the key to every beneficial change lay in the enlistment of public opinion. 'All government is founded in opinion . . . Make men wise, and . . . you make them free.'[38] O'Connell's entire political structure was to rest, ultimately speaking, on these two simple propositions. He himself was overwhelmed by Godwin's argument. Godwin's 'work cannot be too highly praised', he wrote upon turning the last page. 'All mankind are indebted to the author. The cause of despotism never met a more formidable adversary. He goes to the root of every evil that now plagues man and degrades him almost beneath the savage beast. He shows the source whence all the misfortunes of mankind flow. That source he demonstrates to be political government.'[39]

Fittingly, perhaps, O'Connell interleaved his reading of *Political Justice* with his reading of Mary Wollstonecraft's *A Vindication of the Rights of Woman*: she was very shortly to become Godwin's mistress, and then wife. O'Connell regarded the *Vindication* as opening 'the road to truth by clearing away prejudice'. It was not a prejudice that he had shared: 'that mind has no sex, and that women are unjustly enslaved, are opinions I have long entertained.' How precisely, and to what degree, women should exercise political power remained puzzles to him. But Godwin had at least provided a general principle for judgment 'by proving that government to be best which laid fewest restraints upon private judgment. Surely the judgment of the one sex ought to be as unshackled as that of the other.'[40] This too was a significant conclusion for O'Connell. He was not to become a female suffragist or emancipationist; the first half of the nineteenth century was not a kind climate for such beings. From his later conduct we can, perhaps, even infer an acceptance of the prevailing ideology of 'separate spheres'. But, in general terms, laying the fewest possible restraints upon private judgments of every kind epitomized and interlinked O'Connell's reformism across the spectrum.

Paine's *Age of Reason* appears to have been as telling for O'Connell's religious doubt as was *Political Justice* for his social faith. As with his move to radicalism, his drift towards scepticism appears to have been a gradual development from late 1794 to late 1795. In the summer of 1794 he still regarded proximity to a Catholic chapel for Sunday mass as a significant factor in selecting a resort. But a year and a half later he justified his distaste for making a journal entry by his feeling oppressed 'by the same sensations which I used to feel when, formerly, I intended on a day to go to confession'[41] – with the seeming implication that he had for some time given up this practice. *The Age of Reason* was a powerful deist tract, anti-dogmatic, anti-ecclesiastical, anti-revelationary and anti-Christian, except in so far as Christ himself was saluted as a notable philanthropist. O'Connell, who may well have borrowed it from his redoubtable landlady, did not read it in isolation from similar tracts. During the same period he studied, for example, Voltaire's ironic assault upon Catholicism, 'Zapata's' *Questions*, as well as *Receuil Nécessaire*, an anthology of freethinking authors. Doubtless his simultaneous perusal of *Decline and Fall* (which he was of course to re-read later) speeded up the inroads on his inherited religion. But it was *The Age of Reason* which really confirmed O'Connell's unconversion. 'This work gave me a great deal of pleasure', he recorded on 13 January 1796, when he had completed the first volume. 'In treating of the Christian system he [Paine] is clear and concise. He has presented many things to my sight in a point of view in which I never before beheld them.'[42] Six days later O'Connell wrote of the second volume,

> This part has given me more satisfaction than the former. It has put the foundation of the religious question of the Christians in a point of view in which a judgement is easily formed on its solidity. I now have no doubts on this head. I may certainly be mistaken. But I am not wilfuly mistaken, if the expression has any meaning. My mistakes I refer to the mercy of that Being who is wise by excellence. To the God of nature do I turn my heart; to the meditation of His works I turn my thoughts.[43]

Scepticism, however, was not to be embraced completely without nervous *arrières pensées*. As O'Connell himself confessed, 'The prejudices of childhood and youth at times frighten and shake the firmness of my soul.'[44] In short, he asked, was he taking a terrible false step? What if after all Catholicism turned out to be the truth? He tried to console himself with the thought that the benign Deity would never punish error, if honest. 'He will not punish for the unbiassed conviction of the soul. To affirm the contrary would, in my apprehension, be to calumniate.'[45] His attempt to exorcize the past and secure himself against every possibility eventually took this shape:

> These fears, these doubts, perhaps imply a libel on the First Cause, the Great Spirit who created the planetary systems that roll around. It is impossible that He whose justice is *perfect* should punish with eternal torments the belief which is founded on conviction. It appears impossible because the conviction of the mind does not depend on us. We cannot prevent, we cannot change, the belief that our souls form on the perceptions of the senses. Again, these perceptions are not in our power. We receive impressions from the surrounding objects notwithstanding all our efforts to the contrary. It would in fact be as absurd and criminal to say that the Great Spirit would punish me for not believing that it is *now* noon

> as to affirm that He would inflict tortures for not believing another proposition the belief of which is equally impossible.[46]

We can never speak with certainty, or perhaps even confidence, of another's spiritual condition. But the evidence to hand does seem to indicate that O'Connell 'lost his faith' during 1794–5, and committed himself deliberately to another, Paineite deism, early in 1796. In doing so he did not, however, rid himself of doubts. Rather he exchanged doubts that Christianity might not be true for doubts (or at least extra-rational fears) that it might be, after all.

## IV

O'Connell made the last London entry in his journal on 18 February 1796. Possibly this was because his departure for Ireland (though still almost three months distant) was settled on about that date. New regulations had been issued for the Irish bar. These required the keeping of nine terms at the King's Inns, as well as satisfying the requirements of a London Inn. In order to meet both conditions and yet be called to the bar in Dublin in time to go on the summer circuit of 1798, O'Connell would have to begin attendance at the King's Inns by mid-May 1796. So it was arranged. As things turned out, he had also to change from Lincoln's to Gray's Inn for his last London term so that all this could be fitted in. Hence what he himself described as his 'threefold apprenticeship to the law',[47] though in fact the triple apprenticeship meant little more than experiencing three different sorts of dinners.

The new regulations meant heavy additional calls upon Hunting Cap's purse – even the formal transfer to Gray's Inn cost £11 – and he was already angry at what he divined to be O'Connell's folly and extravagance during his last months in London. O'Connell bent himself to counteract this impression. On 26 February he wrote from Chiswick,

> Had I to do with anyone else but you I should deem it politic to mention the different articles at different periods that in the division the bulk of the aggregate may be lost sight of. But with you all low cunning would be as base as it would be useless. Your liberality takes away the will as your penetration does the means of deceit.

| | |
|---|---|
| Fees at Lincoln's Inn | £22. 4.0 |
| Transfer to Gray's Inn if necessary | £11. 0.0 |
| Travelling charges | £12.12.0 |

| Analysis of Travelling charges | |
|---|---|
| Carriage to Holyhead | £5. 0.0 |
| Luggage *as at coming* | £2. 2.0 |
| To guards and coachmen | 15. |
| Passage to Dublin | 10.6 |
| Victuals on the road – suppose | £1. 3.0 |
| | £9.10.6 |

The overplus is £3. 1. 6 in case of no delay whatever at Holyhead but as there is a possibility of delay the impropriety of travelling with only the exact sum necessary for the speediest journey is self-evident.[48]

O'Connell was probably disingenuous. Clearly he expected Hunting Cap to be flattered when he described him as too perspicacious to be cheated; but his words read unpleasantly like a confidence man's opening gambit. Not all O'Connell's justifications of his accounts sound even plausible. He explained the purchase of several pairs of black silk stockings, for example, as prudent because they were cheaper in London and proper because they were *de rigueur* in his future profession. It is certain that he left England in debt; and he later bemoaned his extravagance at Chiswick. 'Indeed, I knew not what it is to be economical in London. I spent foolishly what I bitterly regretted since.'[49]

His spending and his debt were comparatively trivial in amount. They loomed large for O'Connell only because Hunting Cap was his sole resource. From past experience he knew that asking for or accepting money from his father would bring down his uncle's wrath upon him. This explains, if it does not altogether excuse, O'Connell's unctuous pleading and pathetic concealments. His extraordinary dependence on his patron and that patron's automatic parsimony and suspicion nurtured in him some unattractive qualities – bombast, cajolery and deceit – though they also gave him some ultimately useful practice in the art of persuasion and finesse.

Although Hunting Cap would never have recognized, let alone admitted, it, he had received good value for the money spent on O'Connell's London education. Despite his continual dissatisfaction with his own progress, O'Connell succeeded in teaching himself a great deal, as well as learning something from his surroundings. Few bar students of the day would have known as much law as he by the age of twenty-one, and fewer still could have matched him in wider fields; and he had trained himself earnestly in speaking at the Cogers, and in dialectic with his fellow-boarders at Mrs Rigby's. He was industrious to the end of his London days. Even he allowed that he had augmented his hoard of knowledge in 1796. True, he added that his 'acquaintance with the law has not been much, if at all, improved'.[50] But this was surely too gloomy an account, given his steady legal reading.

His recreational life in London is only rarely and fleetingly revealed; but one guesses that it was both inextensive and comparatively innocent. Most of the few companions mentioned in the journal were Irish (Kerry cousins in all but two cases), and his worst misconduct little more than a night's overdrinking and a consequent brawl or scuffle. He recorded nothing which suggests debauchery. Much inclined to priggishness in self-judgment, he none the less noted privately on 31 December 1796, 'During this year there has been no action of mine which ought to bring regret to my conscience or shame to my cheek.'[51] Overall, O'Connell did not greatly exaggerate when, shortly before he left London, he gave Hunting Cap a résumé of his achievements and his hopes:

> I hope to be pretty well master of the subject [law] before I have an opportunity of putting myself forward to public notice. If I can come forward at first with any thing like tolerable *eclat*, there will be an hundred to one in my favour. Though I am extremely anxious to become a greater lawyer, law makes little more than the principal part of my study. I read with attention history, rhetoric, philosophy, and sometimes poetry. While I apply myself to the English language, I endeavour to unite purity of diction to the harmony and arrangement of phraseology . . . And as my life will be a chain of study and application until I appear on the great stage of the world, I will endeavour to appear there with brilliancy and solidity.[52]

It is perhaps significant that, as usual, O'Connell's master metaphors were those of the actor and the stage. Only once does he refer to play-going in his London journal. But other evidence suggests that this was by no means his only visit to the theatre; and we must keep in mind that not only did he record selectively while he kept the journal, but also that he only kept it for only three of the forty months of his London sojourn. The single theatrical entry is however filled with interest, for O'Connell, then only twenty years of age, concentrated his dramatic analysis on rhetoric and elocution. Contrary to the current orthodoxy that John Kemble was a master of rhythm and declamation, O'Connell found him deficient in both. His lines (in Nathaniel Lee's *Alexander the Great*) were, O'Connell noted, poor in matter but with 'a smooth flow of numbers in them pleasing to the ear'. To render them palatable, he continued, 'they should receive from the speaker this the only beauty they possess. Now Kemble, on the contrary, pronounces them as if they consisted of a number of disjointed half-sentences.' Kemble's sister, Mrs Siddons, was by contrast the complete speaker of dramatic lines. 'The strength and modulation of her voice render any character doubly interesting in her hands. With our modern actors it is no small difficulty to understand the dialogue of a tragedy. But Mrs Siddons has the faculty of making herself clearly understood in every part.'[53] O'Connell contemptuously dismissed the performance of a third Kemble, Charles, as impudence without merit – this despite, or possibly because of, Charles Kemble's having been his schoolfellow at Douai. Even so severe a judgment may not have been astray, for the younger Kemble had only recently taken to the stage. O'Connell was well aware that his estimates challenged the contemporary orthodoxy at several points. But whatever the rights of the matter, they certainly revealed an acute and independent intelligence. It is also noteworthy that where O'Connell moved beyond comment upon declamation, it was fire and force which he most admired in acting, and affectation which he excoriated. All in all, even Hunting Cap might not have been dissatisfied had he known what O'Connell had made of his night at Drury Lane. In proper Ciceronian fashion, he had rendered it an exercise for his future work and painfully elaborated his own conception of the forensic art. It is true that London had also transformed, or at least helped to transform, O'Connell into an extreme political radical and a religious sceptic. It is hard to guess which development would have been more abhorrent to Hunting Cap, had he known of the march of his nephew's mind. But he could scarcely have withheld approval altogether from O'Connell's earnest intellectual endeavour, however unfortunate its immediate fruits.

O'Connell had arrived in London a schoolboy of seventeen accustomed to following instructions and set texts and measuring his achievement in terms of the mastery of appointed tasks. He departed a young man of nearly twenty-one accustomed, painfully, to formulating his own judgments, with a heterogeneous accumulation of knowledge and ideas and the main principles of his political philosophy already chosen. Some schoolboy features were still clearly discernible in the bar student of ten terms' standing, in particular unremitting application and ambition. Curiously, there is no indication, apart from the mollificatory transmission of a little London political gossip to Hunting Cap from time to time, that O'Connell took any interest in the parliamentary proceedings at Westminster while he lived in England. This contrasts strikingly with both his earlier and his later enthusiasm for the debates of the Irish House of Commons at College Green. None the less, there is no mistaking the thread of a more or less deliberate political apprenticeship running through O'Connell's adolescence and early manhood from his Douai to his Chiswick days.

*CHAPTER 3*

# Dublin

## *1796–1800*

### I

O'Connell reached Dublin on 12 May 1796, just in time to keep the Trinity term at King's Inns. Hunting Cap, whose influence with various Dublin lawyers had helped to speed up his enrolment, had evidently expressed displeasure with his later London career, for, as soon as he reached Ireland, O'Connell promised amendment now that he had 'as it were arrived at a new stage of my life'.[1] As an earnest of his repentance, he even sought Hunting Cap's approval of the route which he proposed to take on his way to Kerry for the long vacation – to Cork, thence to his MacCartie relatives in the north-west of that county, thence to Carhen and finally to Derrynane. We may take it that this itinerary was sanctioned and successfully fulfilled; but the upshot was not so happy. Some time after he returned to Dublin in October 1796, O'Connell noted that he had quite fallen out of favour with his uncle, who had begun to treat him with suspicion. The explanation is probably to be found in his summer visit to Derrynane. After his departure, Hunting Cap wrote savagely to O'Connell's mother,

> Your son left this ten days ago, and took with him my favourite horse. Had it not been for that, I might have dispensed with his company. He is, I am told, employed in visiting the seats of hares at Keelrelig, the earths of foxes at Tarmons, the caves of otters at Bolus, and the celebration of Miss Burke's wedding at Direen – useful avocations, laudable pursuits, for a nominal student of the law! The many indications he has given of a liberal mind in the expenditure of money has left a vacuum in my purse as well as an impression on my mind not easily eradicated.[2]

O'Connell was to fall into further trouble immediately. On 22 December 1796 a French invasion fleet reached Bantry Bay, and when it departed six days later without having been able to land its troops, it was believed to be bound for some disembarkation point on the Ulster coast. Dublin was therefore in a fever of apprehension for the first week or two of 1797 as well as the last days of 1796; and in the excitement, O'Connell followed the lead of most lawyers and law students and enrolled in the Volunteers on 2 January. Hunting Cap may well have forbidden any such step already. At any rate, it was practically certain that he would disapprove. Yet O'Connell enlisted a day before he asked Hunting Cap's permission to do so. 'I have this day', he noted, on 3 January, 'written to my uncle to get leave – that is in fact money – to enter into this [the Lawyers' Artillery] corps.'[3] He pleaded to Hunting Cap that he was the only young lawyer who had not joined a corps; that it was generally believed that those who refrained would be 'marked by government' as politically disaffected; that if he held back he would be disgraced in his profession and obliged to leave Dublin; and that the Lawyers' Artillery (he said that he *wished* to join it, not that he had already done so) was, with its lace-free uniform, 'the best regulated and least expensive' corps, costing no more than £20 to enter. 'I need not add', O'Connell concluded mendaciously, 'that your decision will be religiously obeyed . . . the whole of my conduct rests with you.'[4] In a later letter, he appears to have added the argument that the lord chancellor, Fitzgibbon, would prohibit his being called to the bar if he failed to enrol in a volunteer company. Hunting Cap's reply has not survived, but it is clear from later correspondence that he angrily rejected O'Connell's application. Worse still, he refused to credit most of O'Connell's assertions. He did not believe for a moment that the government would 'mark down' those who did not join a corps or that the chancellor could determine single-handedly what was properly a matter for the Benchers as a whole. O'Connell's 'threat' to abandon Dublin incensed him most of all.

The situation was potentially disastrous. Hunting Cap had been not only deeply alienated but also deceived. Yet for O'Connell to try to leave the corps now, with his enrolment still undetected by Hunting Cap, presented opposite perils. To disengage himself might be disgraceful, and word of the ensuing stir might well make its way to Derrynane. When on 16 January 1796 O'Connell received Hunting Cap's answer to his initial letter, he was cast into such despair as to write of suicide.

> Good God, what a strange world we live in! How stale, flat, and unprofitable are to me its uses! Would I was quietly in my grave! But what is there to prevent me from going to rest? Unreal mockeries, womanish fears, hence! Do not shake the firmness of my soul. ETERNAL BEING, in whose presence all things exist, look to the wretch who addresses Thee.

> Direct as it has been ordered by Thee. Rule as Thy wisdom pleases. But let not the phantoms of disordered imaginations disturb him who reposes on Thee with confidence.[5]

Perhaps so Hamletish a declaration of *possible* intent should not be taken seriously; it smacks of posturing. Yet O'Connell added in his journal on the same day, apropos an unidentifiable 'Eliza' with whom he had recently fallen in love, 'There must, assuredly there must, be an exquisite pleasure in madness. Would I was mad! Then, Eliza, I would rave of thee; then should I forget my uncle's tyranny, the coldness and unfeelingness of his heart, my own aberrations.'[6] A day later, he noted that his mind was now more calm. 'Study has restored it to tranquillity.'[7] None the less the crisis was real. Attitudinizing about suicide on paper is no guarantee that the attitudinizer will stop at that.

At least the crisis was not protracted. A second letter from Hunting Cap, received only a week after the first, granted O'Connell permission to enrol, albeit with 'almost as [great] harshness as he last week refused to permit me'.[8] Hunting Cap's continuing resentment was shown by his refusal to supply money for a uniform, telling O'Connell to apply to his father instead. There are no clues to explain Hunting Cap's change of mind. The best presumption would seem to be that, as often before, he had been forced to accept that, in preparing O'Connell for a profession, he was also committed to the adoption of that profession's practices and standards. O'Connell may have exaggerated, but there could be no gainsaying the plain facts that bar students were expected to enlist during the current emergency, and that they would lose face with their peers and elders should they fail to do so.

More fundamentally, the surface appearance of things – that is, the unilateral domination of O'Connell by his uncle – may not have truly represented the balance of power between the parties. Hunting Cap had already invested too much in O'Connell to foreclose recklessly. Whatever the outward-seeming relationship, Hunting Cap's commitment to O'Connell's career – in terms of money, vanity, sense of lineage, vicarious ambition and even perhaps affection – had in reality rendered him vulnerable. Doubtless there were still limits to this endurance, and there was still some level of offence at which he would cast O'Connell off. But the limits and level were surely being extended and raised steadily as O'Connell's career advanced. O'Connell may even have sensed this himself, at least subconsciously. In his reply of 23–4 January 1797 to Hunting Cap's churlish submission (of which reply O'Connell insouciantly observed, 'I am well satisfied with my letter to my uncle, but that is no proof that he will be so'[9]), he argued each point raised in anger or disbelief by Hunting Cap pertinaciously. He also carried sarcasm to the very border of insolence – or so his words would seem to read today:

> You had been so long in the habit of treating me as a child that I forgot that I was expressing with too much warmth the danger I was in of being looked upon by the men who are to be my companions and fellow labourers through life, as a coward or a scoundrel, or as both. That I now see my error can be of service only to prevent me from relapsing into a similar error. But of that indeed there can be little danger while I have so good a monitor as your last letter before my eyes. No. Despicable as any possible conjunction of circumstances may make me, dispirited and wretched, I will only shrink into myself; nor dare to raise my eyes so high again.[10]

Hunting Cap may not have caught the note of irony in this fulsome obeisance (though it almost echoed his own in reply to the antiquarian Smyth many years before), but, privy to O'Connell's journal, we cannot fail to detect the underlying hostility which it expressed.

The episode was significant in marking, as it were, a coming-of-age in O'Connell's relations with his patron. Not only had he won the bout but he had even persisted in his defence after victory. Moreoever he soon set about conciliation. By flattery and attentions, he won his way back into Hunting Cap's good graces well before his legal education was complete. We might also note that the episode prefigures, in lineaments if not in outcome, a much more important later happening, O'Connell's secret marriage in defiance of Hunting Cap's plans. Possibly O'Connell over-relied on the lessons of history in supposing, then, that the coup of January 1797 could simply be repeated.

## II

Professionally speaking, O'Connell's eagerness to enlist in a Volunteer Corps was quite comprehensible. But in any event his temperament would have driven him strongly in the same direction. He fell in love immediately with the colour and self-important bustle of gentlemanly soldiering: the smart uniforms of scarlet faced with blue, parades before the *ton* in Phoenix Park, all the happy business of cannon-loading and the guns, and excited manoeuvring. His journal regularly deplored the consequent neglect of study. But there can be no doubt that he enjoyed what was in effect a form of holiday – perhaps even the correction of an imbalance stemming from his long and lonely labours. 'Certain it is', he noted on 23 February 1797, 'that I should have read and written much more if I did not enter into any corps. Yet the recollection of having been in one will hereafter be pleasant. It will be still more pleasant to be always able to say, "I was a volunteer".'[11] But politically O'Connell's move was curious, to say the least. The immediate cause of the wave of volunteering in Dublin in late 1796, after O'Connell had returned from his long vacation at Derrynane, was, first, the threat and then the materialization of a French expeditionary army. But the purpose of a French invasion was to join forces with the potentially revolutionary movement in Ireland, the United Irishmen and possibly also the Catholic agrarian conspiracies. Thus volunteer corps such as the Lawyers' Artillery were automatically aligned with the causes of authoritarian control and repression. In the event of armed conflict they would rapidly become an integral element of the state's machinery of defence. How then did O'Connell square his enlistment with his Godwinite radical beliefs, not to mention his Godwinite pacifism?

He was certainly dismayed by the news of the arrival of a French fleet at Bantry Bay. His immediate reaction on 29 December 1796 took the form of:

> Liberty is in my bosom less a principle than a passion. But I know that the victories of the French would be attended with bad consequences. The Irish people are not yet sufficiently enlightened to be able to bear the sun of freedom. Freedom would soon dwindle into licentiousness. They would rob; they would murder. The altar of liberty totters when it is cemented only with blood, when it is supported only with carcases.[12]

Over the next four months – until 1 May 1797 when the journal entries end in mid-sentence with the next pages torn out, probably to avoid some form of incrimination – O'Connell returned several times to the subject of revolution. Two notes struck in his initial reaction of 29 December to the news from Bantry Bay – distrust of the French and fear of the masses in Ireland – were repeated shortly after, with the firm conclusion, 'A revolution would not produce the happiness of the Irish nation.'[13] He soon constructed a corollary of his position: 'Of real patriotism moderation is the chief mark.'[14] By this O'Connell meant that demagoguery and violence were as inimical to political liberty as oligarchy and repression. After a Sunday walk with Bennett and another friend on 22 January 1797, he noted:

> We talked some pure, because moderate, democracy. Hail, Liberty! How cheering is thy name! How happy should mankind be if thou wast

universally diffused! Strange it might appear that thou shouldst be hateful to any. But thou are calumniated, as thou art disgraced by the nominal advocates. The interested, those who grow fat on the miseries of mankind, the tyrant, and the demagogue condemn thee. The one raises his voice aloud and is heard in the public places to declaim against thee; the other more effectually damns thee by his support.[15]

For all these fine words, he worried increasingly whether self-interest lay at the bottom of his passion for 'moderation'. By the end of March 1797, there were indications that he was drifting towards bolder courses, as Dublin Castle adopted ever more brutal suppressive measures, and gave the Orange Society its head, more or less, in debasing Catholics. On 25 March O'Connell 'trembled' as he asked himself whether his own likely fate coloured his 'desire or dread of a revolution'.[16] Six days later he followed this up with another Hamlet-like soliloquy – the romantic-dramatic strain in him was still evidently running strong:

It is impossible for any young man at the present day to guess with probable success at the mode in which his existence will terminate. This opinion has been in my mind these two days past. I have in consequence been accustoming myself to consider death without shrinking. Much yet remains to be done before I can familiarise myself with the idea . . .

I must avoid disclosing my political sentiments so frequently as I do at present. It would be a devilish unpleasant thing to get *caged*! Nonsense! *Liberality* can never become dangerous.[17]

It seems likely that the mood of O'Connell's last sentence took over temporarily as 1797 proceeded, and that he was led a fair way down the path of 'immoderation'; the torn-out pages would suggest as much. We also have O'Connell's own testimony that his closest friend, Bennett, was 'an adjunct to the Directory of United Irishmen' and that he himself actually joined the movement – probably under Bennett's influence – later in the year. He recalled, moreover, attending about this time a meeting of radical lawyers, at which the United Irish leader, John Sheares, was present, adding, 'It was fortunate for me that I could not then participate in the proceedings. I felt warmly – and a young Catholic student stepping prominently forth in opposition to the Government would have been in all probability hanged.'[18] It seems clear then, that O'Connell moved into the penumbra of Irish revolution and conspiracy in 1797. This is not surprising given the government's gross provocations throughout that year to Catholics, liberals and even merely chivalric or decent-thinking men. It was to be a common enough experience in Ireland over almost the next two centuries that moderates should be driven temporarily to the left by bouts of official brutality. But it seems equally clear that the outer edge of the United Irish movement and the left-wing of the Irish bar represented the full extent of O'Connell's deviation from 'moderation', and that in his case the tide receded rapidly from its high-water mark. We can be tolerably certain that this fairly summarizes the history of his political opinions in 1796–8. But it still leaves us with the original question – how to explain his enthusiastic service in the 'para-forces' of the crown?

There is no indication that this question ever concerned or even occurred to O'Connell himself. Almost side by side in his journal he recorded, on the one hand, his delight in corps drill and on the other the increasing chances of his ending on the wrong side of a revolution. Beyond reasons of pride, prudence and even companionship, enlistment was, in O'Connell's eyes, equated with 'Volunteering'; and the Volunteers of the early 1780s, formed to repel invasion but soon to be turned into an instrument for winning Ireland's 'constitutional liberty', were for him a heroic (and perhaps also an imitable) body. In fact, the original Volunteers had soon moved on in various directions. Some corps became nurseries of radicalism, and even here and there of violent revolution; others ended, virtually en bloc, as Orange lodges. These extremities emblemize the complexities of Irish political choices and destinations during 1780–1800. Ultimately the basic Irish pattern of Protestant Ascendancy and Catholic disaffection reasserted itself overall. But in between there were several phases of flux and change, and not a few individuals deviated, temporarily or permanently, from their hereditary alignments – sometimes, it would seem, with quite small chances determining their final points of arrival.

O'Connell was certainly in the midst of such a phase in 1797. We must be careful not to impose retrospective rigidities, the logic of a later century, upon him. His own political position was by now a tolerably settled one; but such a position in such a place at such a time was bound to be more or less ambiguous. Where the contrary winds of the day might blow him could not be foretold. This is not to remove our question altogether. Whatever the pressures, he had voluntarily joined a force under the direction of Dublin Castle while yet a political radical and formally a member of a proclaimed organization. None the less, the ideological turmoil and confusion of the later 1790s in Ireland surely clears him of any suspicion of double-dealing or cold calculation. The essence of it all would seem to be that he was, from the first to last, a young man of the centre struggling to find his place on a spectrum of ever – and quickly – changing length and range. This is confirmed by another line of journal entries which coincided with and in effect overrode his gloomy speculations upon revolution.

## III

O'Connell's ambition did not diminish as he came to manhood or even – a still more effective puncturer of pretension, perhaps – to Dublin. If anything, it grew in purposiveness and precision. True, he occasionally doubted whether he could 'estimate' his talents accurately; he feared, when low in spirits, that he would never rise above mediocrity. But sometimes '– and this indeed happens most frequently – I am led away by vanity and ambition to imagine that I shall cut a great figure on the theatre of the world . . . Distant prospects rise unbidden to my sight. They are not unwelcome to my heart.'[19] Often the prospects were distant in the sense of being unspecifically 'patriotic', though also astonishingly large for a student who had just reached his majority. 'I will endeavour to give liberty to my country',[20] ran one such solemn resolution. In another he gravely dedicated his 'public life' to 'the good of my country'.[21] But by the beginning of 1797 his ambition was also taking on a much more definite form. He commenced to delineate his future in terms of a parliamentary career. On the face of it, this was extraordinary. Less than two years before, on 5 May 1795, the Irish House of Commons had rejected a bill to admit Catholics to membership by a majority of more than three to one; and currently the British government was set upon a course of Catholic repression. Yet on 28 January 1797 O'Connell noted, 'I have been this day thinking on the plan to be pursued *when I come into Parliament*.'[22] Four weeks later he attended a Commons debate on the defence of Ireland, and, struck by the mediocrity of the major speech, exclaimed. 'I too will be a member. Young as I am, unacquainted with the ways of the world, I should not even now appear contemptible.'[23]

Moreover, O'Connell was already considering the party and the parliamentary line to which he should attach himself. It was out of the question that he should be a government member. Support of a repressive, corrupt and oligarchic regime was anathema. But though he might rocket into fame 'by becoming a violent oppositionist', this also would run athwart his essential purpose in entering politics, 'to serve my country'.[24] As before, a line of 'moderation', which would eschew both the venal and coercive and the mob-pandering and reckless parties, was O'Connell's choice. In contemporary Irish parliamentary terms, this would probably have placed him in or close to Grattan's camp, as an 'advanced' whig.

But there was also a prophetic strain of nineteenth-century radicalism in O'Connell's early speculations on his coming political career. Concurrently, he was reading *The Jockey Club*, a merciless indictment of royal and aristocratic corruption in England, much in the vein of John Wade's later *Black Book*; and this may explain his self-dedication to the task of eliminating one specific source of 'the misery of man' from government. 'Oppression harasses his [man's] faculties. Privilege confined by *accident* insults his understanding. His industry is consumed to support the follies and vices of men who help him not.'[25] Albeit in idealistic and generalized form, O'Connell was marking out already a political and parliamentary position not dissimilar to that actually adopted by him at Westminster in the 1830s. There were of course to be important changes. When he came to Parliament at last, it was a British not an Irish House of Commons that he entered, and this very fact constituted his overriding grievance. Otherwise, however, the O'Connell of 1837 was anticipated to a remarkable degree in the O'Connell of forty years before. Economical and administrative reform, and war upon almost every form of civil discrimination – all handled 'moderately' or pragmatically of course – linked the naive aspirant and the hardened parliamentary performer. For in 1797 his hitherto inchoate ambition had begun to take definite shape, his career to have a clear direction; the gears, so to say, were starting to engage. Yet in all probability this was the very year in which he associated himself, formally at least, with the United Irishmen.

As with the puzzle of his enlistment in a corps, the explanation of this seeming dualism probably lies in the turmoil and fluidity of contemporary Irish politics. If anything could have projected O'Connell in the direction of armed resistance, it would have been the course of brutal repression and virulent no-popery on which the Irish government was embarking. But no provocation could have driven him deeply, let alone permanently, into the camp of revolutionary conspiracy. He found disorder and unrest abhorrent; the sudden or violent disruption of the social fabric represented the supreme danger. His French experience had driven these lessons home. In short, his leftward lurches of 1797–8 were quite uncharacteristic, though also perhaps inevitable in the circumstances. It was not these but the focusing of his ambition upon constitutional reform through parliamentary methods which lay along the true trajectory of his life.

## IV

Throughout all the excitements, O'Connell continued his humdrum student life, although inevitably with differences from London. Dublin, where he was to dwell for most of the remainder of his life, was not a large city; its population was then little above 200,000. But 'O'Connell's Dublin' was in effect still smaller. If one stood in the centre of College Green and drew a circle of about a mile in radius, one would cover the area in which practically his entire life in the capital was lived out. This circle contained rookeries of the utmost squalor, but it also embraced the main glories of the Georgian city and its principal institutional ornaments. It was the opulent and noble thoroughfares which O'Connell generally trod. Perhaps his familiar townscape reinforced his socio-political choices. Certainly, when he spoke – as he often did – of Ireland's poor, it was invariably to agrarian rather than urban impoverishment that he referred; and when he spoke – as again he often did – of Ireland's regeneration it was the native capture of Dublin Castle and College Green, and equal treatment in the Four Courts, University, Banks and Exchanges, Corporation Chamber and Mansion House, which he had in sight.

His first Dublin lodgings – with a Mrs Jones for almost eighteen months, and then with one Regan, a fruiterer 'by appointment' to Dublin Castle – were a far cry from the Chiswick *ménage*. He set down the Joneses immediately as 'a most pleasant family', while Regan, as we shall see, was to interpose paternally to save him from himself. It is possible that the 'sweet Eliza' with whom he was infatuated early in 1797 was a Jones daughter. This might account for both the apparent frequency of his encounters with her and the silence of his worship. 'Sweet Eliza', he rhapsodized in his journal on 28 January, 'let me again offer up to you the tribute of my silent wishes. Now by myself, in the lonesomeness of my heart I reflect on thee with satisfaction and delight.'[26] It might also explain his sudden departure later for Mr Regan's. 'I left Mrs Jones's this day [13 January 1798]. Some other time I will descant on my reasons. My heart is now sick.'[27]

In contrast to his later London days, O'Connell's early Dublin life was spent in the heart of the city, mostly within a radius of half a mile or so of Dublin Castle. His lodgings were much less important to him than his room had been at Chiswick. He spent four days a week, and did the bulk of his reading, at the Dublin Library in Eustace Street; he had expended two guineas ('a great sum of money for me'[28]) to join the Library soon after he had settled in the capital. 'My life', he noted on 10 December 1796, 'though it is not in any degree insipid, is monotonous and unchequered. I spend the greater part of the day in the library. In the perusal of a favourite author I feel not the time slip away. Was the library to remain open till one o'clock, I am sure I should frequently be there at that hour. As it shuts at ten, I am forced very reluctantly to leave it at that hour.'[29] There were other excursions about the city, with the Artillery Corps, of course, but also to listen to speeches from the gallery of the House of Commons, to eat dinners in the Inns, to join in moots and debates at Trinity College (although he was not an undergraduate) and to sup at nights in taverns. So far as it goes, the fragmentary evidence of the journal suggests a much fuller and more varied life than he had led in London. Curiously, almost all the companions whom O'Connell mentions in the 1796–7 Dublin entries were young Irish Protestants, several of them members of Kerry gentry families. Two of these figures appear in a strangely boyish passage, in which O'Connell, while cloaking himself in mystery, day-dreams of later friendships.

> I like [Ralph] Marshall very much, as everybody must who knows his character. He *knows* me not; yet he wishes to be acquainted with my heart, my disposition. I will not hurry his knowledge of it. Let time unfold by degrees that which it would not be easy to show at once. A man, I believe, meets with many difficulties in playing even his own character. I am anxious for the friendship of Marshall and Bland. I think we will make a valuable triumvirate. I can here indulge what elsewhere would be deemed vanity.[30]

In fact, Marshall did become O'Connell's friend. Like Bennett, he was an advanced liberal, but probably more congenial to O'Connell politically in being both an anti-revolutionist and a Francophobe.

Young Kerry gentlemen were not O'Connell's only links with the Anglo-Irish Ascendancy. In compliment to Hunting Cap, various lawyers with whom he had dealt over the years extended invitations to his nephew. Amongst these were the Frankses, the Rices and the Days, the last two of whom belonged to Kerry county families into the bargain. O'Connell was immediately – but not too grievously – oppressed by a sense of inferiority. After dining with 'the three Rices' (one of whom, Dominick, was to sign the memorial for his call to the bar) on 4 January 1797, he noted, 'Stephen Rice seems to me to possess more information than any man in whose company I have ever been. How different, how decisively superior, is his knowledge to mine! He made me creep into my ignorance. Yet I am at times apt to be vain of what little I know . . . He is by no means obtrusive in his learning.'[31]

Seven weeks later he dined with Robert Day, another barrister, who was to become a circuit judge in the following year, with much the same effect. 'I wish', he wrote on returning home, 'I had that smoothness which society bestows on its frequenters.'[32] Later still, he even called upon Lord Kenmare, a Kerry magnate, at Hunting Cap's indirect suggestion.

It may seem strange that O'Connell, a twenty-one-year-old Catholic student, should have been able to breach at least the outer circle of the Ascendancy, and that so many of his Dublin associations were with Anglicans. It was not however truly surprising. Hunting Cap was rich and influential, and O'Connell himself destined to become a barrister. The Irish bar was still almost exclusively Protestant; O'Connell belonged to the very first wave of Catholic aspirants. But if the profession *had* to include Catholics (and not a few of its members were former Catholics who had conformed to enable them to practise), it was only sensible to include them also in its social traffic. Moreover, this was still 1797, before the outbreak of the Wexford rising and the re-embitterment of Protestant-Catholic relations which followed in its wake. Further still, O'Connell was especially favoured by his own cleverness and charm. But even if readily explicable, his movement into the outskirts of Protestant society is of considerable interest. It shows the possibilities of Irish Protestant and Catholic intersection in the late eighteenth century, even in the inner sanctuary of the home. More particularly, it made clear that Catholics at the Irish bar would be treated more or less as equals in personal and communal relations by the incumbent Protestant brethren. The mess at least would never be divided. It also signalled in advance something of the later variety and complexity of O'Connell's intercourse with Irish Protestants. The inherent contradictions in this intercourse were still mercifully hidden from the great 'non-sectarian'.

Although it is proper to stress O'Connell's religious affiliation as of crucial social and political significance, he continued to be a Catholic in name and form rather than materially. Apparently he attended Sunday mass in Dublin, perhaps even regularly. There is even evidence to suggest that he may have toyed with the idea of attempting to recover his lost faith. On 13 December 1796 he reported the receipt of a letter from his cousin Henry Baldwin, 'advising me to go to confession to Mr Beattie [probably the celebrated Fr Betagh], a Jesuit, etc., etc.'.[33] But Sabbath churchgoing was then a general observance for the respectable; and when Baldwin proposed a confessor for O'Connell, he may have been acting entirely on his own initiative.

Certainly, there is nothing in the journal to suggest that O'Connell ever visited the priest. On the other hand, there is abundant confirmation of O'Connell's continuance in deism punctuated by scepticism. 'Virtue' and 'Philosophy' were frequently apostrophized. Established churches were anathemized: 'Oh, Religion, how much have mankind suffered to [*sic*] thee . . . Christianity has had her millions of victims. The great Moore [*sic*] fell beneath her axe.'[34] A friend's death led to gloomy reflections on the dissolution of 'the particles that composed his frame';[35] thoughts of ghosts to the brave conclusion, 'Philosophy teaches me there can be none.'[36] Overall O'Connell appears to have adhered steadily to Godwinite philanthropy, albeit with some nervous self-reassurances should Catholicism turn out, after all, to have been the truth. 'I would, and I trust I will, serve man', he wrote on 7 January 1797,

> . . . I will endeavour to increase the portion of the knowledge and virtue of mankind. Oh, ETERNAL BEING, Thou seest the purity of my heart, the sincerity of my promises. Should I appear before your august tribunal after having performed them, shall not I be entitled to call for my reward? Will the omission of a superstitious action, will the disbelief of an unreasonable dogma, that day rise in judgement against me? Oh, God, how hast Thou been calumniated![37]

Despite his jeremiads on the time taken up by the Lawyers' Artillery and other dissipations, O'Connell's general reading remained extraordinarily extensive. During the two months from mid-December 1796 to mid-February 1797, for example, he not only re-read Gibbon, Godwin, Buffon and other favourites of his Chiswick days but also broke new ground in several directions. Irish antiquity, through Grose and Ledwich and the *Transactions of the Royal Irish Academy*, was one such fresh field; English history, through Henry and Whitaker (*History of Manchester*), another; diplomacy, through Bolingbroke, Condorcet, John Adams and Baron d'Holbach, a third. O'Connell covered not only more chemistry along his accustomed lines but also Cassini on astronomy. He read Barthelemy on ancient Greece, Colquhoun on the policing of London and even a little metaphysics. Johnson became an absorbing subject. Having worked carefully through Boswell's *Life*, he proceeded to Johnson's *Poems of London*, *Vanity of Human Wishes*, *Lives of the Poets* and *Rambler* essays. This listing, though not exhaustive, is surely sufficient to establish the seriousness, persistence and depth of O'Connell's preparation for the greater world.

We know little about O'Connell's law studies after he removed to Dublin. He no longer mentioned his legal reading in his journal, beyond bemoaning the inroads made upon his working time by the calls of the artillery. Eventually, he made a major resolution to amend his ways. 'I misspent my time during the summer', he wrote on 13 January 1798, 'and have done very little better since my return to town [in November 1797]. I am now to take up the study of the law with all the ardour which my situation requires.'[38] Doubtless, as usual, he exaggerated his own shortcomings. Two of the scanty journal references to what he actually did in Dublin suggest as much. On 29 December 1796 he noted, after a law students' test at Trinity College, 'I knew the part of Blackstone in which we were examined, I may safely say, better than any individual';[39] and on 25 January 1797 he recorded his attendance at a technically interesting writ of error case at King's Bench.

O'Connell's stern resolution of 13 January 1798 probably sprang from the imminence of his call to the bar, which might, all going well, take place in the next law term. Hunting Cap was agreeable to his being called then, provided that no 'rub or obstruction could be thrown in the way to impede';[40] he raised no 'rub' himself to meeting the formidable bills which admission to the bar entailed. But O'Connell did fear another sort of obstruction: 'such is the complexion of affairs', he had added on 13 January, 'that it must appear extremely doubtful whether I shall be called to the bar.'[41] In part, O'Connell had in mind the 'odium against the Catholics', which, he told Hunting Cap on 1 March 1798, 'is becoming every day more inveterate. The Chancellor [Fitzgibbon] seems hardly disposed to leave them the privileges which they enjoy at present.'[42] Fitzgibbon was also hellbent against sedition amongst the student body. He had already secured the postponement *sine die* of the call of a politically radical law student, and he was shortly to conduct a purge of Trinity College resulting in the expulsion of nineteen undergraduates who were members or supposed to be members of the United Irishmen. Thus O'Connell felt doubly vulnerable.

He may have been even more vulnerable than he thought. On 7 March 1798, Francis Higgins, the government's principal secret agent, reported to Dublin Castle that O'Connell had covertly received a despatch from one of the leading revolutionaries-in-exile, Napper Tandy. 'Connell holds a commission from France (a Colonel's). He was to be called to the Bar here to please a very rich old uncle, but he is one of the most abominable and bloodthirsty republicans I ever heard of. The place of rendezvous is the Public Library in Eustace Street, where a private room is devoted to the leaders of the United Irish Society'.[43] This was of course a farrago – but by no means total nonsense. Higgins had confused O'Connell with his *emigré* uncle, and stated precisely the opposite of the truth in describing O'Connell as 'bloodthirsty' or, in the French sense at least, a 'republican'. None the less it was undeniable that O'Connell had flirted with United Irishmen in the preceding year, or that the Dublin Library was the United Irish haunt. Young men were to be hanged – let alone denied entry to a profession – on no more damning evidence than this during 1798 and 1799.

There are moreover certain indications that O'Connell moved radical-wards again in the early spring of 1798. He entered nothing in his journal between 13 January and 31 December 1798; but in a posthumous memoir his son John described a dinner party held 'about March 1798' by O'Connell's intimate friend, Murray, a cheese merchant, at which O'Connell, flown with wine, talked politics indiscreetly. He was subsequently warned by his landlord, Regan, whose work rendered him au fait with the gossip of Dublin Castle, against committing himself publicly. In later years, Murray's son, Peter, recalled another fateful evening at his father's house:

> I well remember O'Connell one night at my father's house, during the spring of 1798, so carried away by the political excitement of the day and by the ardour of his innate patriotism, calling for a prayer-book to swear in some zealous young men as United Irishmen at a meeting of the body in a neighbouring street. Councillor — was there, and offered to accompany O'Connell on his perilous mission. My father, though an Irishman of advanced liberal views and strong patriotism, was not a United Irishman, and endeavoured without effect to deter his young and gifted friend from the rash course in which he seemed embarked. Dublin was in an extremely disturbed state, and the outburst of a bloody insurrection seemed hourly imminent. My father resolved to exert to the uttermost the influence which it was well known he possessed over his young friend. He made him accompany him to the canal bridge at Leeson Street, and, after an earnest conversation, succeeded in persuading the future Liberator to step into a turf boat that was then leaving Dublin. That night my father's house was searched by Major Sirr, accompanied by the Attorneys' Corps of Yeomanry, who pillaged it to their heart's content. There can be no doubt that private information of O'Connell's tendencies and haunts had been communicated to the Government.[44]

It is difficult to evaluate this statement. Though highly circumstantial, it was made long after O'Connell's death and may well have been a second-hand reminiscence. Certainly, if O'Connell did leave Dublin in the spring of 1798, it cannot have been for long; and it seems quite out of character with O'Connell of the *Journal* to try to embroil others in a perilous conspiracy. On the other hand, the Castle's witch-hunt in Dublin in March and April, not least among the student population, might have produced a desperate reaction – especially in a moment of pot-valour; and the very vehemence of O'Connell's later denunciations of conspiracy, as the natural begetter of informers, betrayal and ruin, might well have sprung from a sense that he himself had narrowly escaped the trap.

Whatever the degree of his political entanglement, however, O'Connell kept his eye fixed upon his call to the bar. Hunting Cap was applied to long in advance for money for the call, as well as help in securing the necessary memorials of support from practising senior counsel. Evidently pleased that the first staging-post in O'Connell's career was now in sight, Hunting Cap responded with unusual benignity, in addition to his invariable efficiency and despatch. He could not resist playing Polonius for a while; the role was both congenial and practically demanded by the occasion. 'One maxim you should always keep in view, which is, that it is, by much, more decent and reputable to advance gradually and as circumstances will prudently admit, in expense, than to set out ostentatiously and soon be obliged to recede and retrench.'[45] But platitudes broke no bones. O'Connell was now provided with all he needed for his admission, and despite Fitzgibbon's hostility to Catholics and pursuit of the disaffected, and even Higgins's delation of him on 7 March, he safely attained the rank of barrister in the earliest possible law term, Easter 1798.

Within five days of O'Connell's admission the United Irish rebellion, which was also a massive agrarian and sectarian revolt, broke out in Wexford. For a time Dublin itself seemed threatened, and almost a month passed before the final decisive defeat of the insurgents at Vinegar Hill, near Enniscorthy, on 21 June. Meanwhile, legal work was disrupted for the remainder of the term. O'Connell must have left for Kerry soon after the courts were suspended, for land communication with the interior was still cut off when he departed: 'so eighteen of us sailed for Cork in a potato boat, bound for Courtmasherry [*sic*]'. Disembarking at the Cove of Cork, 'after a capital passage of thirty-six hours', he proceeded overland to Carhen.[46] Before the summer assizes (much delayed) commenced, O'Connell fell gravely ill. 'I did not go to it [the summer circuit], as I was confined to my uncle's house by a violent fever, of which I was near to perish.'[47] Possibly his malady was rheumatic fever; at any rate, it was brought on by sleeping in wet clothes and accompanied by bouts of delirium. It lasted for several weeks; for long his life was in danger. 'During my illness', O'Connell later recalled, 'I used to quote from the tragedy of Douglas these lines:

> *Unknown I die; no tongue shall speak of me;*
> *Some noble spirits, judging by themselves,*
> *May yet conjecture what I might have proved;*
> *And think life only wanting to my fame.'* [48]

How revealing was this choice of verse! There is no reason to suppose that O'Connell's memory played him false; but even if it did, even if he picked these lines not upon his sick-bed but retroactively, how very suggestive his selection still would be.

It was November 1798 before O'Connell returned to Dublin and his 'practice'. This last had yielded him but a single guinea since his call to the bar six months before. Yet his involuntary idleness of the summer is not to be set down as an unmitigated misfortune. Possibly – though he himself would doubtless have been amazed at such a thought – he needed a long respite from strain and striving. Certainly, he gained from his remove from the storm-centre of Irish politics; Kerry was quite untouched by the insurrection or its bloody aftermath. Not only did he escape all governmental attention in the inquisitory months which followed the collapse at Vinegar Hill but also he could watch the development of Irish revolution at a philosophic distance, and learn from it two lessons which he was to prize throughout his life. One was the danger and the debauchery of conspiracy. The post-rebellion trials furnished much painful evidence of cowardice and treachery, of spies, informers and *agents provocateurs*. The other was a deep distrust of (as well as pity for) the masses, once they were unloosed from 'rational' control. 'I dined today with Bennett', he wrote in his journal on 2 January 1799. 'We talked much of the late unhappy rebellion. A great deal of innocent blood was shed on the occasion. Good God! what a brute man becomes when ignorant and oppressed! Oh, Liberty, what horrors are perpetrated in thy name! May every virtuous revolutionist remember the horrors of Wexford!'[49] No less interesting however is the opening of the sentence which preceded this particular entry in the journal: 'I finished my notes of *Fee Tail* out of *Coke on Littleton* today.' Two days later, he added, 'In the course of another year I shall be a tolerably good lawyer. My present method of studying the common and statute law I believe to be the best. When I have proceeded in it for some time, I will commence equity on the same plan.'[50] The industrious apprentice was clearly back on course. As with Sieyès' celebrated estimate of his achievement in the French Revolution, O'Connell could say of 1798, 'J'ai vécu'.[51]

## V

O'Connell had been called to the bar on 19 May 1798, and earned his first guinea five days later for drawing up a declaration on a promissory note. But practically speaking his legal career did not commence until the following February. The law year had been much disturbed in 1798, and in any event, as we have seen, O'Connell's illness prevented his going on circuit. In 1799, however, he made a brave beginning at the bar, earning twenty-three guineas from sixteen fees. Ten of these fees came from the attorney who had given him his first brief in 1798, James Connor of Tralee. Connor may have acted from old friendship. He was a remote connection of O'Connell by marriage; but a very distant link could scarcely have been counted for much in the almost infinitely intersected society of middle-class Kerry. At any rate, Connor was soon rewarded for his early patronage for O'Connell proved himself, almost immediately, to be a quite extraordinary junior.

The bulk of O'Connell's earliest work at the bar was more or less mechanical, drawing up declarations, composing petitions for compensation from the local rates for cattle houghed, and the like. But he was briefed as junior by Connor in a case of some magnitude – possibly concerning a challenge to a duel – at the Tralee summer assizes of 1799. It was then the Irish practice for senior and junior counsel to cross-examine witnesses in turn, but also for inexperienced juniors to waive their 'right' to cross-examine if the cross-examination looked like being more than merely formal. But O'Connell, although still only twenty-three years old and in his first few months of effective practice, refused to pass up his chance of glory. As he later described it,

> There was one of the witnesses of the other party whose cross-examination was thrown upon *me* by the opposite counsel. I did not do, as I have seen fifty young counsel do; namely, hand the cross-examination over to my senior. I thought it due to myself to attempt it, hit or miss; and I cross-examined him right well. I remember he stated that he had *his share* of a pint of whisky; whereupon I asked him *whether his share was not all except the pewter?* He confessed that it was: and the oddity of my mode of putting the question was very successful, and created a general and

> hearty laugh. Jerry Keller [a leading counsel on the Munster circuit] repeated the encouragement Robert Hickson had already bestowed upon my activity, in the very same words: 'You'll *do*, young gentleman! You'll do'.[52]

Despite possible high-colouring by its hero, the episode points to several of the courtroom qualities for which O'Connell was later to be celebrated. First, his controlled audacity: here it manifested itself merely – though in the circumstances also strikingly – in taking a considerable risk in the hope of leaping into a local reputation. But it was soon to operate more grandly. O'Connell was to become remarkable for the boldness with which (having calculated carefully beforehand) he struck out his strategic legal line, and also for his indomitable resistance to, and even contemptuous counter-attacks upon, bullying or exorbitant judges. Secondly, his Tralee performance illustrates his speed of response and flexibility in cross-examination. Finally, it exhibits already a strength for which he was to be often and justly celebrated – his capacity to read the minds of ordinary Irish people. In this instance, he understood immediately the shadowy balance between fear of the legal and spiritual consequences of perjury and the desire to avoid the admission of fatal evidence. The consequent word-play, unschooled but cunning casuistry, and blithe differentiation of the *suggestio falsi* from the false – these were characteristic features of a mental world that he could enter and move about in with consummate ease.

Jerry Keller proved a good prophet. O'Connell '*did*', and '*did*' very quickly, at the bar. In his second year proper in practice his gross earnings exceeded £400, and although he earned a little less in 1801, the decline was temporary. By his thirtieth year, 1805, his fees brought in over £1000, and from then on he climbed rapidly through £2000, £3000 and £3500 per annum. In short, O'Connell was prodigiously successful as a junior counsel. Monetary translations between the centuries are notoriously difficult and dubious; but it would be safe to say that his annual income must have exceeded £100,000, in modern terms, within ten years of his being called. Let us not slide over this achievement easily. Even had he been a Protestant, a tory and a judge's son or nephew, all together, such an early climb would have been accounted a marvel. R. L. Sheil, who shortly followed O'Connell to the bar, wrote of the contemporary profession as he found it: 'There is at the Irish Bar a much larger quantity of affliction than is generally known . . . The struggle between poverty and gentility, which the ostentatious publicity of the profession in Ireland has produced, has, I believe, broken many hearts.'[53] Most were doomed never 'to attain to station . . . to live for years in hope, and to feel the proverbial sickness of the heart arising from its procrastination.'[54] Sheil described the typical beginning of even the most eminent career: 'For some years he remains unemployed: at last gets a brief, creeps into the partialities of a solicitor, and sets up a bag and a wife together.'[55] This should make clear the extraordinariness of O'Connell's initial achievement.

Success of this kind at the bar implied immense labours. Most of O'Connell's fees were small sums, down even to one or two guineas; and much of his work continued to be mechanical and tedious, eating

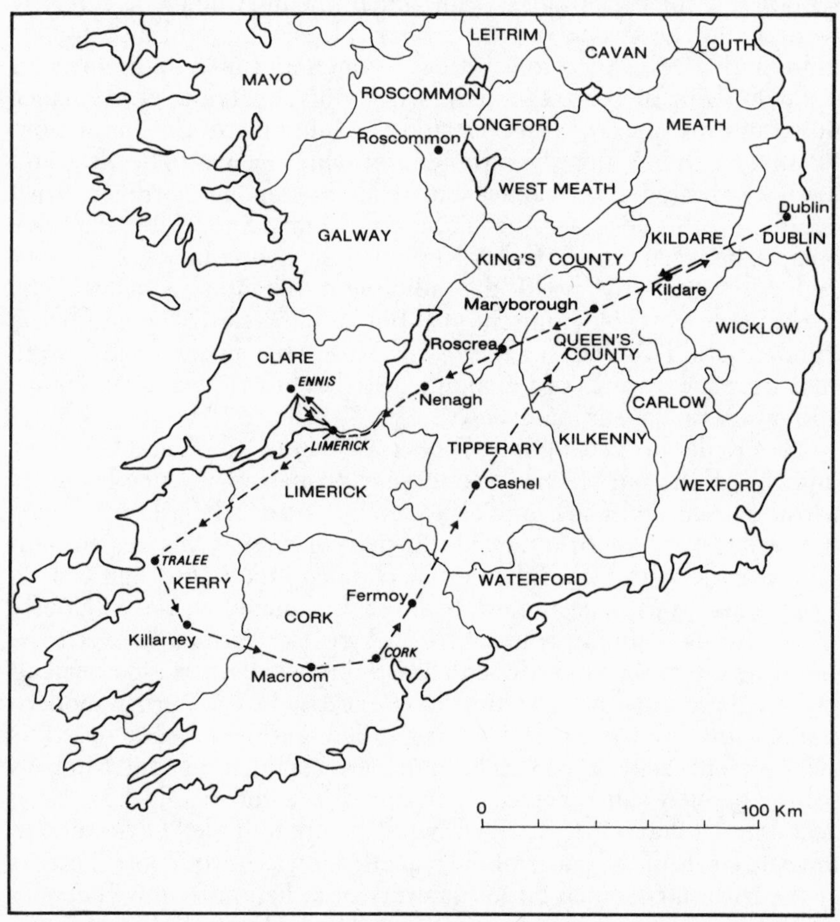


Map 3. The Munster circuit

the hours without compensating stimulation. Extraordinary physical strength, concentration and elasticity of disposition were demanded by such a life, all the more so as it was seasonally peripatetic. Each late spring and each high summer, the young O'Connell undertook by mailcoach, carriage or horse the laborious five- or six-week circuit of Ennis, Limerick, Tralee and Cork. With various deviations, the mere time spent on roads and tracks during a circuit probably accounted for six or seven full days. A great deal of this journeying would have been on execrable surfaces or over rain- and windswept high terrain. Parts of the route, especially north of Tralee and south-west to Macroom, were very difficult: 'if anything were capable of destroying my natural vivacity', wrote O'Connell in 1806, 'it would be those infernal mountains and roads.'[56] A stretch near Kilworth was sometimes brigand-ridden during his early circuit years.

O'Connell's descriptions of parts of two of these journeys survive. One summer morning, almost certainly in 1799, he left Carhen at 4 a.m. and reached Tralee, some fifty miles away, soon after midday.

> I then rode on, and got to Tarbert about five in the afternoon – full sixty miles, Irish, [over ninety statute miles] from Carhen. There wasn't one book to be had at the inn. I had no acquaintance in the town; and I felt my spirits low enough at the prospect of a long, stupid evening. But I was relieved, by the sudden appearance of Ralph Marshall, an old friend of mine, who came to the inn to dress for a ball that took place in Tarbert that night. He asked me to accompany him to the ball. 'Why,' said I, 'I have ridden sixty miles'. 'Oh, you don't seem in the least tired,' said he, 'so come along'. Accordingly I went, and sat up until two o'clock in the morning, dancing. I arose next day at half-past eight, and rode to the Limerick assizes.[57]

Two years later, while crossing the mountains from Killarney to Kenmare en route for the Cork assizes, he brooded upon the passage of the Act of Union:

> my heart was heavy at the loss that Ireland had sustained, and the day was wild and gloomy. That desert district, too, was congenial to impressions of solemnity and sadness. There was not a human habitation to be seen for many miles; black, giant clouds sailed slowly through the sky, and rested on the tops of the huge mountains: my soul felt dreary, and I had many wild and *Ossianic* inspirations as I traversed the bleak solitudes.[58]

These contrasting vignettes enable us to feel, as it were, a little of the texture of O'Connell's circuitry under our hands. But it would probably be misleading to use light and shade in equal proportions in any sketch of his first years as a working barrister. Toil, gloom and struggle there certainly were. But the predominant impression given off by the evidence – scanty though it be – is of O'Connell's delight in his young powers and in the variety and colour of his experiences and companionship. In 'chambers' (which meant, in Dublin, the Law Library and one's home study), O'Connell was succeeding; and for all its discomforts, circuit life was bustling and exciting – at any rate, for a confident junior growing rapidly, twice-yearly, in reputation. Admittedly, much of the material from which one's sense of the fun, glamour and camaraderie of the Munster Bar at the turn of the eighteenth century derives, consists of reminiscenses; and these are notoriously selective. Even if it was larger than life, however, it was a real life which was being twopenny-coloured. The world of dashing chaises and sudden briefs, of ramshackle inns and clarety bar messes, of challenges, and even duels, and contesting wits, of judicial ogres and oddities and 'characters' to fill each courtroom role, had a basis in actuality. (Even the blackly-comic story of O'Connell's being challenged to a duel by a hostile witness, who withdrew the challenge on recalling that O'Connel's was one of the three lives on which his lease depended, but offered to repeat it if O'Connell would insure his life, may well have been substantially true.) Such a world was the young O'Connell's oyster. Tall, handsome, quick, dextrous, brilliant and assured, he could exult in it and exploit it, in more or less equal parts.

## CHAPTER 4

# Love and Money

## 1800–15

### I

O'Connell entered into a secret engagement with Mary O'Connell late in 1800, probably when he was in Tralee for the second assizes of that year. He was then twenty-five years old, she three years younger. He may have known her long, since she was a distant cousin. But his intimacy with her was new, and probably arose from her being sister-in-law to his friend and chief professional support at the time, James Connor of Tralee. O'Connell fell in love, if not absolutely at first sight, at any rate on first seeing Mary with fresh eyes. He acted with corresponding dispatch. As he recalled almost forty years later, 'I said to her, "Are you engaged, Miss O'Connell?" – She answered, "I am not." "Then," said I "will you engage yourself to me?" – "I will," was her reply. – And I said I would devote my life to make her happy. She deserved that I should – she gave me thirty-four years of the purest happiness that man ever enjoyed.'[1]

Mary O'Connell was one of eight children, whose father, Thomas O'Connell, a Tralee physician, had died fifteen years before. She was consequently penniless; and it was this which led O'Connell to insist upon the strictest secrecy in their engagement. It was all too likely that Hunting Cap would disinherit him, and perhaps even break with him entirely, if he discovered that he meant to marry a dowerless girl. 'You know as well as I do', O'Connell wrote to Mary on 28 November 1800, in what was probably his first letter to his future wife, 'how much *we* have at stake in keeping the business secret. I have certainly more at stake than ever I had before or I really believe if I fail at present I shall ever have again. Secrecy is therefore a favour I earnestly beg of you.'[2] It was also the case that Mary's brothers, taking their religion from their father, were Protestants, and impecunious ones at that.

Mary was quite willing to flout convention. A concealed engagement was highly improper, but scarcely less so was the illicit correspondence in which she was now to be employed for eighteen months. O'Connell may, as he said, have loathed the subterfuges and lies which such a correspondence demanded. But he was always a capable intriguer. He induced another, much closer, cousin, also named Daniel O'Connell but generally known as Splinter, to act as receiver of his letters from Dublin to Mary in Tralee. Whenever Splinter, another attorney, was in Dublin on business, *he* addressed O'Connell's letters directly to Mary. This led to difficulties when Splinter was not where he was needed: 'he is not to be found. He is very inconsiderate',[3] O'Connell once complained. It also produced a potentially dangerous situation when in June 1801 Mary's brother, Rick, identified Splinter's handwriting on a cover addressed to Mary. So furious was he at her impropriety in corresponding with the young attorney, that at one point a challenge to Splinter was impending. Rick's bellicosity probably owed something to Splinter's being a notoriously bad match. This crisis led to a temporary suspension of the correspondence. Later, when James Connor was admitted to the secret, he was used in Splinter's place, again with unhappy results. When Connor's wife Betsey saw a cover addressed to Mary in his handwriting, she assumed that he was suffering from a grave illness which he wished to conceal from her! Betsey too had to be told of the engagement, much against O'Connell's wishes.

There were also misunderstandings between the engaged couple. O'Connell was curiously insensitive to women's feelings – at any rate, at this particular time and to a woman of lower social standing than himself. There were distinct elements of Frank Churchill's conduct to Jane Fairfax in his behaviour. When in Kerry in the late spring of 1801, he deliberately fostered the idea that there was an 'understanding' between Mary and another local barrister in order to divert suspicion from himself. 'You are probably indebted to me', he wrote to Mary on 28 April, 'for all the jokes you suffer about Peter Hussey.'[4] O'Connell also forced clothes and finery upon her. At first, Mary resisted. She felt a 'delicacy', she told him, about being given articles which she had asked him to buy for her in Dublin. Behind this there doubtless lay some resentment of his Cophetua-like indulgence; Mary was acutely sensitive about her poverty. But she did enjoy Tralee's envy of her new veil; and in the end O'Connell's persistent argument that she was already effectively, though not legally, his wife, wore her down. By the close of 1801 he was writing of the kerchief and the '*few* pairs of white stockings' which he had purchased for her, and of her 'loose coat' in the tailor's hands.[5]

On the other hand, Mary rebelled mildly, once or twice, against the constraints of O'Connell's secrecy and the consequences of his finesse. The most serious quarrel of the betrothal arose from her writing to him in mock-formal terms, in January 1802, because his letters had fallen off. Angry and fearful, O'Connell misunderstood Mary's tactic and offered (or perhaps we should say threatened indirectly) to end the relationship should she maintain her caprice. His lapse in correspondence, he told her indignantly, had been for prudential reasons. There had been no safe conduit for letters at the time. Full of his own virtue in restraining his pen and in plotting laboriously for concealment, he was furious at what he regarded as Mary's petty and wanton revenge. She was mistaken, he wrote,

> I did not laugh at your former letter to me. Indeed, its producing a comical effect on me would be directly contrary to every impression I entertain of you. I trust and am pretty confident that this experiment will suffice and that you will not in future sport with the feelings which you know are too sensitive to bear being played on. How could you, my only darling, treat me so coldly on so slight an occasion for you had not insisted that I should write to you by every post . . . Judge then how mortified I felt at finding so small an offence – shall I call it an offence? – put every idea of tenderness out of your bosom . . . I beg of you, my love, humbly but as a favour which I think my respectful regard for you merits, that you will consider seriously before you treat me with such coldness. Indeed, indeed, I am unable to bear it.[6]

Mary learnt her lesson. Quizzing and pique were to be the male's preserve.

Despite this, the attachment, passionate from the start on either side, grew rapidly in depth. Mary could express her love the more effectively, at least in correspondence. In yielding to O'Connell's claims to provide for her as if they were already married, she wrote, simply,

> Let me then hope you are satisfied I do consider you as my husband, as my dearest and only love. Indeed, Dan, you are dearer to me than I can express. I have told you before and I will now tell it to you again that you are the only man I could ever love or wish myself united with . . . I am indeed very well convinced of my darling's love, and trust he is also convinced of mine for him.[7]

Mary had, as O'Connell himself observed twenty years later, 'a clear and distinct mind'.[8] By contrast, he could not avoid inflation.

> In disposition and in heart she ['my little woman'] is all excellence, in

> temper all sweetness, in person all that painting can express or youthful poets fancy when they love. To tell you how much I love my little woman would be to express that of which no image can be formed. Think how much you love me and then add ten hundred thousand times as much . . .[9]

But the fact that one could write straightforwardly, and the other only through a zig-zag of rhetorical postures, does not mean that their emotional commitments were unequal; the future was to show that O'Connell was Mary's peer in love.

No wedding date or plan is mentioned in the pre-marital correspondence, which stretches from November 1800 to May 1802. Presumably Hunting Cap was to be bearded before a date could be set, but O'Connell feared to hazard such a step. Meanwhile, their meetings alone must have been few and hurried, as well as covert. From the start, O'Connell had counted much on a projected visit to Dublin by Mary. 'I anxiously hope you will come up to town after Christmas with Mrs Connor', he wrote in his initial letter of 28 November 1800. 'Here I would have many more opportunities of seeing and conversing with you than in that prying, curious, *busy* town of Tralee.'[10] Presumably, it was hoped that this would afford them the chance of settling their future. But a year and a half were to pass before the visit could be managed. In the end, it did need the help of James and Betsey Connor (whom O'Connell had tried again to use, to get Mary to Derrynane, in August 1801) to bring the lovers together for a considerable time. Mary accompanied the Connors to Dublin, at last, on 12 May 1802.

It is most unlikely that a wedding in Dublin was planned beforehand. Neither O'Connell's nor Mary's letters suggest, in any way, that this was in contemplation before she left Tralee. But on 24 July, a day or two before the Connors had to return to Kerry, a private marriage did take place in the Connors' Dublin lodgings. How the celebrant, a local parish priest, was persuaded to act in such secrecy, it is impossible to say. Nor do we know why O'Connell left his own family entirely in the dark; none of them as yet had heard anything of even the betrothal, although it was by now quite widely known among Mary's close relations. Possibly O'Connell reasoned that – Hunting Cap perhaps apart – the best course was the boldest, that of presenting them later on with a fait accompli. But the most probable explanation is that the decision to marry was a very sudden one, taken in the light of the imminent separation. There are times when, all in a flash, waiting can become unendurable, and prudence crumble.

## II

The public deception continued long after the wedding had taken place. Mary returned to Tralee with the Connors within two days of her marriage, lived with them there for a few weeks, and then, with her mother, took new lodgings. It was two months before she next saw O'Connell when he visited Tralee in the course of his annual Kerry vacation. All this time, and indeed throughout the remainder of 1802, she lived as a single girl. O'Connell himself addressed her, on the cover of her letters, as 'Miss Maria O'Connell'. Even when, in September, he told his sister Ellen in confidence of '*our secret*', it was the 'attachment' only that he revealed and not the marriage.[11] By the beginning of November however O'Connell knew that his wife was pregnant; the period of possible concealment was now limited. He set the time of disclosure for his Christmas visit to his relations. On 30 December 1802, O'Connell wrote to Mary from his father's home, Carhen,

> I am just going to Derrynane. I will remain there nine days, then three here – one in Killorglin on business and the following I shall embrace the best, most amiable and most beloved little woman in the world. I wish to God *my story* was told to the old Gentleman [Hunting Cap]. I shall feel devilish awkward. But I am full of hope and know no reason to be otherwise. If contrary to my sanguine expectations I should find my uncle desperate in not *permitting me to marry without a fortune*, I will not go further but you and your mother shall (if I get hers and your consent) come to Dublin on your way to join Maurice [Mary's brother]. But this is a scheme which I am determined not to want although I mention it. For I will not quit my uncle until I tell him of our marriage. At all events do not expect to hear from me till you see me as I shall like to be the bearer of my own good news.[12]

O'Connell's optimism, if ever genuine, was short-lived. In the event, his courage failed him and he did not dare to tell Hunting Cap of his marriage, face to face. Instead, on returning to Dublin at the end of January 1803, he left a letter of confession with his brother, John, to be handed to Hunting Cap at a propitious moment.

The result was disastrous. Hunting Cap, in 'a most violent flood of tears', was 'grieved and exasperated' beyond expectation. 'I never witnessed', wrote John, 'such a struggle as was exhibited by him between affection and displeasure.' Displeasure carried the day. He ceased to regard or treat O'Connell as his heir; relations between the two became merely formal. O'Connell fared far better with his own family. His father, John reported, disapproved of the marriage only in so far as it would injure him in the estimation of his uncle. 'At any moment you please, he is satisfied to receive Mary at Carhen. You may easily suppose she will meet with every attention from the rest of the family.'[13]

Hunting Cap's anger was to have been expected. He had, characteristically, planned an advantageous match for O'Connell, and had one such actually in train. Now his will was permanently thwarted. It was not the Protestant strain – the fruit of a comparatively recent conformity – in Mary's family which he found offensive, but rather their poverty and social decline. He had spent half a century securing himself and his relatives from both. O'Connell quite failed to understand how deeply he had wounded Hunting Cap; successful manoeuvres such as that which secured his membership of the Lawyers' Artillery may have rendered him carelessly confident. At first, he looked to a further letter, which he had 'written with feeling and I think with some degree of talent',[14] to coax his uncle out of his resentment. Two months later he still airily asserted that 'what remains of his displeasure will be apt to vanish when we come to converse soberly'.[15] By the end of 1803, however, Hunting Cap had brought home to him the intensity of his resentment by knotting the purse strings absolutely. It was now O'Connell's turn to try to allay his wounded pride. He professed himself surprised and 'almost ashamed' that he had reigned so long as his uncle's favourite. 'He could not but perceive that in every action my mind scorned the narrow bounds of his.'[16]

O'Connell's immediate family however proved altogether compliant. At first sight this is surprising. Marrying both money and social equals or superiors was a family article of faith – marriage for sentimental preference anathema. In November 1802, his parents had compelled his sister Ellen 'to give up that foolish attachment' to her cousin, Splinter. 'Sure it would have been hard', wrote his mother, still ignorant of O'Connell's own secret marriage, 'that my ever dear Ellen should refuse to act as each of her sisters did, who gave up early prepossessions to gratify me who they well know had their interests only at heart.'[17] Yet O'Connell's breach of this marriage code was never openly condemned – a testimony to his commanding position within his own family. John did not exaggerate when he wrote that his father's displeasure was vicarious not personal, for Morgan's treatment of Mary appears to have been consistently affectionate and kind. There are many indications that Catherine O'Connell resented her son's marriage and his bride, not only immediately but also for several years after the disclosure. But this was no extraordinary reaction for a mother in such a situation; and Catherine certainly did not spare herself in helping the young couple in the first years of their marriage.

The marriage's 'external relations' were however a secondary affair; its interior proved sound. O'Connell's passion grew. Often he expressed it in terms at once cloying and bombastic. 'Sweet Mary, I rave of you! I think only of you! I sigh for you, I weep for you! I almost pray to you!'[18] But a professional rhetorician and advocate is perhaps bound to stumble in the language of the heart. Moreover, his letters to Mary were in the strictest sense private communications, and as he himself once observed,

> Love, I conceive that an indifferent person would smile at a *husband's* writing thus to his wife after being married even so long as we are; but I should be truly ashamed if any person felt more fondness, or passion or did or suffered more for the object of illicit and criminal love than I would cheerfully do for my Mary. And yet I see men endure every hardship for the obtaining the possession of women whose persons alone can be desirable.[19]

A crisis came suddenly upon them at the end of January 1803, after O'Connell had returned to Dublin, leaving Mary in her lodgings in Tralee under her mother's charge. It was from her mother that he learnt that Mary had fallen so ill in pregnancy that her life was in danger. On 1 February he wrote frantically, trying to convey 'an idea of the black agony that harrows up my soul of souls'.

> If you were well I care not for uncle, relatives, or fortune. I would accept poverty, tortures and death to give you either happiness or even a single proof of the unceasing and consuming passion which devours whilst it consumes this anguished heart of mine . . .
>
> Mary, sweet, sweet Mary, I cannot, indeed, I cannot live without you. You are my life, my comfort. If I were a religionist I should spend every moment in praying for you – and this miserable philosophy which I have taken up and been proud of – in the room of religion, affords me now no consolation in my misery. How much truth do not I now feel in the assertion that man is a creature more of the heart than the reason. Sweet, dearest darling, write to me as soon as you can but do not hurry yourself until you are quite recovered, for you must indeed, my own Mary, you must recover. I have the insolence [*sic*] madness to say it must not be otherwise, or if it be, depend on soon meeting your husband, if a spirit so pure as yours will elsewhere consort with such a vile being as mine.[20]

Mary recovered quickly, O'Connell's letter actually crossing one of hers written from her sick-bed on 3 February. His anxieties for her were fully matched by her fears that he would break down under his uncle's displeasure which 'will I know give you more real sorrow than the loss of his fortune'.

> I beg and entreat of you then, my heart's dearest treasure, to take care of yourself and not give way to unavailing grief. I know from experience how injurious it is to the health. Consider, darling, if you do make yourself unhappy you will make one whose existence depends on yours the most miserable of beings.[21]

The O'Connells' reciprocal misery was succeeded by reciprocal joy as each learnt of the other's recovery from real or supposed distress. Happy letters of relief soon flowed in either direction. But one great difficulty, probably an ill-consequence of the rupture with Hunting Cap, remained. O'Connell had been searching for a house (presumably to rent, and not to buy) in Dublin. This quest was now abandoned. His prospects had been dimmed and his usual recourse in extremities – further support from Hunting Cap – would certainly not be forthcoming. It was clear that Mary would have to remain in lodgings in Tralee until her baby was born. Some time before the birth took place on 27 June 1803, however, O'Connell's parents must have agreed to take in the mother and newborn child as soon as practicable after the confinement.

Although the house at Carhen was comparatively modest in scale, the elder O'Connells provided a home for Mary and her children for most of the two and a quarter years which followed the birth of her first child, Maurice. When she went to Tralee for the birth of her second son, Morgan, in October 1804, Maurice remained in the care of his grandparents at Carhen. For the next year, they were virtually his parents, and apparently so regarded by Maurice himself. 'Our sweet Maurice is perfectly well', wrote Mary to O'Connell soon after her reunion with her elder son. 'He is much attached to me though he sometimes calls me a bitch and desires me to go to Tralee to Dada Dan.'[22]

Mary had not found it easy to regain her niche at Carhen after her second accouchement at Tralee. On 9 November 1804, ten days after Morgan's birth, she sounded out her husband in Dublin,

> Tell me, darling, did you write to your father requesting he would permit his namesake [Morgan] to stay at Carhen until after Christmas? If you did not, I wish you would on receipt of this without mentioning that I had wrote or spoke to you on the subject, and do not omit mentioning if your mother has no objection to it. Perhaps it would be better for you [to] write to herself about [it]. In my opinion it would. The two nurses and the children could sleep in my room very well.[23]

A week later, she followed this up, rather despondently. 'You did not tell me if you wrote to your mother. What I would give to have her keep my little darling [Morgan] at Carhen while I remained there, but I fear I have no chance.'[24] It is clear from the December 1804 correspondence between O'Connell and his wife that they expected to achieve the removal to Carhen before Christmas. But, for whatever reason, this fell through and Mary's return was delayed until mid-April 1805, by which time some seven months had probably elapsed since she had seen her elder child. Evidently the interval – or Mary's first period of residence with her parents-in-law – had created soreness on either side. On 16 April 1805, upon her eventual return to Carhen, she wrote to O'Connell:

> I arrived here late yesterday evening and was met by James [O'Connell's youngest brother] at Filemore who told me he had come at the instance of his father and mother to request I would go down to Carhen. To gratify you, my heart, I agreed to do so. Your father came to the gate to meet me and welcomed me in the kindest manner. Your mother was out walking but soon came in and received me rather stiffly. However, I don't mind that as she is coming off of it this day. I found our darling Maurice much improved. He talks a great deal but all in Irish. He is already taken with me and calls me Mama Mary. He is very fond of your picture since morning, kisses it and calls it Dan.[25]

But such jarring was after all a natural concomitant of the awkward situation in which all the O'Connells – Daniel himself perhaps excepted – were placed by his improvident match. For the first three years of her marriage, Mary had mostly to live apart from her husband, either with his parents or in lodgings in a provincial town. Catherine O'Connell had to provide for O'Connell's family, or part of it, for over two years, and to care for the children on her own on two occasions in mid-1805 when Mary visited Dublin. As Mary herself acknowledged, it was very hard for old people to look after infants for considerable periods at a stretch.

Meanwhile, from July 1802 to July 1805 O'Connell had endured a solitary life in Dublin lodgings or circuit inns for at least three-quarters of each year. He often expressed a longing for Mary and his children. 'Darling,' he wrote towards the end of 1803, 'I doat of you with an affection which absence only increases – and which renders the air I breathe poison until I shall have clasped to my breast at least *the thoughts* of my beloved . . . Tell me how my sweet boy gets on. My darling infant, how I doat of him because he is yours.'[26] However effusive or even foolish the expression, the feeling was real enough.

The steady rain of O'Connell's letters and his scarcely-to-be-credited exertions to join Mary in almost every interstice of his pressing professional life were proof of this. Equally, he was an anxious, eager, boastful father. On one of the very rare occasions on which the children were in his sole charge, he told his wife,

> I have not seen Morgan yet [he was being wet-nursed on Valentia Island] but am just going in to him. He is, however, I am informed, the sweetest and finest creature imaginable. Your son Maurice is as like you as two eggs – and has all that sauciness of temper and disposition. He is a wonderful favourite and the most affectionate little villain in the world. His temper is certainly hasty but he is never for one moment sulky or sullen and I already perceive that there would be little difficulty in bringing him into proper discipline.[27]

It was doubtless the accumulated strain of protracted separations which induced O'Connell, at last, to set up his own household in Dublin. His purchase of no. 1 Westland Row in mid-1805 was financially imprudent. On the other hand, by the time his wife and children moved there in November 1805, he had been a married man without a home for well over three years and his third child was shortly to be born. Much more provident husbands than O'Connell might have taken this leap long before.

Doubtless Mary had suffered much more than he from the delay. Countless humiliations and embarrassments – as well as a great deal of tedium – must have flown from her enforced residence with her husband's parents, especially in the long months of his absences. But the senior O'Connells also had much to bear, and O'Connell's father and two at least of his sisters, Ellen and Kitty, seem to have given Mary constant comfort and affection. In fact O'Connell's extraordinary marriage was more striking for the comparative amity and decent restraints on all sides than for the occasional brushes and the underlying resentments and domestic wounds. Correspondingly, O'Connell's own magnanimity was quite as remarkable as the family's acknowledgement of his continued leadership or its corporate capacity to absorb the blow. Even his brother John's elevation, at the end of 1803, to the station of Hunting Cap's heir-presumptive, in the place of Daniel, did little to weaken the ties of affection and cross-support between the brothers. John seems to have striven honestly to maintain Daniel in Hunting Cap's favour. Reciprocally, Daniel and Mary attached no blame to John when he replaced O'Connell – in part at least – in his uncle's will. Mary privately execrated the 'old sinner' for his treatment of her husband, but John altogether escaped her condemnation. Again, when two years later O'Connell's father re-wrote his will and passed over some of the estate intended for him to his youngest brother, James, and O'Connell quarrelled with the new beneficiary, Mary wrote:

> It grieves me, my darling, that you should have any difference with any of your family, more particularly as I feel myself unintentionally the cause of your present quarrel with James. Don't refuse me this request, my own darling, and consider that you have every prospect of making a fortune independently of the dirty trifle taken from you and left to James, and consider also, heart, that you have a wife who doats of you and who would equally be as fond of you were you in poverty as in affluence. I know I need say no more to you on this subject. Write to me on receipt and let me know if you will gratify me. Indeed I am sure you will. [28]

O'Connell did so immediately. The family, and O'Connell's headship of the entire concern, had triumphed again, much to his own ultimate advantage, as James was loyally, however querulously, to support him in many a crisis over the next two decades and a half.

Even Hunting Cap was partly reconciled to O'Connell in the end. Evidently O'Connell took the initiative early in 1805, passing on information to his uncle which would be useful to him in both his proprietorial and his smuggling roles. Gradually, they slipped back into their old business relationship, with O'Connell helping Hunting Cap with trifles of legal work or counsel, though still formally addressing him as 'Sir'. A year later they met in Tralee when O'Connell was on his spring circuit. 'As to the meeting with my uncle', he told Mary on 31 March 1806, 'nothing could be pleasanter to me. He told me of the hereditary property being mine and gave me most distinctly to understand that he intended all the rest for me. He told Robin Hickson that he had forgiven me and I felt it completely.'[29] As usual O'Connell was over-sanguine. But the restored cordiality deepened steadily until by 1809 Hunting Cap was settling property on O'Connell, while Mary was a-flutter over the purchase of a new bed for his visit to their home in Dublin. Mary attributed the change in Hunting Cap partly to family feeling but also to pride in O'Connell's rising fame. A characteristic comment was that of 11 October 1810: 'Surely your uncle is the kindest of men but, my heart, independent of his affections for you, he feels quite proud of you. The *noise* which you make here and the esteem in which you are held must flatter him greatly.'[30] Mary's judgment of people was always shrewd.

# III

The O'Connells' regular married life began with their removal to Dublin towards the end of 1805. By then their third child, Ellen, had been born. Four others followed soon: Kate in March 1807, Edward in July 1808, Betsey in February 1810 and John in December 1810. Edward died when he was one year old, but all the rest flourished; and within ten years of their marriage, the O'Connells had a family of six, ranging from eight years downwards. During this time their life settled to a pattern. O'Connell was on circuit for almost a quarter of each year, five to six weeks or even longer in March–May and again in July–September. He was also from home at other times, generally for a week or two, for special assizes, arbitration or as legal officer at parliamentary elections. Posterity is the gainer, as the bulk of the letters passing between O'Connell and his wife from 1805 onwards derived from these absences. But the absences forced Mary to serve as family manager and decision-maker for considerable periods of time. This was markedly the case after 1809 when the O'Connells moved upwards socially in Dublin by purchasing no. 30 Merrion Square. Mary had to negotiate and supervise extensions to their new home, manage a larger household and act, to some extent, as O'Connell's banker and man-of-business, in ever more complicated financial circumstances, while he was away.

Moreover, her place in Dublin society was now more demanding and her children required much more attention once they commenced school. On hearing of one particular dinner invitation while he was on circuit, O'Connell wrote (with remarkable marital tact) to Mary, 'I hope you went to Mrs Blaquiere and that you were pleasant there. But, my heart, I have a strange notion floating in my mind that she is not precisely the kind of woman I should be anxious to have you intimate with.'[31] On another occasion, Mary told O'Connell of her distress at having to chastise her five-year-old daughter.

> My poor Nell, such a scene as I had with her yesterday. You may suppose how bold she must have been when I was obliged to beat her with a rod, all occasioned by fear and terror of going to school. The day before, Mrs Bishop [the proprietoress, a sister of Mary Wollstonecraft] beat and punished her for not having her hymn, and doubled her task for yesterday in consequence of which the poor infant made every resistance to going to school. You would hardly believe what a complete battle she had not to go.
>
> She never ceased crying from the time she got up in the morning and entreating of me not to send her any more to Mrs Bishop's, but when I

would not listen to her she threw herself on the stairs and I assure you it was a difficult matter to take her up. However, she was at length forced to school.[32]

O'Connell warmly applauded Mary's resolution, 'I am greatly obliged to you for your firmness with my poor Nell. If you had given up the point she would have conquered you for life.'[33] It was easy to be an armchair disciplinarian 160 miles away, but again hard for Mary to have to act alone.

She was often fearful or fretful when O'Connell was away, especially when – though it was rarely the case – several days elapsed between his letters. Her special terror was that he would be forced to a duel, either on his own account or through his belligerent brother, John. 'All I dread', she once wrote, typically, 'is that John (who I know is very hasty) may try to be avenged on Mr S[egerson]. and thereby involve you but for my sake, darling, . . . do not think it worth your while to take notice of anything he says or does for he is beneath your notice.'[34] These fears were far from groundless. O'Connell had apparently come quite close to having to fight the same Segerson on two occasions already. Pistols were a common resort of the quarrelsome Kerry gentry and the Munster bar; and eventually O'Connell was indeed embroiled. One reason for Mary's dislike of his taking in Kerry, and in particular 'going into Iveragh', when he was on circuit or vacation was that, in the early years at least, these were most likely places for challenges. Another was the difficulty of extricating O'Connell from Kerry once he had reintegrated himself into beloved kinship networks and sporting life. Mary's letters were often punctuated with little jibes of the kind dispatched by her to, respectively, Derrynane and Tralee on 29 September and 1 October 1812, 'Perhaps, love, you were *induced* to remain for the pattern [festival] of this day', and 'I have at length the satisfaction to hear you are arrived in Tralee and have fixed your departure from thence on Monday next . . . let nothing induce you to put it off any longer.'[35]

But the most important reason of all for Mary's fear of Kerry was O'Connell's propensity to spend heavily and to incur fresh obligations there. O'Connell was not only the crown prince – or even already reigning king – of his own family, but also embedded in countless other connexions of blood, dependency or friendship. He found it extremely difficult – not that he ever really tried – to deny applications for loans of money, and, still more, to deny applications to act as guarantor for the loans of others, these being conveniently distant and hypothetical obligations. Conversely, he found it fatally easy to borrow small sums and incur other debts. Mary was soon painfully aware of the danger of these Kerry entanglements. When, in the spring of 1809, she was in such straits in Dublin as to write, '*I want money, love*',[36] he had to excuse the paucity of his remittance with – 'I had several debts to pay in Kerry.'[37] This was a harbinger of the crisis which was almost to engulf O'Connell, once and for all, in 1815.

A further though minor difficulty which O'Connell's Kerry perambulations threw up for Mary was the promised hospitality which he cast about. Invitations to stay or to dine or to use his horses when in Dublin were scattered far and wide. Perhaps Mary did not much wish him to be sparing in this particular regard. But it certainly bore hard upon her. On several occasions she complained to O'Connell of the extreme awkwardness of her finding (or even having!) reasons for putting off the relations whom he had asked to stay at Merrion Square. As to his horses, she wrote sharply on 15 January 1809 when his cousin Connell was taking up O'Connell's proferred loan,

> William [the O'Connell manservant] will not nor cannot attend to the mare and, if every person who wishes for it is to get it, you must hire a groom to convenience them . . . if you wish Mr O'Connell should get her, his servant must make her up when he brings her home every day, for John [the O'Connell coachman] cannot attend me if he is to attend him. [38]

O'Connell had worries of his own arising from his long absences. Sometimes his first letters from circuit spoke of his black depression or his agitation at the tearful parting or his concern for Mary's apprehensions. He also left behind him an ever more precarious financial house of cards. Dublin outgoings and receipts were invariably in a delicate balance, depending on Mary and various other agents delaying payments until he could send back enough of his bar earnings to meet the bills. None the less, even Mary realized that circuit work, with its clamour, dash and triumphs, was her husband's breath of life. 'I ought not, darling,' she wrote in 1810, 'regret so much your going circuit, for in general the change and bustle of it is of use to you . . . and then, heart, the pleasure you have in looking forward to the time you will be with your *little woman* and your babes again makes up to you in a great measure for being away from them.'[39] This was fair comment. And apart from the exhilaration of the court-room combat and the crowding clients, O'Connell usually enjoyed, and even exulted in, the pull of home as each circuit drew to its weary close. As he himself once put it, when handing over his final brief to a fellow-counsel in order to save a day, he was riotously joyful as a schoolboy on the eve of term's breaking-up. Moreover, in the early years at least, he rejoiced in reporting to Mary, assize town by assize town, the mounting total of his earnings. These were a measure of both the demand for his services and his success in fulfilling the role of family hunter and gatherer. Not least (as he once said) were the thoughts of his 'sweet bedfellow'[40] as the time for their reunion drew near.

## IV

The greatest shadow over O'Connell's marriage, down to 1829 at any rate, was money. In the last analysis, it was lack of money which drove him to conceal his betrothal, to marry in secret and to board his wife and children with his parents for most of the second and third years of his married life. From 1805 onwards it was the magnitude of his expenditure rather than the meagreness of his income which caused the trouble. The upshot was however much the same. In the immortal words of Mr Micawber (whom O'Connell came to resemble strikingly in certain ways), 'Annual income twenty pounds, annual expenditure twenty pounds ought and six, result misery. The blossom is blighted, the leaf is withered, the God of day goes down upon the dreary scene, and – in short you are for ever floored.'[41] Of what avail was it for O'Connell to multiply his income rapidly and enormously if the ought-and-sixes grew just as fast?

In the year in which he became engaged, 1800, O'Connell earned about £420 at the bar. To some extent, this figure was misleading as £175, two-fifths of the whole, derived from a single extraordinarily protracted case, *Segerson* v. *Butler*, at Tralee. His next year's total, £387, should not therefore be taken as marking a real decline in business; this is confirmed by the 1802 earnings, £522. Hunting Cap may well have supplemented O'Connell's income in these early years, as it was not to be expected that a barrister should support himself initially; he could certainly not have lived off his fees in 1798 or 1799. If this is so, perhaps £150–200 annually should be added to these figures. Most likely, Hunting Cap simply continued the allowance made to O'Connell as a student, which was probably within this range. Conversely, O'Connell had inescapable professional expenses, Law Library fees, books, copying, travel, mess charges and accommodation in the assizes towns. At a guess – and it is nothing more – these outgoings would have counterbalanced, at the very least, Hunting Cap's hypothetical allowance. Thus, at the apex of our airy pyramid of surmise we are left with a net income of something like

£500 for O'Connell, in the year of his marriage, 1802. Had the 1800s been a classificatory decade this would have placed him, at the age of twenty-seven, in, say, the B1 or possibly even A2 rank of incomes; he would not have been subject, we should remember, to any form of direct taxation. None the less, he was probably in debt already. Marriage certainly increased his outgoings without any compensating accession of capital. But in 1802–3 Mary lived substantially the same life as she had done as a single girl, and over the next two years she and her children were largely supported by O'Connell's parents. The wedded state, therefore, added less immediately to O'Connell's expenditure than would ordinarily have been the case, although it led undoubtedly to the loss of his uncle's allowance from 1803 on, if this were still being maintained.

In 1805, however, O'Connell was pushed onto a much higher level of spending when he bought a house in Dublin and set up the usual middle-class domestic establishment. Professor M. R. O'Connell believes that 'O'Connell said goodbye to solvency when he purchased No. 1 Westland Row'.[42] Certainly he was forced to borrow substantially – and, he hoped, secretly. To one friend he wrote – it is possible that similar letters were sent to others – 'The purchase of my house and the first expenses of getting into it have made it extremely desirable to me to get the use of £200 for a year, but it is still much more necessary for me that no third person should know that I wanted or got the money.'[43] In 1805 O'Connell earned £841 in fees and in 1806 £1,077, which probably meant net incomes of about £600 and £800, respectively. Though these were considerable sums, they were clearly insufficient for his altered circumstances. There were several signals of financial difficulties in 1806. In April O'Connell evidently borrowed (or received as a gift) £50 from his father, and both Ralph Marshall and an unidentified 'Zeb Mac' in Kerry lent him further sums. Zeb Mac's £100 went towards staving off a sheriff's execution upon the property of his old confederate, Splinter. All this time, O'Connell, with amazing buoyancy, spoke to his wife only of his increasing income. 'Darling', he wrote from Cork on 15 April 1806, 'I have made a little fortune here – and have I believe laid the foundation for a *much greater*.'[44] From the summer circuit he reported that he had done extraordinarily well at Ennis, that Limerick had proved 'a *spendid* assizes', that he had had his full share of the meagre business at Tralee and that Cork, where he was 'one of the foremost in briefs and bustle', had provided 'an *immense* deal to do'.[45] Characteristically, not only did he set up his wife and children in Tralee for a long vacation in the summer, but he also insisted on Mary's engaging a carriage to go sea-bathing. 'The only reason that can operate to prevent you is the expense and if we could not afford that I confess I would applaud your prudence in avoiding it. But, sweet love, I can well, very well afford it.'[46]

O'Connell continued in this exultant strain in 1807. Early in the spring circuit he wrote, 'Ennis was very well'. From Limerick came a 'spare fifty guineas' with expressions of delight in the prospect of giving his wife 'every convenience' and later every 'comfortable luxury': 'I doat of you, my sweet Mary, and nothing can give me such pleasure as seeing you in affluence.'[47] Cork was as usual the crown of all. 'I am really getting a load of money', he reported from there on 26 March 1807,

> At this rate you shall soon have not only carriages but a country house. It is an infinite pleasure to me to succeed thus as it enables me to give my sweetest little woman all the luxuries of life. We loved each other, darling, when we were poor, and as we were really so, it was almost our only consolation to love each other. And now that we are becoming rich it is the chief sweetener of life.[48]

It may be difficult for the more provident portion of humanity to understand how a man, who was almost certainly sinking deeper into debt year by year, could write persistently in such a strain. But, *experto crede*, there is another sort of person who can empathize with O'Connell all too readily. He will immediately recognize the illusory glow generated by sudden cash inflows. It was very easy for O'Connell, dazzled by a flood of coin and notes at the assizes, to forget the distant, daily drain of a household of wife and children, housekeeper and five or six servants in Dublin. Again, it was only to be expected that he should draw a wildly rising income curve upon his imaginary graph of the future. He really *was* succeeding prodigiously. In 1806 not only had he earned well over £1,000 at the bar, but he had also entered the highly profitable field of special engagements. The £2,000 per annum barrier was to be broken in 1807, and the £3,000 barrier within four years. The trouble was that the counter curve – that of expenditure and monetary obligation – was gradually drawing ahead. But what man of O'Connell's temperament ever projected the two lines with an equal hand?

Finally, we must bear in mind the likely effects upon O'Connell's outlook of his partial reconciliation with Hunting Cap in 1806. He was actually guaranteed no more than the eventual reversion of the hereditary O'Connell lands. But as we have seen he leapt to the conclusion that this was merely the first step towards total restoration as his uncle's heir. We must also remember that Hunting Cap was seventy-eight years old in 1806, and had already suffered at least one serious illness. O'Connell must have assumed that a fortune lay more or less close to hand. Why count the pennies or withhold subscriptions or displease friends petitioning for loans or guarantees when so massive an accession of wealth as to render each individual item negligible was just around the corner?

Mary was not entirely ignorant of the true situation. When in 1806 a Kerry kinsman, Mountain Mahony, unexpectedly repaid O'Connell a loan of £100, she wrote lightheartedly, 'I wish all those who owe you money would *surprise* you as he has done', and added, her husband being on circuit, 'Remember, darling, I expect you will bring a great *purse* home with you.'[49] By 1808 she was deeply involved in, and therefore privy in part to, O'Connell's affairs. His letter of 2 April from Limerick is a comparatively simple example of the dealings in which she was to be henceforth embroiled.

> You have enclosed a bill for £115.10.7 out of which you will have two large payments to make, the one of £70 – a bill of mine to Hickson, the woollen draper, which will be due the 14th of April and other of £26 and some shillings which will be due a few days after. This second bill I gave McKenna for his work in the house . . .
>
> There is also a note or bill of mine out for £50 which you are not to pay, darling, unless you get money for that purpose from a Mr Clarke, an attorney. You may in the event of its not being sent to you, I mean the money, by Mr Clarke allow it to be protested [i.e. dishonoured]. I am not one bit uneasy about it.[50]

She was already apprehensive, as a letter from her to O'Connell which probably crossed his of 2 April 1808 makes very clear: 'should you, my darling, not send me up the money as you earn it, you will be *tempted* to distribute it when you go to Kerry. It is there all the claims are on you, putting *Splinter first of all*.'[51]

Things worsened in 1809. On the face of it, this may seem very strange. Not only did O'Connell's bar earnings exceed £2,700 in that year but he also received £750 from Hunting Cap to buy land in Iveragh and inherited the bulk of his father's property when he died in May. In fact, it may well have been the improvement in income and prospects which led O'Connell to take the fateful step of moving from Westland Row to the nearby but much more fashionable Merrion Square in September. If O'Connell was still within hailing distance of solvency after buying his first house, he was certainly far removed from it by the purchase of his second, and the consequent elevation of his family and himself to the most expensive reaches of Dublin professional life. Mary realized this fully. Late in the month, she wrote to him, desperately,

> For God's sake, darling love, let me entreat of you to give up this house in the Square if it is in your power as I see no other way for you to get out of difficulties. If you borrow this money [one thousand guineas] for Ruxton how will you pay it back? In short, love, I scarce know what I write I am so unhappy about this business.[52]

None the less the purchase of no. 30 Merrion Square went ahead.

Mary's worst fear however was that O'Connell would ruin himself by going security for friends and relations, and she apparently wrung from him a solemn undertaking to abandon this practice, or at least to indulge it only if she were fully informed. A much shrewder head than Mary's, Hunting Cap's, also saw this as the chief source of danger. When in 1811 Hunting Cap heard rumours that O'Connell was about to become guarantor for a large sum for John Primrose, a friend and kinsman whose son was later to become O'Connell's steward, he warned him of the consequences with the utmost portentousness:

> I can scarcely express to you the uneasiness I feel since this matter has occurred to me, well knowing as I before mentioned the softness and facility of your disposition and with what ease designing men may draw you into their measures, when in fact and in truth acceding to such a proposal from Primrose must have the effect of inevitably ruining you beyond redemption. I therefore again and again most earnestly caution you against it and further add that no feeble or temporizing excuses will have any sort of weight with me, and that your neglecting to comply with what I not only so earnestly beseech and request but what I absolutely and decidedly command, will create a breach between us never to be healed, and decidedly determine me during the period of my existence never to exchange a word with you. It distresses me indeed to think that it is necessary to write to you in such strong terms when a bare intimation of my will ought . . . be sufficient . . .[53]

Mary and Hunting Cap were proved right in March 1815, when James O'Leary, a Killarney merchant, went bankrupt. O'Connell, who had gone security for him was liable for £8,000. Mary learnt of the disaster not from her husband but from his brother, James. She wrote so fiercely to O'Connell for the breaking of his promise to her that he destroyed her letter. 'I wept over it for two hours this morning', he replied on 13 March 1815,

> When once suspicion enters the human mind, there is an end of all comfort and security. It is, I see, in vain to make any protestations to you. You are, I see, irrecoverably unhappy. I blame, indeed I do, my brother James for instilling this poison into your mind . . .
>
> Darling believe me, do believe me, you have no cause for your misery. Did I ever deceive you?[54]

Mary's anger could not stand when she found O'Connell so 'exquisitely miserable'. More admirably than accurately, she assured him that it was not in his nature to deceive her – in fact, she was probably still unaware of the magnitude or certainty of the disaster – and went on to entreat him to trust in her love for him and 'forget what is past'.[55]

No such forgiveness would be had from Hunting Cap: he had specifically warned O'Connell long before against dealings with O'Leary. As we shall see, when at last the news of the bankruptcy became widely known, every effort had to be made to conceal O'Connell's involvement from his uncle. The ultimate disaster of being unmasked and repudiated by Hunting Cap was avoided. But short of that O'Connell came quite close to ruin. For an Irish working barrister his income was by now enormous, probably between £6,000 and £7,000 in 1815: property which he had inherited from his father or been given already by Hunting Cap between 1809 and 1811 produced net about £2,000 per annum. Yet by the end of 1815 his debts cannot have been less than £15,000, and were probably much more. It required a sustained effort by his family to save him from bankruptcy. James arranged the necessary loans and pledged himself as guarantor, although he believed that he too would be removed from Hunting Cap's will if word of the transactions came to his uncle's ears. General O'Connell advanced a large sum later to reduce the horrific outflow of interest. Mary not only forgave her husband fully but joined him – perhaps, led him – in battling through the crisis. He had no doubt, he told her on 21 March 1816, that 'we will work over the difficulties into which my most absurd credulity involved me. Dearest sweetest, how I *ought* to love you for the manner in which you have met those difficulties.'[56]

There is a certain charm in O'Connell's lightness of spirit and indomitability, not to add in the unbreakable loyalty of both his inner and his outer families. But this should not lead us to forget that O'Connell had wantonly brought his troubles on his own and others' heads, with a trail of subterfuge and concealment, of broken promises and unmet obligations, and of reckless disregard for his brother's interest, in order to indulge the 'softness and facility' of his disposition. *O felix culpa*, however, so far as his marriage was concerned. It appears to have emerged all the stronger and warmer for his pardoned delinquency. Like Captain Wentworth in *Persuasion* he had to brook – and who would brook it more easily? – being happier than he deserved.

## CHAPTER 5

# Public Lives

## *1800–13*

### I

O'Connell had entered public life, dramatically, on 13 January 1800. Earlier, the Irish bar had resolved against the proposed Union of Great Britain and Ireland by an overwhelming majority; among other things, the members believed that it would cost them a great deal of their business. As both a very young and newly called barrister and a Catholic, O'Connell was a mere silent supporter of that course. But all the more did he resent the argument of the Castle faction at the bar that the Irish Catholics en bloc favoured the amalgamation of the two kingdoms. It was probably this which drove him to take a leading part in organizing a Catholic meeting at the Royal Exchange in Dublin in January 1800 to repudiate 'so horrible a calumny'. The Catholic resolutions, which he introduced and largely composed, were milder than those carried by the Irish bar. This was a caution well justified by the event, for the town major, Sirr, appeared at the commencement, examined the agenda and only reluctantly accepted it as anodyne, before he would allow the meeting to proceed. O'Connell was foremost in checking panic in the crowd when the military drew up in front of the Exchange, and also in the preliminary parleys with the major. It was an extraordinary initiative for a young man of twenty-four years to take, all the more so as it implied a further defiance of Hunting Cap. The Castle faction had been substantially right in claiming that the Union had the backing of the Irish Catholics, for the bishops believed that the British government was committed to full Emancipation in return for their support. Hunting Cap himself, and another of O'Connell's uncles and his brother, John, were among those working up a pro-Union campaign in Kerry. Thus O'Connell's stand was even more daring than it publicly appeared.

Essentially, O'Connell argued that Catholic interests should be subordinated to 'Irish'. He even denied that there *was* any special

Catholic interest. 'The enlightened mind of the Catholics', he told the meeting, 'had taught them the impolicy, the illiberality, and the injustice of separating themselves on any occasion from the rest of the people of Ireland. The Catholics had therefore resolved, and they had wisely resolved, never more to appear before the public as a distinct and separate body.' Of course, the fact that they were accused of having a distinctive sectarian policy on the Union had compelled them to come forward 'as a distinct body'. But they did so 'for the last time' and only to repudiate the foul charge that they 'were ready to sell their country for a price, or, what was still more depraved, to abandon it on account of the unfortunate animosities which the wretched temper of the times had produced'. Even in his first public speech, O'Connell used extravagance for purposes of emphasis; 'let every man who feels with me proclaim', his climax ran,

> that if the alternative were offered him of union, or the re-enactment of the penal code in all its pristine horrors, that he would prefer without hesitation the latter, as the lesser and more sufferable evil; that he would rather confide in the justice of his brethren, the Protestants of Ireland, who have already liberated him, than lay his country at the feet of foreigners. (This sentiment was met with much and marked approbation).[1]

The condemnatory resolutions – which in fact sound rather tame after such a flight – passed unopposed, and would have passed presently into oblivion had they not occasioned O'Connell's first declaration of political faith. Broadly speaking, his claim to have adhered to this faith throughout his life was justified.

When Hunting Cap expostulated on O'Connell's performance at the Royal Exchange – it was widely reported in the newspapers – he took the traditional line of Irish Catholics of substance, that the Protestant Ascendancy was their true enemy, and the British government their only agent of their relief.[2] Nothing could make clearer the nature of O'Connell's departure. He had taken colour – permanently – from the peculiar epoch in which he had grown up. The fifteen years 1778–93 were marked by a train of concessions to the Irish Catholics; it was natural for the young O'Connell to regard the penal code as both anachronistic and in a steady process of dissolution. The same years were also marked by various apparent triumphs for Irish liberalism, *vis-à-vis* both Great Britain and the rule of caste at home. Again, it was natural for the young O'Connell to take these at their face value, and also as heralds of a new harmony of sects and classes. The idealizations of the growing boy crystallized into lasting certitudes. On 14 April 1843 O'Connell wrote that when Irish Protestants combined 'to make our beloved fatherland a nation again . . . the utmost cordiality will prevail, as in 1782, between all Irishmen and we will be able to make the mighty change [repeal of the Act of Union] with perfect safety to person and property, and to the continuance of the connection between the two countries'.[3] Seriously meant, this gives us a measure of the indestructibility of O'Connell's early visions.

In immediate terms, O'Connell's stand at the Royal Exchange was an isolated episode. True, the subsequent enforcement of the Union enraged him. Later he recalled his feelings on 1 January 1801 when he heard the bells of St Patrick's Cathedral pealing out in joy at the surrender: 'My blood boiled, and I vowed, on that morning, that the foul dishonour should not last, if *I* could ever put an end to it.'[4] But there was nothing to be done. Ireland lay inert in the aftermath of the Union; even the Catholic question fell away once Pitt was forced out of office because of his promise to press it upon the united Parliament. O'Connell had only abhorrence for Robert Emmet's Dublin insurrection of 1803, the solitary demonstration of resistance to British rule in Ireland in the first post-Union years. Emmet, he wrote on 28 August of that year, 'merits and will suffer the severest punishment. For my part I think pity would be almost thrown away upon the contriver of the affair of the 23rd of July. A man who could coolly prepare so much bloodshed, so many murders – and such horrors of every kind has ceased to be an object of compassion.'[5] His wife did nothing to mitigate O'Connell's deep-set anti-revolutionism. Although he had remained a serving member of the Lawyers' Artillery, regularly called upon for guard and patrol duty in Dublin, he evidently decided to join the Kerry yeomanry as well, in the alarm which followed Emmet's rising. 'I am quite delighted', Mary told him on 18 November 1803,

> that you should enroll yourself in Sir Edward Denny's corps though, if it could be helped, I had rather you were not in any. However, it is a great consolation to me, should the French land, not to have you obliged to remain in Dublin. Kerry will be the last place they come to and the yeomanry, I trust in God, will be able to keep down the common people. *They are the* only [one word missing] I dread in this part of the world.[6]

Perhaps O'Connell had indoctrinated his wife with his original fears of both revolution and the masses. If so, the pupil was all too ready to turn teacher. This way or that, they seem to have reinforced each other in these particular forms of reaction.

Pitt's restoration as prime minister in May 1804 revived Catholic hopes in Ireland. The Catholic Board, which had been put down in the general welter of repression in the preceding year, now reconstituted itself as the Catholic Committee. In either form it was a far from radical body, being dominated by noblemen and landed proprietors. The most able member, the veteran John Keogh, belonged to the Dublin merchant class which had been prominent in the Board in former years; but his participation was by now intermittent. A new group, the Catholic barristers, were however beginning to push their way forward. Of these much the ablest was O'Connell; but he was not the most senior, nor had he, apparently, taken any part in Catholic politics before the new Committee met on 16 November 1804. Neither his earlier abstention nor his participation on 16 November should cause surprise. Each is readily explicable in terms of his profession and his marriage. Down to 1804 these naturally absorbed his mind and energies, all the more so as the Irish politics of 1801–3 were at once dangerous and torpid. But by the end of 1804 his earnings at the bar had risen to almost £800, and his second son was born. On both counts he found himself suddenly face to face with the practical penalties of being a Catholic in his own land. Were he not excluded from the inner bar by his religion, he could have looked forward to taking silk soon, and to a glorious professional career ending in the mastership of the rolls or the chief baronship of the exchequer, at the very least. Correspondingly he was bitter that his sons were starting their race of life already shackled by their religion. In his first reported speech to the Committee he presented himself as an epitome of Catholic disabilities. He was not only a young man artificially prevented from rising in his profession, but also the father of children doomed to the same fate: 'It was the liberties of those children the present petition sought – would they postpone for an hour that sacred blessing?'[7]

O'Connell pushed himself to the front so vigorously on the Catholic Committee that he was appointed to both the standing committee of twenty-five, and the small sub-committee charged with drafting the parliamentary petition. He was delighted to rub shoulders with the peers and baronets who graced the first, and proud of his responsibilities on the second. 'Dearest', he wrote to Mary on 4 December 1804,

> I am very busy at present in framing the Catholic petition. The fate of millions perhaps depends on my poor pen – at least so in my enthusiasm I say to myself and *to you* – But to you, *you alone*. There are five appointed for *this* purpose. We must have the petition ready on Sunday. Until then

> believe me that I shall sleep little. Heart, my *law* business goes on right well.[8]

Constantly, he assured Mary that his professional work was not suffering because of his labours for the Committee. But unknown to her he was prepared to sacrifice his career, to a limited extent at least, in the pursuit of new glory. On 19 December he proposed himself to Denys Scully (an older Catholic barrister and the acknowledged master of the Catholic question) as an appropriate person to go 'to London on the business of the petition'.[9] O'Connell was prepared to be reimbursed his expenses but nothing more. Professionally, the journey to London would truly be 'both inconvenient and injurious', he told Scully, 'nor should I upon any terms consent to *be paid*. The fact is that even in my humble situation at the Bar no money could repay me for the loss *consequent* to absence during term.'[10] In the event, a large party, including Scully and another barrister, accompanied the petition, but O'Connell – presumably because he was still comparatively unknown and undistinguished – was not selected. He had not done badly in his first Catholic venture. His was the seventeenth name on the petition, and he acted, in effect, as the Dublin political manager of the petition-bearers while they negotiated in London. A certain measure of wounded vanity, however, may be detected in the would-be facetious opening of his letter to Scully on 19 March 1805, reporting on the Dublin end of things.

> High and Mighty!
>
> For certainly the great Rustifusti or the greater Miamouchi was a mere dandle compared with the representative of four million, five hundred thousand of the creatures in Ireland styled *men*. Out of the excess of your dignity your recollection has been thrown away and you have not a thought *to throw away* upon your former acquaintance.[11]

Whether O'Connell's volunteering to go to London is to be explained by vanity or ambition or a sense of his own superiority, it was certainly an act of familial irresponsibility. His wife and children were still without a home, and he was soon to be forced further into debt in order to buy even a comparatively modest house. Yet, quite unprompted, he had offered to forgo a quarter or more of his year's earnings so that he could cut a public figure in the metropolis. Domestically speaking it was an ominous political debut.

# II

The Irish Catholic 'initiative' of 1804–5 failed dismally. Pitt not only refused to act on behalf of the deputation but even told them roundly that he would now oppose any measure of Catholic relief. The dismayed delegates found his rival Charles James Fox perfectly agreeable to stepping into Pitt's discarded shoes. But on 14 May 1805 Fox's motion for a Relief Bill was rejected in the House of Commons by a majority of three to one. The Catholic Committee had been routed; but in one sense the débâcle represented a triumph for O'Connell. He was easily the foremost in its ranks in opposing the Act of Union, and the Catholic case for support of the Union had always rested upon Pitt's promise to carry Emancipation and the assumption that the British Parliament would prove more tolerant of Catholic claims than had its Irish counterpart. Pitt's defection and Westminster's contemptuous rejection of the Committee's petition swept away the old pro-Union case. O'Connell had proved the better prophet. But in 1805 he still lacked the standing to mount a challenge to the ruling junta on the Committee, backed – as it was generally believed they were – by the Irish episcopate. Moreover, the dominant 'cautious party' was given a fresh lease when Pitt died and the 'Ministry of All the Talents' came to office in February 1806. Fox, who was now in government, had assured them that he would press their claims, even if he could not do so immediately with the struggle against Napoleon at its crisis. Despite O'Connell's dissatisfaction, the Committee agreed that their illustrious 'friend' should be placed under no pressure for the present. But Fox fell ill in July 1806 and died two months later, without ever having raised the Catholic question since attaining office.

The division within the Committee sharpened. Keogh and his aristocratic allies desired only to entrust their cause to the discretion of their surviving well-wishers in the ministry. But O'Connell had no faith in well-wishing and no taste for patrician restraint. At the aggregate meeting of 17 February 1807, in anticipation of the coming parliamentary session, his fiery oratory produced a majority in favour of petitioning for Emancipation once again. He was aided by the accident of Keogh's absence from the meeting and his own tactical skill in drawing into light the hereditary servility which really underlay the aristocratic plea for dignity of bearing. He also repeated his denunciation of the Act of Union as the immediate cause of the continued degradation of the Irish Catholics. Keogh, warmly supported by the nobility and squires, was furious at the passage of O'Connell's aggressive motion. O'Connell's charge, that Keogh would prefer a measure to fail than that it should be carried by another leader, may not have been wide of the mark. At any rate, Keogh procured a second aggregate meeting at which his authority and numbers carried the day, and O'Connell's motion in favour of petitioning was rescinded. None the less, O'Connell had made progress. At least he had forced himself to the forefront of both the 'forward' element and what might be termed the 'barristers' faction' in the Committee.

The battle was refought in 1808, the Ministry of All the Talents having meanwhile fallen. Petitioning was again proposed at the aggregate meeting of 19 January, only to be met with a contrary amendment grounded on the Keoghite argument that a petition would 'only expose us to the mockery and insult of men in power; to division, rejection and defeat'.[12] At this point O'Connell intervened, acknowledging that Catholic division was deplorable, but arguing that even division was preferable to the loss of self-respect. He refused to be cowed by the British mighty, in earnest of which he treated them to a round of fishwife's abuse. Irish Catholics, he said, 'had little to fear from the barren petulance of the ex-advocate, Perceval, or the frothy declamations of the poetaster, Canning – they might meet with equal contempt the upstart pride of the Jenkinsons [Lord Liverpool], and with more than contempt the pompous inanity of that Lord Castlereagh.'[13] The effect on the meeting was electrifying. It may puzzle us to understand why such rhetoric was accounted admirable, or why O'Connell descended to such vapid and vulgar personalities or jogtrot, over-laden cadences. They were henceforth to constitute one of his characteristic styles, particularly before a popular audience. The answer would seem to be, in part, that we cannot see the look and gesture, or hear the voice, which apparently transformed these banalities; in part, that telling oratory is the creature of its own time; and in part, as O'Connell himself frequently confessed, that lapses into Billingsgate were a fault which he could never overcome. But it is probably also true that such language was calculated to reduce his political enemies to a level with Catholics, Irish or any other category of inferior beings; that it was designed to counteract the instinctive cringe of the oppressed, and to force the proud and disdainful to engage with them upon equal terms. At any rate, O'Connell's coarse eloquence certainly helped him to achieve his object on 19 January 1808. Keogh, who arrived late for the meeting, proffered no reply, and his supporters withdrew their amendment and allowed O'Connell's motion in favour of a petition to pass unchallenged. In the battle of the young and old bull seals, O'Connell had triumphed comparatively quickly. 'From that day', as Dunlop puts it, though with some exaggeration, 'he and not Keogh was the leader of the Catholics.'[14]

When the motions in favour of Catholic relief arising from the petition came before Parliament in May 1808, they were heavily defeated in both Houses. However, the proposers in the Commons, the whig leader George Ponsonby and the veteran Henry Grattan, were confident that a compromise could be reached. Accordingly, they offered the British government, on behalf of the Irish Catholic hierarchy, at least a negative veto on all Irish episcopal appointments. Their speeches also disclosed the fact that in 1799 the ten Irish archbishops and bishops who constituted the trustees of Maynooth had tendered Pitt just such a veto, as well as acceptance of state payment of the Irish clergy, in return for Emancipation. Now the fat was in the fire. It was true that Bishop Milner, vicar-apostolic of the Midland District and the English agent of the Irish bishops, had not had time to consult his principals before coming to the agreement with Ponsonby and Grattan which had led them to make their offer. It was also true that Milner's concessions fell far short of warranting Ponsonby's final assurance to the House of Commons that 'the appointment [of every Irish bishop] should finally rest with the King'.[15] None the less, Milner, who had reason to expect considerable Irish episcopal support, had placed no specific limitation upon the practical use of the veto. As to the Maynooth trustees' 'surrender' of 1799, this was indisputable, though hitherto no hint of it had reached the Irish public.

O'Connell, who had been quite as much in the dark as the laity in general, was outraged by these disclosures. Arguing that any form of veto would render the bishops, in time, so many puppets of a government dedicated to the retention of both the Protestant and British Ascendancy in Ireland, he set about organizing and deploying a popular furore. This was done mainly through the press, which was fortunately provided with a vent when Milner visited Ireland in the following August. As Milner himself described his reception,

> It is a fact that all the newspapers, particularly the *Dublin Evening Herald*, and also the *Irish Magazine*, are full of abuse against Lord Fingall and his friends Dr Troy [Archbishop of Dublin], Dr Moylan [Bishop of Cork] and myself, as having pledged ourselves and the body to acknowledge the royal Ecclesiastic supremacy by giving the nomination of Prelates to the Crown.

> Not only the many-headed mob have taken the alarm, but also most of the inferior clergy, and a great portion of the Bishops; in short they are to meet about it on the 14th September.[16]

O'Connell spoke of Milner's visit as a 'vetoistical mission'. Whether or not this was justified, his description of the outcome – that the Irish people 'rejected the mission and the missionary'[17] – was undeniable. More to the point, the Irish bishops followed substantially the same course as 'the Irish people'. To some extent, the members of the hierarchy, denied the Emancipation which had been tacitly promised in 1799, must have shared O'Connell's anger at their treatment at the hands of British politicians. But doubtless they were also moved by the excited, even threatening, lay agitation. The National Synod which had been hastily convened in Dublin in September 1808 condemned, by the overwhelming majority of twenty-three to three, every form of interference by the crown in appointments or other matters of government of the Irish church. Even the three recalcitrants would haved voted for the resolution had 'at present' been added to its wording.

Obviously this marked a further advance in O'Connell's influence in Irish affairs, especially in demonstrating his willingness and capacity to call in popular forces to help pressurize his domestic opponents. But the price was division in the Catholic movement. Although this was not fully apparent for another four years, the foundation for a 'vetoistical' party within the Catholic Committee had been laid. In itself, the anti-O'Connell faction, comprising the small aristocratic element with a few old Keoghites and some of the more malleable lawyers, did not look formidable. But it had episcopal sympathizers, if not outright supporters. Troy and Moylan, for example, while subscribing in 1810, like all the rest, to sixteen resolutions reaffirming the Irish episcopate's hostility to the veto, were always prone to compromise on the issue. Moreover, the English Catholic Board, dominated by noblemen and squires, was decidedly vetoist in inclination, as well as influential at both Westminster and Rome. Thus, although insignificant in terms of numbers, O'Connell's Irish lay opponents were far from negligible as a force. Over the next fourteen years, they were to constitute his 'running sore'.

There was however one significant, though hidden, change preceding this particular conflict which should be noted. Mary O'Connell's letter of 21 March 1809 to her husband makes its nature clear:

> I hope, darling, you did not eat meat on Friday or Saturday since you left this and surely I need not beg you to abstain from meat next [Holy] week. You can't be at a loss for fish in Cork. And Good Friday the *judges* will go to prayers and certainly you can then *spare time* to go. At all events I hope you will hear prayers on Easter Sunday. You see, heart, how good I want you to be. I do, darling, because I doat of you. I would wish you to be attentive to your religion and thankful to God for all his blessings and favours to both of us. I often with delight, darling, heard you say you were the happiest of men and I say with truth I am the happiest of women. In gratitude to the Almighty then we should at least attend to the duties of our religion and, darling, I can't tell you what real happiness it gives me to have you this sometime back say your prayers and attend Mass so regularly, not to say anything of your observance of the days of abstinence. I will, heart, say no more on this subject until we meet.[18]

All this suggests that comparatively, though not very, recently, O'Connell (who had unquestionably still been a deist in 1803) had returned to the practice of Catholicism. It also suggests that it was under pressure from Mary that he first began to move in this direction, and that as yet he was 'infervent' if not precisely 'lukewarm'. But fervour would come; and meanwhile it was certainly something that a Catholic leader should have again become, apparently, a believing Catholic.

## III

O'Connell's success at home in 1808 was directly related to the failure of Emancipation in Parliament. Not only were the Catholic claims decisively rejected yet again, but also leading parliamentary 'friends' had been embarrassed by the public wrangles over what Milner had really conceded or could properly concede. The final Irish rejection of the veto was an open rebuff to Ponsonby, Grattan and the whigs in general. Worse still perhaps, it was impossible for them really to comprehend the Catholic objection to the veto, since parliamentary supremacy over the Church and ultimate lay control of the clergy were fundamental presuppositions in the Anglican tradition. In these circumstances, there seemed no prospect of success for another petition or campaign after the 1805–8 pattern, and no move was made during the 1809 session. Indeed, Keogh would claim to have been vindicated in his earlier opposition to petitioning on the ground that it led only to humiliating rebuffs in both houses and internal discord. O'Connell may have stood at the head of the Irish Catholic movement from 1808 on, but it was a stationary and covertly divided column which he led.

It is not surprising then that he turned joyfully in another political direction when an opening unexpectedly appeared – all the more so as it brought the matter back to what he regarded as first principles. Although a Protestant redoubt, the Dublin mercantile interests had never been reconciled to the Act of Union. The commerce, trades and petty industry which the Corporation represented had suffered heavily from the disappearance of the Irish Parliament and its complex of social appendages; and after a decade's experience, they had convinced themselves that the Union spelt the ruin of business. Accordingly, on 20 July 1810 the Corporation resolved that only the restoration of the Irish Parliament could halt the city's decay. A consequent aggregate meeting on 18 September (to which Catholic as well as Protestant freeholders were invited) determined to petition for Repeal. O'Connell, who had of course thrown himself into the movement from the moment that it spread itself beyond the guilds, was one of the nine selected to draw up the parliamentary petition.

Later in the aggregate meeting O'Connell produced the second of his now-celebrated rhetorical set pieces. Essentially, it repeated his original anti-Union speech of 13 January 1800, although the range of the appeal was wider and its force much increased by many bitter words upon the faithlessness of British politicians as revealed by their collective conduct since 1801. 'What sympathy can we in our sufferings, expect from those men? . . . What are they to Ireland, or Ireland to them?' As before – indeed as always – O'Connell explained Irish subjection in terms of Irish disunion, 'which the enemies of Ireland have created, and continued, and seek to perpetuate amongst ourselves, by telling us of, and separating us into wretched sections and miserable subdivisions.' Conversely, combination was strength.

> The Protestant alone could not expect to liberate his country – the Roman Catholic alone could not do it – neither could the Presbyterian – but amalgamate the three into the Irishman, and the Union is repealed. Learn discretion from your enemies – they have crushed your country by fomenting religious discord – serve her by abandoning it for ever . . . I require no equivalent from you – whatever course you shall take, my mind is fixed – I trample under foot the Catholic claims, if they can interfere with the Repeal; I abandon all wish for emancipation, if it delays that Repeal. Nay, were Mr Perceval, to-morrow, to offer me the Repeal of the Union, upon the terms of re-enacting the entire penal code, I declare it from my heart, and in the presence of my God, that I would most cheerfully embrace

> his offer. Let us then, my beloved countrymen, sacrifice our wicked and groundless animosities on the altar of our country . . . – let us rally round the standard of Old Ireland, and we shall easily procure that greatest of political blessings, an Irish King, an Irish House of Lords, and an Irish House of Commons.[19]

O'Connell was received with acclaim though his audience was largely Protestant and Orange in composition. Immediately, he became a public figure in the capital in a larger sense than domination in the Catholic Committee. It was evidently this speech which he had in mind when, in later life, he recalled seeing his portrait in a Dublin shop window after a meeting in 1810 'at which I had attracted public notice . . . [I] said to myself with a smile, "Here are my boyish dreams of glory realized".'[20] But for all its early sparkle this political stream soon ended in the sands. Though noisy, the mercantile discontent was neither deep nor lasting; and the 'wretched sections and miserable subdivisions' of religious hatred rapidly reasserted their normal supremacy over political fraternity. There are indications that Dublin Castle had stirred itself to restore this particular form of Irish normalcy, and also not a few which suggest that O'Connell was now well on the way to becoming a marked man in its dossiers.

Although the interdenominational anti-Unionism of 1810 proved a political cul-de-sac – to be closed off almost as soon as entered – O'Connell's fierce espousal of the cause is worth some consideration. In the first place, it reiterated his concept of Irish nationality as essentially locational, to be determined solely by Irish birth or residence. These dwarfed every difference of class, interest, culture, language or even religion. It was significant that in his original anti-Union speech of 1800 O'Connell had deliberately thrown into antithesis 'Catholics' and 'country' and 'sect' and 'people', as well as proclaiming, in the name of his co-religionists, that even the humiliation and deprivations of the penal code were preferable to political subordination to Great Britain. Rhetoric could be stretched no farther to drive home the notion that Irish nationality was both an affair of place and superior in its claims to any other form of self-identity. There remained the difficulty that considerable bodies of Irish Protestants and Irish Catholics alike had favoured the Union in 1800. Worse still – the Dublin Corporation notwithstanding – there could be no doubt that by 1810 the Union was supported vehemently by the great majority of the Church of Ireland and the Presbyterian communions.

How was the British allegiance of so many Irishmen to be

explained? O'Connell's answer – his second principle, in effect – was – by Britain's steady practice of divide and conquer, in particular, by her 'artificial' fomenting of religious discord. It is important to note that thus far O'Connell's position was identical with that of another founding father of Irish nationalism, Theobald Wolfe Tone. Of course, Tone and O'Connell stand at the heads of opposed traditions, the violent and the non-violent movements. But both put the same gloss on the idealistic Grattanism of their youth. Both argued or assumed that Ireland was indivisible politically and inherently a sovereign nation; that sectarian distinctions (and *a fortiori* any lesser principles of segregation) were irrelevant to national identity and equality; and that Irish subjection to Great Britain was the fruit of Britain's determination to bribe, divide and confuse sufficient natives to keep the entire island under her ultimate control.

There was however a third element in O'Connell's apologia of 18 September 1810 which has had no counterpart in the revolutionary camp. His speech marks one extremity in what was to prove a life-long tactical oscillation. The poles of O'Connell's practical politics were, on the one hand, attempts to collaborate with British whigs, liberals or radicals and, on the other, attempts to make common cause with Irish (generally Orange to tory) Protestants, in order to achieve an end. Movement between these poles, in response to some particular discouragement or defeat, or the exhaustion of some earlier initiative, constituted a basic pattern over O'Connell's entire career. The effort to capitalize upon Dublin Corporation's anti-Unionist fling of 1810, following the parliamentary débâcles of 1808, is the first clear manifestation of the phenomenon.

Finally, another characteristic constituent of O'Connell's grammar of politics was introduced in his peroration. The final words of his speech of 18 September apostrophized 'an Irish King, an Irish House of Lords and an Irish House of Commons' as the 'greatest of political blessings'.[21] This and similar phraseology served two important purposes. To the utmost practicable extent, they secured his flank against charges of revolutionism: 'King, Lords and Commons' was the most solemn incantation of all in the liturgy of the high and dry constitutionalists. They also suggested that his programme was moderate, to the point of being, literally speaking, reactionary. After all, he proposed repeal of the Act of Union in terms of a return to the condition of 1800. This *restorative* emphasis masked – perhaps even from himself – the essential radicalism of his objectives. For he could not have meant what he appeared to mean, a simple turning back of the hands of the constitutional clock. To no one was the narrow, rigged, corrupt and externally manipulated Irish parliamentary system of 1782–1800 more of an anathema.

As if in response to the 'law of oscillation', new hopes of an advance at Westminster sprang up almost as soon as the old hopes of collaboration with the Dublin Protestant merchants were quenched. George III's 'madness' returned in November 1810; a regency bill was introduced in the Commons on 20 December. The Catholic Committee in Dublin took it that the Prince of Wales, an old friend of Fox and Sheridan and widely assumed to share their political liberalism, would prove a *deus ex machina* for Emancipation. O'Connell led the field in organizing a royal address. But in doing so he ran foul of the conservative faction on the Committee. First, they were both shocked and frightened by the scurrilous abuse of the prime minister, Perceval, with which O'Connell inter-wove his laudation of the Prince. Where O'Connell sought to flaunt his defiance of, and break the spell cast by the British political class, the Catholic conservatives sought to appease it and to demonstrate their parity as gentlemen. Their motion to forbid reports of the meeting because of O'Connell's provocative language was, however, defeated. Secondly, the conservatives feared O'Connell's increasing power within the movement. In the spring of 1810 he had acted for several weeks as secretary of the Committee while its permanent secretary, Edward Hay, was conducting Catholic business in London, and later in the year he organized a national testimonial to Hay to reward him for his services to the cause. These opened up for him connections with London politicians, the Irish hierarchy and above all the network of prominent Catholics scattered across the counties. *A la* Stalin and Khrushchev in later days, control of communications through the general secretaryship meant a further access to power! O'Connell was also resented as the leader of a supposed barristers' party in the Committee. At a meeting early in January 1811 Lord Ffrench, himself a truculent boor, accused the lawyers of self-seeking – they 'ought to be suspected, having more to expect than any other description of Catholic' – and announced his intention to 'put [them] down'.[22]

Having been steadily worsted on the Committee, Ffrench proposed that its decisions be referred to aggregate – open, public – meetings for ratification. He failed to see the irony of a gentry appeal to the populace against the influence of the professional class. Nothing could have better suited O'Connell's book. He also was disenchanted with the Committee – but for its timorousness and obeisance to respectability. The more popular (and perhaps we should add, vulgar) the agitation, the greater his own leverage and the leverage of the movement generally. The primary obstacle to 'going public' was the Convention Act of 1793 which had been designed to prevent Irish Catholics from forming a representative body. O'Connell hoped to steer a safe way amongst its provisions by issuing a general invitation to the Catholics of Ireland to appoint 'managers' of the Catholic petition in each county. When a number of these 'managers' turned up at the Committee meeting of 2 February 1811, at which the petition was being drawn up, the Ffrench–Keogh party bitterly opposed their attendance as opening the way to prosecution under the Convention Act. O'Connell beat off this internal attack with the argument that since the Committee itself was not a representative body its attenders could not be, legally speaking, representatives. But the Irish chief secretary, Wellesley Pole, responded almost immediately by issuing on 12 February 1811 a circular to all sheriffs and magistrates instructing them to proceed immediately, under the Convention Act, against any person involved in appointing representatives to the Committee.

Before the month was out, magistrates broke into and attempted to disperse an ordinary meeting of the Catholic Committee. Ffrench and his opponents joined ranks. Advised by O'Connell and other barristers, Ffrench refused to leave the chair unless charged with a specific offence or forcibly removed. The legal battle was finally transferred to a conference to be held at the Castle itself. It never took place; for the time being O'Connell was triumphant. Aggregate meetings, with the ostensible purpose of preparing petitions, were held in March and July 1811 without governmental intervention. At both O'Connell, as lawyer, dictated the tactics and tone: caution and attempted conciliation were the order of the day. None the less O'Connell had been emboldened by his success in February, and at the aggregate meeting of 9 July he strongly supported a resolution to add to the Committee not only all Catholic peers, baronets and prelates but also ten persons chosen by the Catholics of each county, and five from each Dublin parish. That he understood the risk involved is clear from his offering himself as a parish candidate ready to give bail so that the legal issue could be determined. One wonders what Hunting Cap made of the newspaper reports of this particular piece of heroics! He had written a few months before, 'Nor would reason or experience in any degree bear him [O'Connell] out in the vain expectation that he could resume with any prospect of success a profession which he had once, though partially, withdrawn from or relinquished.'[23]

On 30 July 1811 the Irish Administration responded to the second challenge with a proclamation, under the Convention Act, declaring illegal the appointment of county or parish representatives. The indictment of a number of people concerned in these elections (but not of O'Connell or any other leading member of the Catholic Committee) followed swiftly, although the magistrates bungled the next step – attempting to disperse the subsequent meeting of the Committee – by arriving in force after its conclusion. The first trial, that of Dr Edward Sheridan, was held on 21–2 November. Although he could not of course lead in the case, O'Connell designed the defence upon the construction to be placed on a single word in the Convention Act, 'pretence'. The chief justice summed up heavily, but vainly, against such a line of argument; the jury found for Sheridan. Now the battle was really joined. Foolishly, the Committee counter-prosecuted the chief justice for illegal arrest, and suffered its first defeat of the year; and when it assembled for its next meeting on 23 December, it found a police magistrate, Hare, already in possession of the hall. There followed one of the great set-pieces of early-nineteenth-century agitation, with O'Connell dictating the Committee's moves stage by stage.

When Hare demanded to know the purpose of the meeting, the chairman, Lord Fingall, replied obliquely with a tangential formula of O'Connell's devising. When Hare took this to be an admission that the meeting was one of the Catholic Committee, as defined by its own resolution of 9 July 1811, O'Connell insisted that this could be only a private and not a judicial opinion. When Hare none the less declared the assembly to be illegal, O'Connell advised submission, under protest, to what was now a magisterial action, but also that the chairman await formal arrest so as to provide the basis for a future law suit. When Hare used token force to remove Fingall, another peer, Lord Netterville, and, on his being deposed in turn, Lord Ffrench, were voted into the chair. Next, the Committee transferred itself to a private house, where the magistrate followed them and a further imbroglio transpired. In the end, the meeting was transformed into a 'gathering of private individuals', and Hare declared that Fingall and Netterville had not been arrested after all!

Despite the vein of farce running through all the proceedings and the absurdity of their conclusion, the interplay was significant. First, it signalled the Irish government's absolute determination to check any expansion of the Catholic movement either socially or geographically; it was acting on the secret instructions of the Catholics' supposed friend, the Prince Regent. Secondly, although Hare's intervention was not wholly successful, he had so disrupted and threatened the future activity of the Committee that O'Connell decided on 29 December that it should be replaced by a new 'Catholic Board', designated as a mere petitioning body. Moreover, despite the acquittal of Sheridan on 22 November, Dublin Castle persisted with its prosecutions, and on 3 February 1812 secured a verdict against another of the offenders, Kirwan. On the other hand, O'Connell was well aware that, ju-jitsu like, the very force of his opponents' charge could be turned to his own account, if handled cunningly. Both the uproar and the government's insolent and secure exorbitance on 23 December 1811 provided tinder for future agitation. O'Connell ensured that the episode was exploited for publicity, making it in turn the subject of meetings of protest not only in the capital but also in the provinces, in particular in the circuit towns and cities. The success of any individual move or counter-move in the new game of cat-and-mouse mattered comparatively little as against maintaining, and if possible raising, the level of political excitement.

O'Connell was now well into his apprenticeship as agitator. It was he who had been primarily responsible for the changes in form and emphasis of the Catholic movement during 1811. Basically, he had set out to widen, render national and, to a limited degree, popularize the campaign. The Convention Act of 1793 made it almost certain that such moves would precipitate a legal and constitutional conflict. This he welcomed both from professional and natural inclination and because it placed the direction of the campaign in his own hands. From February 1811 onwards even the aristocratic leaders in the Committee acted almost as his chessmen in the game of common and statute law which he was playing with his Castle counterparts.

We might also note that it was during 1811 that politics began seriously to compete with his profession for O'Connell's time. Some thirty years later, he replied bitterly to the Earl of Shrewsbury's charge that he was greedy in accepting the public's financial support:

> At a period when my minutes counted by the guinea, when my emoluments were limited only by the extent of my physical and waking powers, when my meals were shortened to the narrowest span, and my sleep restricted to the earliest hours before dawn – at that period, and for more than twenty years, there was no day that I did not devote from one to two hours, often much more, to the working out of the Catholic cause . . . For four years I bore the entire expenses of Catholic agitation, without receiving the contributions of others to a greater amount than £74 in the whole. Who

> shall repay me for the years of my buoyant youth and cheerful manhood? Who shall repay me for the lost opportunities of acquiring professional celebrity, or for the wealth which such distinctions would ensure?[24]

There were to be fluctuations in the extent of his political commitments. In certain phases, 1816–17 for instance, no expenditure of energy or talent could set or keep a serious agitation in motion. But in general, O'Connell understated, if anything, his outpouring of time, money and physical, nervous and mental energy in the public cause in the decades 1811–30. Already in 1811 the pattern was being set in which, 'Busy all day long, either on circuit or in the law-courts, he could still find time to arrange meetings, draw up resolutions, make speeches and in short direct the whole business of the Catholics.'[25] The student who could not rise in the mornings had by now reduced his sleep to six hours a night, now rose at 5 a.m., toiled as a lawyer for nine hours or more, and then took up his other career again each afternoon. It had become a life of Hercules and Sisyphus in one.

## IV

By the opening of 1812, the Catholic Committee had been effectively stifled; there is no evidence that O'Connell ever contemplated putting his assertions of the illegality of its suppression to the test. But some cards still remained in Irish Catholic hands. Foremost was the war with France, now entering perhaps its most critical year of all. For a variety of reasons, ranging from the international influence of the Papacy to the high proportion of Irish Catholics among recruits to both the army and navy, this was the factor which had impelled successive British governments since 1793 to toy with Emancipation. Secondly, the Catholic question had begun to divide British politicians deeply and, still more significant, cross-factionally. Cabinet building, the management of the Commons and the quality of the war administration all suffered from the consequences of this extraneous source of contention, with corresponding incentives to end it by some final settlement. Thirdly, and most immediately, there remained the traditional English 'rights' of petition and assembly to be exploited, and these O'Connell continued to exploit in the early months of 1812. County or other aggregate meetings were held during the spring assizes, with O'Connell to the forefront in Ennis, Limerick and Tralee; their business spread rapidly from protests against Hare's conduct to denunciations of 'That grave of Irish prosperity, the Legislative Union'.[26] Meanwhile the new Catholic Board, despite its self-imposed limitations, conducted itself in substantially the same fashion as the Committee had done, with meetings reported in the press and a deputation sent to London for the parliamentary session. In all this, O'Connell was the master figure; already the cult of personality was manifest. At the Limerick meeting of 24 July he told the enthusiastic crowd:

> I feel it my duty as a 'Professed Agitator' to address this meeting; it is merely the exercise of my office of Agitation . . . If the Emancipation Bill passes, next Sessions, as it is likely to do; and that no other candidate offers, I myself will bring your present member to the poll. I probably will have little chance of success; but I will have the satisfaction of shewing this City and the County, what the freeborn mind might achieve, if it were properly seconded. [*Here the Applause became so great, as to prevent the Speaker for some minutes, from proceeding.*][27]

After Kirwan's conviction on 3 February 1812, the Irish government did nothing to check the Catholic movement for several months. A serious effort was being made in London to resolve the Catholic question once and for all; it was no time for further stirring of the hornet's nest. When at last Canning showed his hand it was to give notice on 6 May that he would move in the Commons for 'the consideration of such securities as might be necessary to fence the Established Church' in the event of Emancipation.[28] Simultaneously, it was rumoured that the prime minister, Perceval, was attempting to reach a settlement with the Irish Catholic hierarchy behind the backs of the Catholic Board, and at successive meetings of the Board on 12 and 16 May O'Connell denounced this 'insidious' move and expressed his conviction that 'no such proposition had been made'. As Professor M. R. O'Connell suggests, however, 'O'Connell's denunciation on 12 May may well have been mere kite-flying in order to discover whether there was any truth in . . . [the] information.'[29]

In between these meetings of the Board news had reached Dublin of Perceval's assassination on 11 May. Immediately hopes had risen that the reconstituted government would prove more favourable to the Catholic claims, and O'Connell held off calling an aggregate meeting in Dublin until he saw how things would shape themselves. It was soon apparent that they would shape themselves badly. The illusion that the Prince Regent was the Catholics' friend, awaiting only opportunity or political encouragement to liberate them, was rapidly destroyed by his refusal to grant a personal interview to the delegates of the Irish Catholic Board, and his ready acceptance of a new ministry constructed by Lord Liverpool upon the familiar anti-Catholic lines.

Catholic anger expressed itself in the subsequently notorious 'witchery' resolutions passed at the Dublin aggregate meeting of 18 June – the witchery being that of the Prince's current mistress, Lady Hertford.

> We learn with deep disappointment and anguish, how cruelly the promised boon of Catholic freedom has been intercepted by the fatal witchery of an unworthy secret influence, hostile to our fairest hopes, spurning alike the sanctions of public and private virtue, the demands of personal gratitude, and the sacred obligations of plighted honour. To this impure source we trace, but too distinctly, our afflicted hopes and protracted servitude, the arrogant invasion of the undoubted right of petitioning, the acrimony of illegal state prosecutions, the surrender of Ireland to prolonged oppression . . .[30]

The ringing phrases were Denys Scully's but it was O'Connell who, boldly and savagely, applied them directly to the Prince. The disclosures had transformed him into an absolute intransigent, much to the fright and chagrin of the cautious party in the Board.

The formation of the new government, however, worked for as well as against the Catholic interest. The fact that such able tories as Canning and Wellesley had been prevented from joining a tory administration, at a time of supreme national crisis, solely because the Catholic question remained unsettled, had its effect upon high political opinion. The ground was ready for an attempt to remove the question once for all from British politics by some agreed solution, to be worked out essentially by the various contestants at Westminster. Accordingly, when Canning proposed on 22 June 1812 that the issue of Catholic disabilities should be tackled at last in the next parliamentary session, the Commons supported him by the overwhelming majority of 235 to 106.

O'Connell, unlike many, perhaps most, members of the Irish Board, reacted with uncompromising hostility. At an aggregate meeting on 2 July he called upon Irish Catholics to redouble instead of relaxing their agitation. They should settle for nothing less than unqualified Emancipation; the cry for 'securities' to allay Protestant fears was an insult to free men and in itself a sort of confirmation of Catholic servility. Borrowing a Grattanite slogan of the early 1780s, O'Connell ran 'Simple Repeal' up the masthead. This presaged a fundamental cleavage in the Board; but during the summer of 1812 there was no public repudiation of O'Connell's call for intransigence, although he repeated it at every aggregate meeting on the assize circuit. Did he really mean to reject all adulterated forms of Catholic relief? Or was his primary purpose to build up Catholic bargaining power against the moment of eventual compromise, or to popularize the movement, or to out-manoeuvre his opponents in the Board, or generally to extend the practice of agitation, the habit of defiance and the sight of his co-religionists bearing themselves as equals? We lack the evidence to make a choice of motive, but he himself would doubtless have liked us to select the last. Perhaps it was in earnest of this passion for equality that he sought to drag down in ridicule the new Irish chief secretary, Robert Peel, appointed on 4 August 1812 at the age of twenty-four. Instantly, O'Connell employed the obvious derogation, 'Orange' Peel.

Nine months were to pass, however, before the two engaged closely in combat. It took Peel time to establish his domination over the permanent officials at the Castle and to form an alliance with its most effective member, William Saurin, the attorney-general; it took the lucky accident of the near-simultaneous departure of the viceroy and a permanent under-secretary in May 1813, to clear his way to over-riding power. Meanwhile, the Catholic cause had at least held its ground. O'Connell's fortunes had been mixed in the autumn of 1812. The opportunity of demonstrating Irish Catholic electoral strength in the general election of October was neither well-seen nor well-seized: pro-Catholic borough seats were actually lost in Cork and Newry. Worse still, in the course of the subsequent recriminations, the Catholic Board, despite O'Connell's earnest protest, carried a motion on 28 November condemning and repudiating those Catholics who had failed to support the Emancipationist candidates. 'One would suppose', O'Connell told the meeting, 'that Ireland was not sufficiently divided and distracted already, but that division and dissension in the Catholic Board could be afforded in addition.'[31] Later, summoning all his influence, he managed to have the condemnatory resolution rescinded, but by then the charges of cowardice and self-serving had worked their poison on personal relations.

On the other hand, the lost and unwon Irish seats seemed scarcely to matter when the new House of Commons assembled at the beginning of 1813. Grattan's resolution in favour of Catholic relief was carried by a majority of forty; his motion in committee on 1 March, that all Catholic disabilities be removed, subject only to 'securities' to guarantee the Protestant establishment, passed still more easily and the bill derived from this motion was read for the first time on 30 April. The 'securities' prescribed in the bill consisted essentially of an oath of allegiance to be taken by all Catholics, lay and clerical alike, swearing to uphold the Protestant succession, Protestant property and the established church, and to reject the episcopal nomination of any candidate whose loyalty and 'tranquil disposition' was in doubt. All this was in the eighteenth-century style. Substantially the same oath had been freely sworn by Irish Catholics of the preceding generation; in practice, it constituted little more than a ritual of abasement.

The very symbolism of subservience, revived in Grattan's bill, may explain the ferocity of O'Connell's opposition to the new measure when it was considered *in camera* by the Catholic Board on 1 May 1813. But although most supported his condemnation of the bill, several members were prepared to close with Grattan's 'offer'. O'Connell countered these by 'leaking' an account of the proceedings to the newspapers; he wished to rally popular support to intimidate the compromisers. When challenged at the next Board meeting, he agreed to allow a statement to be sent forth that the Board had come to no determination on the bill. He had already achieved his objective, the silencing, temporarily at least, of his opponents. At the same time, O'Connell sought to guard his other flank by threatening the bishops obliquely. While he noisily proclaimed his belief that the clerical order might be trusted to safeguard its own independence, he also made it clear that he would resist it strongly should the last relic of national pride and honour, an unmanaged Church, be tarnished by episcopal compromise. Whether or not influenced by this warning, the Irish hierarchy publicly condemned the ecclesiastical clauses of Grattan's bill in the strongest terms on 29 May. In fact, the bishops' action was unnecessary; two nights before, the House of Commons had so emasculated the bill that its supporters withdrew it as now worthless. O'Connell was fortunate that this news had not reached Dublin until after the bishops met, for their resolution practically enlisted them in his ranks in the current struggle.

His sense of triumph was unbounded. At the next Board meeting, he lauded the prelates to the skies for saving the Irish people from the perpetuation of their 'degradation'. Cleverly, he capitalized upon this line of argument by using the bill's proposal that there should be a governmental commission to control Irish episcopal appointments as a means of denigrating its likely members – as to whom, incidentally, his guesses were remarkably accurate. The chief victim of his invective was 'Orange' Peel, 'a raw youth squeezed out of the workings of I know not what factory in England, and sent over to Ireland before he had got rid of the foppery of perfumed handkerchiefs and thin shoes, upon the simple ground that, having vindicated the murderous Walcheren expedition, he was thought to be a lad ready to vindicate anything and everything'.[32] Such vituperation could scarcely have been quite without design. But O'Connell may have been carried along by the tide of his own thoughts, by his smarting under the vision of the perpetual 'degradation' just avoided, as he strove to force down a brutally disdainful caste to the common level.

The price of gross abuse was the making of personal enemies in politics: we may plausibly date Peel's lifelong aversion to O'Connell from this occasion, just as we may date the Prince Regent's from O'Connell's elaboration of the 'witchery' resolutions. A further cost was the tearing apart of the Irish Catholic movement. O'Connell's motion of gratitude to the hierarchy was bitterly resisted at the Catholic Board meeting of 29 May 1813. Twenty members opposed it, and they and their friends seceded permanently from the Board after they had been defeated. Henceforth there was an Irish 'vetoist' party in schism from the O'Connell-dominated majority. The division was not quite on the lines of social class, still less of generation, and not quite as marked in the provincial cities as in the capital. Certainly, the 'vetoists' comprised, by and large, the Irish Catholics of the highest social rank. But they also included a number from the professional and mercantile classes and, especially important, some of the ablest men of the rising generation, such as Richard Lalor Sheil and Thomas Wyse, and some of the most ambitious of the young Catholic barristers, such as Nicholas Ball and Stephen Woulfe. This was in part a matter of self-interest. But the perennially attractive political argument that substantial gains might be made for only the cost of insubstantial guarantees of good behaviour could also be deployed. As one critic put the point, the anti-vetoists, like the Gregorian calendarists, 'found out an evil which did nobody any harm, and provided a remedy which did nobody any good'.[33] The critic himself went on to suggest that the leading vetoists saw government influence over the Irish clergy as a remedy which might do *them* a little good. They feared, he wrote, O'Connell's efforts to build up a clerical caste. '[The] aristocracy would not forget the humble origin of most of the priests . . . This was never mentioned in the whole *veto* controversy, but it was really the point at issue. The aristocracy sought the *veto*, because they hoped that the government would use its influence to preserve the prelacy at least "*unvulgarized*".'[34]

At any rate, it was clear that O'Connell could no longer rely on the aristocratic and professionally-pushing factions even to form a common front in emergencies. He signalized as much by summoning a public meeting at Fishamble Street theatre on 15 June 1813 at which he specifically adopted the principle of popular agitation. This marked a radical departure. Making a virtue of necessity, O'Connell pointed to the benefit of the postponement of full Emancipation – a mere delay, of course, for nothing was more certain than its eventual passage. The interval of frustrated hope would inevitably breed agitators, and agitators were bound to accustom 'the popular mind' to consider public issues, to awaken it to a knowledge of its wrongs and to lead it into the passions and machinations of politics. Once aroused and directed, 'the people' would prove irresistible in the end. But the condition precedent of their success was to eschew all violence or even illegality and to rely exclusively upon 'the repetition of your constitutional demands by petition, and still more by the pressure of circumstances and the great progress of events'. In the most solemn words, O'Connell warned his audience that should any crime or illegality in the movement bring down upon them a renewed reign of terror, he himself would be found in the ranks of the suppressors. 'There would not be so heavy a heart; but there would not be a more ready hand to sustain the constitution against every enemy.'[35]

This very curious declaration set out the philosophy of political action which was to govern O'Connell's entire agitatory career. The philosophy was complete already, even if the machinery of implementation remained to be invented. It represented a specific repudiation of the revolutionary tradition, just as it also repudiated directly the republican objective. O'Connell confined political action to the limits of the British constitution, and the goal of all such action to a full, fair and equal place within that constitution. It was an extraordinary doctrine and recipe for a demogogue to offer the masses whom he intended to 'create'. But, albeit inert and hidden for at least a decade, it contained the dynamite which would eventually blow apart the old Protestant Ascendancy in Ireland.

There remains the question, why did O'Connell adopt the role of absolute intransigent during 1812–13? In many ways it was out of character. By temperament he was averse to extreme positions, by training a settler out of court in doubtful issues. Moreover, he himself probably stood to gain more from Grattan's original bill, in terms of eventual status and income alike, than anyone in the vetoist cliques. The answer is, partly, that current and future compromise in the bill would be mainly at the expense of the Irish Catholic Church's autonomy, and O'Connell was sincere in regarding this – *vis-à-vis* Great Britain at least – as integral to Irish independence. Secondly, he still rated the French threat to Britain as powerful enough to force her to come to a satisfactory accommodation with Irish Catholicism, if only the Irish Catholics pressed hard. But, most important of all perhaps, he judged it unlikely that the House of Commons of 1813, with Liverpool's anti-Catholic ministry in office and the Prince Regent the ultimate determinant, would yield anything of substance unless intimidated by Irish agitation or disorder. A half or a quarter measure now, drawing off most of the lay Catholics on the make, might render it impossible to mount another major offensive for many years. O'Connell's political judgment was probably correct at every point.

CHAPTER 6

# Championing

## 1813–15

### I

During 1813, O'Connell began to manifest a new style, suited to a wider and more popular audience. He had already become a daily public spectacle in Dublin's streets, known to and watched with awe by multitudes. A perceptive observer later described his half-hour morning walk from Merrion Square to Arran Quay:

> When breakfast was over, his burly form excited attention, as he moved towards the Four Courts, at a pace which compelled panting attorneys to toil after him in vain. His umbrella shouldered like a pike, was his invariable companion; the military step which he had acquired in the yeomanry, strangely blended with the trot characteristic of an active sportsman on the mountains of Kerry, gave him the appearance of a Highland chieftain – a similarity increased, when his celebrity as an agitator began to ensure him a 'tail' of admiring followers whenever he appeared in public.[1]

In a comparatively small city, politics could become personalized in a specific and physical as well as a large and metaphorical sense.

With his violent direct assaults upon the Regent and Peel, O'Connell had, to some extent, assumed the role of gladiator engaging enemies in personal combat. This development reached its apotheosis in the Magee trial of 26–7 July 1813. On 3 June, John Magee, the Protestant proprietor of the main pro-Catholic newspaper, the *Dublin Evening Post*, was arrested on a charge of publishing a libel on the lately departed viceroy, the Duke of Richmond. The arrest was part of a deliberate campaign, by Peel, to destroy or intimidate the opposition press. Already two other pro-Catholic publishers, Cox and Fitzpatrick, had been gaoled. But Magee was much the most important victim of the new Castle offensive, and O'Connell decided to turn the consequent publicity to account by rendering the trial, in effect, a political tournament. There was of course a full array of counsel on either side, but he was to dominate the defendant's, just as the attorney-general, Saurin, a narrow, bitter but upright and competent Protestant zealot and Ascendancy man, was to dominate the prosecution.

O'Connell and Saurin had clashed already in Fitzpatrick's case, when O'Connell electrified the court by demanding that both the attorney-general and a judge, Norbury, be summoned as witnesses – Saurin's and Norbury's conduct in a recent capital case being a leading item in Fitzpatrick's 'libel'. Saurin had been breathtaken by the measure of O'Connell's insolence in attempting to arraign the entire administration of justice, and to reduce two of its ornaments to the level of mere cross-examinees. 'Were they', he exclaimed, 'to convert the trial of a person charged with libel, into a trial of his Majesty's Government?'[2] This described precisely O'Connell's objectives in the Magee affair. When he rose to address the court at the outset of the trial's second day, it was to hold 'the law' (and the whole governmental system) up to ridicule and scorn. He began with Saurin's opening indictment:

> That which yesterday excited my anger, now appears to me to be an object of pity; and that which then roused my indignation, now only moves to *contempt* . . .
>
> It was a discourse in which you could not discover either order, or method, or eloquence; it contained very little logic, and no poetry at all; violent and virulent, it was a confused and disjointed tissue of bigotry, amalgamated with congenial vulgarity. He accused my client of using Billingsgate and he accused him of it in language suited exclusively for that meridian . . .
>
> I cannot repress my astonishment, how Mr Attorney-General could have *preserved* this dialect in its native purity; he has been now for nearly thirty years in the class of polished society; he has, for some years, mixed amongst the highest orders in the state; he has had the honour to belong for thirty years to the first profession in the world – to the only profession, with the single exception, perhaps, of the military, to which a high-minded gentleman could condescend to belong – the Irish bar. To that bar, at which he has seen and heard a Burgh and a Duquery; at which he must have listened to a Burston, a Ponsonby, and a Curran; to a bar which still contains a Plunket, a Ball, and despite of politics, I will add, a Bushe. With this galaxy of glory, flinging their light around him, how can he alone have remained in darkness? . . . Devoid of taste and of genius, how can he have had memory enough to preserve this original vulgarity? He is, indeed, an object of compassion . . .[3]

These lacerating words were directed at two audiences. The first was the ruling powers – the chief justice and his companion judges on the bench, and the chief secretary Peel, the Irish chancellor of the exchequer, the Irish commander-in-chief and all the lesser potentates of Dublin Castle ranged beneath it. They sat stunned by the onslaught, in a stupor of disbelief that a papist junior counsel should charge the first officer of the Irish Government, in open court, with congenital and irremediable vulgarity. The second audience, on the rear benches and in the gallery, was but a token of the shadowy masses whom O'Connell was addressing from afar, the Irish Catholic millions whom he was telling not to crouch, not to admit inferiority, not to fear. The public humilation of Saurin was meant to be a demonstration lesson, so to say, for raw pupils on their first day at school. Far into his address, O'Connell was checked at last by the chief justice. Under a very transparent disguise, he had just spoken of Saurin as 'an infamous and profligate *liar*!' for charging the Catholic Board with sedition.

> CHIEF JUSTICE: What, Mr O'Connell, can this have to do with the question which the jury are to try?
> MR O'CONNELL: You heard the Attorney-General traduce and calumniate us – you heard him with patience and with temper – listen now to our vindication![4]

There were no further interruptions.

The alleged 'libel' was based on a sentence in the *Evening Post* ending, 'but truly . . . they [the people of Ireland] must find themselves at a loss to discover any striking feature in his Grace's [Richmond's] administration, that makes it superior to the worst of his predecessors'[5]: the review had described earlier viceroys in such terms as 'the profligate, unprincipled Westmorland', 'the cold-hearted and cruel Camden' and 'the artful and treacherous Cornwallis'. O'Connell first tackled the charge by attempting to justify these descriptions of Richmond's predecessors, and he had no difficulty in producing similar condemnations by their various British political enemies. As for Richmond himself, O'Connell distinguished the honourable private individual from the public man guilty of all the customary sorts of Irish misgovernment. Together, these lines of defence enabled O'Connell to survey, systematically and scarifyingly, the entire course of British management of Ireland over the preceding quarter of a century. Again the Bench and the 'quality' in court sat amazed under the attack, their world suddenly turned upside down, their ears hearing audacity beyond belief. Peel epitomized their reaction when he later declared that if Magee had published a gross libel, O'Connell was uttering one even more atrocious – and doing so with impunity.

But such an Ascendancy form of judgment was undercut completely by O'Connell's second, concurrent defence tactic. This was his 'honest and conscientious opinion . . . that in the discussion of *public subjects*, and of the administration of *public men*, *truth* is a duty and not *a crime*'.[6] Flat or facile though this may read in the late twentieth century, it was the simple, almost the sole issue in mid-1813. Today Magee's diatribe might disgust as vulgar, inflated or wild, but only in a deeply totalitarian state would it so much as occur to an official that it constituted a seditious or defamatory statement. Unerringly, O'Connell traced the British coercion of his time to its source – the Star Chamber mentality, which had lived on in those eighteenth-century English and early-nineteenth-century Irish courts, where 'Servility at the Bar, and profligacy on the Bench, have not been wanting to aid every construction unfavourable to freedom, and at length it is taken as granted and as clear law, that truth or falsehood are quite immaterial, circumstances constituting no part of either guilt or innocence.'[7] As this indicates, the libel action against Magee was – in our terms – a mere mechanism of political censorship, with cruel penalties being imposed retrospectively for breaches of an unspecified and unpromulgated code.

O'Connell threaded his libel defence with further assaults upon the current Irish Administration, and in particular Saurin. He mocked the packed Protestant jury as 'suppressors of vice and Bible distributers' (a reference to the repressive and proselytizing societies to which most of them belonged), demanding of them, 'Are you sincere, or are you, to use your own phraseology, whitewashed tombs – painted charnel-houses? Be ye hypocrites?'[8] He assailed Peel directly as the briber of the newspapers in Dublin Castle's pay. 'Would I could see the man', he exclaimed, staring Peel in the face, 'who pays this proclamation money and these pensions . . . I would ask him whether . . . this be the legitimate use of the public purse.'[9] But it was Saurin above all whom O'Connell continued to hound down. Because of his Huguenot ancestry, he was depicted as a carpet-bagger, a 'bigoted and intemperate stranger', filled with '*French* insolence, than which there is nothing so permanent – even transplanted, it exhibits itself to the third and fourth generation.'[10] In 'putting an imaginary case' (*à la* Mr Jaggers), O'Connell heaped scorn upon Saurin's 'church-wardening piety' and 'maidenly decorum of manners'; but also pictured him, bigotted, prejudiced, pompous, vain and loaded with the booty of the attorney-generalship, using, once raised to the Bench, 'that character for SANCTITY which has served to promote him, as a sword, to hew down the struggling liberties of his country'.[11] The climax of this terrible rending was probably O'Connell's rehearsal of Saurin's political career before the Union.

> The charge of being a Jacobin, was at that time made against the present Attorney-General – him, plain William Saurin – in the very terms, and with just as much truth as he now applies it to my client. His reply shall serve for that of Mr Magee; I take it from the anti-Union of the 22nd March, 1800.
>
> > 'To the charge of Jacobin, Mr Saurin said he knew not what it meant, as applied to him, *except it was an opposition to the will of the British minister.*'
>
> So says Mr Magee; but, gentlemen, my eye lights upon another passage of Mr Saurin's, in the same speech from which I have quoted the above. It was in these words:-
>
> > 'Mr Saurin admitted, that debates might sometimes produce *agitations*, but that was the PRICE *necessarily paid for liberty.*'
>
> Oh, how I thank this good Jew for the word. Yes, agitation is, as Mr Saurin well remarked, the price necessarily paid for liberty. We have paid the price, gentlemen, and the honest man refuses to give us the goods. (*Much laughing.*)

In the end O'Connell implied a charge of selling principles for profit, when he asked, 'But, gentlemen, is the Attorney-General at liberty to change the nature of things with his own official and professional prospects?'[12]

O'Connell's address concluded with a brilliant sustained appeal-by-role-reversal. He asked the jury to suppose themselves inhabitants of a Portugal, four-fifths Protestant in composition and ruled, through a viceroy, by a repressive foreign Catholic power:

> your native land shall be to you the country of strangers; you shall be aliens in the soil that gave you birth, and whilst every foreigner may, in the land of your forefathers, attain rank, station, emolument, honours, you alone shall be excluded . . .
>
> Only think, gentlemen, of the scandalous injustice of punishing you because you are Protestants. With what scorn – with what contempt – do you not listen to the stale pretences – to the miserable excuses by which, under the name of state reasons and political arguments, your exclusion and degradation are sought to be justified![13]

He proceeded to outline, in acerbic detail, the full course of Richmond's administration – all in the form of a Catholic viceroy's oppression of Protestant Portugal. At last he reached the stage matching that at which the genuinely Irish Protestant Magee had published his 'libel' upon Richmond's rule.

> But if at such a moment some ardent and enthusiastic Papist [in 'Portugal'], regardless of his interests, and roused by the crimes that were thus committed against you, should describe, in measured, and cautious, and cold language, scenes of oppression and iniquity . . . if this liberal Papist, for this, were dragged to the Inquisition, as for a crime, and menaced with a dungeon for years, good and gracious God! how would you revolt at and abominate the men who could consign him to that dungeon! . . . What pity would you not feel for the advocate who heavily, and without hope, laboured in his defence![14]

The final words challenged the jurors on their home ground, 'earnest', fundamentalist, evangelical religion. O'Connell demanded that they show whether they were sincere believers, whether with 'all this zeal – with all this piety', there was a single conscience among the twelve, or a single soul which felt terror at violating the sacred oath. If he had 'alarmed religion . . . in one breast amongst you, Mr Magee is safe . . . but if there is none – if you be slaves and hypocrites, he will await your verdict, and despise it.'[15]

O'Connell failed to 'alarm religion' in, or otherwise disturb, a single juror-breast. Magee was quickly declared guilty, although his sentencing was postponed until the next law term. O'Connell was generally condemned at the time for sacrificing his client's interest to his own political ends, and by and large posterity has endorsed this verdict. But such a judgment seems superficial. It was morally certain that the carefully culled ultra-Protestant jury would find against Magee whatever conventional line of defence was chosen. O'Connell's bold and wonderfully executed strategy – to try to bring home to even one juror an understanding of his proper function or of the plain brute oppression which the so-called Irish Government merely masked, or to awaken a scruple or qualm in a single juror's conscience – may well have represented the sole hope of securing a hung jury, if not acquittal. An acute contemporary, who was by no means an uncritical admirer of O'Connell, adjudged that he 'did not neglect any material point in his client's defence; and even if he had confined himself strictly to his duties as an advocate, the issue would still have been the same'.[16]

Nevertheless it is true that Magee's fate was a secondary consideration. O'Connell used the trial first and foremost to assert, in a more public and telling form than had ever been available to him before, that Catholics were fully the equals, rank for rank, of their Protestant counterparts. For once, he could, literally, confront his enemies; they were bound to their seats in court, bound to hear him in silence, by the weight of their own mores and self-regard. For once it was they who were on the triangle, and for four and a half hours O'Connell lashed them with irony and scorn. On only one occasion had the court attempted to wrest the scourge from O'Connell; and it had been almost contemptuously swept back. The address, magnificently structured and endlessly fertile in invention and allusion, was probably O'Connell's master forensic display. It also marked a new stage of Catholic pretension, even arrogance.

O'Connell's speech was reported extensively in the Irish newspapers, Magee's *Evening Post* reprinting it in full. It was also issued immediately as a pamphlet, as well as translated into French and Spanish – though not Portuguese! All this of course multiplied O'Connell's offence in Castle eyes. But (to anticipate Mr Gladstone) the resources of 'civilization' were not exhausted. On 10 August, 1813, Peel wrote to Lord Desart, 'I hope the Chief Justice [Downes] will not allow the Court to be again insulted and made the vehicle of treason, but that he will . . . interrupt his [O'Connell's] harangue by committing him to Newgate for contempt of court.'[17] No doubt this message was conveyed to Downes; already the government had told him that O'Connell's performance at Magee's trial had disgraced his court. It was not surprising therefore that when Magee came up for sentencing on 27 November 1813, Saurin, himself still smarting from the trouncing he had received on 27 July, should have presented O'Connell's advocacy and Magee's publication of his address in full as an aggravation of the original crime. 'For I do say', declared Saurin of O'Connell's 'blustering and bravadoing' performance, 'such an outrage on public decency has not occurred in the memory of man.'[18] When the attorney-general went on to imply that O'Connell had participated in Magee's criminality, O'Connell replied that Saurin had done well to store up his resentment for four months so that he could express it in the safety of the courtroom: otherwise he would have received the chastisement he deserved. Downes and his brother judges were aghast; two, Daly and Osborne, threatened O'Connell with immediate committal for a criminal offence. But he stood his ground until Saurin was induced to withdraw any imputation that O'Connell had participated in Magee's crime. Then, flushed with victory, O'Connell went on – under the thin veil of a vision of the future – to depict Saurin as 'some creature – narrow-minded, mean, calumnious, of inveterate bigotry, and dastard disposition', and their Lordships as interrupting and threatening defence counsel 'lest he should wipe off the disgrace of his adversary'.[19] The Bench sat silent now.

Although O'Connell seemed to have won yet another round, he had in fact overreached himself. His renewed violence and insolence towards the Bench so frightened Magee that he suddenly threw him over in the hope of a lighter sentence. Wallace, another advocate, announced that Mr O'Connell was dismissed and disavowed as Magee's counsel; he urged that the defendant should not suffer for O'Connell's 'abuse of the forensic robe'.[20] This did not save Magee from a sentence of two years' imprisonment as well as a fine of £500 and the threat of further retribution should he ever resume his radical political journalism. But O'Connell also suffered grievously. He was deeply humiliated by being thrown over by his client, and widely spoken of as incompetent or self-seeking in his conduct of the defence. Hunting Cap, whom he dared not offend again, was gravely displeased by the contretemps. 'I have therefore', he warned O'Connell on 14 December 1813,

> most earnestly to request, and will even add to insist, that you will in future conduct yourself with calmness, temperance and moderation towards him [Saurin], and that you will not suffer yourself to be hurried by hate or violence of passions to use any language unbecoming the calm and intelligent barrister or the judicious and well-bred gentleman, or that may tend to expose you to the reprehension . . . of the court.[21]

In addition, the Catholic cause had been further injured by the crushing of its supporting press (what editor would dare to step into the breach left by the *Evening Post*?) and by the desertions from O'Connell's camp within the movement. His dwindling band of political friends tried to stem the adverse tide by suscribing a thousand guineas to present him with a service of plate in recognition of his indominability and matchless powers. In making the presentation John Finlay, a fellow barrister and member of the Catholic Board, depicted him as a sort of latter-day Cuchulainn, striving to hold back single-handed the government's onslaughts upon the independence of press and bar. Finlay concluded with a gloss upon some lines from Scott's *Marmion*:

*Let him but stand in spite of power,*
*A watchman on the lonely tower*
*His thrilling trump will rouse the land*
*When fraud or danger is at hand*
*By him, as by the beacon light,*
*The pilot must keep course aright.*[22]

As 1813 drew to a close, neither his trump nor his light was much regarded. It was true enough, however, that he still stood in spite of power.

## II

Not altogether coincidentally, the weakening of O'Connell's position during 1813 was paralleled by Napoleon's decline. By the beginning of 1814 all Bonaparte's gains since the first Italian campaign of 1797 had been dissipated; the French had been practically driven back to the lines of the Rhine and the Pyrenees, and the fear of defeat, and even the sense of being engaged in a life-or-death struggle had been lifted at last from Britain. Nor was it altogether a coincidence that Rome's decision on an appeal from the English Catholic Board against the Irish Catholic bishops' condemnation of the veto in 1808, which had been meandering for years about the channels of the curia, should have been declared early in 1814 (16 February) or that it should have met substantially the desires of the British government. The Roman rescript recommended acceptance of the veto on the ground that the British crown desired it only for reasons of public security, and not at all to wean Irish Catholics from their religion, which was, moreover, 'friendly to public authority, gives stability to thrones, and makes subjects obedient, faithful, and emulous of their country's welfare'.[23]

This rescript produced consternation in the Irish laity, apart from the still small though growing faction of vetoists; O'Connell was appalled. Some comfort was eventually derived from the fact that it had been signed by Mgr Quarantotti, the vice-prefect (Dublin was soon to translate this as 'a mere understrapper') of Propaganda. It was argued that the document was 'non-pontifical' because Pius VII, at that time Napoleon's prisoner, had not seen the rescript before its despatch. O'Connell did not however commit the cause wholly to casuistry, but set about organizing a series of fiery protest meetings, both open and at the Catholic Board, at which he threw down the gauntlet in the plainest language. At one he roundly declared, 'I would as soon receive my politics from Constantinople as from Rome.'[24] It is interesting to note that, as with the Union in 1800, O'Connell took – and maintained – his stand upon a simple liberal principle: any Roman intervention would constitute an invasion of civil liberty, and better that Irish Catholics should remain forever without Emancipation than that they should purchase it at such a price. Meanwhile, he had placed pressure, whether necessarily or not, upon the Irish hierarchy, and their private meeting on 27 May 1814 issued in a unanimous decision to reject the veto in any form. Daniel Murray, co-adjutor Archbishop of Dublin since 1809, was dispatched to Rome 'to inform his Holiness of the real state and interests of the Roman Catholic Church in Ireland'.[25] These turbulent and defiant reactions were so successful that the Quarantotti rescript was withdrawn for re-examination by the pope and Propaganda.

At best this represented a successful holding action, and simultaneously O'Connell was undergoing a further humiliation because of the unfortunate Magee. Peel insisted that Magee be subjected to a second prosecution. On 10 August 1813 the *Dublin Evening Post* had published resolutions passed at a public meeting in Kilkenny congratulating O'Connell on his address of 27 July 1813 as 'calculated to control the partialities of the Bench, to shame and stigmatise the bigotry of a selected jury, and to rebuke into native insignificance the vain and vulgar law officer'. In pressing for this to be punished, Peel had no particular animus against Magee. 'I shall be disappointed', he wrote almost immediately after the Kilkenny meeting, 'if we cannot strike at higher game than the printer. I hope those who presided at their [the resolutions'] birth may have the manliness to avow themselves as the authors.'[26] Doubtless he had the chairman of the Kilkenny meeting, Major George Bryan, a wealthy and active O'Connellite, and Denys Scully, the author of the resolutions, in his sights. But another Magee trial would also further counteract O'Connell's original triumph of 27 July. Re-engaged by Magee, O'Connell would not dare to repeat the 'insolence' which had led Magee to repudiate him on 27 November. In fact Dublin Castle was in an even stronger position here than Peel could realize, for, before the second Magee trial came on, Hunting Cap specifically enjoined O'Connell: 'I have not only to entreat, but decidedly to insist, that on your part they [the coming exchanges with Saurin] will be carried on with calmness, discretion and decency, and that you will not in any degree glance at anything that has passed between you on former occasions or animadvert with severity or strained conclusion on what may fall from him.'[27]

At the second trial, held on 23 February 1814, O'Connell did indeed comport himself with 'calmness, discretion and decency' – in itself a sort of admission of defeat. As to the rest, Bryan refused to accept any responsibility for the Kilkenny resolutions; Scully failed to take the stand; and poor Magee ended with a further six months' imprisonment and a further £1000 fine. But even the 'escape' of Bryan and Scully turned out to be another victory for the Administration. Magee made it clear that he felt betrayed by the Catholic Board. As the solicitor-general put it, 'the Catholic Board entered into partnership with the traverser, but left the jail part of the concern exclusively to him'.[28] Bryan was widely condemned by Catholics, even among the membership of the Catholic Board, for pusillanimity. Yet O'Connell – as befitted a political boss demonstrating loyalty to the loyal and also anxious to retain a very wealthy and influential supporter – championed Bryan warmly. In an attempted pre-emptive strike, he moved at the commencement of the next Board meeting that Bryan take the chair. A rival Catholic demagogue from Belfast, the journalist-barrister John Lawless, countered with a motion strongly deploring Bryan's behaviour. For the first time, O'Connell found himself in conflict with the 'democratic' section of his movement; he was even hissed and shouted down when he attempted a defence of Bryan. He at once tacked masterfully, throwing himself upon the mercy of the crowd. 'These cries convince me that in some instances I have fallen into error. I do not consider myself infallible, and this I know, that my countrymen will impute my mistakes not to any dereliction of principle, not to the errors of my heart, but of my judgement. [Great and prolonged applause.][29] In the end O'Connell secured a resolution which merely reproved Bryan for an error of judgment while praising him personally as 'pure, independent, honourable, and efficient'.[30] At the same time the Board resolved to make good to Magee his pecuniary losses. In this fashion, O'Connell escaped from the second Magee affair as best he could. He had probably minimized the damage to himself; but even the minimum damage was considerable.

On 22 March 1814 Mary O'Connell wrote to her husband, then on circuit at Tralee:

> As to politics I am indeed a very bad judge but I much fear there is little chance for Emancipation. Every *thing* seems to be against it and surely, while the Catholics continue to disagree among themselves, what can they expect? The Convention Act will be carried and, what I consider worse, the veto. I hear there is to be a great meeting of the Board on Saturday relative to a letter from Lord Donoughmore. His Lordship, like all the other *seeming friends* to the cause, wishes to give it up.[31]

Mary was in fact a very shrewd rather than a very bad judge. No new 'Convention Act' eventuated because Peel and Saurin finally concluded that the Catholic Board could be suppressed without one, and the veto continued to hang fire. But otherwise her comments and prophecies were justified. They amply indicate the third field in which O'Connell was embattled in the first six months of 1814: internal Catholic policies. The Quarantotti rescript embarrassed the Board profoundly in its annual parliamentary offensive, for it provided a ready pretext for its 'spokesmen', Grattan and Lord Donoughmore, to refuse all directions, or even so-called 'suggestions', as to the presentation of the petitions. In fact Grattan merely tabled the petition in his charge, with a bald announcement that he would introduce neither bill nor motion in 1814. Donoughmore rebuffed the Board with equal insolence.

To try to find some counter to this latest blow, O'Connell summoned a meeting of the Board for 3 June 1814. So demoralized and divided were the members, however, that even an hour after the advertised time, the attendance was still seven short of a quorum. At this point, the Castle delivered the *coup de grâce* when its messenger entered the room and handed O'Connell a proclamation suppressing the Catholic Board, under the provisions of the 1793 Convention Act, as a body which assembled only 'under pretence of presenting petitions to Parliament on behalf of the Catholics of Ireland'.[32] O'Connell immediately denied the legality of this action, and announced – by then it was quite safe to do so! – that the meeting would proceed if a quorum materialized. None the less, when what remained of the Board gathered a few days later it did so in O'Connell's own drawing room and under agreement not to name itself the 'Catholic Board' any longer or to agitate further except by way of aggregate meetings. In short, Peel and Saurin had achieved the last of their objectives. Already they had effectively emasculated the pro-Catholic press, largely offset O'Connell's humiliation of the Irish Bench and Administration ten months before, and capitalized upon the schism in the Irish Catholic movement which the veto had rendered deep and open. Now they had destroyed even its basic organization.

O'Connell's spirits can scarcely have been raised by a jobation received from his Uncle Daniel in Paris, hard on the heels of the Board's suppression. 'I cannot refrain myself', wrote the Count on 16 June 1814,

> from congratulating you on the fair opportunity the late proclamation affords you of bidding farewell to the late Catholic council or committee of Dublin, as well as to all your political pursuits, and to confine yourself in future solely to the practice of your profession . . . It has always been my

> steady opinion that the only effectual way to attain that desirable end [Emancipation] can only consist in gaining the good will and confidence of government and of those of the Established Church by a prudent, peaceable and loyal deportment, and that tumultuous assemblies or meetings of what denomination soever, intemperate speeches and hasty resolutions are better calculated to defeat than to promote that object . . . allow me, my dear nephew, most earnestly to entreat you to submit and conform your conduct to the letter and spirit of the Lord Lieutenant's late proclamation, and to listen to no proposal nor suggestion that could tend to elude or counteract the intent or scope of it. Let me add that to pursue a different course would be folly in the extreme and only expose you to a rigorous and, I must say, a merited prosecution.[33]

But O'Connell's wife was made of much sterner stuff; in this period her influence was always thrown against, rather than for, more cautious courses. When in September 1814 the Cork Catholics meekly accepted some contemptuous responses from Grattan and Donoughmore but resolved none the less to commit their parliamentary petitions to them once again, Mary wrote fierily, 'Did you ever read such an insulting letter as Lord Donoughmore's? What little spirit the Catholics of Cork show in leaving their petitions in his hands.'[34] O'Connell, who had himself, at an earlier stage, spoken in Cork in favour of just such a course, now held his heroic place in Mary's eyes by answering, 'The letter of Lord Donoughmore was excessively impertinent and insolent and the *submission* of the people of Cork seems to me to prove they are fit to be slaves. I am very, very sorry I was not at the meeting. I never would have consented to have put that presumptuous peer in charge of the petition. I can scarce tell you how angry I felt at his letter.'[35] This was mere private and, practically, meaningless indigation. But for O'Connell to work himself up in such a fashion, and before his wife, may have had its own uses for him in so bleak a season.

## III

Towards the end of 1814 rumours began to spread in Ireland that the papacy had agreed to yield the veto to the British government in return for the restoration of the Papal States, the future of Italy being then under negotiation at the Congress of Vienna. Simultaneously, the Irish vetoist and anti-vetoist factions were faced with the problems of whether, in whose name, through whom, and for what, to petition in the approaching parliamentary session. On 10 January 1815, Lord Fingall summoned a private meeting of the leading Catholics of each group in his house. For this the rising (indeed the only) vetoist star, the brilliant young dramatist-barrister Richard Lalor Sheil, had prepared a draft petition. It was elegantly composed but also – in O'Connell's view – servile and compromising. O'Connell's powerful opposition secured its rejection together with the formation of a committee (he himself being a member) to frame an alternative petition. This in turn failed to produce agreement on anything more than that some petition or other should be presented.

O'Connell now proceeded to raise the stakes alarmingly *vis-à-vis* both Rome and Westminster. At an aggregate meeting which he organized at Clarendon St Church in Dublin on 24 January 1815, he proclaimed his absolute and undying opposition to the veto. 'Let our determination never to assent reach Rome . . . [and] should it fail I am still determined to resist. I am sincerely a Catholic but I am not a Papist.' He went on to repudiate in advance the Pope's power to bind the consciences of Irish Catholicism in any particular whatsoever without the Irish bishops' assent. He felt, he said, that he could count on the Irish episcopate; but if

> the present clergy shall descend from the high station they hold to become the vile slaves of the clerks of the Castle – a thing I believe impossible – but should it occur, I warn them in time to look to their masters for support, for the people will despise them too much to contribute (*Great applause*). The people would imitate their forefathers. They would communicate only with some holy priest who never bowed to the Dagon of power, and the Castle clergy would preach to still thinner numbers than attend in Munster or Connaught the reverend gentlemen of the present established Church.[36]

This was Gallicanism with a vengeance, except that it now rested on popular instead of monarchical power; and that it was not altogether a rhetorical ploy in a game of political pressures is indicated by O'Connell's private references to relying upon the regular clergy should the seculars fail. In a later letter to the Knight of Kerry, for example, he declared:

> if they enact restrictions, the effect will be worse than the present state of affairs. The *Crown Priests* will be despised and deserted by the people, who will be amply supplied with enthusiastic anti-anglican friars from the Continent. There is a tendency *already* to substitute friars for any priests who are supposed to favour the Veto. It is very marked in Dublin, and they know little of Ireland who supposed that they could *abolish friars* by law.[37]

Certainly, the friars appear to have constituted a species of ecclesiastical left wing at this particular stage. It may be significant that the church in which O'Connell spoke belonged to the Carmelite order; and that the Carmelite prior, William L'Estrange, was a fervent admirer of O'Connell and, by the standards of the day, an advanced nationalist.

O'Connell's dramatic oration from the altar steps of Clarendon St Church marked a new level of lay assertion and defiance in Ireland. It also scandalized the staid and delighted the masses, and put the greatest possible weight upon the Irish bishops to fall into line. But it had no effect upon the politicians at Westminster. Grattan announced that he would promote the Catholic cause in 1815 only on his own terms, that is, qualified concessions with, in all probability, a veto. This was angrily rejected by O'Connell at the next private Catholic meeting on 15 February; and he and his faction immediately set about framing a petition which would express, and finding a member who would introduce, their demand for simple and total Emancipation. For the immediate purpose, O'Connell established his first, short-lived, 'Catholic Association'; it was essentially a front organization for the petition, and in drawing it up O'Connell avoided, with elephantine care, any structural element that might draw it within the ambit of the Convention Act. All this labour bore little fruit. Not until 23 April 1815 did he find a compliant member of the Commons in the Irish whig, Sir Henry Parnell – his 'own' M.P., the Knight of Kerry, had tactfully evaded him on the ground of his relative insignificance as a politican. When on 18 May Parnell sought to introduce several resolutions embodying the Catholic claims (according to the O'Connellite version), the first met such disapproval from the House that he withdrew it and abandoned the remainder. Even his motion, twelve days later, that the House go into committee to consider the claims, was resoundingly defeated by a majority of 81. Worse still, the Knight told O'Connell, 'were we to go to a vote on unqualified relief, we should not divide with fifteen'.[38] O'Connell was then reduced to urging on Parnell and the Knight a ludicrous proposal for squaring the Anglo-Irish political circle – the concession of unqualified relief to be followed by the imposition of 'securities'!

He had been sustained throughout the spring of 1815 by the joyous news of Bonaparte's return from Elba and resumption of the French throne. On first hearing of the escape on 17 March he wrote to Mary, 'and then, love, the public news – the public news!! I can scarce draw my breath. Good God, how I die with impatience for the next packet.'[39] She reciprocated, 'I am told that he [James Sugrue, a kinsman and later agent of O'Connell] is in great spirits since the *good* news came.'[40] When Bonaparte was opposed, O'Connell reassured her, 'Do not be uneasy about the Allies. They will only tend to consolidate the great man's power if they attempt to attack him. His popularity with the French people is the most glorious and extraordinary of his achievements.'[41] In all this, O'Connell saw England's difficulty as the Irish Catholics' opportunity; and he did what he could to frighten the parliamentarians accordingly. 'The fall of prices has beggared the peasantry and ruined the farmers', he told Parnell on 13 June 1815. 'The restoration of Buonaparte has given a new direction to their hopes and wishes.'[42] Correspondingly, the outcome and aftermath of Waterloo cast him into utter – though being O'Connell, only temporary – political despair. 'I am horribly out of spirits', he wrote to Mary from Ennis on 12 July. 'There is all the bad news confirmed even beyond our fears and liberty for ever crushed in France.'[43]

Meanwhile the news was bad again on the final, Roman front. Long preceded by the usual accurate rumours in Dublin, the new rescript from Propaganda, published in May 1815, realized almost, if not quite, the worst fears of the majority of Irish Catholics. It was found that, although the Quarantotti concessions had been modified in several respects, the papacy was quite prepared to submit the names of candidates for vacant sees to the crown for approval. Of the various forms of allowing the temporal power to influence episcopal appointments, this was perhaps the least obnoxious; Rome already allowed it freely in its dealings with other Protestant states. None the less it represented an inverted veto, and was as such anathema to O'Connell. Much now depended on the reaction of the Irish hierarchy. Whether because of O'Connell's earlier intimidatory campaign or from native inclination, they fortunately swung round to the most outspoken support of their flocks. At a National Synod held on 23–4 August 1815, the bishops resolved unanimously that they should 'at all times, and under all circumstances, deprecate and oppose, in every canonical and constitutional way, any such interference . . . [It] must essentially injure, and may eventually subvert the Roman Catholic religion in this country.' They added that Murray, who had presented their 'very energetic memorial' at Rome in the preceding year, was far more 'competent to inform his Holiness of the real state and interests of the Roman Catholic Church in Ireland, than any other whom he is said to have consulted'.[44] The episcopal declaration was greeted rapturously at a mass meeting organized by O'Connell five days later, and he carried, with acclamation, a series of still more violent resolutions against any attempt by the papacy to exercise temporal power in Ireland, which '[we] would, if necessary, resist at the peril of our lives'.[45] He followed this up by a 'remonstrance', to be taken hotfoot to Rome by a contumacious friar, Rev. Richard Hayes, O.F.M., protesting 'against the interference of your Holiness, or any other foreign prelate, state, or potentate, in the control of our temporal conduct, or in the arrangement of our political concerns'.[46] Defiance could go no further. In due course the pope curtly replied that he merely followed the Holy See's invariable rule of appointing none to bishoprics whose loyalty was suspect or who were otherwise displeasing to the Powers concerned; and Hayes himself was destined to undergo a very knotty time in Rome, ending in his forcible deportation from the Papal States. But perhaps the worst damage of all, from O'Connell's standpoint, was that both the parliamentary shufflers and the vetoist cliques could now claim, without challenge, the support of the ultimate ecclesiastical authority.

## IV

The supreme form of championship was single combat, at the risk of life, on behalf of one's adherents; this also fell to O'Connell's lot in 1815. For the preceding twenty years he had lived in duelling times and circles, and had inevitably come close to an actual engagement on several occasions. He had even invited one in 1800 or 1801 when he had struck his cousin, John Sigerson, with a cane in open court after Sigerson, whose cause he was opposing, had sprung up from his chair to abuse O'Connell. On 13 August 1813 he was on the very brink of fighting. Again the origin of the quarrel was a 'scene' in court. During a case at Limerick assizes O'Connell had shouted 'That's a lie, Maurice' at the opposing counsel – a friend – Magrath. Magrath had responded by hurling a volume of statutes at O'Connell's head and kicking O'Connell's shins, the upshot being a challenge from O'Connell and a meeting next day at Limerick's *place de duel*, the Windmill Fields. The contest was one of prominent Catholic barristers, surrounded by other prominent Catholic barristers, merchants, squireens and attornies, and one of these, N. P. Leader, interposed, just before the firing, with the '*very dextrous proposition*' that O'Connell should declare that 'he was about to fight a man against whom he entertained no enmity'.[47] His friends and second prevailed upon O'Connell to make the declaration, upon which Magrath and he were 'reconciled', without exchanging shots.

Even at the time O'Connell was unhappy at his own conduct. 'I have now, my dear Dan', wrote his second, Nicholas Purcell O'Gorman, a few days later, 'to request you will give yourself no uneasiness on this topic. You were advised by some of the bravest and most skilful men on those subjects in existence'.[48] In Protestant quarters however he was soon spoken of as a poltroon. 'I do not know', Peel told his intimate, J. W. Croker, 'a finer subject for speculation than one which now presents itself; namely: given, a kick upon the posteriors of O'Connell by a brother counsel at Limerick, and an acquiescence in the said kick on the part of O'Connell, to determine the effect which will be produced in the Catholic Board.'[49] Nor was it only his enemies who felt that O'Connell had failed in courage. Even his own brother-in-law, Rick O'Connell, confessed later that 'the unfavourable impression that remained fixed on my mind and which I could not divest myself of, relative to the manner in which your affair with Mr Magrath was patched up by that miserable meddler in Catholic affairs [Leader], gave me the most serious uneasiness'.[50] The episode threw a heavy shadow over O'Connell as a public man. True, his baiting of Saurin and his near-open invitation to the attorney-general to challenge him during the course of the Magee trials of 1814 could be construed as reckless bellicosity. But many construed it otherwise, simply writing Saurin off as the greater coward of the two, and O'Connell's brave words as a safe exercise in bombast.

Between them, the Magrath and Saurin by-plays probably go far to explain the D'Esterre duel of 1 February 1815. On the one hand, it was expected that O'Connell would not fight; on the other, Saurin's humiliation needed to be avenged. Ten days before the duel O'Connell had described the Dublin Corporation – then petitioning against Emancipation – as 'beggarly'. Ironically, it was this (for O'Connell) mildest of abusive epithets which produced the fatal challenge. By a further irony the challenge came from one of the few pro-Emancipationist Dublin Protestants and the only member of the Common Council of Dublin Corporation to have opposed the anti-Catholic petition. John D'Esterre, a provision merchant and naval contractor on the brink of bankruptcy, chose to interpret O'Connell's word as having a personal application. He was also currently a candidate for the lucrative office of city sheriff and may have hoped to ensure his election by stepping forth as the Orange champion against O'Connell.

D'Esterre was certainly no coward, being celebrated for his physical courage. He was both a deadly marksman and the hero of one of the more dramatic incidents of the Nore mutiny of 1797, when, with the noose about his neck and bound hand and foot, he was given a last chance by the mutineers to join them but replied, 'No, never! Hang away and be damned! God save the King.'[51] Thus the probable explanation of his hesitant course of conduct before the duel is not that he was frightened, but that he never expected to have to fight O'Connell, assuming instead that O'Connell would eventually eat humble pie and he himself emerge with all the éclat of the paladin who had exposed the braggart. But O'Connell responded effectively to D'Esterre's first call for an explanation by refusing either to confirm or to repudiate the newspaper account of his words, or to answer any further letter. A second letter from D'Esterre was returned unopened, and a third greeted by a message expressing O'Connell's astonishment that he had not 'heard from' D'Esterre in the usual fashion – if indeed he were really serious in his protestations. By now four days had passed since D'Esterre first wrote; all Dublin was a-buzz with the exchange; and, unfortunately for D'Esterre, he and O'Connell had been transformed into symbols of the Protestant-Catholic conflict, and forced to move about with bodies of supporters. On 31 January 1815, D'Esterre, manouevred by events into the role of Orange bravo, proceeded to the Four Courts with a horse-whip to chastise O'Connell; his accompanying party included Saurin's son, and Alderman Bradley King, formerly lord mayor. As O'Connell described the outcome:

> The ruffian appeared in the Hall [of the Four Courts] for a moment with a whip. The instant I heard it I left the King's Bench and he disappeared. He paraded the quay with his whip. R[ichard] O'Gorman [N. P. O'Gorman's brother] met him, asked him did he want me, for that I told him I would fight him (D'Esterre) in three minutes whenever he chose; that he had but to send me a message and that he should be instantly met. He (D'Esterre) said the message ought to come *from me*, at which O'Gorman laughed. The fellow then took post at Briscoe and Dicksons [drapers] in College Green. I came there with my friend, Major MacNamara, but the delinquent had fled . . .
>
> The crowd accumulated so fast that I took refuge in Exchequer Street, where Judge Day followed me and bound me to keep the peace on *my honour*. Was there ever such a scene?[52]

Despite the 'impeccability' of his behaviour up to now, O'Connell had begun to lose reputation. His old adversary in the Magee trials, Lord Norbury, who was said to 'have shot himself up to the bench', had laid down the rule for the Irish bar that 'the first report of a duel should be that of the pistols';[53] and the D'Esterre affair was quickly degenerating from high drama to low farce. So when next day Sir Edward Stanley, barrack-master at Dublin Castle, called upon O'Connell on D'Esterre's behalf and attempted to settle the matter with 'explanations', O'Connell refused to hear a word and directed him peremptorily to Major MacNamara. In turn, MacNamara, a noted duellist and fire-eating petty country gentleman in the best Lever tradition, also declined to enter into 'explanations', leaving Stanley with nothing to deliver but – at last – the challenge. This was accepted with alarming alacrity, MacNamara insisting on a meeting within three hours.

In fact, D'Esterre was late in arriving at the appointed field, just across the border of co. Kildare and some thirteen miles from the city; and the duel did not take place until 4.40 p.m. By this time the light had begun to fail, despite the white covering of snow upon the ground. When the handkerchief fell, D'Esterre missed but O'Connell's shot hit hip and stomach. It was not realized then that D'Esterre had been fatally wounded. Indeed, Stanley and MacNamara shook hands upon the fact that the duel had ended without loss of life. Stanley had particular reason for his relief. Earlier he had been apprehensive that the expected outcome – O'Connell's death – would endanger D'Esterre and his whole entourage. The long delay had multiplied the number of O'Connell's supporters on the scene, including hundreds of local peasantry. In fact, O'Connell's returning carriage passed a party of dragoons which had been despatched from Dublin to maintain order upon a false report that D'Esterre had killed his man. Whatever the sentiments of the combatants, their respective publics insisted on regarding the contest as a deadly tournament of orange and green.

O'Connell did not regard himself as yet out of difficulty by any means. Fearing Castle vengeance, he went into hiding in Denys Scully's house on the evening of the fight, also warning his wife, 'If any suspicious person should come do not send *here* at all.'[54] He was moreover apprehensive of the ecclesiastical reaction: duelling, condemned as a grave sin by the Council of Trent, was sternly prohibited by the Irish bishops. But O'Connell's concern proved needless on both accounts. Immediately after D'Esterre's death on 3 February, Stanley reassured him: 'Lest your professional avocations should be interrupted by an apprehension of any proceeding being in contemplation in consequence of the late melancholy event, I have the honour to inform you that there is not the most distant intention of any prosecution whatever on the part of the family or friends of the late Mr D'Esterre.'[55] Meanwhile O'Connell's brother, James, who had 'supported' him at the duel, set out to propitiate Archbishop Murray. This passed off with equal ease. Murray is reputed to have greeted James with, 'Heaven be praised! Ireland is safe!'[56] Even if Murray's words were actually less grandiloquent, the report is morally true in stressing both the blind eye which the Church turned towards O'Connell's offence and the fact that Murray, like most other churchmen and the entire laity, looked upon O'Connell as the 'Catholic' and 'national' champion.

This last was of course the popular attitude in Dublin, and the night of the duel, 1 February, was accordingly celebrated with bonfires in the city, though the rejoicing was also said to have been decently muted out of feeling for the fallen D'Esterre. O'Connell's social peers certainly made their approval plain. Scores of cards were left next day at his house in Merrion Square. Perhaps the most pleasing tribute came from Rick O'Connell's unschooled pen:

> I was decidedly aware, whenever it came to the point and when you were fairly committed and left to your own judgment and with such a friend as Mr McNamara, that you would have conducted yourself with that steadiness, carriage and coolness which are the true and leading characteristics of an O'Connell . . . You have laid low the champion of intolerance and the beggarly Corporation of Dublin, to use your own words, who selected the unfortunate D'Esterre as the man, the only man, they could prevail upon of that highly respectable body to put down the troublesome Counsellor O'Connell.[57]

Initially O'Connell felt quite justified. On 6 February he wrote to Major Bryan, 'The affair was forced on . . . I could not have acted otherwise and I am therefore free from self-reproach . . . *Those are*, my dear friend, the consequences of labouring for the country';[58] while he told Mary, 'however to be regretted, [it] will purchase years of safety'.[59] But he was soon overtaken by remorse, as well. Characteristically, this took dramatic, even theatrical, forms. Already half-sunk in debt, he offered to share his income with D'Esterre's widow and orphaned children! He was said thereafter to have raised his hat each time he passed D'Esterre's house on Bachelor's Walk on his way to and from the courts, and to have worn a black glove on his duelling hand whenever he received Communion. But this was simply – or rather complexly – O'Connell's style; he was temperamentally incapable of the plain or unobtrusive. Extravagance was far from insincerity. O'Connell's heart was extraordinarily soft, his disposition extraordinarily sentimental, and his conscience, in the narrowest Catholic sense, increasingly merciless in its judgments upon himself. Meanwhile, his common life went on. Even the sententious paterfamilias rapidly regained the shoes of the desperate, fugitive husband. Within a month of D'Esterre's death, he was writing – from co. Kildare! – to Mary, 'Kate's breath this morning smelt most terribly of worms. Darling, see what can be done for her.'[60]

## V

As with innumerable other early-nineteenth-century affairs of honour (including D'Esterre's), O'Connell's next duel sprang from ludicrous blunderings and misunderstandings. It would probably never even have reached the stage of challenges had not Peel and O'Connell been designated as champions by their respective factions. On 30 May 1815 Peel had told the House of Commons that O'Connell's Association would not merely present itself as dissatisfied but also pose as an aggrieved party if granted anything less than its full demands. From newspaper accounts of the speech, O'Connell took this to be a charge of dishonesty against himself. He interpreted it thus before a Catholic meeting of 4 July 1815 in Dublin, adding that Peel would not abuse him to his face, 'personal prudence [being] a quality in which he [Peel] was said to be not at all deficient'.[61] This having passed unchallenged, O'Connell took the further step, at another Catholic meeting on 29 August, of accusing Peel of sheltering behind parliamentary privilege in impugning his honour; and he called upon the police reporter to place his remark on record.

Now Peel acted. With the approval and encouragement of the lord lieutenant, he sent his friend, Sir Charles Saxton, a former Irish under-secretary, to tell O'Connell that he was ready to avow publicly whatever he had said in Parliament. Saxton could have brought the matter to a rapid close when he saw O'Connell on 1 September. For so far from regarding the message as an affront, O'Connell proceeded to expiate on Peel's 'handsome and gentlemanlike' conduct until Saxton interrupted with a virtual demand that O'Connell challenge the chief secretary immediately. It is evident that the Castle party thought that O'Connell might be driven into a humiliating retreat. The lord lieutenant described O'Connell's speech as 'an attempt at intimidation, but O'Connell mistook his man';[62] William Gregory, Saxton's successor as under-secretary, added that O'Connell, though he killed D'Esterre, 'remains the same man who was kicked by Magrath'.[63] In fact, O'Connell had expected to fight from the moment that Saxton left him. Forced into a corner by Sir Charles, he had nominated a 'Protestant country gentleman', George Lidwill, to serve as his 'friend'. 'Do just as you please', he told his prospective second,

> I only think the county of Kildare ought to be the place. I care not where there. Everything will be ready expeditiously. My family would be less alarmed if we postpone it till morning; but do just as you please.[64]

On meeting Saxton, Lidwill told him that the challenge, if any, should come from Peel, as the aggrieved party. In the interview it also emerged that Peel had in fact not imputed dishonourable behaviour to O'Connell in his speech of 30 May, and Lidwill duly expressed regrets for O'Connell's mistaken reaction.

There is no doubt the entire business should have ended then. At least at second hand, Peel had made it clear that he had not intended to offend and O'Connell had apologised for his error. But Saxton – whether in pique at O'Connell's supposed escape or in the hope of forcing on a contest after all – at once published a sententious 'statement' of the affair. Lidwill claimed that Saxton had misrepresented him as well as O'Connell, and proceeded to challenge Saxton on his own account. For his part, O'Connell replied with an angry public letter accusing Peel of 'a paltry trick' and of 'ultimately [preferring] a paper war'.[65] Now it may have been *he* who calculated that his opponent would not fight; the opening sentence of his note on the evening on which his letter was published seems to indicate some surprise: 'Peel has sent me a *challenge*'.[66] None the less, he set out to find another 'friend' (Saxton and Lidwill being now, in all senses, otherwise engaged), and apparently found the Knight of Kerry acquiescent. But before the Knight could make arrangements with Peel's new second, Colonel Samuel Browne, deputy quartermaster-general at the Castle, O'Connell was immobilized by his wife's intervention.

Mary O'Connell had probably known nothing of the quarrel before Saxton and O'Connell appeared in print. But within a few hours of the publication of O'Connell's letter in the Dublin evening papers of 4 September she acted decisively. After O'Connell had set arrangements for the duel in train and gone to bed – probably about 10 p.m. – she sent covertly for the sheriff to place her husband under arrest. This proved to be a form of house arrest, for next morning he asked the Knight to call on him at his home where he was being confined. Later he received there a humiliating message from Colonel Browne who found 'himself under the painful necessity of reminding Mr O'Connell of the letter which he delivered yesterday from Mr Peel and of the impropriety of any delay in a case of so much delicacy'.[67] Already O'Connell was suffering from the disparity in treatment which was to injure him throughout the business. Peel was given ample forewarning of the sheriff's visit to him, and was able to remove himself at leisure to a comfortable hiding place. While his valour was being extolled by the Castle clique, pasquinades on O'Connell's use of his wife to secure him from combat were beginning to be circulated.

Meanwhile O'Connell was driven into a tangle of subterfuge which was meant to end in a meeting with Peel in Ostend as soon as both men could make their way to Belgium. For Peel the change in plan presented no difficulty. 'It is much better', he told Gregory, 'to go to Ostend than to be, in any event, knocked on the head in the country of Kildare, which "ought" to be the place, in Mr O'Connell's opinion.'[68] For O'Connell, however, even the first stage of the journey involved escorting Mary and the children into Kerry for a supposed family vacation and then doubling back secretly to Waterford (under the pretence of an urgent, unexpected case in Cork) to catch the cross-channel packet.

These tortuous manoeuvres took time and Peel was already in Calais (practising his marksmanship, according to the O'Connellites) before O'Connell even took ship for Wales. Dublin gossip was well abreast, if not ahead, of events. The Castle press openly (and jubilantly) reported the progress of Peel and Saxton and their respective seconds across England on their way to France. Far otherwise with O'Connell. It took him a week to reach Waterford by way of Killarney, where he at last succeeded in breaking away from the unsuspecting Mary, and to arrange that his new second, R. N. Bennett, meet him at the embarkation point. O'Connell elaborated his plan to join Bennett with even more than characteristic deviousness, by means of 'my letter to [Eneas] MacDonnell [which] . . . contained a letter for Sugrue . . . Bennett's letter was enclosed in Sugrue's'![69] The cloak-and-daggerism probably derived from O'Connell's fear that Mary would learn of the Ostend arrangement. It was both extraordinary and most fortunate for his reputation that she failed to do so. As Lidwill pointed out after it was all over,

> It was very lucky she never suspected anything as, besides her uneasiness, she might have attempted to have you bound over which, coming from any of *your* friends, would destroy [you] for ever and encourage the enemy to do that which he otherwise would not, to send you a message.[70]

Apparently, O'Connell did not expect to be apprehended as he journeyed from Milford Haven to Dover, although he was surprised when, on disembarking at Milford on 14 September 1815, '*our names* were carefully inquired into . . . What was this done for? No matter.'[71] In fact the British government had determined that he and Lidwill should be stopped. Constables and Bow Street runners were stationed at Dover and Ramsgate and some even sent ahead to Calais. As things fell out, these particular precautions proved unnecessary. Both men were arrested in London, O'Connell as he was boarding a chaise for Dover on 18 September. There is little doubt that the arrests were arranged by the Home Office; and Conant, the chief magistrate at Bow Street, made it clear that the government meant business by warning O'Connell that, if he killed Peel in a duel, he would be rigorously prosecuted *in England* and assuredly executed, if convicted. '*They* have got their wicked will of us', O'Connell wrote bitterly to Scully. 'Our hands are tied behind our backs and they have full liberty to abuse us. What a glorious opportunity have they not deprived me of – living or dying – but regret is vain and would console our enemies.'[72]

He had counted on victory over Peel. 'It is perhaps absurd', he had written on his way through Cheltenham, 'but I cannot bring myself even to doubt success.' His own fate apart, however, 'the real value to poor Ireland is the contest itself. There never was such a battle. Waterloo was nothing to it.'[73] In Irish imaginations it truly had assumed the proportions of a meeting of Bonaparte and Wellington without their armies. As the O'Connellite *Dublin Chronicle*, for example, put it,

> Who does not see that the entire quarrel is that of public men? English placemen on one side, the favourites of Ireland on the other, patrons of Orangemen against the advocates of religious freedom, the hirelings of an iron rule seeking the lives of the champions of Ireland, and indeed for the second time the life of Mr O'Connell . . . Mr Peel, Colonel Brown, Sir Charles Saxton and a Mr Dickenson . . . all Englishmen, all placemen, all feeding upon Irish salaries, lodged in Irish mansions . . . are the four champions of the Castle.
>
> Can it be believed for a moment that a mere personal difference, a private quarrel, can have arisen between such persons and Mr Lidwill, Mr O'Connell, and their friends? The one class belonging to the relentless foes of Ireland, the other to her ardent and resolute protectors. What can have brought into conflict such men but the cause of Ireland alone?[74]

Peel was also, to some extent, the tool or instrument of his party. He was no friend to duelling. When he had wished to laud the late prime minister, Perceval, to the skies, he had said of him that no consideration would have induced him to fight. Some of the English advice which Peel received was very different from the Castle's urging. Two of his evangelical friends condemned his challenge as an outright sin, one adding that to fight was 'arrant cowardice to man, contempt of God and hardy defiance which can receive no mercy.'[75] Peel's brother-in-law, William Cockburn, argued that O'Connell had been within his rights up to the point where he had spoken of 'a paltry trick' and of Peel's preferring 'a paper war'. But, he went on, such 'immaterial trumpery expressions . . . used too in the heat of the moment' were not worth fighting over, and 'the slightest apology, the most simple explanation' by O'Connell should be seized upon to bring the deplorable business to a close.[76] But by then Peel, as much as O'Connell, was locked into Irish paladinhood. It was, however, much easier to play the role of government paladin than that of people. Notwithstanding the Home Office's preventive measures, 'our adversaries', as O'Connell complained, 'advertised themselves at every stage, and were allowed to go on unimpeded. This is called "*activity*".'[77] O'Connell was made to cut a rather hangdog figure in London, while Peel was proving his 'manhood' costlessly in Calais. In the battle of public images, which the affair largely represented, official manoeuvres ensured that Peel would take the palm.

After O'Connell's being bound over, the projected duel had to be abandoned once and for all, and the protagonists wound their way gradually back to Ireland. On reaching Dublin, O'Connell wrote to Mary in Killarney,

> My darling Heart,
> . . . I left London on Monday [25 September 1815] and posted to Shrewsbury, and travelled thence in the day-coach to Holyhead. We reached the Head on Thursday at one o'clock, and sailed at three. The night came to blow tremendously and the packet was crowded to excess. Not a berth could be had for love or money. I lay on the cabin floor as sick as a dog, with three gentlemen's legs on my breast and stomach, and the sea water dripping in on my knees and feet. I was never so completely punished . . .[78]

O'Connell's penitence, real or assumed, is curious. His wife's stance, to be inferred from her actions and his concealments alike, seems to present no difficulties for the interpreter. She loved O'Connell deeply; the eldest of her six children was barely twelve years old; the family lived extravagantly and was at that stage head over heels in debt;

financial and social ruin was certain if O'Connell died. By no means least, she knew that duelling was a mortal sin and one for which, practically by definition, there was no opportunity for repentance if one fell to the opponent's shot. Why should Mary stop at anything to prevent her husband hazarding his life and soul within nine months of the last blessed escape? Perhaps a real gentlewoman would have feigned ignorance or at least refrained from public intervention in a men's matter of such apparent importance. But Mary had not been bred a real gentlewoman. She was merely clear-headed and afraid.

But O'Connell neither would nor could elude the gentlemanly code. Reduced to the individual level, his political *raison d'être* was to establish his absolute equality with Protestants of the same 'class'. Nothing would have been more wounding socially than rejection as too 'low' to be challenged or to have one's challenge taken seriously. The Cato Street conspirator, Thistlewood, turned to assassination only after the home secretary, Lord Sidmouth, refused to fight him 'honourably', thereby placing him in the blackguardly classes. The clear corollary of admission to the circle of gentility was obedience to the laws of honour. Correspondingly, O'Connell's leadership of the Catholic movement demanded that he prove his courage and defiance in the most elemental fashion, by personal combat on behalf of the cause which he was held to epitomize. So far, all is self-evident. But gentlemen were also meant to keep all knowledge of affairs of honour from their womenfolk, or at the very least to see to it that the women maintained a decent show of ignorance. That women should seek to control them was beyond all bounds. Mary had broken the sacred code and exposed O'Connell to ridicule and shame.

Yet it was O'Connell who excused himself to Mary, not she to him. How is this to be explained? Partly, perhaps, by O'Connell's own moral unease. His attempts to make atonement to D'Esterre's family suggest that, while he could exonerate himself completely when his conscience held open court, he could never argue away the fact that he had killed; the black glove worn on his fatal hand was a symbol of guilt, even if 'guiltless' guilt. Secondly, although there is no evidence that such was the case, it would have been quite in character for O'Connell to have promised Mary to eschew duelling forever, in the excited aftermath of the D'Esterre affair. No one was more accessible to remorse or softened feeling, nor was there ever a readier promiser than he. Last but far from least, Mary was used to moral domination in their mutual relationship. She was the perpetual forgiver; it was she who took up and held the strong positions. This is not to say that she would have thought, for a moment, in such adversary terms, still less that she was ruler of the marriage. Indeed the very language of conflict and mastery is most malapropos in so interpenetrant a union. None the less fifteen years as the virtual pronouncer of judgment on such ethical questions as arose between them had rendered her confident in decision. Conversely, O'Connell was habituated to surface acquiescence and covert circumvention. When, emboldened by fright and love, she did not hesitate to place the saving of his life above the saving of his 'honour', it was much more likely that he would follow his accustomed course and deceive her rather than round upon her. This was their particular way. Perhaps Tolstoy was wrong in proclaiming that happy families are all the same. Instead, they seem to rest upon a myriad of almost imperceptible accommodations. In this case, even the public world of championship seems to have failed when it clashed with the private world of intimate marital balance.

# CHAPTER 7

# Entr'acte

## *1816*

### I

During 1816, O'Connell reached the age of forty, a sort of meridian of life. Let us attempt to cast a balance sheet-cum-profit and loss account for him in this particular year.

How did he stand in politics? Since 1813 he had decidedly lost ground. First, the general climate of affairs had worsened. From the late autumn of 1813, the defeat of France seemed certain, and accordingly the British need to conciliate Irish Catholics diminished, if not disappeared. The Hundred Days of 1815 was too short and hectic a span to produce even a temporary change in this disposition. Its conclusion, at Waterloo, confirmed the government in its new-found disinclination to concede; Protestant toryism was firmly in the saddle once again. Moreover, peace precipitated an agricultural depression. As Robert Owen put it, on the day the war ended the great customer of all the producers simply went off the market. The consequent distress emasculated the politics of rights and principle in Ireland. On the one hand, support for the abstract justice of Emancipation fell off, even in the towns; not one Catholic in ten thousand would either earn or eat more if it were granted in the morning. On the other, constitutional agitation withered in the face of fresh outbursts of agrarian violence.

Rome had also played a part recently in dimming the prospects of full Emancipation. O'Connell's remarkable achievement in mobilizing both popular and episcopal resistance to – and even virtual defiance of – the Papal rescript of February 1815 had been partially offset within a year. As we have seen, Pius VII dismissed the Irish remonstrance against the modified form of veto which he had sanctioned, pointing out that it conformed to common practice in the Church's treatment of Protestant powers; the Hayes mission itself was treated contemptuously. It was all too evident moreover that the Papacy was set on conciliating Britain to the utmost possible extent during the phase of post-war settlements and restoration. The pope's final and formal rejection of the remonstrance on 1 February 1816 consolidated the vetoist party in Ireland and deepened the gulf between them and the O'Connellites. Antagonistic petitions were presented to Parliament by the two factions later in the spring. At a meeting at Lord Trimleston's house on 13 February the vetoists resolved to accept 'qualified' Emancipation, and Grattan assured the House of Commons that they would cheerfully agree to 'securities'. O'Connell's Association, which still demanded full Emancipation, used Sir Henry Parnell as spokesman. Parnell was no firebrand; he advised O'Connell to reason rather than demand in his petition: 'The former course would obtain converts but the latter never will, though it will certainly give new life to your enemies.'[1] O'Connell had the dark satisfaction of seeing his rivals' hopes – he could scarcely have held any for the success of his own petition – dashed when on 15 May 1816 the Commons by a majority of 31 refused even to consider the Catholic question. So much for Roman and genteel Irish conciliation!

The growing sense of futility in Irish Catholic ranks increased rather than diminished internal conflict. Not only in Dublin but also in Cork and other cities, the vetoists and O'Connellites challenged each other openly. In even so small a place as Skibbereen, rows broke out in the Catholic chapel on 17 and 22 March as signatures were sought for the rival parliamentary petitions, with the parish priest denouncing the vetoists violently and being violently denounced in turn. 'What a shocking scene has taken place in Skibbereen Chapel', wrote Mary O'Connell on 2 April. 'I think Mr Sandy Tim [Alexander O'Driscoll, a leading Cork vetoist] has no great cause to be proud of himself. I could forgive him anything but attacking the clergyman in the house of God. I fear the Veto will do more mischief.'[2] Almost alone among the liberal Catholic leaders, O'Connell struggled on to restrict the mischief. During the spring circuit, he secured strongly anti-vetoist resolutions from aggregate meetings at Limerick and Cork, and he maintained some semblance of a central organization from his own pocket. But his enemies discounted what they called meaningless huzzas at popular assemblies, and the decline of his Association in the capital was signalled by its removal from Capel St to a still cheaper and meaner room in Crow St.

Characteristically, O'Connell found another tack to follow before the year was out. The spread throughout England during 1816 of Hampden Clubs dedicated to the extreme of parliamentary reform set O'Connell upon his first venture in making common cause with British radicals. His adoption of Hampdenism was understandable. The unreformed House of Commons had proved a persistent stumbling block to even partial Emancipation, and O'Connell had never wavered from his faith in full and free political representation. But the agitation for parliamentary reform in 1816, especially in this 'root and branch' version, carried overtones of religious scepticism, moral licence and social instability. It was besides an essentially British movement. For these reasons there was considerable danger that it would repel not merely 'respectable' Irish Catholicism (generally vetoist in sympathy at this particular juncture) but also clerical and popular Irish Catholicism into the bargain. None the less O'Connell took the first step safely at an aggregate meeting held in Cork on 6 September 1816 at the end of the summer assizes. There he secured a resolution attributing the succession of Catholic failures to the corruption and inequity of the parliamentary system, and urging 'our fellow subjects of every religious persuasion, to leave no constitutional means untried in order to procure a full, free, and frequent election of Real Representatives of the people of these Nations in the Commons' House [of] Parliament'.[3] When, however, the equivalent aggregate meeting took place in Dublin three months later, the parliamentary reform issue proved so divisive that O'Connell refrained from moving his intended resolution in its favour. By this stage his efforts had attracted the attention and approval of such well-known radicals as Major Cartwright and John Hancock, and he persisted for a month or two with moves to stir up an Irish reform agitation. But the Catholic public was unresponsive; the movement – if it deserved such a name – petered out early in 1817.

O'Connell's political fortunes between 1811 and 1815 had generally conformed to a pattern of remarkable advances followed by considerable losses of ground. He had attained the leadership of a heterogeneous Catholic agitation and rendered it a comparatively well-organized and effective pressure group, which also embraced many lower-middle and upper-working-class Catholics in the larger towns. Yet by 1816 he stood at the head of only one wing of an ailing movement, and his 'organization' was both penniless (or, more exactly, heavily indebted because it had been saddled with the unpaid costs of earlier Catholic petitions) and practically dependent for survival on his exertions as an individual.

O'Connell had also built up a vigorous, metropolitan pro-Catholic press to support the Catholic Committee. But this too had been punished and bullied almost out of existence by the successful prosecutions of Cox, Fitzpatrick and Magee in 1813–14. In 1816 the Irish Government stamped just as hard upon a smouldering ember when it arraigned the *Cork Mercantile Chronicle* for reporting a speech of O'Connell of the previous year in which he had criticized the administration of justice in Ireland. In the libel action heard on 18 May 1816, Saurin accused O'Connell of inciting rebellion, while O'Connell denounced him as an incompetent. It was a pale shadow of the Magee affair, but O'Connell suffered defeat once more; the unfortunate printer was fined £300 and sentenced to two years' imprisonment. O'Connell's plea for clemency because his client was both old and poor was cursorily dismissed. The case diminished further the éclat which he had won by his original excoriation of the attorney-general and the entire Irish legal apparatus on 27 July 1813. Not only was another sympathetic newspaper silenced but also Saurin had ridden through O'Connell's abuse once more to carry off the verdict. Even O'Connell's triumph in the D'Esterre duel had been offset by the dismal – and, worse, in parts comic – failure of his attempt to meet Peel later in the year. The effects of this débâcle lasted into 1816: it was widely expected that he and Peel would face each other when the original alarms had died away, and his reputation was certainly not enhanced as the months passed by eventlessly.

Peel's arrival in Ireland as chief secretary had proved the turning point in O'Connell's early political career. Peel had given direction and determination to the Castle's counter-attack during the later war years. It is true that Bonaparte's decline and, ultimately, defeat had provided the new chief secretary with favourable conditions, and also that he had gained from the British government's skilful exploitation of the Papacy's vulnerability in a phase of European reconstruction. But, having chosen Saurin for his leading acolyte, he had seized his chances to divide the Irish Catholic body deeply; to destroy the major Catholic organization, without even needing, in the end, a new form of the Convention Act; and to weaken O'Connell's standing as the Catholic hero.

Yet O'Connell's original achievements could not be altogether effaced. He had demonstrated more clearly than any predecessor the power of Catholic combination and discovered already some of the potentialities of a Catholic mass movement. On the crucial veto issue, he had won over to his side almost the entire Irish episcopate; this support he never really lost, despite some temporary shuffling later on. His defiance and abasement of the Irish Administration even for one glorious day had destroyed the assumption that it was, and must always be, effortlessly superior; he had forced it onto level ground and into dirty war in order to circumvent himself.

For the contest between O'Connell and the Castle was no fair fight. The Government could, in large measure, extend the offence of 'libel' as it wished, and count upon its packed juries for favourable verdicts and its subservient judges for favourable rulings and court management. It could afford to run its own press and force opposition newspapers out of business – at any rate, out of the business of criticizing its members or activities. It could even use its executive powers to enable its chief secretary to cut a fine public figure, and ensure that O'Connell would cut a sorry one. But the inequity of such a use of official force could be neither entirely concealed nor sustained forever. *'Ní h-é lá na gaoithe lá na scoilb'* – the windy day is not the thatcher's day, runs a Gaelic proverb. It all depended on whether O'Connell would remain in the thatching business until the adverse gale abated. He did: herein lies the significance of his lonely persistence, against all the odds, throughout 1816 and the following hopeless years.

## II

O'Connell may well have had more at stake in the Catholic question, materially speaking, than any other person in the United Kingdom. By 1816 he stood head and shoulders above any other junior at the Irish Bar. Had his religion not barred the way, he would have taken silk long before that year. Although many before and since have found that they lost instead of gaining money by being called to the inner bar, O'Connell, with transcendant abilities and national fame, was surely justified in his conviction that he would both augment his income and halve his work were he a King's Counsel. As it was, his professional life was more or less a treadmill. Nearly a quarter of a century later, even the bitterly inimical *Dublin University Magazine* admitted the reasonableness of his grievance:

> If O'Connell appears regardless of truth and justice in his persecutions of the Protestants, let them recollect what must have been the feelings naturally excited in his soul by the laws to which he was subjected in the earlier part of his life. With talents which he must have felt sufficient to raise him to eminence in his profession, or to enable him to act an important part in the grand theatre of politics, he found himself precluded by our Protestant institutions from all hope of attaining the rank and honours which are the legitimate rewards of success in his profession, and

> condemned to pass his life in the drudgery of a stuff-gown lawyer . . . Even those who may be disposed to defend those restrictions as necessary for the protection of our Protestant institutions, will at least admit that they were not calculated to excite any kind of feeling towards those institutions in the breasts of those who suffered from them.[4]

During the spring circuit of 1816 even the indomitable O'Connell owned to arriving at his first stage, Nenagh, very weary as well as very late, only to be lodged 'there in a wretched cold room'. A few days later he 'left it [Limerick] at five in the [Monday] morning and did not get here [Tralee] till near nine [p.m.], very much fatigued, having *worked* at my trade till past twelve on Sunday night, and of course . . . slept very little'.[5] At Cork 'Judge Mayne sat so early and Judge Day so late that there was not a moment left for me to breathe in'.[6] During the summer assizes of 1816 he spent over ten hours daily (from before 9 a.m. till after 7 p.m.) in court at Cork, and the spring assizes, with both judges 'miserably slow',[7] would have been quite as bad. Yet with the spring circuit of 1816 coinciding with Lent, which he observed most strictly, he was without food during all his time in court, sometimes until as late as ten o'clock at night. Even Mary urged him to relax his extraordinary mortification while he was on circuit: 'Wednesday, Friday and Saturday would be quite sufficient for you to fast from breakfast.'[8] But he ignored her counsel. O'Connell never complained of hardships – a most endearing, as well as very rare quality in a husband. Fasting, he told Mary repeatedly, 'agrees perfectly with me in every respect'. 'Sweetest love', he wrote from Limerick, 'I am as well, notwithstanding my fasting, as any man in Ireland.'[9] After his long journey to his 'wretched cold room' in Nenagh, 'instead of finding myself the worse for it I am considerably better, indeed quite rid of the cold in my head of which every symptom has vanished'.[10] But for all this brave front, it was beyond human nature that he should not often have felt his stuff gown to cling to him like a hair shirt, if not indeed a very shirt of Nessus.

O'Connell earned considerably more on circuit than any other counsel, including his seniors, at the Munster Bar. 'My business', as he assured Mary on 13 March 1816, 'is far beyond that of any other barrister. I am quite and without any rival at the head of this circuit. I am not drawing upon my vanity in telling you so. I am saying just what is the simple truth.'[11] He was briefed in every 'record' (civil action) in Ennis, and in all but one in both the city and county suits at Limerick. It took him more than a fortnight to work off his briefs in Cork, and after that he had to turn to his '*chamber business*' there, and return to

Limerick for more. None the less it was a lean circuit. From Limerick O'Connell had already reported it as 'bad' for business; from Tralee he wrote, 'Only *two* records . . . so that for the first time since I was called to the Bar I have had [? but one] record brief.'[12] Litigation was as depressed as any other gainful activity in Ireland in 1816. As Mary observed, 'In truth I believe the people had not money *even* for law';[13] O'Connell himself bemoaned the change in the times on 18 March. Desperate for money in 1816, he engaged himself heavily in the less remunerative criminal work. Perhaps his 'chamber business' in Cork and Limerick is another indication of his straits, although it was probably true, as his wife argued, that he would have earned as much at his desk in Dublin as at Cork. One way or another it was grinding labour for small rewards that year.

Much of it was also distasteful. Many of the criminal briefs were for capital offences, usually the product of agrarian violence. O'Connell's feelings about such cases may be gauged from his note to his daughter, Ellen, from Tralee on 1 April, 'I am . . . a little out of spirits as this was a very bloody assizes . . . seven men capitally convicted and I really believe they will all be executed.'[14] Conversely, when he defended successfully in Cork in August, he exulted, 'I am, dearest, in the gayest spirits. I will suffocate my Nell for her darling letter. I am just out of court after a *great* acquittal and as soon as I dine I will go to the play.'[15] Verdicts for the crown in these cases cast him into gloom; even pending 'capital' briefs rendered him apprehensive. For counsel were not distanced from the ultimate consequences of adverse verdicts in the Ireland of 1816. The convicted were often hanged within a day or two, and generally before the legal train had moved on to the next assizes. The drudgery of the stuff gown was not the worst experience of a circuit.

Bitterest of all perhaps was O'Connell's sense that he was systematically belittled. He was good-humouredly contemptuous of the circuit judges. 'We have hourly the most ludicrous scenes with Judge Mayne', he told Mary on 13 March. 'He is *an animal*, easily managed, and he and I agree perfectly and I have the pleasure of laughing at him by the hour.'[16] It seems true that he and Mayne dealt well together. Later in the year Mayne took much trouble to facilitate an effort by O'Connell to win a reprieve for a client condemned to almost immediate execution. But O'Connell believed himself to be incomparably superior as a lawyer not merely to Mayne but also to the great majority of the judiciary. He also felt himself to be at least the equal of the leading Irish silks. He dismissed the great Curran, who was to have led him in a major defamation action, *Bruce* v. *Grady*, heard at Limerick on 7–9 August 1816, as 'a wavering inconsistent fellow!';[17] and he adjudged the statement of the case in this action by the almost equally renowned silk, Goold, as 'an excellent speech . . . but very tedious'. As a junior in this case his role was limited to the opening address for the defence; but he had no doubt that his was the triumph of the affair: 'It was *my* best speech I think and the entire Bar think so too.'[18]

Thus the toil was doubly irksome. When every possible penny had to be grasped, juniors' work included much dull routine and many mechanical legal operations. Yet O'Connell had to bear a senior's responsibility in significant political cases (such as those arising from the Skibbereen Catholic fracas or the *Cork Mercantile Chronicle* 'libel') and celebrated civil suits (such as *Bruce* v. *Grady*) without a senior's rewards or a senior's increase in profitable reputation. Miltonic allusions may ill-fit an overworked, stout, middle-aged barrister. But just as O'Connell, in his political nadir of 1816, suggests *maligré lui* Lucifer's

> *What though the field be lost?*
> *All is not lost; th' unconquerable will . . .*
> *And courage never to submit or yield:*
> *And what is else not to be overcome?*,

so, too, his diurnal course on circuit may suggest even Samson's

> *Eyeless in Gaza, at the mill with slaves.*

## III

The prime cause of O'Connell's money-hunt of 1816 was the O'Leary bankruptcy, gazetted at last on 13 February. The most important thing of all was to keep knowledge of O'Connell's involvement in the crash from Hunting Cap. O'Connell's brother James reassured him on 4 January: 'I think it is now almost impossible he can hear it.'[19] One of his Kerry cousins, Myles McSwiney, reported on 16 February after a meeting with Hunting Cap that he had no suspicion of O'Connell's entanglement. Next day James wrote more fully from Derrynane:

> He repeatedly asked me if you were engaged for him for any sum. I assured him you were not. Indeed, he was at first so earnest and particular in his inquiries that I feared some person had made him acquainted with the facts, but on my *solemnly* assuring him you would not lose a guinea by the fellow as you never became security for him to any amount, he seemed

Daniel O'Connell at the age of forty-two, painted by John Gubbins

Maurice (Hunting Cap) O'Connell, 1728–1825. Uncle of Daniel and master of Derrynane

.-General Count Daniel O'Connell, 1745–1833, painted by Paulin Guerin. Uncle of Daniel

Mary O'Connell, Daniel's wife, with her youngest son Daniel Jr, painted by John Gubbin
1817–18

Morgan, O'Connell's second son, in the uniform of the Irish Legion to South America, painted in 1820

The ruins of Carhen, near which O'Connell was born in 1775

Derrynane House today, from the south-east

e old summer house at
rrynane

e sea shore near Derrynane

O'Connell statue, Ennis, co. Clare, erected where his return as MP for the county was declared in 1828

quite satisfied and says that you possibly may loan something to this blackguard but that he himself told you last year O'Leary would unquestionably snap from the expensive manner in which he lived. I, of course, allow him to take what merit he pleases for his friendly caution.

You have a right to feel much obliged to Ellen [his sister] for her exertions in preventing my uncle from hearing this unfortunate business. She had two confidential men stationed, one at the upper gate and the other at the strand, to caution every person who was coming to Derrynane not to mention this business. This, I assure you, was a very necessary caution as every individual in this country knows every circumstance connected with O'Leary's failure. I now hope we have little to fear but we must still keep a sharp look out.[20]

James had lied to Hunting Cap already. To explain the delay in his visit to Derrynane – caused in fact by the O'Leary business – he had invented a bout of illness. He was well aware of the danger he was running for his brother's sake: 'should this affair come to the knowledge of my Uncle Maurice I am convinced he will never give me a guinea.'[21]

The most immediate problem however was to raise enough money to cover O'Connell's new liabilities. James having failed to negotiate a loan of £4000 from their uncle Daniel, O'Connell was driven to borrow most of that sum from his banker-agent, John Hickson, at the beginning of the year. While acknowledging that O'Connell was entirely at Hickson's mercy, James deplored both Hickson's 'very *unfair and usurious* terms' and O'Connell's 'too sanguine disposition [which] makes you calculate on some ideal *good* that may never occur'.[22] James determined that somehow or other a less exacting creditor must be substituted for Hickson before 1816 was out. Meanwhile, much more money was required, and on 16 January O'Connell went to Cork to 'work [?for] funds enough to keep myself above water'.[23] Funds enough to keep O'Connell above water would have been funds indeed! But at least he secured another very considerable sum, although at the expense of James who had to join him as guarantor. Poor James was painfully aware that he had put his small patrimony in hazard. 'You will have this *precious deed* [signed by himself] by Thursday morning', he informed O'Connell savagely on 22 January 1816,

and I sincerely hope it will be the means of saving you from *destruction*, whatever my fate may be, but now *that the die is cast* I can with truth say that I am, by being made a party to this business, exquisitely miserable as I am no longer master of my own time or of the very limited property I inherited in right of my father . . . I was well aware when I affixed my name to this accursed deed that in all human probability my prospects in life were for ever blasted. I again repeat, whatever my sufferings may be, I will never be guilty of the folly of blaming any person as, alas, alas, I am too well aware of the consequences . . . I now conclude this, to me, most disagreeable subject by saying you have involved me in the ruin you have been so long preparing for your amiable wife and interesting family.[24]

But these were only two, though probably the largest, of the fresh obligations which O'Connell incurred or sought. Within a fortnight of receiving James's guarantee, he employed his friend Bennett to arrange a further loan of £2000. The terms were onerous; in addition to interest, '£2,200 [was] payable within two months after my uncle's death or in four years, whichever shall first happen.'[25] Even that leading signal of nineteenth-century ruin, the *post-obit*, had made its appearance. Still the pressure continued, and even Mary took a hand. 'I called to see Mrs O'Sullivan', she wrote on 26 March,

and, in the course of our conversation, she told me her niece, Mary Coppinger, had at present a £1,000 to put at interst. *It* immediately occurred to me that you may wish to get it, and Mrs O'S joined me in opinion that Mrs Coppinger would give it. What would you think of writing to her on the subject without mentioning her aunt's name but, except you want the money very much, darling, I should prefer your not taking it. Interest money to you must be so heavy just now.[26]

Income was problem enough without interest and capital repayments. James, who was then acting as O'Connell's principal agent for his Kerry lands, bemoaned on 17 February 1816 the 'wretched state of this country with respect to money'; he would not be able to collect enough for O'Connell to pay even the head rents falling due. 'What is to become of us if the times do not improve! I have had recourse to the harshest methods to try and extort some payments from your tenants for the last week, all the pounds of the country filled with their cows but all to no purpose.'[27] On 31 May Myles McSwiney, who also acted for O'Connell and would soon take over the major role, told him that he could get in no rents; he could not even pay an old woman's jointure which O'Connell owed locally. O'Connell himself had the same story to tell when he visited Iveragh in September. 'The rents are coming very slowly', he wrote to Mary, 'and between the fall of prices and the dreadful weather there is nothing but rain and wretchedness.'[28]

All this threw a greater burden on O'Connell's bar earnings. But despite his utmost exertions these remained depressed. The summer circuit appears to have been still worse than the spring. That

O'Connell failed to report to Mary his takings in some of the assize towns, a rare occurrence, probably told its own story. 'I hope, heart', she wrote to him from Dublin on 21 August, 'you will be more fortunate in Cork than you have been in Tralee. You did not tell me what you made at Ennis and Limerick. I don't suppose (excepting your first assizes in Tralee) you ever got so trifling a sum as you did this time [thirty-four guineas] but if the business was there you would get it.'[29] Mary had good reason to be anxious. At different stages during the circuits she had to press O'Connell for money to pay the governess's, the nurse's and the housekeeper's wages; in the last case, ten days elapsed before she received the long-overdue ten guineas. On one occasion Mary and Hickson were in dispute over £30: each had received one half of every banknote. 'From your letter', Mary wrote on 8 April, 'he understood the money was for him, but surely, darling, you very plainly told me to send to Hickson for the remaining halves of *these* you sent me.'[30] Evidently Hickson won the tussle of the half-notes, for five days later came a cry from Mary, 'No letter from you this day, which is indeed a very great disappointment as I have not one farthing of money and Saturday with me is always *pay* day.'[31]

The last resort in these straits was personal and family economy. O'Connell was profuse in resolutions and even in self-congratulations. In his first spring circuit letter from Ennis he assured his wife, 'Darling, I am become one of the most attentive fellows living, taking most excellent care of my money',[32] and following this up from Limerick with, 'Darling, I am become really an economist.'[33] Mary reciprocated with equal professions of virtue, 'I have kept a regular account of every shilling I received and of every penny I laid out since you left home with the strictest economy . . . not a penny was laid out that could in any way be avoided.'[34] But the O'Connells were not the stuff of which financial martyrs are made. Mary's 'strictest economy' ran at over £16 per week (more than twenty times a contemporary labourer's wage) on ordinary household expenses; simultaneously, she reported to O'Connell that she could get only two dozen bottles of white wine and half-a-dozen bottles of port from his usual supplier and asked where she should purchase a further dozen and a half of port 'as it will be necessary, love [?to have] it in before your return'.[35]

Characteristic was her approach to buying a new piano. 'I would rather, darling,' she told O'Connell on 4 April, 'you would at once say to me buy or don't buy it, for I feel delicate in putting you to any expense at present, though, as I before told you, I think we ought to trespass a little for the advantage of our children.'[36] The sly wife could not have doubted for a moment that such a husband as O'Connell would respond by '*commanding*' an immediate purchase.[37] In the event he was lucky in that Mary failed to find a desirable instrument on her first foray. For his part, he pressed her irresistibly to accept a staying guest in order to oblige a useful friend, and James wrote apropos his autumn vacation of 1816 'your *own personal expenses*, which I know from what occurred when last you were in Iveragh, are to a man circumstanced as you are, ruinously heavy'.[38] It was a true marriage of untrue minds, blossoming from moral sleight of hand. O'Connell never ceased to thank her for the generosity with which she forgave his former folly, and Mary never ceased to shift the blame from his to other shoulders, in particular the iniquitous O'Leary's. 'My dearest Love', she wrote to him on 9 August,

> Dumas [a Kerry attorney] told me there was not a greater buck in Bond Street than Mr James O'Leary, dashing away at his usual rate and most elegantly dressed, at the opera and theatres every night, and living at one of the most expensive taverns in London. This is the way, darling, he is spending your eight thousand pounds. My God, what a horrid perjured fellow he is. Surely, heart, you will never think of signing his certificate. Believe me, you owe to your own character not to do so and I ask you as a favour not to sign it.[39]

Antiphonally, O'Connell replied, 'I promise you, darling, not to sign O'Leary's certificate. I only despise myself heartily for allowing so contemptible a scoundrel to impose on me.'[40]

None the less reality could not be altogether kept at bay. When the piano campaign re-opened in August, O'Connell was compelled to respond – and there could have been no greater measure of his financial desperation – 'Tell my sweet Nell that she shall have the piano as speedily as I can possibly get it for her but, love, the fact is that I have still near £1,700 of guarantees or bills of that scoundrel O'Leary outstanding and I want every shilling which I can put together to avoid being obliged to have my bills protested, and myself sued.' Although the pill was sweetened with, 'Nobody can be more prudent that you are, *that* is quite certain',[41] the fact remained that O'Connell was forced to confess to Mary (probably for the first time in their married life) that he could not afford a family good. Early in 1817 James thrust upon O'Connell a list of debts, as known by him at the end of 1816, with the comment, 'My dearest fellow, what do you mean by saying that in two years the far greater part of your debts will be discharged? Surely, when you speak in this way, you are not aware of the magnitude of them.' James's list, a compilation pitiful in the host of small sums owed to relatives, clients and friends, and including £130 'due of you to Maurice, my uncle's clerk' and £3000 'Due of you in Iveragh to common men in *all at least*', totalled nearly £19,000,[42] and James recognized that there were probably many other debts and outstanding obligations of which he had been told nothing. It is all too easy to cast O'Connell as the glorious skimming bird and James as the croaking raven. But, if only thoughtlessly, O'Connell was a heartless man with others' money. What did he care about the security of 'Widow Connor of Killarney', or of his uncle's clerk, or of the common men of Iveragh who had been flattered into doing a favour for the local Sun King? When James told him, after signing the fatal deed on 22 January 1816, 'by the contents of your letters you seem to think I have the egregious folly to suppose I am doing a mere act of courtesy',[43] his scorn for O'Connell's vacuous and convenient optimism was all too well deserved. But it was long since such barbs had penetrated the time-toughened hide.

O'Connell and his wife were never more loving towards or deeply in accord with one another than in 1816. Evidently the crises of the autumn and winter of 1815, the Peel duel and the O'Leary failure, ending in penitence and resolutions of amendment on O'Connell's part, and the exercise of the sweet power of absolution on Mary's, had brought them closer. O'Connell's first letter in 1816 lauded her as 'the greatest blessing that ever man had';[44] at the close of the summer circuit, he wrote, 'darling, I owe you my deepest debt of gratitude for the manner in which you have borne the privations which my absurd credulity has compelled you to endure.'[45] Mary reciprocated with still more warmth and expressions of trust than usual; implicitly and explicitly she told him that he was – in her eyes – faultless for all his faults. She had become pregnant again in the preceding November; she was also probably responding to O'Connell's new religious fervour which may well have dated from about the same time.

The effect of this last change was apparent from the beginning of 1816. On 13 January O'Connell wrote to Mary from Tralee, 'Tell [Rev.] Mr L'Estrange [he had become O'Connell's spiritual director], darling, that I long to be back with him. I promise you, love, I feel myself beyond any comparison happier in *this* change which, with the grace of God, I hope will prove complete. Pray for me, darling, fervently and often.'[46] The note of extraordinary piety was unprecedented, the implication that of a Methodist-like conversion. In fact that very word was used by either O'Connell's wife or his eldest son to describe the spiritual transformation. Maurice, wrote Mary on

11 April 1816, 'had many questions to ask about you, thanked God with his hands clasped for your *conversion*'.[47] Since O'Connell had returned to Catholic belief and practice by 1809, and possibly even for some years before then, the reference is probably to the replacement of conventional by 'vital' religion: the evangelical sea-change of the soul was by no means confined to Evangelicals in 1815. L'Estrange was almost certainly the instrument, but the trigger may well have been O'Connell's latest and greatest financial trouble and the consequent confession to Mary of his broken promises. 'We will be ourselves a great deal the better for it',[48] he told her on 13 January apropos O'Leary's bankruptcy; from Limerick he wrote two months later, 'We shall be, I hope we are, the happiest and the better for *this* event. As to the happier, that alone relates to you for better, sweetheart, you could not be';[49] and there are other comments apparently connecting his reformation to his near-disaster. His near-duel with Peel, however, may also have contributed something to his change of heart.

That O'Connell's 'conversion' was a family as well as his own affair is made clear by Mary's letter of 26 March 1816.

> You have indeed, my darling, a great deal of merit for your attention at present to your religious duties, and it is a delightful reflection to me that amidst all your bustle and business you continue a pattern of piety to all of us. I had yesterday the happiness of being at Communion and as my *health* will now permit me to be more regular than I have been this time back, I shall with the assistance of God try to follow your example. God be thanked, darling, the times are changed. You are now the better *Christian*. My girls are to pay [Rev.] Mr Walsh a visit this week and, as for our darling boys, I need have no fears that their religion will be neglected.[50]

Mary's own religious practice intensified; on the eve of her confinement she attended no less than three Sunday masses; and L'Estrange became her regular visitor. Maurice's fervour was perhaps less attractive, though due allowance must be made for twelve-year-old piety. He prayed God that he would fulfil his promise to his father to study harder, adding 'I think a lecture from Mr L'Estrange would do him [his younger brother, Morgan] a great deal of good.'[51] O'Connell's resolutions of amendment probably included a determination to give his children more time, attention and (though he had always been a loving father) affection. In 1816 he added to his circuit labours a warm correspondence with each of his elder sons and elder daughters; they of course eagerly competed for his letters and open praise. When Morgan fell ill O'Connell reproached himself for his habitual severity in dealing with his rather idle, though winning, second son: 'I felt as if I had treated the poor fellow badly and my grief was embittered by a very painful sensation like remorse.' He sent a message through Maurice that he 'doated' upon Morgan 'with the tenderest affection'. Morgan, he added, 'has every promise of being a delightful fellow . . . I intend to be more punctual in writing to you and your brother than I have been. Tell my Morgan so.'[52] It was however difficult to remain forever in such a state of parental grace. When O'Connell heard the results of the summer examinations at the boys' school, a new Jesuit foundation, Clongowes Wood, he could not altogether repress the stirrings of vicarious ambition. 'I must own', he told Maurice, 'I felt a passing shade of disappointment that you are not higher in your class. I am very willing to believe that it was not your fault, and do not blame you; and yet, my child, I consider *you could* have worked out a better place. However, be assured I say this without one particle of anything like anger. Will you make an effort to gratify me next time?'[53] Next came Morgan's turn. 'The truth is that if you took it into your red head you could easily be head of the class . . . but a little laziness and a little carelessness combine to keep you down . . . Do, my sweet Morgan, take the trouble.'[54] Neither could O'Connell maintain the volume of children's correspondence. He was reproached by Mary on 17 October: 'He [Maurice] complains as Morgan *does* of your not writing to him since you went to the country.'[55] Five weeks later O'Connell had to apologize to Morgan for a broken promise to visit him at school: 'Professional hurry makes me forget those things, but your mother does not love you better or more tenderly than I do.'[56] The way of paternal perfection was very hard.

The old Adam was not to be put down altogether even in O'Connell's dealings with his wife. The beginning of September found him still winding up the business of the summer assizes at Cork, and he apparently considered going directly to Kerry for his annual vacation without returning to his wife, who had been delivered of her seventh child in Dublin only nine days before. At any rate he told her that neither his mother's illness nor his friend Butler's marriage settlement was really so urgent that he could not 'afford to run to see you' for a few days, 'but . . . only for a few days'.[57] Mary replied with justified asperity:

> Had you gone to Kerry without coming to see me and my boys, I should be most highly *offended* with you. Your mother is not in that dangerous state that you should hurry off to her, and James Butler having lived so long a bachelor, the delay of a week cannot add much to his *age* . . . As to your

> being back from Iveragh until November I have not a hope nor do I expect it. I own I would rather you did not spend much of your time in *that* country. A fortnight to amuse you is all I should *allow* and a week to spend entirely with your uncle.[58]

Iveragh of course brought on the old Adam by leaps and bounds. James's later comments make it clear that O'Connell spent and borrowed in his customary reckless way during his autumn vacation of 1816. O'Connell also wrote angrily to Mary from Kerry when she failed to forward business (probably money) papers because she was uncertain of his whereabouts or time of return to Dublin. '*This nasty* letter from Carhen has dispirited me', she replied on 17 October. 'It is the first *serious* letter I ever got from you and I exactly feel like a *spoiled child*.'[59] But it would be wrong to suppose that the occasional exchange of hot words between O'Connell and his wife, or even his pecuniary relapses in Kerry, amounted to more than a ruffling of the marital surface: they could not dwell forever at the high altitude of fervid reconciliation. While O'Connell was still in Iveragh, Mary's love for him passed a sterner test than squabbles over his absence or her neglect of business. She received a series of anonymous letters in Dublin denigrating her husband, and apparently accusing him of unmet obligations and other misbehaviour. Her sole concern was that he should be comforted and supported. 'I am quite displeased that you should for a moment suffer the slightest uneasiness on *this* subject. Believe me, my *own* Dan, when I assure you that the machinations of *our anonymous friend* has [*sic*] not lessened my confidence in you. I should indeed be most ungrateful for your tenderness and affection if I allowed myself to fret or felt less happy than I did before the receipt of those contemptible scrolls.'[60] This struck the true note of their marriage, after fourteen years.

O'Connell ended 1816 with a significant political past but seemingly no political future, somewhat tarnished as hero in the public eye, trapped as a labouring junior counsel, monstrously indebted with no real prospect of relief beyond his precarious expectations from Hunting Cap, and pressed as well as blessed by teeming family affections. But though forty, defeated, burdened and hemmed in, he was still never to be repressed. 'Darling', he wrote to Mary from Derrynane on 26 September, 'I will be at Carhen on Saturday and we are to have great racing at the pattern. All my schoolboy feelings are alive again and I am as merry as ever I was.'[61] This too was an authentic voice.

*CHAPTER 8*

# Ploughing Sands

## *1817–22*

### I

'By no kind of means', wrote O'Connell's son, John, of the post-war years, 'by no manner of exertion, and he *did* look about for means, and *did* use a thousand exertions, could he arouse the Catholics to action, or even to a defensive position.'[1] Between 1815 and 1823 O'Connell's political exertions were ever varying and ever futile – at first sight a kaleidoscope of failures. But we must not forget that this was how he learned his trade and tested his later instruments and courses.

In mid-1817 he formally wound up his first Catholic Association – it was a pronouncement that life was extinct rather than a mercy-killing – and called an aggregate meeting in Dublin on 3 July to try to reconstitute the movement. The meeting agreed that 'individuals who belonged to the late Catholic Board and Association', and such others as they admitted to their ranks, should come together to draw up a petition for unqualified Emancipation.[2] The new group, generally known as the reorganized Catholic Board, met for the first time on 12 July 1817. Initially, O'Connell was fortunate in finding a piece of ready-made business for the revived body. Rev. Richard Hayes, O.F.M., who had taken the Catholic remonstrance against the veto proposals to Rome two years before, was on the point of being expelled from the Holy See, and O'Connell proposed that the Board draft a 'Letter of Complaint' to His Holiness. Even this produced much wrangling – Nicholas Mahon and his nephews, Nicholas and Richard O'Gorman, opposed the move – but a watered-down version of the letter was accepted at a later meeting. There was however much more to be squeezed out of the business than a futile epistle to the pope. O'Connell saw to it that the new Board sent one circular to all the Irish bishops, and a second to the clergy generally, expressing alarm at Hayes's ill-treatment. The first circular struck the note of chauvinism, pretending to outrage that Ireland should still fall within the sphere of Propaganda 'as if this were a mere missionary country without a national church'. The second raised the spectre of covert British influence at the Curia. Both seized the opportunity to rehearse the anti-vetoist case and to pressurize the clergy once again. The bishops were urged to see to it that the pope guaranteed them 'Domestic Nomination' to the episcopate and thus 'confirm[ed] the Irish Church in her National Independence'.[3]

In part, O'Connell was really worried lest the bishops weaken in their resistance to the veto. Archbishop Murray had already expressed anger at a violently political sermon delivered at the Carmelite Clarendon St Chapel (the meeting-place for the Dublin aggregates) by L'Estrange on 9 March 1817. O'Connell soon came to suspect that Archbishop Troy, whom he regarded as a truckler to Dublin Castle, had won over his coadjutor to his side. The joint reply from Troy and Murray to the reorganized Board's episcopal circular seemed to suggest that they might compromise on the veto issue; at any rate, they had responded coldly to the anti-vetoists. O'Connell wrote excitedly to Edward Hay, the secretary to the new Board, on 27 July,

> I perceive 'the pliant Trojan' [O'Connell's habitual nickname for Troy] has got Dr Murray's support for the Veto. Their publication of their letter to you was intended to intimidate other bishops from that zealous opposition to the Veto which the people look for and the times require . . . I am, I own, greatly shocked at the part Dr Murray is taking. I had the highest opinion of him and the greatest respect for him. But I see he wishes, with Dr Troy's see, to inherit the patronage of the Catholic Church of Ireland. Oh! it is melancholy to think of his falling off – he who compared the Vetoists to Judas. As to Dr Troy, better could not be expected from him. His traffic at the Castle is long notorious. But the sneer at the Board and the suppressed anger of those prelates would be ludicrous if the subject were not too important and vital. Are they angry because we urge not the *name* but the reality of Domestic Nomination? Alas, the fact is, that is just the cause of their ill temper and the source of their attack upon us.

O'Connell instructed Hay to publish immediately the other bishops' replies 'reprobatory of the Veto and favourable to Domestic Nomination', and this was done during August 1817. He also used aggregate meetings to demonstrate popular support and revived in oblique form his old threat that the people would repudiate vetoist priests and bishops: 'The Methodists were never in so fair a way of making converts.'[4] But by the end of the summer this rather factitious storm in a teacup had been altogether stilled. Whatever Troy's and Murray's original intentions they had been pulled back into the ranks of a solidly anti-vetoist episcopate. But the victory left the new Board practically bereft of business. On 26 September O'Connell spoke of Ireland as 'most wretched – fever – poverty – party spirit and *want of animation*'.[5] The only other excitement of the year was the miserable one of O'Connell's being challenged to a duel for his abuse of a member of a leading Ascendancy family, J. F. Leslie, at the meeting of 4 December 1817; the affair was finally patched up by O'Connell conceding that he had spoken of Leslie, not as an individual, but as a public man. Thereafter the new Board ceased to meet; it decided not even to petition Parliament during the spring and early summer session of 1818. O'Connell himself pronounced the requiem on 21 December of the same year: 'The Board is defunct . . . There are many debts due – there is a great indisposition to *organize*.'[6]

The ill-starred new Catholic Board did not exhaust O'Connell's efforts to agitate during 1817–18. In the first half of 1817, he took up the issue of proselytism at the Dublin House of Industry, and was condemned by the Castle press for dragging the name of the lord lieutenant into the row. He also denounced Orange supremacism at one public meeting and Anglican pretensions to a monopoly of loyalty to the crown at another. By the second half of 1818, however, his emphasis had changed from the politics of sectarianism to the politics of ecumenism: in between he had striven to conjoin the Catholic cause and that of moderate parliamentary reform. Ceaselessly, backwards and forwards, he probed for some weakness in the government's front which a new agitation might exploit. Meanwhile, he struggled to bring into being again, and then support, a sympathetic press. In 1817 he indemnified the official guarantor of Eneas MacDonnell's pro-Emancipation newspaper, the *Dublin Chronicle*, and on 24 August 1818 assured Michael Staunton, his new ally as editor of the *Freeman's Journal*, 'I have been and am exerting myself to get your paper into the clubs here [co. Kerry]. You are now the *longe et facile primus* of the Irish press.'[7] But it was all uphill and ill-rewarded work.

The humiliations, pettinesses and generally derided endeavours of 1816–18 were all the more galling because O'Connell, no prophet in his own land, discovered himself to be remarkably prophetical in London. In the early summer of 1817 Mary was sent to Clifton, near Bristol, to recover her lost health. Having installed her there, O'Connell spent a week in London, his first visit (apart from the Peel episode) since his student days. He was lionized in a mild though thoroughly flattering degree. As soon as he arrived, Charles Butler, the foremost English Catholic commoner, waited upon him and introduced him to the Duke of Norfolk, Sir John Throckmorton and all the 'great men' of the English Board; he also met leading parliamentary liberals although he missed Brougham, 'the very first man in England', who was then ill. On 4 June 1817 the prominent 'Anglo-Irish lawyer' Anthony Blake

> splendidly entertained [me] . . . at his house with a large party of English Catholics of the first rank. And the next day Lord Fingall and I were entertained in a similar party at the Thatched House Tavern in St James Street – with that name it is one of the first taverns in the world. Our feast was turtle – turbot, champagne, etc. On Thursday I . . . paid and received many visits. I could not tell you the lords and commoners to whom I was introduced nor the attention I met with.[8]

It was a bitter, as well as sweet, experience. In every meeting and conversation O'Connell felt conscious of his superiority to the host of 'men of high names' who feted him. 'Darling', he told Mary on 10 June,

> do not smile at my vanity, but your credulity with respect to anything in my favour will easily make you believe that I felt how cruel the Penal Laws are which exclude me from a fair trial with men whom *I look on* as so much my inferiors . . .
>
> I saw the English Bar, darling, in its strength and be assured, heart, they are just nothing to the Irish Bar. I felt *that* easily and strongly. I spent almost the entire day on Friday in the King's Bench . . .[9]

The resentment of his debased station was political no less than personal. On his next visit to Mary in September 1817 he wrote from Clifton, 'I have seen nothing here but stupid loyal slavish English, who for a rise of one per cent in the funds would truck a republic for the government of slaves.'[10] To be systematically degraded by such people was hardly endurable.

## II

In O'Connell, however, hope was always tinder-dry; at any spark it blazed. On 2 November 1818 he wrote excitedly to Owen O'Conor (The O'Conor Don) of Balanagare, a country gentleman of ancient Catholic family, 'I have just heard from a credible person in London that Emancipation is certain. *I believe it*.'[11] It was enough to galvanize O'Connell once again. O'Conor, respected, honourable and sensible, was his principal ally in the new campaign; O'Connell summoned him up from co. Roscommon repeatedly. But he also had hopes of a rapprochement with Lord Fingall (and through him with the aristocratic faction of Catholics) and of making common cause with the Irish whigs and in particular with their most eminent personage, the Duke of Leinster. Fingall, as he told O'Conor on 21 December 1818, proved immovable. None the less, O'Connell was 'decidedly for petitioning. If I petition alone, I *will* petition.'[12] He cast one of his favourite flies over O'Conor by asking *him* to lay out a course of action, assuring him that he would fall in gratefully with whatever O'Conor might propose. But meanwhile he had hit on a device of his own. He would compose a public letter to the Catholics of Ireland for publication on the opening day of the new year: in fact, this turned out to be the first of O'Connell's celebrated New Year letters to his supposed national flock – pronouncements *urbi et orbi* so to say.

Of course, O'Connell did not really wait upon O'Conor's inspiration. While not despairing altogether of Fingall, he set about organizing an Irish Protestant lobby for Emancipation. Eventually, he managed to persuade eight sympathetic peers, headed by the Duke of Leinster, and four M.P.'s, headed by Henry Grattan, to requisition the lord mayor of Dublin (Thomas McKenny, another sympathizer) for a Protestant meeting to petition for Catholic relief. Despite Castle opposition, the meeting held on 11 February 1819 was successful, securing a wide and respectable Protestant support for a petition. O'Connell was exultant. 'Are you not delighted', he wrote to O'Conor that evening, 'that you did not stay in the country and plead, as you might, business &c &c?'[13] It was certainly a triumph for O'Connell, now forced to operate without any organization of his own, and with still very feeble press support. He had not got as close to Grattan, the great embodiment of '1782', as he now desired. To Grattan's memory of O'Connell's coarse repudiation of him in 1815 had been added that of being hooted by a mob of O'Connell's Dublin sympathizers in the general election of 1818. Still, by the beginning of 1819 the two were on civil terms at least; even this was a partial triumph.

But a price would ultimately be exacted for such a move to the right in Catholic politics. Publicly, Eneas MacDonnell pointed out that O'Connell's address of 1 January 1819 had omitted all reference to the veto, and that O'Connell had earlier alleged popular apathy and episcopal division on the subject. The veteran Presbyterian radical, William Drennan, who was organizing pro-Emancipation meetings in Belfast, assumed that O'Connell would beat some retreat upon this vital issue, though on balance he granted him both prudence and probity. 'I see', he told O'Connell on 30 January 1819,

> the whole matter is settled. The Veto in operation already. Well, you must balance the *much* you may receive against the *comparatively* little you lose. The Catholic *regium donum* will follow the Presbyterian *regium donum*, but the love of laymen for liberty will overcome and quench the ecclesiastical proneness to prostration. Take what you *can* get and trust to the future, nor cast away your civil rights in compliment to those who degrade the dignity and sanctity of the latter . . .
>
> *You* will always act the honest part, not the poor spirited and aspiring character of the day. I would not condescend to compliment you or anyone without grounds, but I sincerely think you possess many of the characteristics of Charles Fox, his manly spirit, his openness and candour, his ability and perhaps a little of his gullibility, the weak part of an otherwise impregnable stronghold of honesty and honour. I was going to say to you, as I would have said to him, oddly as it may sound, 'Beware of the goodness of your heart. Your paper, which blinked the Veto, called for an answer and got it. Eneas fought with Achilles. Your reply has vindicated your consistency and politically accounted for your omission.' . . . It is a ticklish station but with moral integrity that disdains the juggling and *leger-de-main* of speculating politicians, your object will be obtained and your name be recorded in History.[14]

Clearly O'Connell was prepared, early in 1819, to compromise, to some extent, upon the veto issue in order to secure a Relief Act immediately; he may well have hoped – insofar as he planned ahead at all – that 'Domestic Nomination' would prove nebulous enough to accommodate the various conflicting interests. But the issue did not come to the test at once. Grattan's motion of 3 May 1819 for a committee to inquire into the laws affecting Catholics was defeated – although, cheeringly, by only two votes.

O'Connell was certainly not dismayed by this result. Attributing their failure to the lateness with which the question had been brought on in the Commons, he told O'Conor soon after the defeat that they must 'recommence operations' much earlier than usual, and if possible before Parliament sat again in the first week in November 1819. 'We have been materially injured by the late period in which the question has always come on.' He also called on O'Conor to help immediately in 'perfecting' the reunion of the Irish Catholic forces.[15] Correspondingly, he was careful to continue to cultivate the whigs, English no less than Irish. When in August 1819 Edward Hay (now estranged from O'Connell) 'leaked' to the *Dublin Evening Post* (also estranged by now) the 'information' that the notorious witchery resolutions of 1812 had been inspired by the English whigs, and in particular by

George Ponsonby, O'Connell quickly issued a public denial to save his English allies from embarrassment.

He even cut short his sacred Kerry vacation to make an early start in the new season's agitation. On 21 October 1819 he wrote to O'Conor from Dublin:

> I intend instantly to set the cause in motion. This great experiment is worth making. I think you will let me have your assistance. I write by this post to Lord Fingall. I am strongly prompted by our friends in Parliament. I wish to God you could come up *at once* to help me. If we *show out* before the Regent's speech is prepared, perhaps we may be remembered in it. If you agree with me that this time requires a sacrifice, you will come up. My own opinion is that we will be emancipated *now or never*.
>
> I came to town only yesterday, and already I have many irons in the fire to raise the blaze which should lead us to victory. I want you much, and the cause wants you more.[16]

At this stage O'Connell argued that another failure of Emancipation would render the argument for parliamentary reform irrefutable and demonstrate 'a disposition to make use of bigotry as an instrument to perpetuate the divisions, dissensions and consequent degradation and oppression of Ireland'.[17] He did not however develop this into a distinct threat to turn to Reform or Repeal, if disappointed. On the contrary, he instructed his 'countrymen' in his encyclical of October 1819:

> You will be told that you should despise emancipation as a minor and unworthy consideration, and join the almost universal cry of reform. Do not be carried away by any such incitement . . . we have a previous duty to perform; a favourable opportunity now presents itself to add to the general stock of liberty, by obtaining our emancipation; and the man would, in my judgment, be a false patriot, who, for the chance of uncertain reform, would fling away the present most propitious moment to realize a most important and almost certain advantage.[18]

Moreover, he continued to court the Irish Protestants and whigs. Early in November 1819 he strove to revive their interest in the cause through the device of a subscription for McKenny 'for his virtuous and independent conduct in calling and presiding at the Meeting of the Protestant Friends of Roman Catholic freedom . . . in Febuary last'.[19] In fact, probably for lack of support, the advertised dinner had to be postponed and it was almost six months before it eventually took place early in May 1820. In the interval, O'Connell fell into further difficulties when he rashly declared that the Duke of Leinster and

Lords Fingall and Cloncurry would act with him in resigning from the Kildare Place Society (the semi-state body entrusted with promoting national elementary education) because it permitted the proselytizing of the Catholic children. But he apparently made plausible explanations to, and in due course peace with, his aristocratic patrons. In the end, Grattan departed for Westminster on 20 May 1820 – even later in the session than usual, for all O'Connell's original aspirations. He was armed with a bundle of petitions from Irish Protestants and Catholics alike, and accompanied by even higher hopes than in 1819.

The expedition could not have ended more unfortunately. Grattan fell ill when he arrived in London and died on 4 June. O'Connell apostrophized the dead hero with 'I should exhaust the dictionary three times told, ere I could enumerate [his] virtues';[20] perhaps he half-meant this at least, for much later, speaking privately, he placed Grattan second only to himself among Irish statesmen. The demise brought discord and delay. The choice of a substitute spokesman divided the Irish Catholic deputation which accompanied Grattan. In the end – surprisingly – William Plunket, who had told the deputation that 'securities' or conditions upon Catholic relief were both just and necessary, was preferred (by a casting vote) to the much less accommodating Knight of Kerry, O'Connell's particular friend. When the news reached Dublin, O'Connell denounced the deputation furiously. But though sinister in its implications for the future, the decision had no bearing on the present. By now the session was so far advanced that the government could play out time upon the Catholic claims; the petitions were never presented. Thus by a mixture of ill-luck and ill-management 'the best opportunity', as O'Connell put it, 'I have ever known of pressing emancipation on the ministry, [has] been thrown away and lost for ever'.[21] Worse still, the Irish Catholics had been rent asunder once again and, from the anti-vetoist standpoint, the choice of Plunket had sold all possible passes in advance. The conciliatory strategy which O'Connell had followed for more than twenty months was now in ruins.

## III

The travails of the past year had however been partially offset by an agreeable political distraction. The apparent revival of liberalism abroad during 1819–20 had fired O'Connell's ardour. In March 1820 he was overjoyed to learn that Ferdinand VII of Spain had been forced to restore the constitution of 1812.

> I am in great spirits. The complete revolution in Spain is so auspicious a circumstance that I hail it as the first of a series of events useful to human liberty and human happiness. Until *the last* papers I was not without my fears of a failure, but now my mind is quite at ease and I enjoy this revolution as all the scoundrels of society enjoyed the battle of Waterloo.[22]

But it was the revolt of the Spanish colonies in South America which seemed to him most apropos the Irish plight. At a dinner which he organized in Dublin on 19 July 1819 to celebrate South American freedom, he came into close relation with John Devereux, who was currently raising an Irish Legion to fight with Bolivar in Venezuela. Devereux, for long a political exile in the United States for his part in the 1798 rebellion, was a vain and unscrupulous adventurer. But O'Connell, completely taken in, 'stood by him even after charges had been made, probably with much truth, that he had organized the Irish Legion for his own financial benefit'.[23]

Devereux's grant of a commission to one of O'Connell's nephews was followed by his making out another, seemingly on his own initiative, for O'Connell's son Morgan, still only fourteen years of age. 'I shall name [him] as on my staff', he told O'Connell on 3 August 1819, 'although it may be no other than a mere compliment yet it will serve to record that affection and respect for you – and for virtues and merits which I feel too strongly to express by words.'[24] O'Connell was now fairly caught. Morgan, with boyish vanity, seized upon Devereux's 'document' and subscribed himself in a letter to his father of 27 August, 'Captain, 1st Regt. of Fusiliers and Aide-de-camp to General D'Evereux, Irish Legion.'[25] In fact, disaster befell the first contingent of the Legion when it landed on the island of Margarita in August 1819; news of its ill-fate reached Dublin months later; and demands for an inquiry into Devereux's conduct – he was widely blamed – followed fast. But the effect on O'Connell was merely to turn him into Devereux's foremost partisan. First, Morgan clung to his commission and hopes of a South American adventure, and therefore to his faith in Devereux, and this predisposed a fond father to take an indulgent view of Morgan's patron. Next, O'Connell had been charmed and flattered by the General 'and mingling his mighty cause with his kindly self I became and in the worst of times continued and am his friend'. Most important of all, O'Connell argued, was the cause itself. 'One more land of liberty is a conquest over despotism and over legitimacy which they cannot afford.'[26] The whole enterprise also touched chords of romance and ambition in the Catholic middle class, not least in O'Connell himself. In one light, it seemed a renewal of the

'Flight of the Wild Geese' in which from the 1690s onwards young Irish Catholics, deprived and depressed at home, sought fame and fortune in the Continental armies of the *ancien régime*. In another, it seemed to renew the age of the conquistadores (though now under liberal banners), for lavish land grants and honours in the freed colonies seemed assured. We must always paint in this glowing foreground if we are fully to account for the intensity of the Irish enthusiasm, however shortlived, for the bizarre undertaking.

For O'Connell there was the additional attraction that Bolivar seemed his political mirror image, half way across the globe. He made no such claim publicly, of course. A letter which he gave Morgan to deliver to Bolivar opened with stately deference,

> Illustrious Sir,
>
> A stranger and unknown, I take the liberty of addressing you. I am encouraged to do so by my respect for your high character and by my attachment to that sacred cause which your talents, valour and virtue have gloriously sustained – I mean the cause of Liberty and national independence.
>
> Hitherto I have been able to bestow only good wishes upon that noble cause. But now I have a son able to wield a sword in its defence, and I send him, Illustrious Sir, to admire and profit by your example . . .[27]

But it would have come as no surprise to learn from Morgan, after he had arrived at Margarita on 12 June 1820, that praise was heaped upon 'the Irish liberator' in the welcoming after-dinner speeches in the mess. O'Connell was toasted 'as "the most enlightened, the most independent, and the most patriotic man, not only in Great Britain, but in all Europe". This was drunk with great acclamations, and Col. Low's son, standing up on his chair shouted: "Viva el Councellor O'Connell".'[28] Bolivar himself was respectful of O'Connell's fame, though he turned it neatly to account by postponing the addition of Morgan to his staff because 'I have numberless hardships to go through which I would not bring him into for the character of his father is well known to me.'[29]

It was accepted in Venezuela that the Irish Legion depended largely for its expansion on O'Connell's reputation and vociferous support. Certainly, he was heavily engaged in defending and justifying its projector in Dublin during the early months of 1820; in addition to his own writings and speeches in Devereux's favour and his efforts to secure him a favourable press, he acted as his lawyer and probably – of all things! – his 'banker' at certain stages. But by the time of Morgan's arrival at Margarita, things had gone badly awry with the expeditionary force. The initial contingent of approximately 1000 had mutinied and, for the most part, been shipped out of trouble to Jamaica. Four months later, on 4 October 1820, a letter from Admiral Brion, Bolivar's naval commander, condemning the remainder, was published in the Dublin newspapers. Brion described Devereux's newly arrived forces as banditti, and declared that Bolivar's troops at Baranquilla had refused to receive them. Dogged loyalty still held O'Connell back from abandoning Devereux and the Legion; but the venture was now hopelessly discredited, and he was reduced to consoling Mary on 13 October 1820 with, 'Make your mind easy about my darling Morgan. His share of the evils which befell the Irish Legion are small indeed. He has means to supply his wants and can return when he pleases.'[30] Morgan did return safely at the very end of 1821, although only after he had undergone attacks of ague and fever, two shipwrecks and successive rescues by, first, a long-lost illegitimate O'Connell cousin who was soon to be murdered by an Italian boatswain and die in Morgan's arms, next, an Irish naval officer who had lost his commission for refusing to take the prescribed anti-Catholic oaths and now sailed under Danish colours, and finally an Irish lieutenant R.N. commanding the sloop *Raleigh* who landed him eventually at Chatham. Characteristically, O'Connell cast a roseate wash over Morgan's entire madcap adventure. 'His trip to South America', he wrote on 5 January 1822, 'has done him nothing but good as it would otherwise have been difficult to tame him down to the sobriety of business.' Without having so much as seen him for more than eighteen months, he was none the less assured that Morgan was now 'very prudent in money matters'![31] By this stage the affair of the Irish Legion was receding into memory, apart from occasional scandalous allegations about and counter-charges from Devereux. O'Connell had certainly not enhanced his reputation in Dublin Catholic circles by his persistent credulity or even his obstinate loyalty to his protégé. Yet there was more to it all than a trivial exhibition of ill-judgment. Bolivar remained an ideal for O'Connell all his life, neither was it a coincidence that he came to bear with pride the title invented originally for Bolivar – 'The Liberator'.

From one distraction to another: just as the Devereux business was entering its darkest phase, O'Connell found another welcome political diversion. Upon returning from his Iveragh vacation at the end of October 1820, he conceived the notion that he should be instated as Queen Caroline's Irish attorney-general. Despite the inherent implausibility, it was no mad dream. The Queen's affair was now at its hottest pitch of excitement and agitation; O'Connell's sympathies (liberal and Irish alike) had of course been with her and against her husband from the start; and the whig lawyers Brougham and Thomas Denman had been appointed, respectively, her attorney- and solicitor-general earlier in 1820. Although such appointments to a royal consort traditionally carried with them admission to the inner bar, it is not clear whether O'Connell had any such hope in pressing his own case. The statutory prohibition on Roman Catholics taking silk still stood. He said that his appointment as the Queen's Irish attorney-general 'would be of great use to my clients [in] that I should not be flung into the back row'[32] – an indeterminate aspiration. But he may well have felt that the commotion which would follow his nomination might precipitate a crisis ending in the removal of the bar on Catholics. O'Connell himself told Lord Cloncurry on 16 November 1820 that 'my leading motive in looking for this office is to annoy some of the greatest scoundrels in society and, of course, the bitterest enemies of Ireland.'[33] Whether or not this really was his leading motive, there could be no doubt that such an elevation would infuriate every tory – not to add a considerable majority of the whigs – in the United Kingdom.

Seized with his extraordinary scheme, O'Connell dispatched letters in all directions to concert a campaign for his own appointment. He emphasized, as was essential, that in his view the 'Penal Laws do not exclude a Catholic from being Attorney-General to the Queen.'[34] Through Cloncurry, he tried to ensure the patronage of the Duke of Leinster; through Thomas Spring-Rice, the newly elected whig member for Limerick city, he sought an entrée to Brougham, the Queen's principal legal adviser. From Alexander Wood, an Irish journalist working on the London *Traveller*, he obtained an analysis of the power structure of Caroline's court; Wood advised him to enlist Sir Henry Parnell's aid, to gain introductions to the influential Earl Grey and Lord Darnley and, above all, to try to 'move through' Alderman Wood as well as Brougham 'for when two great orbs spin in the same direction, there is, you know, an eclipse of one!'[35]

At first it seemed as if O'Connell's *coup de main* would carry the day. On 24 November 1820 his former pupil, John Bric, wrote triumphantly from London on the strength of a chain of reports said to have the ultimate authority of Alderman Wood, 'My dear Sir, You are the attorney-general of Ireland for Her Majesty.'[36] Two days later O'Connell described himself as 'Her Majesty's Attorney-General' in replying formally to an invitation from Cloncurry.[37] Doubtless he was also responsible for the news item appearing in a Dublin newspaper, *Carrick's Morning Post*, on 27 November under the headline, 'APPOINTMENT OF HER MAJESTY'S ATTORNEY-GENERAL FOR IRELAND'.

But it was Brougham who held the key to the situation, and he fell at once into the role of the archetypical 'slippery whig' with whom one could neither disagree nor cooperate. His sympathy with O'Connell's objective was boundless, his courtesy unfailing, his tone respectful almost to the point of deference – but there were always difficulties. Brougham first asked O'Connell to seek a precedent for the appointment of consort's legal officer – of whatever religion – in Ireland, and to suggest a Protestant who might be his partner. Later he begged O'Connell to state a case on which Denman and he might give an opinion. O'Connell could find no precedent (he fairly pointed to the deplorable state of Irish public records) but argued vigorously that the only possibly prohibitory legislation referred solely to male consorts. He relied however upon his own professional judgment and the strategy of transferring the onus to the crown by compelling them to challenge his appointment – 'without allowing a thought of the expense of the contest coming from any other person than myself'. As he put it in a letter to Brougham of 15 December 1820,

> My opinion is that I should be entitled to a *mandamus*. A barrister in this country is not a mere creature of courtesy as in England but is called to the Bar by force of a Statute of the reign of Henry VIII and, having that legal capacity, I consider that I should, by her Majesty's appointment, be enabled by a *mandamus* to compel the Chancellor to admit me. I may be wrong but, if so, I am wrong very *premeditatedly*. I may be sneered at for giving myself a wrong opinion though, whether right or wrong, I fancy I do at present give as many – probably more opinions – to others than any Irish barrister. I cannot except one.[38]

It was not easy to counter O'Connell's proposal that he be appointed forthwith, thus forcing the government, if it so determined, to try to disallow the move. At worst, as Bric pointed out, 'their refusal to ratify your appointment, that is, to swear you into office would furnish an excellent topic for invective'.[39] But despite a case stated and 'further letters' from O'Connell, Brougham succeeded in delaying a definitive reply until 8 May 1821 when he told O'Connell that Denman and he did not consider 'the right in question . . . sufficiently established . . . to authorize us to give our advice to H.M. in favour of trying it.'[40] Well before then, however, it was clear that Brougham was opposed. In fact, such a realization probably explains the bitter hostility to working with the current British parliamentarians which, unexpectedly, O'Connell expressed in his annual address to the Irish people on 1 January 1821.

## IV

The address of 1821 constituted a complete turnabout. It recommended that the issue of Emancipation be shelved entirely in favour of that of parliamentary reform. O'Connell now spurned the yearly farce and humiliation of a rejected or burked Catholic petition and told his co-religionists no longer to

> *... kneel before their masters doors,*
> *And hawk their wrongs, as beggars do their sores.*[41]

His further plans were vague to the point of vapidity. They consisted essentially in an appeal to all Irishmen – the by-now hallowed 'Catholic, Protestant and Dissenter' – to stand by their common nationality and strike for their common constitutional rights as a nation, without regard to their particular preferences as to modes of political reform. As a programme this was absurd; but the challenge to the right wing of Irish Catholics, and especially to the vetoists, was unmistakeable. Sheil took up the gauntlet on their behalf with a savage 'Answer to Mr O'Connell's Address' which cast doubts upon O'Connell's sincerity as either Emancipationist or patriot. The war between the Irish Catholic factions had broken out once more, and O'Connell responded with a bitter lampoon of Sheil's literary pretensions, ending by imploring him 'with all the earnestness of the plainest prose, to refrain from his sneering sarcasms, directed against ... the long-suffering and very wretched people of Ireland'.[42] Only with the greatest difficulty was Sheil persuaded against inflicting the final blow on the Irish cause by calling O'Connell out.

O'Connell was awkwardly placed when on 7 March 1821 Plunket introduced bills amounting to Emancipation with 'securities' in the Commons. The bills had the warm support of the English Catholic body as a whole, as well as that of the Irish vetoists, and the omens were good for a parliamentary majority, at least in the lower house. But O'Connell did not hesitate to denounce Plunket and his proposals violently. From Limerick, where he was on circuit, he issued a public letter condemning the measures as 'more *strictly*, *literally*, and *emphatically* a *penal* and *persecuting bill* than any or all the statutes passed in the darkest and most bigoted periods';[43] he made much play of the danger to even the secrets of the confessional which the supervisory board proposed by Plunket presented. He also arranged meetings of protest in the assize cities, stirred the local Catholic clergy (who would be subjected to an abjuring oath under the new order) to indignation, and worked upon his parliamentary friends to oppose Plunket. 'If the Bill [Plunket's two proposals had by now been consolidated into one] passes in its present shape', he told the Knight of Kerry on 8 April 1821, 'it will tend to exasperate and render matters worse in point of popular tranquillity.'[44] None the less, he remained nervous. Six days later, he confessed to Mary, 'I wish with all my heart that the present rascally Catholic Bill was flung out. While I am travelling on Monday [16 April] morning the rascals will be debating.'[45] He might have guessed, however, that the upper house would muster sufficient 'rascals' to defeat Emancipation, however qualified. Although the combined measure passed the House of Commons, the Lords finally rejected it by 159 votes to 120 on 17 April. O'Connell rejoiced that a disastrous compromise, which might have covered over, without destroying, the essential evil for a generation, had been averted, and no less at the discomfiture of his domestic enemies. 'Even the Vetoists', he wrote, 'must admit that *securities* do no good because we are kicked out as unceremoniously with them as without them.' None the less, it left the Irish Catholics of all sorts stranded and virtually hopeless. As he put it to O'Conor on 23 April 1821, 'What is to be done now? That is the question.'[46]

To the thoroughgoing opportunist, however, almost anything can provide an opportunity. The forthcoming coronation of George IV on 19 July 1821 and his promised visit to Ireland in the following month (the first by a reigning English monarch since Richard II's expedition of 1399) might not seem promising material for a revival of Irish Catholic politics. But O'Connell determined to turn them to account. At first, he intended to combine with a loyal address a fresh statement upon Emancipation. But O'Conor, on whose respectability and standing he relied for the successful requisitioning of a general Catholic meeting, insisted that the business be confined to the address, lest 'we shall be again split into parties and consequently weakened'.[47] This course was rendered more palatable to O'Connell by an overture on 10 July 1821 from the (mainly Orange) corporation of Dublin asking that Protestant-Catholic hostility be set aside for the king's visit and that George IV be received by all under the common denomination of loyal Irishmen. Nothing could have fitted better the volte face which O'Connell had announced in his public pronouncement of the previous 1 January. He also maintained in later years that he was serving the cause of Emancipation as well as Ireland's national interest by his extreme conciliatoriness – not to say, servility – before, during and immediately after the king's descent upon the country.

> This was the most critical period of my political life, and that in which I had the good fortune to be most successful. If I have any merit for the success of the Catholic cause, it is principally to be found in the mode in which I neutralised the most untoward events and converted the most sinister appearances and circumstances into the utmost extent of practical usefulness to the cause of which I was the manager . . . I was able to convert the King's visit to Ireland from being a source of weakness and discomfiture to the Catholics into a future claim for practical relief and political equalisation.[48]

Undoubtedly, O'Connell came to believe this strange claim in retrospect. But there is little evidence that his thoughts ran upon these lines at the time. In fact, he and Sheil pursued their ill-tempered rivalry throughout the whole affair.

No one could have exceeded O'Connell in forbearance when, against the spirit of the entente, members of the corporation offered various Orange provocations. Dublin Catholics were entertained by the piquant spectacle of O'Connell preaching restraint – successfully in the end – to Sheil and his fellow-vetoists. O'Connell was also foremost in public obeisance to the king, as with the extravagance of his welcome. 'In sorrow and bitterness', he orated, 'I have for the last fifteen years laboured for my unhappy country. But this bright day has realised all my fond expectations. It is said of St Patrick that he banished venomous reptiles from our isle, but his Majesty has performed a greater moral miracle. The announcement of his approach has allayed the dissensions of centuries.'[49] During the royal sojourn, O'Connell presented himself loyally to George IV, and, as he was departing, held out to him a laurel crown 'intended with all humility to be replaced by one of Emeralds'.[50] O'Connell also added his name to the subscription list for the erection of a palace to commemorate the king's visit (in the end the money sufficed only to build a bridge), and founded a 'Loyal Union, or Royal George Club' to perpetuate the 'affectionate gratitude towards his Majesty King George the Fourth (whom God preserve,) which now animates every Irish bosom'.[51] The club (curiously similar in detail to O'Connell's later Order of Liberators!) was to meet and dine regularly together and to wear a species of uniform made from cloth of Irish manufacture. He was also reported to boast that a new fur cap he wore was a present from the king. Nicholas Mahon derided this supposed piece of flunkyism soon afterwards in Cork, but O'Connell claimed to have turned the tables on his persistent critic. 'I had great fun at the county meeting. You never saw or heard of anything that took better than my hit at Mahon in reply to his attack on my cap. I concluded by saying "I would call my cap the cap of unanimity, but then the cap would not fit Mr Mahon".'[52]

Both then and later O'Connell proferred a political defence of his season of obsequiousness. He was ever loyal to the crown, as King or Queen of Ireland; and as loyalism (with claims to exclusive rights therein) was the Irish Protestant's stock-in-trade, it behoved the Irish Catholic to express his fidelity in the most unmistakable terms. O'Connell also distinguished between the office and person of the head of state; it was to the crowned monarch, not George himself, that he proclaimed his undying attachment. Moreover, the prime objective of an Irish statesman should be able to find common ground for Irish Catholics and Protestants, and where better to do so than in their joint allegiance to the king?

Despite the thin rationality of all this, a fawning and courtier-like O'Connell presented a pitiful change of front. As reported, with some malicious exaggeration, by the London press, his conduct during the royal visit aroused disgust and contempt among liberals in England. Tom Moore was appalled by the 'bad servile style in which Paddy has received him [George IV] – Mr O'Connell pre-eminent in blarney and inconsistency'.[53] Byron lashed him in verse:

> *. . . O'Connell, proclaim*
> *His accomplishments!* His !!! *and thy country convince*
> *Half an age's contempt was an error of fame . . .*
>
> *Shout, drink, feast, and flatter! Oh! Erin, how low*
> *Wert thou sunk by misfortune and tyranny, till*
> *Thy welcome of tyrants has plunged thee below*
> *The depth of thy deep in a deeper gulf still.*[54]

To the very close of 1821 O'Connell struggled to retain the illusion that the royal foray into Irish affairs was, as George IV declared, the harbinger of the end of faction, and the prelude to Catholic equality. In his annual address at the beginning of the year, O'Connell had called for the sinking of Irish sectarian differences and the display of a united Irish manliness of comportment in the face of Britain's contemptuous neglect of their common country. It was ironic that this should have ended in Catholic abasement before both Orange supremacism and the throne.

## V

During 1822 O'Connell's new-found conciliatoriness and loyalism took on another form. In December 1821 the Marquess of Wellesley, a supporter of the Catholic claims, became Irish lord lieutenant, though this was deliberately balanced by the appointment of the ultra-tory Henry Goulburn as chief secretary. As a sort of counter-compensation, Wellesley replaced Saurin (much to Saurin's fury – in anger he refused both an English peerage and the chief justiceship of King's Bench) by Plunket as Irish attorney-general. O'Connell took all this to mean the inauguration of an era of non-factional government in Ireland; and as Wellesley was specifically the crown's alter ego it was easy to transfer the hopes and deference of the later months of 1821 to the viceroy. In moving the address of welcome at a general Catholic meeting on 7 January 1822, O'Connell proclaimed him to be the 'representative, not only of the person, but also of the kindly disposition of our beloved Sovereign'.[55]

At the same time O'Connell decided to test the water on whether or not he should make a fresh bid for Emancipation. He announced that after consulting Plunket (Plunket had probably done no more than listen politely) he had framed a scheme of Domestic Nomination which he believed would give the state reasonable securities while not infringing on the essential liberty of the Irish Catholic Church. But he would not, he added, force the issue if it were to revive the bitter division of the veto controversy or if others felt that it endangered ecclesiastical independence. This uncharacteristically tentative proposal did not bode well for further action; and although a Dublin aggregate meeting of 13 February 1822 resolved in favour of petitioning again, this never happened. Later in the spring, O'Connell attributed his restraint to the wave of agrarian outrages currently ravaging cos. Limerick, Kerry and Cork: these had already brought down upon Ireland a grievously repressive Insurrection Act as well as the suspension of Habeas Corpus. For O'Connell to launch an agitation, however 'constitutional', at such a stage might well have been paraded by the malignant as colluding with rural terrorism. Nothing could be further from O'Connell's intention; but it was reasonable for him, from past experience, to fear even so gross a misrepresentation.

But the decisive reason for O'Connell's failure to act was probably Plunket's blank refusal to raise the Catholic question during 1822. On 4 April O'Connell pleaded with him that the mere advertisement, in the debate, of the loyalty of the priests in the present disturbances would more than compensate for the defeat of a motion in favour of Emancipation.

> The Catholic clergy of the second order are unanimous in wishing for it because they are convinced that at this moment every man in the House must admit the zeal and energy the Catholic clergy have evinced during the present disturbances. This testimony you will cheerfully bear. This testimony Mr Goulburn, our mortal enemy, and even Mr Peel *must* now admit to be true . . . These will at all events be precious advantages – to have admitted in Parliament *the innocence* of the Catholic religion as any part of *the immediate* cause of the troubles now raging and also to have praised and *admired* by all parties the exertions and loyalty of the Catholic clergy.[56]

In the name of parliamentary tactics, Plunket vigorously resisted the re-airing of the Catholic question, and indeed the notion that the Catholic question should form the matter for a regular pitched battle in the Commons every session.

> It would not only lose its interest but its friends who, though willing to expose themselves to some unpleasant differences with their constituents (I mean the English Members for counties and open places) in order to carry, or essentially to advance the measure, will not submit to be annually dragged forward merely for discussion. In addition to this there are many persons on the ministerial side of the House who have been amongst the steadiest and most efficient friends of the Roman Catholics who may feel themselves placed in a situation of some awkwardness if in consequence of a determination to bring it on every session, the question should become liable to be considered as one of attack and embarrassment.[57]

With O'Connell still committed to the policy of supporting the crown's representative in Ireland, in the hope of even-handed government at last from Dublin Castle, Plunket's outright opposition was bound to be decisive.

But despite the initial triumph of Saurin's humiliation, O'Connell had by now good reason to doubt the even-handness of Wellesley's rule. The lord lieutenant had early disabused Irish Catholics of any idea that he might act to support their claims: he had come, he told them in reply to one address, to 'administer the laws, not to alter them'.[58] He had proceeded to recommend an Insurrection Act – which, as an agitator, O'Connell disliked, however much, as a landowner, he might acquiesce in its necessity – and the suspension of Habeas Corpus – which, as a common lawyer, O'Connell instinctively repudiated. Then Plunket had stamped upon any discussion of the

Catholic grievances in the Commons. By 1 July 1822 O'Connell had reached the point of writing satirically to Plunket, apropos of a gross misuse of their legal offices for political ends by Saurin and Norbury which had just been discovered accidentally,

> I am not so foolish or so uncandid as to assert that the case of a Protestant who conspires to injure the Catholics' case can in the present temper of Society in these countries, and under the present system, with at least one half the administration in both decided enemies of Catholic rights and liberties – I am not, I say, so foolish and uncandid as to assert that under such a system the crimes of Catholics and Protestants against each other should be weighed in the same scales of gold; neither theory nor practice warrant me to say so.[59]

O'Connell decided to put Wellesley to the proof. On 11 July he addressed a public letter to the lord lieutenant asking that he 'administer' (that is, enforce) the law next day by prohibiting the traditional Orange celebration of 'the Twelfth' in Dublin: 'it is a direct provocation to tumult.'[60] Wellesley attempted to compromise. He would not enjoin, but pleaded with the Orange leaders to forgo their marches. The appeal was contemptuously dismissed.

Wellesley had failed the test. But where was O'Connell to go from there? Fortunately, since this was a question to which there was no ready answer, he was engrossed for the remainder of the summer and most of the autumn of 1822 by domestic matters; most of September and October were spent with his family, then 'in exile' in France. Still more fortunately, just after his return to Dublin, his remonstrance of 11 July to Wellesley was crowned with a belated success. The lord lieutenant prohibited the secondary Orange celebration of 4 November (to commemorate William III's birth date) and enforced his prohibition by a military guard about William's statue. It was the Orange Society's first public rebuff since its formation, the first official rejection of the implicit Orange assumption of supremacy – with corresponding outrage on the one side and triumph upon the other. Orange demonstrations of increasing virulence against Wellesley followed, culminating in a riot in the Theatre Royal on 14 December 1822 (perhaps the play, *She Stoops to Conquer*, was ironically appropriate!) in which the lord lieutenant's box was pelted by Orange hooligans with fruit, an empty quart bottle and the timber of a watchman's rattle.

Nothing could have suited O'Connell better in his role of true-blue constitutionalist. He led the way in virtuous Catholic indignation at the Orange *lèse-majesté*, and could make common cause upon the issue not only with liberal Protestants but even with the moderate Irish tories. A 'mixed' aggregate held in Dublin on 20 December to express sympathy with Wellesley and abhorrence of the 'outrage' was addressed by peers and members of the Commons, knights and barristers, Protestants and Catholics, indifferently. 'There never was such a meeting in Ireland', O'Connell reported. 'The Exchange was crowded to the greatest excess. I was the only person who made himself heard throughout. There was the greatest unanimity and good feeling, and the Orange faction were branded with deserved reprobation. Not a human being to defend the miscreants or to say one word in their favour.' Next day he wrote to Mary, 'You may imagine what a curious revolution it is in Dublin when the Catholics are admitted to be the only genuine loyalists. For the first time has this truth reached the Castle.'[61] On Christmas Eve he crowned it all when, as a member of the sympathizing 'Committee of 21' and in court dress, he waited upon the lord lieutenant in St Patrick's Hall.

All this may have been magnificent but it was certainly not war for an agitator. There were of course profound psychological satisfactions in even the temporary disgrace of his hereditary enemies and his own entry into viceregal favour. But the course of Emancipation had not been and was not being advanced an inch. Instead the old whig-liberal confidence trick was being played upon the Catholics once again. Thomas Wyse's sombre judgement upon the 'experiment' of 1821–2 seems irrefutable:

> It was then, if ever since the first formation of their committees, that the Catholics had attained that perfect state of 'temperance and moderation', which has been so frequently recommended to them by friend and enemy. Nothing contributed to break it for two entire years: neither petition, nor remonstrance, nor speech, nor assembly of any note, was heard of. The entire body seemed to have relapsed into their ancient sluggishness, and to have surrendered their cause to the arbitration of blind chance, or the choice and convenience of their enemies. It was a wretched and successless policy.[62]

The Christmas Eve levee-ing at Dublin Castle was the apogee of O'Connell's 'purple' or romantic phase: in one form or another it had endured since he had taken up the cause of Spanish American liberation in July 1819. The other O'Connell, the cold political calculator, would however very soon re-emerge. Within a very few days, possibly even on Christmas Day itself, he was to project the new Catholic Association. Ultimately, this would spell the doom not only of the *ancien régime* in Ireland but also of historic toryism in Great Britain.

*CHAPTER 9*

# Reaping Whirlwinds

## *1817–27*

### I

Mary O'Connell fell into ill-health in the late spring of 1817. The cause is unknown. It might have been some bronchial or pulmonary weakness; there were numerous, though vague, references to her coughs and chest troubles over the years. Alternatively, she might have been paying the penalty for the stresses of 1815 and 1816 and many pregnancies; she had borne nine children, seven of them surviving, already, and was thirty-seven years of age when confined with the youngest, Daniel, only six months before. There was no hint of a collapse of health in her letters to O'Connell while he was on circuit in March and April 1817. She wrote of the usual things – their children, Dublin prices, her pride in the reports of his successes – and was solicitous only for him. On 9 April she laid her 'positive *commands* upon you not to go in a *steam*boat while in Cork. I read this morning [of] a melancholy accident which occurred in England.'[1] Two days later she wrote again to Cork,

> I wish to God you could contrive to get out of court for a quarter of an hour during the middle of the day to take a bowl of soup or a snack of some kind. Surely, though you may not be able to spare time to go to a tavern, could not James [his servant] get anything you wished for from the Bar mess at your lodgings, which is merely a *step* from the Court-house? Do, my love, try to accomplish *this* for really I am quite unhappy to have you fasting from an early hour in the morning until nine or ten o'clock at night. I wish I was with you to make you take care of yourself. I am quite sure there is not another barrister on your circuit would go through half the fatigue you do without taking necessary nourishment.[2]

O'Connell replied in a joking, untroubled strain, 'You order me at once out of steamboats and into cook shops. Now the fact is that I like steamboats much and hate cook shops excessively. So darling, darling, sweetest love, let us compromise our quarrel and have neither the one nor the other.'[3] But upon his return to Dublin, in late April 1817, he discovered that Mary was in serious distress and on 7 May he asked his brother James to sound Hunting Cap 'with respect to getting a few hundreds to pay the expense' of Mary's taking the waters at Clifton and also about lodging the boys with him at Derrynane.[4] It seems clear that Mary had hidden her illness from O'Connell while he was on circuit. He wrote to her a little later, 'You *never deceived* me save about your health and it now, I may say, corrodes my soul to think that you may still imagine you were doing me a kindness by concealing from me the exact state of your health.'[5]

Despite Hunting Cap's deafness to James's '*strong hints*' as to the 'few hundreds' (he was, however, willing to receive the boys at Derrynane), O'Connell took Mary to Clifton immediately. It was a characteristic O'Connell exercise. Mary was accompanied by Miss Gaghran, the governess, a maidservant and her five youngest children, and no sooner was she installed in lodgings than she set off to sample the delights of marketing in Bristol – it was her first experience of another country. 'Really', she told O'Connell on 12 June, 'the exertion I am obliged to make here is of infinite use to me. The quiet, still life I lead at home cannot be conducive to my health.'[6] Correspondingly, O'Connell and she had considered her moving to the south of France for the remainder of 1817. But in this scheme her health and the 'finishing' of her children may have been intermingled, for she now told him, 'If I continue to improve in health as I have since I came here, a journey to France will be unnecessary until the time arrives when it will be an advantage to my boys and girls to spend some time in France. Then, darling, you will be on the Bench and a *little* more your own master than you are at present.'[7]

Two months later the French excursion seemed likely to come about. Mary's health worsened again and her Clifton doctor recommended removal to Toulon or its neighbourhood – he was decidedly against Toulouse! Apparently this advice was accepted; on 11 August 1817 Mary spoke of her '*banishment* (if I may call it so)' as fixed, and canvassed such details as whether or not to take the family carriage to France.[8] But when O'Connell joined her at Clifton in late September, he found that 'Mary is daily recovering and has not, the doctor assures me, one single consumptive symptom.' France was no longer necessary; instead, the family would 'settle for the winter in a warm part of Devonshire'.[9] Whether they ever got farther south than Bath, where they re-established themselves during October, is unknown. So also is the date of their return to Ireland, although it must have been before 3 March 1818, when O'Connell wrote to Mary in Dublin from his first station on circuit, 'I am dying with anxiety to hear from you. I left you with a cough and such weather was never invented as we have had since.'[10]

No matter how he reasoned as to the necessity of Mary's absence, O'Connell could not, he had written on first leaving her in Clifton, shake off 'the sensation of loneliness'.[11] It certainly was, as she replied, 'a new thing to you to be at home without your family';[12] even the elder boys were now at boarding school. In his isolation, his irritated fancy went the length of jealousy of a remote connection, Lieutenant John O'Connell, whom Mary had met in Bristol. 'Laugh at me, darling', he wrote on 24 June 1817,

> it is what I deserve for being unhappy without any cause. Yet it will perhaps surprise you more when I tell you the absurdity of my reason. It was that in one of your letters you said he was very *respectful* and in another *very kind*. Now what train of thought was it that could put the word *respectful*? How could it be necessary to think of that! Thus, my own darling Mary, did I torture myself asking foolish questions – and then your consulting me about asking him to dine. Darling heart, you see what a very silly and foolish fellow your husband is, and indeed I am quite ashamed of my folly but could not get cured of it completely without thus exposing it to you.[13]

He threw himself into work – or rather work in unprecedented quantities was thrown at him, quite apart from the arrears which had built up while he was settling his wife in Clifton; these placed 'such a load on me as I certainly never before sustained.'[14] His debts goaded him forward; he claimed that he was getting through the O'Leary bills 'constantly and fast',[15] characteristically asserting that he would be so free of obligations by the following spring that '*even you* [Mary] could not be alarmed'.[16] Although the establishment of a second household in England must have greatly swelled the outgoings, O'Connell may actually have gained financially from his lonely state and the consequent accretions of time for professional labour.

There were perhaps some small compensations for the lamentable division of the family. O'Connell paid at least two, and more likely three, visits to England during 1817; and although these did nothing to raise his opinion of the English and positively enflamed his resentment of his own exclusion from Parliament, they also introduced him to a considerable number of leading public men and useful go-betweens. On quite another tack, his long separation from Mary called forth her most serene and happy tributes to him ever, as husband and father, and possibly as lover too. On 14 July 1817 she wrote from Clifton,

> in existence, I don't think there is such a husband and father as you are and always have been. Indeed, I think it quite impossible there could, and if the truest and tenderest affection can repay you, believe me that I feel and bear *it* for you. In truth, my own Dan, I am always at a loss for words to convey to you how I love and doat of you. Many and many a time I exclaim to myself, 'What a happy creature am I! How grateful should I be to Providence for bestowing on me such a husband!' and so indeed I am.[17]

A week later, she added,

> you can have no idea how constantly you are the subject of mine and my children's conversation . . . In your children's opinion and in mine there is not such another man in the world as you are. When a handsome man, a good husband or a good father are mentioned, Ellen and Kate look with such anxiety for my answer to their question, 'Mamma, sure he is not half so handsome or so good as my father?' My reply is just what they wish, and it speaks the real sentiments of my heart.[18]

O'Connell's confidence that he would work through his debts quickly proved quite unjustified. The spring of 1818 brought not the release from bondage which he had anticipated but fresh embarrassments. On 12 March 1818 Mary reported to him on circuit that 'a good many bank notices' had arrived; on 18 May he importuned a cousin who had delayed the repayment of £300, exclaiming that he was 'very grievously pressed for money this day . . . it is the actual want of the money makes me thus urge you.'[19] Like Mr Sowerby in *Framley Parsonage*, 'When he wanted to raise the wind, everything was so important; haste and superhuman efforts, and men running to and fro with blank acceptances in their hands, could alone stave off the crack of doom.'[20] A little over a year later O'Connell applied to his uncle, the General, in Paris to be relieved of interest payments on a borrowed £3600; he had already persuaded his brother James to lend him £800 from a trust which the General had set up for the young O'Connells; and he was soon to wangle £1700 from James and his other brother John from their interest in these moneys. The General, as he told O'Connell in strictest confidence, had stripped himself of all but £750 of his annual income in order to provide for his nephews' younger sons (including O'Connell's children). It was these savings which O'Connell was now attempting – with some success – to bleed. In a letter of 30 July 1819, written in French so that Mary could not read it, the General refused to forgo the interest on his £3600 because this would, to some extent, defeat the purpose of his own abnegation. But he offered to share with O'Connell 'the income [£750 p.a.] which I have reserved for myself if your situation demands the help of your friends'[21] – provided that O'Connell too made sacrifices. He might have spared his ink. Neither the £3600 nor any future interest on it was ever paid; and a plan which the poor General drew up for O'Connell's financial redemption made it all too clear that he had no notion of the magnitude of his nephew's debts. In desperate straits, O'Connell seems to have lost any lingering scruples over the despoiling of his own relations, from honourable elderly uncles down to babes-in-arms. Yet none ever broke with him, whatever the provocation: they wept, but they gave.

By this time O'Connell was beginning to be faced with the problem of his elder sons' careers. Two years before, on 3 August 1817, the headmaster of Clongowes Wood College, their boarding school, assessed the boys in terms remarkably similar to those employed by Dr Stapylton in relation to O'Connell and his brother at St Omer twenty-five years before:

> Of Maurice I have everything good to say. His improvement in classical knowledge has been very considerable. If *you* and we can form him to steady habits of application, we shall get him to do anything. God has given him very ample talents. Exertion and cultivation will make him a solid and conspicuous scholar. Of Morgan I cannot say so much. Less talented, he wants application which alone could supply for the deficiency. His dispositions are good; generous, bold and independent. If he had industry he would be no inconsiderable character.[22]

Unfortunately for himself perhaps, Maurice seemed tailor-made to follow in his father's footsteps, as lawyer and public man. But Morgan, like his dead uncle Maurice, seemed fit only for the army – that is, within the range of gentlemanly occupations. When however O'Connell applied to the General in 1819 to put Morgan 'into the French service' he was brusquely refused: this course, the General responded, was 'neither practical nor desirable';[23] he added (a hopeless recipe) that Morgan needed at least four or five years of close application to military studies if he wished to make the army his career. By now, O'Connell was well into the next stage of family concern: how on earth to settle seven children in the world.

# II

The staple of O'Connell's income remained the bar. His professional earnings probably exceeded £5000 per annum in the decade and a half 1816–29. True, his fee book suggests a lower figure. But the returns recorded there may well have excluded such highly profitable but peripherally legal work as elections and arbitrations. This would account for such a discrepancy as that presented in 1827 when his fee book registered his income at £4868 for the year but he himself observed on 4 December that 'my [legal] income is now a fine one, upwards of £7,000 a year'.[24] However careless his money dealings may have been, his money calculations were generally meticulous. Except in the management of his own affairs, he was a first-rate man of business.

Such prodigious earnings demanded prodigious labour. By 1822 O'Connell was working a sixteen- or seventeen-hour day, punctuated only by meals and his walk to and from the Four Courts. On 14 May of that year, he told Mary, then in France, '*My trade* goes on flourishingly. All the rest of the Bar are complaining but I never was doing so much. In your absence I have nothing to take up a moment of my time but law. I rise at half after four, breakfast at a ¼ after eight, dine at a quarter after five and go to bed between nine and ten.'[25] He had 'an alarm clock fixed between four and half after four';[26] he had also installed a shower bath which completed the awakening. Nor could he have generated his great volume of business – it must never be forgotten that he could still charge only junior's fees – if he had confined himself to his own circuit or circles. Increasingly, he accepted invitations to go 'special' on other circuits; and when a major case, with corresponding rewards, drew him to Galway, Wexford, Sligo or Armagh, he usually took additional local briefs to 'top and tail' his visit. It was of course also politically valuable to spread his knowledge of and influence in fresh fields. Correspondingly, he had to attract Protestant, including many politically hostile Protestant, clients in order to earn so largely. The bulk of the remunerative civil briefs, in commercial, trust, succession, land title and crim. con. suits, derived from the Ascendancy, those with the lion's share of the nation's property, wealth and leisure. Once O'Connell's reputation was established, Irish Protestants seem to have had no hesitation in employing him in such cases. He was of course practically excluded from crown, corporation and specifically 'Orange' business; but otherwise his professional capability was taken to outweigh his offensive or dangerous public conduct. When Peel, in his celebrated reply to a denigrator of O'Connell as a 'low, broguing fellow', declared that there was no one whom he would prefer as counsel in a case in which he had heavy interest, he was probably repeating an opinion common in the class which he supported during his Irish days.

Twenty years' unremitting practice of the law had also shaped O'Connell's mental habits and forensic patterns. It is hardly too much to say that it gives the key to his style of politics. Obviously, the capacities to work closely for long hours, to 'get up' subjects (or rather as much of them as the case demanded) at great speed, to decide instaneously which line of action to adopt and to marshal the appropriate words and arguments as if by second nature, constituted a politician's no less than a barrister's stock in trade. At a deeper level, the lawyer's ineluctable concern with the correctness of forms and formulae, with legal effects rather than moral stances or satisfactions, was already engrained in O'Connell's politics. So also was the advocate's extravagance in framing claims combined with moderation in settling for returns; opening pleas were tactical devices and by no means irreducible demands. Similarly, O'Connell's was a 'verdict mentality', so to say. In one special sense, his politics were passive. He was inured to adverse or otherwise unpleasing decisions being handed down by an exterior authority; only momentarily would these depress or irritate him. There were always other cases, other means. This strange amalgam of acquiesence and resilience, of cutting losses and planning their recoupment – the professional's carapace hardened by the years of practice – was the very stamp of his political behaviour.

O'Connell had also been a landed proprietor since 1809. It was not a role which brought him much satisfaction or reward at first. Perforce, he was an absentee; he was also soon overtaken by agrarian hard times. After 1815 agricultural prices, and *pari passu* rents, fell and remained depressed. His Uncle Daniel was probably close to the mark when he wrote to O'Connell in 1819, 'The income from your lands which was more than £2,000 has presumably fallen to £1,500',[27] and there was worse to come in the immediately succeeding seasons. Moreover, O'Connell seems to have regarded the returns from rents almost as a species of pin money. A great deal of it was earmarked to pay small pensions to former servants or dependants, or the interest on the numerous small debts which he ran up in Kerry. 'Your income by lands', his brother James told him in 1822, the blackest year of all, 'is so cut up by interest of money, annuities to poor relations and to fosterers that, in the best of times, you have but little *to actually touch*.'[28]

O'Connell was a 'traditional' Irish landlord, easy-going, negligent and unimproving. He certainly set his economic rationalism aside when it came to his own fields and tenants. Instead, he followed, if only from habit or as the line of least resistance, a latter-day form of the old clan system, whereby the maintenance of customary positions within the whole complex was placed well ahead of the maximization of profits for anyone. The local repute and responsibility of the O'Connells, as Catholic semi-gentry for several generations, deepened the tribal-feudal character of the relationship with the tenantry. In this regard, as in many others, O'Connell's stance and outlook strikingly resembled Walter Scott's. Typically, O'Connell selected friends or relatives to act as his land agents. His first steward proper, his cousin Myles McSwiney, was amiable but inefficient. He also 'borrowed' heavily from the collected rents, and O'Connell was very lucky to recoup the arrears of several years in 1820 and 1821 when McSwiney received the dubious windfalls of a part in a local road contract and a share in a smuggled cargo of tobacco. Ever the candid friend, James told O'Connell, 'You are yourself much to blame [for McSwiney's poor stewardship] in not having devoted a few hours once a year when you came to Iveragh to look into your affairs.'[29] It was also typical of O'Connell to have delayed the collection of rents in 1820 by his negligence in dealing with requests to set the level of abatements, and to have left it to his brother to announce the change himself when he decided that James should replace McSwiney in 1821. In this last case, however, James rebelled, writing to O'Connell on 19 April 1821, 'I perceive you never said a word to him about your taking your affairs out of his hands, and, until you call on him *either by letter or otherwise* to hand me over his books, I cannot think of calling for them. Did I do so, the entire odium of removing him would be thrown on me which you must admit is not fair or reasonable.'[30]

The 1821 harvest and low prices of 1819–21 brought falling rents and eventually agrarian disturbances in their train. It was James who bore the brunt of O'Connell's proprietorial difficulties. There is no direct evidence on O'Connell's reaction to the sudden spread of 'swearing in' and secret societies (indifferently referred to as Whiteboys and Rockites at the time) in Iveragh towards the end of 1821. But we can confidently infer his wholehearted opposition from his proposal of January 1822 to set up a yeomanry corps of his own to maintain order in the barony. Hunting Cap opposed his nephew's scheme as both unnecessary and likely 'to protect and cover the smuggling of tobacco ... a circumstance which speedily would be represented to Government and would of course bring a blemish on you'.[31] James agreed, adding scornfully, 'who in the name of God were *to compose it*?'[32] James did however ask O'Connell to procure 'a military party' to pacify the district: '*every peasant in the Barony of Iveragh is a Whiteboy*', he told him on 18 January 1822. '*Those nightly legislators* profess great respect for the O'Connell family [but] I hope soon to be able to *prove* to some of the leaders by lodging them in Tralee jail, how well I wish them.'[33]

O'Connell neglected even to reply to this appeal, and James indignantly complained that he seemed 'quite indifferent' to the risk which James ran in taking up residence in the centre of his brother's property and assisting in putting down the foremost of the 'atrocious blood-thirsty rabble who have combined against everything that is respectable in the country'. James even 'calculate[d] on the probability' of assassination. This may have been no more than a characteristic gloomy and irritable flourish, for in the same breath he preened himself upon his achievement in stamping out 'the *mania of Whiteboyism*' in Iveragh.[34] In fact, despite the rhetoric of stern repression which he employed, James adopted, successfully, a conciliatory policy, offering a general amnesty through 'the Chapels' in return for the abandonment of conspiracies, and expressing his private relief at the escape of some of those whom he had set out to apprehend.

Had O'Connell, by default at least, abandoned James to his fate in Kerry? He had certainly failed to provide even moral support. But he might well have claimed, in mitigation, such a lifelong knowledge of the neighbourhood and its inhabitants (James often specified particular farmers, labourers and their sons in his reports) as to feel no real alarm. He cannot be acquitted of farming out his work and responsibilities as a landlord, and giving only the light of a genial presence on rare occasions in return for rents. But, even with James as agent, he and his tenantry were far from being in the sort of adversary or confrontationist relationship prescribed by the new political economy. Doubtless, he was not in the least surprised at the ultimate accommodation of abatement on either side, acquiescence in arrears of rent and further huckstering as to what the distressed smallholders really could afford to pay. While one form of Irish landlordism headed for guerilla war in 1822, another, exemplified by the O'Connells, generated violence of words and postures rather than blood or change.

## III

By the spring of 1822 O'Connell's affairs were in so desperate a state that his home in Dublin was broken up in an effort to economize seriously at last. Initially, he hoped to rent his house in Merrion Square for at least £365 per annum, as well as sell off his carriage and horses; the letting failed, but at least the establishment was reduced. It may well have been 'the dreadful fall in the times' (as he termed the drying up of rents) which proved the last straw and precipitated O'Connell's decision, for as early as 11 March 1822 he sent instructions to Mary to bargain for her passage and those of her five youngest children and servants to Bordeaux. Possibly the result dismayed him, as he consulted James a little later about their moving to Tralee instead. James's reply was both sour and trenchant.

> Whether you will better your situation much by taking J[ames] Connor's house and fixing yourself in Tralee where *you must keep an open house for all your family*, I will not attempt to decide but I trust you have made your entire family acquainted with your real situation. If they and you are serious in wishing to conform yourselves to your embarrassed circumstances, the South of France would in my opinion be the place to fix them. However of this ye are the best judges.[35]

Even O'Connell seems to have resented candour of this exceptional degree, and a temporary coolness sprang up between the brothers. James was replaced, as O'Connell's agent, by John Primrose, junior, and for a time sneered at as closefisted in O'Connell's correspondence with his wife.

In the end, however, the O'Connells did opt for removal to the south of France, and the hire of a small vessel to take the entire company direct from Dublin to Bordeaux. Meanwhile, O'Connell was 'hoarding gold' to frank the expedition, and pointing to silver linings which few but he could have discerned. He assured Mary that they would be 'splendidly independent' if, as now seemed 'highly likely', they could clear their debts altogether before the 'old gentleman' died.[36] He admitted to his daughter Kate that their parting was 'a cruel thing', but added immediately that 'We must in these dreadful times practise economy', and that she and her sisters would gain immeasurable polish during their exile. 'I expect to join you', he concluded, 'in the vintage which is the gayest time of the year, and I flatter myself that the time will not be the less gay for the arrival of your father.'[37]

Before Mary departed for the Continent, however, the strain of money-raising and of the impending separation told suddenly upon O'Connell. The financial tight-rope which he had left Mary to walk in Dublin became ever more dangerous; on 2 or 3 April 1822 she paid a bill to Hickson earlier than he had intended, with disastrous consequences for his self-devised credit 'system'; he despatched (his own later terms) a 'cruel and ferocious letter ... a barbarous one unbecoming a gentleman or a Christian'[38] and then, horror-struck, followed it immediately with a plea for mercy. Mary proved unresentful, and O'Connell poured forth his relief and gratitude. 'If you had a mind, my darling heart's love,' he wrote on 8 April, 'to wring your husband's very soul you would not have done it more effectually than by writing the sweet, gentle, uncomplaining letter I got from you last night ... I find that my own darling thinks she was wrong merely because her husband unjustly accused her.' We can gauge the near-hopelessness of his pecuniary entanglements (as well as of Mary's difficulties as financial agent) by the conclusion of this letter of penitence.

> I perceive by a letter I got last night from James Sugrue that Dr Wilson's bill lies over unpaid. Let it be so, darling, for a few days longer. You have therefore got from me in half-notes between you and James Sugrue £200 and he has got £100 from Roger [O'Connell's clerk] so that, as you gave him the other £50, you will have only to add £12.10.0 to it. Then, giving your mother £15 you will still have £172.10.0 in hands. Take out of that £42.10.0 for house expenses, it will leave you £130 out of which you will, before this reaches you, pay tomorrow £40 – Eyre's bill – and the day you get this £50 Higgins' bill and you will have £40 towards meeting the bills due on Thursday. I believe my letter of yesterday was erroneous in supposing that Eyre's £40 would not be due until Wednesday. I hope this error will not occasion a protest, as in the list I sent I marked down a £40 bill as due the 9th. I will, please God, send you a banker's bill for at least £200. The bills which are to be paid are 9th £40 to Eyre, 10th £50 to Higgins, 11th, £58 *with interest* to Mr Mahon – same day, 11th, £138.10.0 to Dr Wilson, a *fresh* bill not the one already due, 15th £69.19.0 to Roose, 25th £75 Clongowes Wood payable, I think, to Elliot, 28th £50 to Cooper.[39]

On 2 May 1822 Mary, six of her seven children (Morgan accompanied them as protector) and two maidservants sailed from Dublin for Bordeaux. O'Connell was grief-stricken as he moved about the empty house; even the remaining servants had departed, although he partly reconstituted the establishment later on. In his remorse, he cried out, 'My love, do you not now reproach that loose and profligate waste of money to many and many an ungrateful and undeserving object which makes it necessary for us to separate. No, my love, you do not reproach it but my own heart does, and the misery I now endure is nothing but the punishment I deserve.' As the days passed without word from Bordeaux, he began to fear a shipwreck. 'What a vile wretch [I am]!', he exclaimed on 18 May. 'It was for my own follies and idle gratifications that I made it necessary to separate from you and my children.'[40] Three weeks passed before he heard of their safe arrival, and a fortnight more before Mary could try to still his self-accusations. 'My own, own Dan, do not fret . . .', she wrote from Bordeaux,

> You are, heart, much more religious than your Mary and from the moment it was deemed necessary for me to come with my family to France, I put on the resolution to bear it like a Christian. Do not, my own love, make me unhappy by those reproaches you cast upon yourself . . . You never deserved any from me. You have been the best and most beloved of husbands and you will continue such to the last hour of my life.[41]

It was true, as his next letter showed, that O'Connell had become more 'religious' than the remainder of his family. Whether his piety had been growing since 1816 or (more likely) developed further with his troubles, he might fairly have been described as a *devôt* by 1822. He had subjected himself to a regular spiritual director, Rev. Patrick Coleman, whose charming spiritual principle '*beaucoup de piété, beaucoup de gaieté*'[42] he tried to fulfil by being quiet, cheerful and conscientious in adversity. But he also 'practised' his Catholicism with unusual rigour. Persistently, he urged weekly, or at least monthly, communion upon Mary and his elder children when they were abroad; incessantly he fretted over Maurice's negligent attitude towards the sacraments. A long-range battle between him and his wife over his unremitting Lenten fasts ended only when he told her bluntly,

> you say I gratify you in everything else, and are you not therefore bound in common *honesty* to admit I would have great pleasure to gratify in that particular also if I had not that which you will pardon me for calling a higher duty, namely, my obedience to the Church? . . . surely, dearest, I have a *command* to fast if I am able to do it . . .[43]

He was warm in supporting the Catholic cause in current theological controversy and eager in pressing the case for miracles, supposedly flowing from the intercession of the pious Prince Hohenlohe, in 1823. Although he never ceased to revile them as despots, he even found merit in the French Bourbons' support of religion:

> With such a people [as the French] nothing will do but the strong government of the Bourbons, and while the Bourbon government is repressing their political tendency to crime they are also fortunately and, I hope providentially, engaged in the restoration of that pure Catholic worship which alone contained genuine Christianity. The churches will soon be all filled with zealous and active clergy . . .[44]

The voluminous correspondence between O'Connell and his wife during 1822–4 also lifts the curtain on his literary taste in middle life. His circuit letters over many years make it clear that he kept up well with the current quarterlies and monthly magazines, as well as the virtually mandatory law reports and daily papers. But, in the early 1820s at least, Scott's novels were his leading pleasure. Fortunately, they were being published with amazing frequency. O'Connell snapped each up as it appeared, and even his iron regime fell to pieces until he had read it all; he stayed up all one night to finish *Peveril of the Peak*, at 4.45 a.m. Scott struck many chords – sentimental, romantic, costume-historical – in O'Connell; besides he was, to contemporaries, the absolute master of the adventure story. O'Connell also read Byron extensively, even if he agreed with the public at large that his current poetic dramas were a failure. But Moore was his chief delight. 'Tell Ellen', he wrote on 27 December 1822, 'that Moore's *Loves of the Angels* is come out . . . It is short, a mere trifle for such a poet, but exquisitely sweet and not stained with a single indelicate thought . . . In spite of the *Edinburgh Review* Moore is the very prince of poets.' In this case, however, O'Connell had been softened by Moore's description of a separated wife and husband which seemed to him to presage love's renewal.

*All this they bear but not the less*
*Have moments rich in happiness*
*Blest meetings after many a day*
*Of widowhood past far away*
*When the loved fair again is seen.*[45]

The first nine months of the O'Connells' sojourn on the Continent created no tension between Mary and O'Connell. He was however uneasy when they settled initially at Pau, which he supposed, correctly, would prove dry and dusty in the summer; and when he joined his family there on 18 September 1822, he arranged their removal to Tours, where considerable colonies of English and Irish economic refugees, like themselves, resided and where competent masters for the children could be had. Three weeks in Pau were quite enough to revive O'Connell's Francophobia – 'My opinion of France and Frenchmen is not raised by a near inspection.'[46] This animus even increased in violence after his return to Ireland. 'Oh how I hate France', he wrote from Dublin on 6 March 1823, 'I hate it in all moods and tenses, past, present and to come.'[47] Part of his distaste derived from the fact that France was comparatively distant and inaccessible: already it was almost five months since he had last seen his family. He now wished them to remove to the south of England – Exeter was the tentative choice of place – which he could visit more cheaply and more often. 'I am all alive to having you so much nearer me', he went on, 'I was even thinking of getting a furnished house in Kerry, but certainly Devonshire is much better. It is warm and genial too in winter and it would be a seasoning of you on your way home.'[48]

Initially O'Connell planned to meet Mary's party in Paris in August 1823, spend two or three weeks sightseeing there (earlier he had sketched in a possible Italian tour – so much for the Continent as a desperate measure of economy!) and finally lead everyone to Exeter. But when France intervened militarily in Spain, and war with Britain seemed a possibility, he took alarm and pressed for an earlier and more precipitate departure. By the beginning of May 1823 he had – with the utmost difficulty – gathered enough money for the journeys, fixed Paris for the rendezvous about the 20th of that month, rearranged his case-list and even booked his passage on the packet.

It was at this stage that things began to awry between O'Connell and his wife. Mary refused to uproot herself abruptly, and, while still maintaining his ritualistic obeisance to her better judgment, O'Connell responded with a quite uncharacteristic display of malice and self-pity. His reply of 22/3 May 1823 included a reference to a woman whose 'husband should perceive by a thousand little attentions and those manners which sweeten life that his wife was rendered the better woman by embracing a better religion [Catholicism]', and concluded, 'I wish my girls to read more books than you do, sweetest.'[49] Mary was acutely sensitive to criticism, especially of her social origins and education, and a long absence, among the emigrés, had rendered her more peremptory, more ambitious for her children and perhaps also more extravagant. As early as 20 April 1823 she had rejected a proposal from O'Connell, doubtless designed to reduce fresh expenditure, in this decisive, not to say uncivil, manner: 'Now, love, to answer you on the subject of Morgan's becoming an attorney. I totally and entirely disapprove of it. It is a profession I never wished for any son of mine.'[50] She got her way: Morgan was soon launched (through the General's influence) upon the expensive career of Austrian cavalry officer. As was to be expected with her current disposition, Mary fiercely resented O'Connell's letter of 22/3 May. Her reply has not survived, but we can guess its tenor from his complaint of its 'air of coldness and . . . vexation'. He affected surprise that Mary was 'angry with me about what I said of my girls' reading as if I had meant to offend . . . Forgive me, darling, I will avoid such topics in future. How bitterly do I regret that I placed myself in a situation to be compelled to separate from my family.'[51]

Not that he had many honeyed words for the remainder of his family about this time. His sole companion, Maurice, was a daily irritation, as both vacuous and idle. John (his erstwhile '*great great* favourite') 'I perceive by your letter, is turning out badly . . . I work fifteen or sixteen hours out of the 24. I . . . only ask him to work 5 or 6.'[52] 'Even my Kate I am sometimes jealous of. My Betsey never loved her father much and I scolded my Nell so much about growing fat that I suppose she resents it.'[53] 'I wish Kate would write to me but no, love, leave them all in that respect to themselves.' The truth was probably, as he said himself, that he needed pity: 'so long separated from all my heart holds dear . . . I feel that weariness of the heart which the Swiss experience when they think of their fond home.'[54] Mary was merciful. Her letter of 12 June told him that he was in want of '*petting*'; and at that he melted. It was not the end of hurtful exchanges. Mary continued to see slights – generally of a social nature – in various later comments or proposals; and she was to fall into an acute fit of jealousy of Miss Gaghran, the girls' former governess whom she had always disliked, before the year ended. None the less, the worst was over; and on 13 July 1823 the old absurdly joyous, irresponsible and elastic O'Connell reappeared when he wrote of their impending reunion,

> I am excessively anxious that my own girls should see Paris thoroughly. I will, please God, spend three weeks there with you, myself. We will visit Versailles, St Cloud, etc. In short I will endeavour to make you all as happy as I possibly can. I anticipate with pleasure the joy of being with you to see that proud but filthy capital.[55]

The late spring and early summer of 1823 probably marked the nadir of the marriage. Perhaps menopausal depression was in part to blame; Mary was in her forty-fifth year and O'Connell in his forty-eighth. But beyond that each was grievously harassed and hardened by lonely cares. After six months apart, their traffic had begun to lose the smoothness of its flow, to miss or distort its customary signals. It seems to have been the prospect of coming together once again, however briefly, which suddenly cleared the paths.

## IV

O'Connell found it unexpectedly difficult to join Mary in Paris. During 1822 he had regularly reported to her his success in reducing the load of bills and bonds, and called on her for reciprocal economy. But he was ominously silent about money for most of 1823. In fact, the year probably marked the nadir of his pecuniary as well as his marital affairs. At the beginning of September 1823 he still apparently needed £2000 cash to pay for his own journey to and the removal of his family from Paris and their re-establishment in England, and his sole hope, James, could be induced to join him in a new bond only to the extent of £1500. James had been 'shocked to perceive the state of embarrassment you are in'[56] – imprisonment for debt and the consequent interruption of his practice were looming on the horizon – and was correspondingly caustic about 'the plan of economy adopted by you with respect to your family . . . In the course of a few months they move from Dublin to Pau, from that to Tours, now they are in the most expensive part of Paris and will wind up by fixing their residence in England, the dearest country in Europe to live in.'[57] None the less, O'Connell continued to pursue James for the additional £500, for on 11 September 1823 James wrote again, 'I this evening received your voluminous letter of the 9th inst. and now, for *the third and last time, most solemnly declare* I will not give you the small sum I have in the Funds.' James was unusually gentle with O'Connell, naming him 'ever . . . a most affectionate brother' of whom his family had every reason to be proud, and acknowledging that nothing 'but the greatest distress' would have induced him to persist in his supplication. But he pointed out that the security which O'Connell offered was illusory and that there had never been a 'case of a man who [had] ruined and dissipated his own and his children's property, having too scrupulous a regard' for another's.[58]

Still O'Connell kept up his appeal, and five days later James capitulated with bitter self-reproach. 'I will join you', he wrote on 16 September,

> *in another bond* for the remaining £500 but I have *on my knees bound myself by an oath, during the rest of my life never again to join you in bill, bond or note . . . and, further, I have solemnly sworn on my knees never to give you in any one year during my life any sum of money exceeding twenty*

*pounds. This oath I have taken without any evasion, equivocation or mental reservation.*[59]

With this, O'Connell flung aside all cares. 'I have the happiness to tell you', he wrote gaily to Mary from Cork next day, 'that I have made satisfactory arrangements which will permit me to leave this either this evening or tomorrow morning at farthest before day. My heart is light and my spirits revived . . . Darling, all is well.'[60] It was almost enough to make one fall in love with ruin.

During October 1823 O'Connell settled his family in Southampton, not Exeter, probably to enable Maurice, who had joined Mary and was now entered at the Temple, to eat his dinners with comparative ease. For a time after her husband's return to Dublin, Mary thought that she was pregnant, and O'Connell expressed 'most painful disappointment' when he learned on 30 November that this was not so. Extraordinary as it may seem in a man almost sinking beneath the weight of a numerous and most costly family, the disappointment appears to have been heartfelt. More than once over the past five years, he had grieved that Mary was not expecting another child. Money was of course a more grievous worry than ever after his latest expedition. His rents were being paid again and in four weeks in November he earned an unprecedented £760. But his debts were still immense – '*at least* twenty thousand pounds', James estimated on 19 November. Maurice, already extravagant, especially in his tailor's bills, would henceforth cost even more; and a running battle between Denys Scully and O'Connell during the remainder of 1823 for the repayment of even half of the £2000 which O'Connell had borrowed in 1815 upon the faithful promise that it would be refunded within six months may be amusing for the ingenuity of O'Connell's evasions, but must – or at any rate should – also have been extremely wearing and embarrassing for the contestants. The rector of Clongowes attempted a similar, though more polite, dunning of O'Connell on account of the fees, not of O'Connell's own sons, but of two boys whose father had befriended Morgan in Columbia, and whose school charges O'Connell had grandly, impulsively, taken on himself to pay! His letters to Mary in Southampton were however more concerned with spiritual than financial anxieties – with, for example, injunctions to guard her daughters against 'mixed' marriages and to ensure that all received communion together on Christmas Day.

O'Connell's visit to his family for the New Year proved all too successful. Ardent exchanges followed between Mary and himself, and his children were showered with all his former language of xtravagant affection. But this made the fresh parting on 15 January 824 seem all the more painful and his daily round in Dublin all the nore solitary and cheerless. 'How monotonous my life is', he wrote on 7 January,

> The history of one day is the story of all. I rose today at soon after five. I worked till a quarter after eight by the town [clock]. Then breakfast . . . Working then till a quarter before eleven. Then to court. There until near four . . . At four on my way home call at Milliken's [stationers], read the morning papers *for nothing*, then home. Strip off my *day dress*, put on night-shirt, morning gown, *old* wig and so work until a quarter after five by the town. Then dine. In my study again before half after six . . . and so work till this hour, half after nine. Thus in one day you have the history of the entire.[61]

Within a few days his resolution broke and he suddenly proposed that Mary and the children should settle in Killarney, where at least he ould visit them more often and without additional travelling costs or he loss of professional income. He had evidently toyed with some uch idea in the preceding November, for James had told him that quartering his family at Derrynane was out of the question: Hunting Cap was much too enfeebled to bear noise or bustle.

Mary found 'many objections' to the new scheme. First, 'the chiefest bar', her health would not stand the Kerry climate; Dublin was the only place in Ireland where she could be well 'for a long period'. Secondly, the girls would suffer if they were thrust, impoverished, into he society of an Irish country town; 'they should not appear in Ireland intil they can do so as your daughters ought.' Next, 'there would be ittle saving . . . There would be an eternal *relay* of *cousins*.' Finally, O'Connell had 'a respectability to keep up . . . The world is unkind, and *they* would delight to think your embarrassments were such as to oblige you to send your family to live separate from you in the same Kingdom with you, whereas the delicacy of my health and the necessity of having Maurice in England for a few years is a sufficient eason for our living here.'[62] O'Connell bowed to this powerful easoning, but meanwhile James had given his *nihil obstat* to a fresh plan, the return of the family to *Dublin*; and Mary (who had since been ravaged by her recollection of 'the melancholy strain' of O'Connell's letter of May 1823 'on the subject of my *then* objecting to quit' Tours)[63] now changed her mind and joyfully agreed to join O'Connell in their home once more. Dislike of England where as 'an Irish Catholic' she felt often snubbed or patronized may have helped to ilt the balance. But the basic reasons for her turnabout were the futility of their current mode of retrenchment and the prospect of an end at last to 'the bitterness of separation'.[64] Some sense of virtue was kept alive by her resolve to dismiss her housekeeper, reduce her establishment to four servants and forgo horses and a carriage upon her return.

It was now O'Connell's turn to waver and consider Mary's spending a further fifteen months or so in England (this time at Windsor) in the name of complete financial recovery. But his 'prudence' was of the crumbling kind, and even he must occasionally have realized that the debtless state would always be a mirage for the O'Connells. His first reaction to his wife's decision proved to be the lasting one: 'never was blooming bride so welcome to her husband's arms as my own own Mary [will be] to mine.'[65] So in May 1824 the entire entourage returned to the home which they had left two years before. O'Connell would probably have been better off had they simply stayed at home, and the economies adopted in 1824 could have been made quite as easily in 1822. But it had ever been the O'Connells' way to live dramatically; they would not have been comfortable walking except on stilts.

## V

Hunting Cap had never ceased to be a factor in O'Connell's calculations. On 24 January 1823 he confessed to Mary that he had always counted on 'Uncle Maurice's succession as the means of paying off, and I went in debt on that speculation';[66] earlier he had prayed to be delivered from the 'great sin' of 'look[ing] to his death as a desirable event'.[67] The end came at last on 10 February 1825, with Hunting Cap enduring his long final illness with his customary dignity and fortitude, even composing his own epitaph 'least [*sic*] it be too fulsome'. Significantly, the epitaph declared that 'the chief ambition of his long and Prosperous life was to elevate an Ancient Family from unmerited and Unjust Oppression'.[68] His nephew might well have liked to appropriate these words for his own tombstone later on.

Apart from his landed property, Hunting Cap left £52,000 in cash, mortgages, overdue rents and other assets; and after some £6000 of rent arrears have been 'forgiven' at James's suggestion, each of the three brothers among whom the personalty had been equally divided received about £15,000. The land bequeathed to O'Connell (mostly as a life interest) raised his total rental income to £4000 per annum. Had he been the sole or principal heir, as Hunting Cap had originally intended, he would have been some £20–30,000 better off in cash, with the probable addition of more rental property. None the less he was very well endowed, and General O'Connell was at first confident that, having received over £20,000 recently from his two uncles and with an income of almost £10,000 a year (his profession averaging £6000 net), his nephew could not only clear his debts entirely but also put by 'with ease' £5000 annually for his children's benefit.

O'Connell also felt an initial surge of affluence. Immediately after the funeral, he set off for London to support a parliamentary bid for Emancipation, and remained there for three and a half months at a cost of 'upwards of £3000' in expenses and lost legal fees. (Just as the accident of O'Connell's solitary state in Dublin during 1823 and 1824 had enabled him to concentrate upon his supreme political work, the building of the Catholic Association, so the accident of Hunting Cap's death at that particular juncture enabled him to gain priceless direct political experience of Westminster and Whitehall.) In the teeth of James's warnings, he set about greatly enlarging and altering Derrynane which he had also inherited, thus releasing a fresh torrent of expenditure. He fixed his daughter Ellen's dowry at £5000, spread money about on charities and even bought a Kerry hooker to carry fish and other local produce by sea to his home in Dublin.

The first sign that he had overstretched himself appeared on his return from London. Towards the end of a letter which opened in his best reformed-Scrooge style – 'Let everything be snug and warm [at Derrynane] . . . I should delight to spend my Christmas there in old Iveragh festivity. Give us as many bedrooms as you can and, above all things, an excellent barrack room' – he asked, 'Have you made any sales of my stock or have the tenants sold any? I want money very, very much.'[69] Although the brothers made their final settlement of Hunting Cap's estate on 27 August 1825, this was followed by still more clamorous demands on Primrose; O'Connell even told him, on 29 October, to threaten tenants who were grossly in arrears with the non-renewal of their leases. Meanwhile, Mary had been left behind at Derrynane after the summer vacation of 1825 partly to act as quasi-overseer of building, but mostly as a measure of economy. 'Nobody need have a cold at Derrynane', her husband now informed her, 'unless *they* earn it for themselves.' He made it clear to her that they were deep in financial trouble once again. 'I am quite sick of being in debt', he wrote on 1 November, 'if I had but one or two years of strict economy I would be entirely out of debt and be able to pay Kate's fortune *on demand* . . . Only *help* me, darling, to get out of debt and then you will, as you always did, command every shilling I have in the world.'[70] The reference to Kate's dowry touched a tender spot. Mary had, as she owned on 4 December 1825, 'that feeling about me (it is pride I believe) . . . [that] I brought you no *fortune*';[71] she was, correspondingly, both proud of Ellen's £5000 and jealous of the precedent for her second daughter's sake. Mary was no romantic when it came to her daughters' marriages. 'Ellen has a good deal of good sense', she had written while betrothal negotiations were being conducted on her behalf earlier in the year, 'and though she likes Mr [Christopher] F[itz-Simon, whom she married soon after], should anything occur to put a stop to the business, she would be quite satisfied to accede to your wishes and mine.'[72] With such a maternal disposition, Mary was deeply concerned lest Kate's marriage-chances should be injured by O'Connell's renewed impecuniosity. 'You married Ellen at nineteen', she told him on 2 December 1825, 'and *why* should you not marry Kate at least as early? I am [?sorry] you were not able to reserve *her* fortune for I feel quite sure you will be soon called upon.'[73] Doubtless this concern explains Mary's willingness to be immured in Derrynane for half the year; in urging economy, O'Connell repeatedly dangled before her the carrot of accumulating Kate's dowry. Meanwhile the fending off of Scully even still continued: on 2 November 1825 O'Connell proposed a final series of five monthly notes to clear the balance of their 'account'!

Now that the *deus ex machina* of his inheritance from Hunting Cap had come and gone, he was more dependent than ever upon keeping up his professional earnings. This became difficult after 1824 as his political standing and commitments grew rapidly – to say nothing of the donations, subscriptions and free services expected of him as a leading public man. In fact, according to his fee book (this, as has been said, almost certainly excluded some of his legal earnings), his average annual income at the bar fell from £5286 in 1822–4 to £4850 in 1826–8. But the maintenance of so high an annual average in the second triennium – and the amount was rising significantly again year by year from 1825 to 1828 – probably represented a considerable increase in 'real productivity', for the time and energy which O'Connell could devote to law had been much reduced.

In the mid- and late-1820s he was at the zenith of his powers, with as much business and as high fees on offer as any junior counsel could possibly manage or command. The mature O'Connell was no Rupert of the courts – except when the bold dash seemed the safest tactic – but a painstaking and longheaded strategist. D. O. Madden, who was far from favourably disposed, reckoned that in an era when the Munster circuit was thronged with brilliant counsel,

> O'Connell ranked first among the first. His qualities as a professional have never, perhaps, been sufficiently noticed. Caution in conducting a case was his most prominent characteristic. He affected to be careless, but a more wary advocate never stood in a Court of Justice. Perhaps no great advocate ever had the same relish for the legal profession. O'Connell hunted down a case with the gusto of a Kerry fox-hunter in pursuit of Reynard.[74]

Another appraiser of the contemporary bar, J. R. O'Flanagan, considered his supreme quality to be 'oblivion of himself . . . he forgot everything around him, and thought only of bringing off his client victorious. No lust for oratorical display ever tempted him to make a speech dangerous to the party by whom he was retained . . . He was *par excellence* the safest advocate ever trusted with a case.'[75] O'Flanagan went on to compare him in terms of intellect, oratory and legal knowledge with all the other foremost barristers of his day, English as well as Irish, and while he judged some one of them to be his superior in each particular quality, he believed that none could match O'Connell in terms of their effective combination. But this was a precarious form of supremacy, when it came to income. As James kept reminding O'Connell in the 1820s, were he to die, or even to fall ill or suffer an accident or be arrested for debt, the flow of money would cease instantly, with his family left virtually resourceless. Even O'Connell eventually worried about some such catastrophe. He had reason to. On 5 May 1822, the 'father' of the Munster bar, the hero of scores of stories of mess wit and courtroom repartee, Jerry Keller, died suddenly, and penniless. 'He has left his family in dire distress . . .', O'Connell told Mary. 'I hope and trust the Bar will do something for them. I stirred the matter as much as I could this day in the Hall [of the Four Courts]. His children are real objects of compassion.'[76]

Perhaps, after all, happy families really are all the same in one particular sense – that their 'pattern' remains constant. From the start O'Connell intended the renovation of Derrynane to lead to domestic economizing. If Mary and the children still with her lived quietly, out of Dublin, for half the year, the savings should be considerable. Thus O'Connell wrote on 18 March 1826, 'All our buildings [at Derrynane] are going on gaily . . . I hope I will be able to prevail on my daughters to come down very, very early next summer. It would be a great object to me to get rid of £1000 of my debts during the next two terms.'[77] But the venture proved as counter-productive as the family's residence overseas. In the autumn of 1826 O'Connell, in reply to a request for money from Ellen's husband (presumably an instalment of her dowry was overdue), pleaded the building costs as a reason for his inability to comply. A year later he confessed to Mary, 'I laid out a foolish deal of money at Derrynane to practise the economy which we are now suffering under.'[78]

Suffering they certainly were. As before, O'Connell was driven to the ultimate desperate device of trying to get his hands upon his children's money. This time James refused to give him access to a new trust which the General had set up in 1823 for the benefit of O'Connell's younger sons. It would be, James declared, 'a breach of the most solemn promise I made our uncle'.[79] As in 1822–4, O'Connell repeatedly execrated his own folly and extravagance which were leading once more to prolonged – though much lesser – separations from Mary while she rusticated in Kerry. 'Sweetest love', he wrote to her from Dublin on 4 December 1827, when she was in her sixth consecutive month at Derrynane, 'I am most anxious to be with you and yet my affairs are so deranged that I do not know what to do.'[80] Four days later, he unwittingly summed up much of the dark side of their marriage in a passage which, for its pursuit of the will-o'-the-wisp, solvency, could have been penned (mutatis mutandis) any time over the past twenty years.

> How bitterly do I regret that I was not sooner more vigilant and attentive. There is in fact but one resource and that is strict and unremitting economy . . . I have borrowed much money since I came up [to Dublin in October] and so cleared my way for the present, and I am now labouring to make provision for the money so borrowed. What I want is to keep *all* my income for that purpose. One or, at the utmost, two years of my present economy would clear off all my debts and accumulate Kate's fortune. My duty would *then* be performed because all the rest would be easy. But, darling, why should I tease you with these croakings and yet into what bosom should I pour my sorrows but yours? To whom should I look for comfort, consolation and assistance but to you?[81]

But if their difficulties seemed perpetual, so did their solace. In 1825, in his fiftieth year, O'Connell told Mary, 'when you do condescend to write to me in terms of love you cannot imagine what *a drink of honey* these tender expressions are to me . . . but I have come to a time of life when it is not [?possible] that I should have a woman's love'.[82] She replied simply, as usual. 'Oh Dan, it is impossible for me to give you the smallest notion how beloved you are by me. Why should you speak of your age. . . ? I am for a woman much older.'[83]

*CHAPTER 10*

# Four Years of Irish History

## *1823–6*

### I

Looking back from the heights of 1829, Sheil recalled Ireland on the eve of the formation of the Catholic Association in a passage of baroque magnificence:

> I do not exaggerate when I say that the Catholic question was nearly forgotten. No angry resolutions issued from public bodies; the monster abuses of the Church Establishment, the frightful evils of political monopoly, the hideous anomaly in the whole structure of our civil institutions, the unnatural ascendancy of a handful of men over an immense and powerful population . . . were gradually dropping out of the national memory . . . it was a degrading and unwholesome tranquillity. We sat down like galley-slaves in a calm. A general stagnation diffused itself over the national feelings. The public pulse had stopped, the circulation of all generous sentiment had been arrested, and the country was palsied to the heart.[1]

The background to the formation of the Association was almost two decades of near-fruitless exertion and manoeuvring by O'Connell. Between 1805 and 1808 he had struggled to the forefront of the Catholic movement and to induce it to petition and agitate. It had then been riven by class conflict, the veto issue, and the tactical choice of ingratiating itself by passivity or creating formidable pressure by agitation. By 1820 it was again practically at a standstill. In the following year, a new ploy, appeal to the crown coupled with conciliation of the Orange faction, was adopted; by 1822 it was apparent that this too had failed. George IV remained an opponent of concession, and the Irish tories had treated conciliation as a confession of weakness and determined to employ the discriminatory system more ruthlessly than ever. But Orange triumphalism proved in fact the chief precipitant of the Association. The secondary causes of its formation were the effects of time in diminishing the asperities of the veto controversies, and the disorders and renewed Whiteboyism of 1822 which had signalled the danger of loss of control over the peasant masses by both the clergy and the professional men.

At the beginning of January 1823 the long-alienated O'Connell and Sheil were reconciled at a dinner party at Glencullen, co. Wicklow. Whether as effect or cause of the reconciliation, they determined on a renewal of the Catholic movement. Not that their enthusiasm was equal: Sheil doubted whether the time was ripe and, like the other guests, discounted one part of O'Connell's proposal – that as well as full membership of the new society at one guinea per annum, there should be a category of associate members at a subscription of a penny a month. None the less Sheil joined O'Connell in appealing to the leading Catholics for support in the new venture. Some sixty responded in eating their way to cordiality at the initiating dinner at Dempsey's Tavern in Dublin on 25 April 1823; and two weeks later, after endorsement by an aggregate meeting, the Irish Catholic Association was formally instituted, with 'all such legal and constitutional measures as may be most useful to obtain Catholic emancipation' as its particular programme.[2]

The meaning of this programme was the first battleground within the Association. About one-quarter of the original membership was supplied by the nobility and gentry and they wished to limit discussion to the general question of Emancipation, and activity to preparing an annual petition for relief, after the old fashion. But O'Connell's initial purpose was to constitute a Catholic protective organization. As he told the aggregate meeting, the experiment in conciliation of 1821 had not only failed but was also proving dangerous. The masses would not remain passive under an Orange oppression which was virtually unopposed. Already disaffection and disorder were rife, evictions increasing and an additional police force and sectarian yeomanry brought into being. Without a Catholic body, how were the peasantry to be restrained from insurrection or warned against or protected from those who were goading them into crime? As a corollary, O'Connell aimed at raising the consciousness of the Catholic masses by ranging over the entire body of their grievances, and then using their rising and compacted anger as a lever. He had no intention of working immediately for Emancipation. Instead, he insisted that the Association's business should be actual abuses and inequities which would not admit of delay until the day of liberation dawned. In earnest of this, the first issue which he raised at the first regular meeting of the new body, on 20 May 1823, was the appointment of a Catholic chaplain to Newgate prison in Dublin.

The upper-class Catholics, led by Lord Killeen and Sir Edward Bellew, who chaired the early meetings, were rapidly worsted. By June 1823 they had, without exception, ceased to attend Association meetings, and left the field to the lawyers and other professionals and businessmen. This did not mean that O'Connell's policy of enflaming the peasantry was henceforward unopposed. Timid or factious bourgeois members continued to resist extensions of the area of business. Twice at least they attempted to remove the tithe question from the Association's programme. On 19 June 1823 Eneas MacDonnell, often a thorn in O'Connell's side, opposed a protest against Orange processions. Hugh O'Connor, the most persistent advocate of the narrow view of the Association's concerns, condemned the divergences 'from the sole purpose for which it was instituted – Catholic emancipation . . . extraneous topics, and vituperative personalities . . . have done some injury to the Catholic question.'[3] O'Connell, however, was indomitable. Within a month of its foundation, he congratulated the Association on the decline in agrarian crime which it had already occasioned, and thereafter threw himself into work which he himself, practically single-handed, found for it to do, and practically single-handed did. He used every possible occasion to extend the Association's range of agitation, and crushed, none too scrupulously, every attempt at limitation. His majority was secure; and he could always count upon the important support of Sheil. On 15 November 1823 the matter was finally decided in his favour when he secured a resolution that the Association had been formed to watch over Catholic interests and to redress Catholic grievances in general.

In the same month Goulburn, the Irish chief secretary, reported to Peel, now home secretary, that the Association's proceedings were tedious rather than dangerous, and that it would probably die soon of inanition. On the surface, this seemed indisputable. It is unlikely that the total membership exceeded 120 during the first year. No less than six times during 1823, meetings had to be abandoned for lack of a quorum of ten, and on other occasions a tenth member arrived only in the nick of time. Moreover, despite the plethora of committees and apparent press of business, almost everything rested upon a single pair of shoulders. For the rest, the handful of active members served as a stage army relying on the multiplication of their roles to give the illusion of a considerable body.

But the appearance of weakness was misleading. Peel himself realized as much when he observed in April 1824 that 'the insignificance of the members' was more than counter-balanced by the publicity which the Association had received from the beginning. Governmental control of the press had not been maintained, and four of the six most widely circulating newspapers in the country were in its pocket. F. W. Conway, editor of the *Dublin Evening Post*, and M. Staunton, editor of the *Morning Register* and *Weekly Register*, were close allies of O'Connell, as well as deeply involved in the Association; and although the *Freeman's Journal* was hostile to O'Connell himself, it warmly supported the Association. This meant that the media of Catholic Ireland saturated the country with the Association's propaganda. Meetings were reported in a degree of detail which no twentieth-century newspaper would attempt to match. There is abundant evidence that the effective circulation of the newspapers, even in 1823, was far greater than their sales would suggest. As they were passed about and read aloud, their circles of influence widened continually. There is also abundant evidence that the peasantry bowed down before the printed word: type on paper was treated as in itself authoritative. Thus the voices of the dozen barristers and journalists haranguing each other in a little room over Coyne's bookshop in Capel St, Dublin, on Saturday afternoons – above all, the voice of voices, O'Connell's – were magnified a thousandfold by the press, primarily by the nationalist newspapers, but also by broadsheet and pamphlet. Even the government newspapers contributed to the éclat of the Association, reporting its proceedings almost as completely as its rivals. Peel deplored the subsidization of organs which merely advertised O'Connell. But although their readers might receive news of O'Connell's doings with fear, anger or contempt, they had to know about them.

A second reason for the wildly disproportionate national impact of the Association's handful of members in 1823 was the multiplication and noisy canvassing of 'grievances'. Orangeism and Catholic burials provide two early examples of O'Connell's technique of turning a trivial occasion to great account. On 19 June 1823 the Association agreed to petition the lord lieutenant to forbid the traditional Orange procession of 12 July. The petition was rejected; but the procedural wrangles which preceded it and the denunciatory oratory which it unleashed publicized the Orange phenomenon as never before. This launched O'Connell into the set-piece ridicule of the Orange Order with which he was to delight the Catholic masses in later years, as well as a series of legal actions assailing Orange 'oppressions' and pretensions.

Similarly, the refusal in September 1823 by the sexton of St Kevin's churchyard, Dublin – like all cemeteries then, it was in Protestant hands – to turn the usual blind eye to a Catholic priest reciting the *De profoundis* over the grave of a parishioner was brilliantly exploited by O'Connell. Over the next eight months he used the burial issue to prodigious effect. Committees reported on the relevant statutes and common law and pursued the acquisition of a special Catholic burial site in Dublin. Several priests, and in particular Dr Murray, were drawn into the ferment. Somewhat bathetically, this particular phase of the agitation ended when the Association acknowledged that 'As a matter of fact, prayers have constantly been read at Catholic burials.'[4] But by then tens of thousands of Irish Catholics had been brought to recognize another of the badges of their inferiority. Moreover in O'Connell's hands the grievance had spread like a stain. As he expressed it, the Catholics of Dublin were being taxed £20,000 per annum by the Church of Ireland for the right of burial within the city. It was fruitlessly, though bitterly, that the Anglican Archbishop complained that he and his brethren were being 'held up to public contempt and execration by a set of popish priests'.[5] One grievance led smoothly into another and before the year was out the original burial question had proliferated into Association resolutions against tithes, church rates and Protestant Proselytism. Just as the processions of 12 July had been developed into a campaign against the entire system of caste domination, so the momentary bigotry of the sexton was developed into a campaign against the entire system of Anglican discrimination.

Thus beneath the apparent failure to make headway in 1823, the groundwork for a mass movement was being laid. Through the newspapers the Association served more and more as a national sounding board, and through O'Connell's exploitation of Catholic 'grievances' large bodies of people were being quickly politicized. Latterly, the priests also were being entangled. On two seemingly opposite counts, the fewness of the active members and the great and growing extent of their potential public, O'Connell believed that the time had come to popularize the Association according to his original vision.

## II

O'Connell's penny-a-month plan represented the second stage in the development of the Catholic agitation. Neither the idea of a Catholic

'Rent' nor the idea of widespread minute subscriptions was new. As O'Connell himself acknowledged, Lord Kenmare had proposed, as early as 1784, levying a 'rent' of £1 per annum on every Catholic parish to build up a campaign fund for Emancipation; and both the English Methodists and the London radicals had attempted to organize regular penny subscriptions by the poor in the 1790s. The very mechanics of O'Connell's scheme in 1824 had been largely anticipated in a suggestion of William Parnell to Denys Scully several years before. But O'Connell brought a fresh energy, practicality and purpose to the projects. In his hands they actually worked.

O'Connell saw his Rent as the transformer of sentimental support into real commitment. Hundreds, and ultimately thousands, of ordinary middle- and lower-middle-class people would be drawn into the bustle and business of collection, while each poor subscriber of the weekly farthing would feel that he had a stake and a sort of proprietorship in the vast national movement. This may even have been his primary objective. It was in fact through the Association's committee for the increase of membership that he first launched his proposal on 4 February 1824. But the acquisition of capital was far from unimportant in either his or the Association's eyes. O'Connell aimed at £50,000 per annum (one penny per month from the heads of Catholic households was the basis of his calculation). His projected division of expenditure reveals his desire to pursue the objectives of 1823 upon a much grander scale. The bulk, £30,000, was to be spent on legal aid for Catholics – in particular, in cases involving 'Orange' magistrates – and the support of the 'liberal' press. The balance was to be devoted, in equal parts, to the education of the Catholic poor; the provision of priests for the American 'mission'; church and school building; and parliamentary expenses, mainly for petitions. Thus, broadly speaking, two-thirds of the effort was to be directed to mutual defence and propaganda, and the remainder to strengthening of what we would now call the Catholic 'infrastructure'. Thus O'Connell's basic strategy was still defensive, although a future aggressive campaign was none the less possible. As the original resolution for the adoption of the Rent put it, 'there is no rational prospect for emancipation, unless the Catholic Association shall be enabled to adopt more vigorous and effectual measures than have been heretofore pursued by the Catholic people.'[6] There was of course no conflict between the embroiling of the many and the filling of the war chest. But they were sufficiently distinct for O'Connell to insist upon a separate committee for each end.

It was only with the utmost difficulty that O'Connell persuaded the Association to adopt the Rent. On its first proposal, he was met with the argument that they needed to re-involve grandees like Lord Fingall rather than recruit a horde of 'houseless, starving wretches'.[7] Sheil's backing helped him to secure agreement in principle in the end; but so tepid was the support in general that the critical meeting of 4 February failed to muster a quorum at the start, and O'Connell had to send his clerk down to the bookshop beneath where they were meeting in order to snare some unwary, browsing priests who, bewildered, made up the necessary number. The subsequent organizational work of March–October 1824 fell largely upon O'Connell himself. First, he tackled the towns. Urban committees appointed collectors for various districts (or 'walks'), and remitted the money regularly through their secretaries to the central Association. Contiguous rural parishes were next drawn in, and then more remote parishes where practicable. None of this was easy. Even Dublin and Cork proved difficult to organize initially; half the Cork Rent had to be devoted to local charities to enhance its appeal. Laymen could usually be found to initiate and sustain the work in the cities, but hardly ever in the countryside. Here the Church was all-important. Curiously, O'Connell had given the priests no significant role in the beginning. But he very soon changed this. Collections had to be taken at church doors to tap those without dwellings of their own: the armies of servants in the capital were a leading case. Priests had to be called on for advice on who should be appointed as inspectors. Where – as was normally the case outside the towns – no Rent committee existed, the parish priest became perforce the channel for subscriptions. O'Connell had however long foreseen some such need: as the French traveller de Beaumont later put it, 'he judges Ireland too well not to know that nothing can be done except by the influence of Catholicism.'[8] Similarly, he knew that Catholicism could be 'operated' only through the Church. Hence he had moved at a comparatively early stage, on 16 June 1823, that priests should be attracted to the Association by the waiving of subscriptions in their case. This had been strongly opposed, not least by Sheil who had supported a contrary motion, that the clergy be admitted only as 'observers', on the ground that O'Connell's proposal would lead to clerical domination of the movement. O'Connell had however triumphed by 'a large majority'.[9] It was a symbolic victory of first importance.

So far as harnessing the Church to the Rent in 1824 went, the critical precedent was the adhesion of Bishop James Doyle of Kildare and

Leighlin to the Rent scheme and his supplying the Association with a list of the priests in his diocese; very few priests would have ventured into the work without episcopal approval. Murray and other prelates soon followed the lead of Doyle. O'Connell capitalized upon this at once. As early as Sunday, 7 March 1824 he travelled to Navan 'and [? spent] the day with the bishop [of Meath], a very fine old gentleman of the age of 86, and met a large party of his clergy. I made a harangue to the people in the Chapel and set the penny a month subscription agoing. It will succeed.'[10] To this clerical offensive we should add the evangelical work on the Munster and Leinster circuits in the late summer of 1824, as O'Connell, Sheil and the other Catholic members of the bar set about inspiriting and instructing the assize towns and their hinterlands, one by one. Through it all, O'Connell was supreme, in organization, in management, in administrative invention, in incessant toil. Well might the Catholic aggregate meeting of 2 December 1824, looking back upon the preceding nine months, resolve 'that we are peculiarly indebted to that honest, eloquent, and dauntless man, for his sagacity in devising the Catholic Rent, and his skill, judgment, and perseverence in carrying that important measure into effect'.[11]

As it extended itself across the country, the Association also altered its character. The local branches began to hire rooms, hold weekly meetings and discuss political issues, just like the parent body. Politicization became both general and systematic. Secondly, a chain of communication and command developed quickly. By October 1824 hundreds of thousands were within the control – or at least subject to the direct influence – of O'Connell's committees. Thirdly, the Catholics in the various localities were advancing in self-confidence and self-management. Gradually some branches began to assume the functions of tribunals – arbitrating disputes, challenging the magistracy and formulating and publicizing grievances. Most important of all, the movement had thrown up a national leader. Before March 1824 O'Connell had been merely much the best-known of a group of well-known agitators. Now he towered over the remainder. His extraordinary national dominance, which was to last until his death, 23 years later, had been suddenly achieved; all at once he was rewarded for nearly two decades of dreary labour. At the same time, the Irish Catholic movement had taken one particular shape at last, centred about an individual hero and commander.

Down to the end of September 1824, the Rent yielded comparatively little. Then the labours of six months bore fruit. In the last quarter of the year the weekly average leaped to £600, with that sum frequently exceeded. As N. P. O'Gorman, praising 'that wonder-working man, Daniel O'Connell', reported, the last week of November yielded £1032 as against £8 in the first week of February.[12] The weekly average of the first ten weeks of 1825 was higher still, although some of this augmentation must be attributed to appeals for extraordinary subscriptions before the Association was legally suppressed and collections would have to cease. In all, almost £20,000 was raised during the year that the Rent was open, more than nine-tenths of it in the last five months. These vast sums – vast, that is, in the circumstance of the case – were themselves a cause of Catholic exultation. As, at first, each month, then each fortnight and finally almost every week a receipt for £1000 invested in 3 per cents was produced at the Corn Exchange, where the meetings now took place, a sense of power coursed through the proceedings.

Less than one quarter of the Rent collected in 1824–5 was actually spent. Administrative costs were low, mainly for hiring halls and the printing and broadcast of reports and collectors' books. The principal charge was legal expenses, counsels' fees for prosecuting Orangemen or defending Catholics, although these were sometimes waived by Association members. The Rent also furnished £500 for schoolbooks for the Catholic poor, and an uncertain amount – probably very small – for press propaganda. In July 1824 O'Connell proposed that a considerable sum be applied 'towards establishing a [pro-] Catholic paper in London';[13] but when such a paper, the *Morning Register*, was established, he offered no subvention. Doubtless the very excitement generated by the Rent's progress provided sufficient publicity, free of charge.

Thus the money raised proved an even more secondary objective than O'Connell had originally thought. What mattered was the mobilization of Irish Catholicism. If Rent was collected in only half the parishes of Ireland – and this is a low estimate for early 1825 – as many as 30,000 people might have been involved in the business. Local committees varied greatly in size, but in some cases exceeded fifty persons. The number of contributors (women were appealed to as well as men) may eventually have reached half a million, for collections were pressed very hard once the organization took deep root. The priests had taken up the Rent with zeal. By the end of 1824, they were generally the driving force outside the cities. On 24 January 1825, Vesey Fitzgerald, the sitting member for the constituency, told Peel that every parish in co. Clare had been organized: 'in the few instances where the priest has been either cautious or reluctant, a coadjutor of a more daring . . . spirit is sent to take the management out of his hands.'[14] A similar report from co. Limerick spoke of the Rent as being entirely directed by the clergy, whose influence over the people was thereby rapidly increasing. Clearly, the Church had been enlisted with a vengeance. Equally clearly, the process of Rent-gathering was quite as significant as the gathered Rent. As early as November 1824, Peel recognized this when he noted that although the money itself might not be dangerous, 'the organization by means of which it is raised may be very formidable'.[15]

It is difficult to guess how the Rent would have developed if it had not been halted suddenly by the suppression of the Association. So far it had been only triumph; so far the Rent had been virtually its own end. No one, from O'Connell downwards, was apparently concerned that the money was simply mounting, and practically unharnessed to the Association's stated aims. Meanwhile it had at least served the movement's first principle of being: it had embodied agitation.

## III

The third phase of the Catholic movement began with the gathering resistance of the interests threatened by the Association. By November 1824, the Irish tories were pressing for arms to defend themselves, and Wellington was prophesying armed conflict. Goulburn, while dismissing civil war or insurrection as chimerical, none the less feared that some trivial collision might set off a general explosion in the existing state of popular excitement. Wellesley, the lord lieutenant, struck out upon a new line, even-handed suppression. In December he determined on the prosecution of both O'Connell and Sir Howard Lees, an Ulster Orange leader, for seditious language. Both prosecutions failed ignominiously, and O'Connell rose to dizzier heights of popularity in the event. But the action signalled that the government now felt itself threatened by the Association.

When Peel first considered counter-measures, in a letter to Goulburn of 6 November 1824, he presented the choices as three – to trust to dissension among the leaders, or the inherent folly of the enterprise, to break up the Association; to watch for the false step which would enable a successful prosecution to be brought; and to suppress the body by legislation. Wellesley had evidently been following the second course when O'Connell was charged for a speech at the Association on 16 December, in which he had proclaimed that if

Ireland 'were driven mad by persecution, he wished that a new Bolivar may be found'.[16] Of the three, Peel clearly preferred suppression and this was the course fixed on by the British government at the beginning of 1825. But it was suppression of all Irish associations, and not merely the Catholic which was proposed. It was doubtless true, as Brougham observed, that 'it will be only a nominal equity . . . the Catholic Association will be strongly put down with one hand, while the Orange Association will receive only a gentle tap with the other'.[17] None the less, it was of symbolic significance that the principle of impartiality towards the Irish 'factions' was to be enshrined in legislation. With Wellesley's equality in prosecutions, this marked an open retreat from the automatic identification of British and Irish tory interests.

In introducing the suppression bill Goulburn emphasized the danger of a universal body, controlled by O'Connell and his like, 'men of disappointed ambition and considerable talents'. He tried to tarnish the Association by saying that its membership included those 'familiar with the traitors of old times – Tone, Russell, and Emmett' and to diminish its authority by accusing the Catholic nobility and gentry of cowardice and the priests of being mere automata. Worst of all, the 'Association condescended most strictly to imitate . . . [the] forms [of Parliament]. They appointed their committees of grievances – of education also and of finance. They had almost copied verbatim the sessional orders of that House.'[18] Peel spoke of the frightful ease with which such a vast and co-ordinated piece of machinery might be 'converted into a political engine'.[19] Canning supported the suppression upon the ground that the Association was supplanting both government and House of Commons. This was the favourite and most telling argument in the Commons debates. Nothing was said of the fear of Irish Catholic power which was the true reason for the suppression.

The bill passed rapidly and with very large majorities through both houses of Parliament and came into force at the end of March 1825. But long before then it was apparent that a high price might have to be paid for the success. When the bill was announced in early February, the Association determined to send a deputation to Westminster to plead its cause at the bar of the Commons. It was only with great reluctance that O'Connell consented to be a member; he would miss most, if not all, of the spring circuit; it might (as in fact it did) cost him more than £2000.

The ostensible object of the expedition failed at once; the House of

Commons refused to grant a hearing to the delegation. But both houses conceded select committees to consider the general condition of Ireland, and these gave O'Connell an opportunity to assess and allay the opposition. On 25 February 1825, he was examined by the Commons committee on the state of the Irish peasantry and system of land tenure. His competence, clarity and moderation impressed all members. He was also proving successful as an English agitator. His first major speech, of three hours duration to the English Catholics at Freemasons' Tavern on 26 February, was a triumph. 'I have succeeded, love', he told his wife. 'I was sincerely afraid of a failure . . . but . . . I had the meeting as cheering and as enthusiastic as ever a Dublin aggregate could be.'[20] This was confirmed by Sheil, who heard the speech:

> Mr O'Connell appeared to me extremely solicitous about the impression which he should produce, and prepared and arranged his topics with unusual care. In public meetings in Ireland, he is so confident in his powers, that he gives himself little trouble in the selection of his materials, and generally trusts to his emotions for his harangues. He is on that account occasionally desultory and irregular. But there is no man more capable of lucid exposition, when he previously deliberates upon the order in which he should array the topics upon which he intends to dwell . . . [W]hen he advanced into the general consideration of the grievances under which the great body of the people are doomed to labour – when he painted the insolence of the dominant faction – when he shewed the effects of the penal code brought to his own door – he seized with an absolute dominion upon the sympathies of his acclaiming auditors, and poured the full tide of his own emotions into their hearts.[21]

Meanwhile, he was lionized at whig dinners and receptions. 'We had four Dukes . . .', he wrote of a dinner given by Brougham for the deputation on 27 February. 'I was placed between the Dukes of Devonshire and Leinster, and opposite to the Duke of Suffolk . . . I was again most flattered.'[22] At the Duke of Norfolk's dinner in O'Connell's honour on 6 March, four dukes, four earls, six other peers and two baronets sat down to table with him: 'I was placed between the Duke of Devonshire and Earl Grey.'[23] Of the following night's dinner, he reported to Mary,

> You like to be thought the wife of *a great man*. And now to feed that wish I tell you I dined yesterday with Mr Frederick and Lady Barbara Ponsonby in St James Square . . . We had *only* one duke – of Norfolk – only two earls, Grey and Bessborough, but then we had a Marquis of Lansdowne, the senior peer sitting in Parliament being, I believe, the 35th Baron of

> Lixnaw, Sir Francis Burdett and the Knight of Kerry were there . . . Only think that earls are now become so familiar to me that I left out Earls Fitzwilliam and Sefton.[24]

Meanwhile, O'Connell had measured the leading British politicians, and concluded that he himself was superior in calibre to most, and equal to any. 'Darling, they think themselves great men', he wrote home, 'but the foolish pride of your husband would readily make him enter into a contest with them. I have not the least fear of being *looked down on* in Parliament.'[25] Perhaps it was all this agreeable encouragement which induced him to press Burdett, a leading radical, to introduce a motion favouring the Catholic claims, although it is also possible that he had determined to try again for Emancipation before joining the deputation. At any rate, when Burdett did seek leave to introduce a bill on 28 February, it was granted by the respectable majority of thirteen.

It was clear that the Association had suddenly brought Emancipation to the brink of success. To some extent, the Commons vote may have represented a feeling that the proposed suppression implied a *quid pro quo*. But primarily the shift in opinion was caused by fear. The Association might be put down. But it had already demonstrated the power of popular organization, and this might surely be repeated in some other – and perhaps even more subversive – form if the Irish Catholics were constantly frustrated. The most important anti-Catholics were coming to believe that the game was up. Liverpool considered that even if the Lords rejected relief it would be by so small a margin that the next bill would be irresistible, and he wished to resign office to avoid involvement in what he regarded as the inevitable surrender. Peel, on the same reasoning, tried to resign at once, and was persuaded only with difficulty to hold back his resignation until Liverpool's was delivered. There are indications that Wellington was prepared to replace Liverpool as prime minister with the intention of presiding over the concession. Even George IV appears initially to have regarded Emancipation as inevitable. If those at the heart of British politics should have so underestimated the remaining strength of the resistance to relief, O'Connell can scarcely be blamed for his grosser miscalculation.

On the strength of the success of the Commons motion of 28 February, O'Connell collaborated fully with Burdett and Plunket throughout the second week of March in drawing up a Catholic relief bill, together with 'securities' to meet all 'reasonable' Protestant fears. The 'securities' – state payment of the Irish Catholic clergy and the disenfranchisement of the Irish 40s. freehold voters – were to constitute the 'wings' by the aid of which Emancipation itself would be borne through both houses. Clearly O'Connell had concluded that the time had come to cash in these two political assets. In his evidence before the Commons committee, he had decidedly favoured the disenfranchisement of the 40s. freeholders. Despite considerable evidence to the contrary in recent Irish elections, he regarded these as votes in the landlords' pockets. In his evidence before the Lords, he had favoured, though more tentatively and conditionally, state payment of the clergy. After all, Maynooth, which was state supported, had been producing priests for thirty years, and the current complaints were not of their subservience but of their disloyalty to the British government; and even Doyle, the most indomitable of the Irish hierarchy, did not seem absolutely opposed. According to Lord Colchester, Doyle had told the Lords' committee that he was 'unwilling to receive any State provision; rejecting it absolutely unless equality of civil rights were given to the Roman Catholic laity; and even then would accept such provision only as permanently annexed to each benefice or dignity.'[26] At the same time, O'Connell's uneasiness with this 'security' seems evident from the manner in which he disclosed the proposed concession to his wife: 'A provision will be made for our Clergy which, by the by, will be so much the better for the friars as it will leave almost all the individual donations *free*.'[27]

O'Connell does not appear to have anticipated sensible difficulty in carrying Irish Catholic opinion with him on the 'wings'. He informed the chairman of the Association of these in a letter of 7 March 1825, without in any way dissociating himself from either. When this letter found its way to the press, opposition was expressed at once. But this was swallowed up in the larger commotion which followed Jack Lawless's public letter of 15 March denouncing the deputation's treason – 'a furious tirade', O'Connell called it, 'calculated to do extreme mischief here and to raise a flame in Ireland'.[28] Lawless, in his role of *vox populi*, had followed the deputation to London to watch for backsliding – and not in vain. O'Connell was accused of 'selling the people for a silk gown' and succumbing to the flattery and attention of the aristocracy: 'the Circean cup of their hospitality' had drugged and debauched him, and he had surrendered the 40s. freeholders for his own advancement.[29] This was a dangerously plausible account of the recent transactions. England, to use Sheil's phrase, operated as a sedative on O'Connell. 'His deputation to England', Sheil continued playfully, 'produced an almost immediate effect upon him. As we advanced, the din of popular assemblies became more faint; the voice of the multitude was scarcely heard in the distance, and at last died away. He seemed half English at Shrewsbury, and was nearly Saxonized when we entered the murky magnificence of Warwickshire.'[30] O'Connell himself joked with his wife about being 'lost by *flattery*',[31] but doubtless the rain of dukes had some effect. Certainly, he was soon sucked into the Westminster game of factional manoeuvres. None the less he boldly repelled Lawless' onslaught with a public letter of defence, and in early April 1825 returned temporarily to Dublin where he addressed a large aggregate meeting. The 'wings' were not so much as mentioned, and O'Connell repaired to London once again with the negative security that Lawless and his other enemies had not dared to denounce him before a popular audience.

The flank had been temporarily secured and the main battle seemed to be going well. The relief bill passed the Commons with a final majority of twenty-seven; the securities, eventually embodied as separate bills to smooth the path of relief, followed with majorities of almost fifty. Meanwhile, however, the Duke of York, heir to the throne, had taken the lead in organizing resistance in the Lords. In a speech on 25 April he declared that, like his father, he regarded the coronation oath as an insuperable obstacle to granting the royal consent to Emancipation. O'Connell erred in dismissing this as empty gasconade, for the speech emboldened other peers to hold out against concession. It is true that Liverpool still believed that the question would have to be compromised; and although he now took a stronger anti-Catholic stand in public than he had ever done before, it was to prepare the way for his own resignation. But at the critical division in the Lords, on 18 May, Liverpool's stance was largely responsible for the bill's rejection by a decisive forty-eight votes. The government and Liverpool's prime ministership were unexpectedly saved; Catholic relief had been routed. Moreover, Canning after minatory gestures soon made it clear that he would not leave the ministry; the 'open system' (whereby politicians agreed to differ on the issue of Emancipation when it came to holding posts in government) would continue to sap all pro-Catholic efforts in Parliament.

O'Connell, who had long been exultantly confident, was furious, believing that he had been sold. He immediately announced his intention of renewing agitation and reconstituting the Association, and returned to Dublin to resecure his base. Despite his worthless 'surrender' of the 'wings' and the suddenness and ignominy of his defeat, he had comparatively little difficulty in confirming his leadership. His journey from Howth, where he landed, to Dublin was an unbroken ovation; and when a week later, at the aggregate meeting of 8 June, Lawless attempted to impugn the deputation's conduct in London, he was shouted down and forced to withdraw his motion of condemnation. Later Lawless organized a closed meeting of the Bridge St parish, where his main strength lay, to secure some public condemnation of O'Connell's conduct. But O'Connell would not allow even this petty threat to his mastery to go unchallenged. With a body of supporters he forced his way into the meeting, and despite constant interruptions managed to rout the fomenters of 'discord'. But to do so he had to confess openly that his former support of the 'wings' was mistaken, and to claim the backing of Doyle and Murray for his former acquiescence in state payment. At the Bridge St meeting he also asserted that he had received votes of thanks from almost every county in Ireland; and this was probably true. As he went on circuit during August and September he was hailed as a conqueror by vast crowds in each assize town, as well as in Galway and Wexford where he had special retainers. Significantly, the Cork address declared that 'his purity of intention and devotion to the interests of the Irish Catholics continue unimpeached in the public estimation'.[32] The medal struck in honour of his work for the Catholics of Ireland portrayed, in Roman imperial fashion, his bust upon the obverse side and a half-laurel wreath (the other half being shamrocks!) upon the reverse.

It was now clear that O'Connell had ridden successfully over the Lawless challenge, that his campaign of 1825 was estimated a national triumph and that he had risen to an unprecedented height in leadership. Probably, his position would have been secure even if he had made no extraordinary exertions after the débâcle of 18 May. But he had counter-attacked, first, by challenging Lawless at once on each of the three occasions on which he had attempted to arouse opinion against him; secondly, by disclaiming the 'wings' quickly and without reservation; and thirdly, by making good his promise to reconstitute the Association substantially. He was not yet out of the wood. He had, as he himself put it, 'smashed the Bridge St gang';[33] but in doing so he had offended Doyle, who denied that he had ever sanctioned state payment of the clergy. O'Connell was both wounded and astonished. He had taken Doyle's support for granted, and (very reasonably) regarded Doyle's evidence before the Lords' committee as endorsing a circumscribed form of state payment in return for Emancipation. But Doyle could not be treated like Jack Lawless, and O'Connell bowed before the storm. He had not, however, understood Doyle's line of reasoning; and when he unluckily referred to the matter again at a public meeting in October, Doyle replied angrily that he had told the other bishops in London that he would resign his see rather than accept a salary from the crown, 'for if my hand were to be stained with Government money, it should never grasp a crozier, or a mitre ever afterwards be fitted to my brow'.[34] This rhetoric was not perhaps incompatible with acquiescing in state payment for the clergy generally, for Doyle had also declared that he would cause no dissension if the remainder of the episcopate was in favour of the concession. But O'Connell now understood his danger, and made no effort to chop logic with a bishop. Instead, Canossa – he humbly asked for a reconciliation. Doyle was critically important as the boldest and most intelligent and radical of the episcopate.

Meanwhile, O'Connell had set the New Catholic Association afoot in July 1825, defining its objectives in terms of the subjects specifically exempted from the operation of the Suppression Act – religious worship, charity, education and agriculture, and 'such other purposes as are not prohibited by the said statute of the 6th George 4th chap 4'.[35] This permitted engagement in almost every field in which the first Association had worked, from supporting a liberal press to combating arbitrary ejectments. In fact, the very limitations imposed by Geo. IV c.4 led O'Connell to propose effective new activities, for example the compilation of a religious census which promised the double advantage of establishing the paucity of the Irish Protestants and training 'assessors' in resource calculation and local and national organization. The Association could no longer run a direct campaign for Emancipation; petition-work would *ipso facto* render it an illegal body. Henceforth petitioning had to be managed at aggregate meetings and the fourteen-day limitation upon 'aggregates' induced O'Connell to propose the holding of simultaneous petitioning meetings in every county in Ireland. Here again the Suppression Act, ironically, produced a new and more effective mode of agitation; simultaneous county meetings would demonstrate Catholic strength and coherence dramatically. The remaining threat to the Association's work was the prohibition upon the collection and distribution of subscriptions. O'Connell countered this, well before the Act came into force, by vesting the money in a single individual, Lord Killeen, who became, in practice though not in law, the trustee for the balance of the Old Rent.

In all these ways, O'Connell recovered rapidly from the 'downfall' of May 1825. Superficially, his political losses were very grievous. The Association was suppressed, the Rent suspended, his willingness to yield on matters of great principle revealed, his extraordinary tractability disclosed to his British enemies, and a store of ammunition against his own integrity handed to his Irish ones. But he fought back superbly. As he had promised, he restored both the Association and the Rent in other forms, and reorganized the agitation for Emancipation. In the second half of 1825 the Association proper concentrated upon the 'defensive' or preparatory role defined at the outset in 1823 – but with several new objectives and techniques. These implied a return to steady political education, enrollment, and radicalization. Formally separate was the Emancipation campaign, the first major step in which was taken at Limerick on 24 October when a new system of provincial aggregates, to rehearse grievances and prepare parliamentary petitions, was inaugurated.

Meanwhile, he had boldly recanted his 'errors', crushed or conciliated (according to circumstances) his Irish opponents and processed the country as Victor in order to confirm and solidify his further elevation above the ranks of all other agitators. The instinct of the adulatory masses who responded uncritically to this presentation of himself was not mistaken. The near-triumph of March had been O'Connell's own doing. 'You cannot think', he had written to his wife on the 7th, 'how everybody says that it is *I* who am carrying emancipation',[36] and 'everybody' was right. Correspondingly, despite the Lords' vote of 18 May, he had, overall, won a critical Catholic victory. To have been baulked only by peers and against all expert expectation was surely to render success ultimately certain. O'Connell had many seasons of apparently greater triumph, but considering all the odds and turns of fortune against which he had to struggle, 1825 was probably his finest year of all.

## IV

It was however low water for O'Connell and the Association during the first five months of 1826. As planned, the wave of aggregate meetings of late 1825 reached its climax in a fourteen-day session in Dublin in January 1826. But O'Connell feared to press the resultant petition for Emancipation hard lest, with a general election imminent, anti-Catholic sentiment in Britain might be enflamed. Otherwise, the leading event was a dinner held in February to honour liberal Protestant supporters. O'Connell attached great importance to the accompanying parade and oratory of good-will. But we can hardly follow him in this. In fact, his parliamentary 'friends' fobbed off the

Association's efforts to have the Catholic question raised at all during the Parliament's final session. They even persuaded O'Connell that it would be unwise to raise debates on such petitions as they did present. These in themselves indicate the Association's dispirited condition. One prayed that the Treaty of Limerick of 1691 be adhered to; another, that state funds be diverted to Catholic education. Even O'Connell could hardly have supposed that the slightest attention would be paid to either.

Attacks upon O'Connell's leadership were moreover renewed in the Association. Lawless persisted with motions condemning, obliquely, his acceptance of the 'wings' in 1825; on 11 February 1826, a rising young radical, James O'Gorman Mahon, assailed him roundly for condemning the anti-clerical measures of the Spanish Cortes; and two days later, the *Freeman's Journal* denounced 'that violent and vulgar abuse which he [O'Connell] has so long been notorious for pouring out upon every person whom he cannot wheedle or bend to his purposes . . . his most slavish sycophants must admit him to be, inconsistent, ungrateful, capricious, vindictive.' We should not perhaps attach much weight to all these challenges. Dublin was not Ireland: O'Connell continued to be received with all the customary deference and adulation at provincial meetings. He could besides still dominate in Dublin whenever he chose to exert himself. But he forwent several of the Dublin meetings on account, he said, of professional business; one at least he attended in wig and gown. At another, a mere handful of hostile members carried some damaging resolutions in his absence. It was all, however, symptomatic of low morale and lack of direction rather than a breakdown of his power. In so far as O'Connell possessed a strategy in the first half of 1826, it was only to petition once more, through aggregate meetings, for a relief bill, after the general election in mid-year had produced a new House of Commons. He never guessed that the election itself would provide a dramatic change in fortune.

To a degree, the critical innovation of the Association in 1826 was both accidental and independent of the official organization. It began with an affront to Catholics in Waterford, a county dominated by the Beresfords, an Ascendancy family remarkable for its resistance to all Catholic claims and for the extent of the patronage at its disposal. Coincidentally Waterford was the home of a Catholic mercantile dynasty, the Wyses, whose latest representative, Thomas, junior, was a young man of extraordinary sophistication and cool judgment, in terms of the circle of agitators among whom he found himself. He was foremost in the long planning of a riposte to the Beresfords. Rev. J. Sheehan of Ballybricken, one of the first and shrewdest of the new breed of political priests and, in effect, O'Connell's agent for Waterford, was also critically important. But it was largely Wyse who devised and managed the systematic Waterford programme of 1825–6.

The objective of the campaign was to wrest one of the county seats from Lord George Beresford. To find a good opponent proved unexpectedly easy. Villiers Stuart, a young liberal landowner and pledged Emancipationist, was so eager to stand as to hasten back from the Tyrol for the contest. But the quality of the candidate was comparatively unimportant. It was the revolutionary methods of Wyse and Sheehan which really counted. A general committee was set up in the city with a subordinate committee in every barony and local agents in each parish. Priests were committee members *ex officio*. Weekly, the local agents and parish priests reported to the baronial committees which reported in turn to the centre, from which they received instructions which were passed down along the same line to the localities. Everyone concerned kept a register of the voters in his district. These, when forwarded to the central committee shortly before the election, predicted correctly the choice of practically every voter in the county.

Of course the purpose of all this work was not mere enumeration – though this was certainly important – but rather to induce the great body of the enfranchised, the 40s., freeholders, to defy the directions of their landlords. The organization used three wedges to split the ruling bond of proprietor and freeholder. First, the Beresfords were presented as historically the very centre-piece of the exclusive Ascendancy system and the most resolute Irish opponents of Catholicism. Secondly, it was reiterated that electors who took both the Beresford shillings (Beresford was attempting wholesale bribery) and the obligatory oath that they had not been bribed were guilty of the mortal sin of perjury. Finally, since many proprietors threated to evict every freeholder who supported Stuart, a local fund, collecting both money and alternative holdings, was set up to provide for the prospective victims of landlord revenge. These themes were repeated in chapel after chapel, Sunday by Sunday, for at least two months before the election; and meetings harangued by peripatetic agitators as well as the local priests enlisted the force of community pressure upon the side of defiance. Families were made to feel the shame of 'demean[ing] themselves before all the county'.[37]

But moving and sustaining bodies was just as important as fixing minds. The carriage of voters to the city, where polling took place; their maintenance there for several days; and discipline, sobriety and direction at the booths, required extraordinary planning. The preparatory network readily provided the requisite machinery, and the central committee used the tradesmen of the city as a sort of police force within Waterford itself. The result stunned contemporaries. Stuart was leading Beresford by 1357 votes to 527 when Beresford called off the contest. At that point Stuart had still several hundred votes in reserve, so that the true Emancipationist majority easily exceeded three to one. Even the Beresford tenants had supported Stuart.

At almost the twelfth hour, a few other counties attempted to imitate Waterford, in general with remarkable success. Louth, Westmeath, Monaghan and Armagh were won by a sudden mobilization-in-revolt of the Catholic freeholders. In some respects, Louth was an even more striking victory than Waterford. Only ten days before the election, a candidate of little name, fame, money or connexions, who refused moreover to pay a penny towards his own expenses, announced himself. Conjuring up the aid of the Association and its lawyers and agitators, and of the Archbishop of Armagh and his priests, he trounced the anti-Emancipation candidates whose families had had the constituency to themselves for half a century. None the less, the Waterford contest was the really significant phenomenon. It was the inspiration of all the rest; it alone was thoroughly planned and systematically executed; it alone was unmarred by violence and disorder, and marked by perfect discipline; and, numerically speaking, it was much the clearest demonstration of the political potential of the 'revolt'.

O'Connell had played a leading part in the Waterford triumph, spending several days before the poll electioneering throughout the county, and several more as Stuart's counsel in Waterford once voting had begun. On the second day of the campaign, he wrote from Stuart's house to his wife:

> We breakfasted at Kilmacthomas, a town belonging to the Beresfords but the people belong to us. They came out to meet us with green boughs and such shouting you can have no idea of. I harangued them from the window of the inn, and we had a good deal of laughing at the bloody Beresfords. Judge what the popular feeling must be when in this, a Beresford town, every man their tenant, we had such a reception. A few miles farther on we found a chapel with the congregation assembled before mass. The Priest

> made me come out and I addressed his flock, being my second speech. The freeholders here were the tenants of a Mr Palliser, who is on the adverse interest, but almost all of them will vote for us . . . We had a most tremendous meeting here [Dungarvan]; we harangued the people from a platform erected by the walls of a new chapel. I never could form a notion of the great effect of popular declamation before yesterday. The clergy of the town most zealously assisted us. We have, I believe, completely triumphed . . .[38]

Everywhere, O'Connell was received even more rapturously than Stuart and the remainder of the entourage. He served as the epitome of defiance and success. Yet his function in Waterford was essentially confirmative. He may have been the foremost harvester; but others, in particular Wyse and Sheehan, had done the work.

For despite the precedents of the general election of 1818 when the 40s. freeholders, mobilized by the priests, had wrested three counties from anti-Emancipation candidates, and the co. Dublin by-election of 1823 when he himself led a similar successful challenge, O'Connell, like the rest of the leadership, had failed altogether to appreciate the weapon that lay to hand in 1826. He did not even bother to register the vote for which he himself was qualified in Waterford. Six months before the election he still asserted in public that the 40s. freehold vote impeded the Catholic cause. When O'Connell was convinced, after only three days' electioneering, that Waterford would be won, he blamed his earlier faintheartedness on bad local advice. 'I took my former opinions from timid persons here.'[39] This is implausible. As early as February 1826, optimistic reports from Waterford were discussed by the Association in Dublin; and Sheehan, O'Connell's own 'man' in Waterford, had supported Stuart's candidature enthusiastically from the start. The truth is, probably, that O'Connell and Sheil simply failed to think out beforehand the possibilities and implications of the new experiment. Metropolitan bickering and manoeuvres always absorbed too much attention in Dublin; and the 40s. freeholders naturally, if altogether illogically, suffered in reputation from having been once thrown over.

All this changed of course with the dramatic events of the general election. Sheil, who had played in Louth the equivalent of O'Connell's part in Waterford, perceived their significance immediately.

> A simultaneous and universal revolt against the aristocracy has taken place, – Ireland has been to a certain extent revolutionised. How has this come to pass? How has this extraordinary change in the public mind been effected? . . . I do not exaggerate, when I say, that we behold in the events which are passing around us, the results of the Catholic Association.[40]

O'Connell '*read his recantation*' as he himself put it, at the first meeting of the Association to be held after the elections closed. Hitherto he had supported the 40s. freeholders 'for the sake of preserving unanimity' but his 'private judgement' was otherwise.[41] Now they had so completely proved him wrong that he proposed a motion (which passed unanimously, of course), pledging the Association ever to reject Emancipation if it were coupled with their disfranchisement.

This was excellent so far as it went. Unity of heart as well as word had been restored; a treasury of political power had been, almost accidently, stumbled on; an animating programme – to organize the Catholic freeholders in all the other Irish counties – presented itself ready-made. There could be no doubt that almost the entire Irish county representation could be won. The Mr Palliser whose tenants O'Connell had poached wrote, bemusedly, towards the close of polling in Waterford,

> men who in the year 1798 with exemplary loyalty assisted me to keep Rebellion out of these parishes, and in the last year resisted to a man the payment of the Catholic Rent, although called upon by the priests from the altar to contribute, have been now compelled to bow to this Popish Inquisition . . . none but my five Protestant tenants have been polled out of this large estate, and Lord Doneraile who has upwards of an hundred, has not been able to bring to the poll more than his seven Protestant tenants . . . all the remainder have polled against him, as have even Lord Waterford's own tenants.[42]

All this was readily repeatable over most of Ireland.

But there were also difficulties. First, seven years might elapse before the next general election. An agitation which might not come to a head until 1833 could scarcely be white-hot. Secondly, the retaliation of many landlords upon their upsurgent tenants provoked fresh discord in the Catholic movement. There was of course no disagreement that the tenants threatened with eviction (by distress for rent arrears) should be supported. They had, as O'Connell declared, 'made great sacrifices, and it was right they should be protected and indemnified';[43] it was also only prudent. Nor was the extent of the problem ever clear. Reports from the rebellious constituencies were confused, and accusations of landlord vengeance sometimes found to be baseless; and though there can be little doubt that the proprietors concerted counter-action in some places, its precise character cannot be determined. None the less, the threat was unquestionably grave.

Almost £10,000 had to be expended over the next six months in tenant 'protection'.

Where such a sum was to come from was the issue which divided the Association. O'Connell got his blow in first by proposing on 7 July 1826 a New Catholic Rent for the specific purpose of supporting threatened freeholders, with 'the overplus of the fund . . . appropriated to the purposes of education'. Significantly, he had already talked over the proposal with several priests, and he meant the Church to serve as the main engine of money-raising: 'in eight and forty hours after the plan was announced, the Catholic Clergy would go the rounds of their respective parishes'.[44] Collections began promptly, but with modest results: the weekly average was £100 at first, although some of the money raised in the embattled counties appears to have been distributed directly instead of forwarded to Dublin. The trouble was that cries for the immediate dispatch of quite large amounts, £300 or £400, began to go up from Monaghan, Westmeath and elsewhere, as particular landlords suddenly moved against their freeholders. In fact, the demands never did exceed what the New Rent and the county protection associations could provide. But throughout the autumn they seemed ever on the verge of outstripping these particular resources. Naturally, people looked to the balance of the Old Rent (over £13,000), left behind after the original Catholic Association had been suppressed in 1825, to meet the likely deficiencies. This proved to be the field of battle.

O'Connell strenuously opposed drawing upon the Old Rent on behalf of the 40s. freeholders. He argued that it was illegal to use it for such a purpose, and was probably sincere in this opinion. But – more important – he was also convinced that Rent was the most effective means of recreating and galvanizing a mass movement, and that the clergy would throw themselves wholeheartedly into a campaign for this particular purpose. Nor did he wish the 'sacred fund' of the Old Rent to be dissipated. It was still needed for his original purposes of opposing Orangeism in the courts, press propaganda and education.

It was not to be expected that O'Connell's apparent coolness towards the victims of 'the grand revolt' would pass unchallenged. As early as 14 August 1826, his loyal supporter Edward Dwyer, secretary of the Association since 1825, warned him:

> the greatest surprise is . . . felt at the withholding such assistance to the persecuted 40/- freeholders as we have in our power to give. They say, 'Why not devote a portion of that fund collected from the poor, for their relief now in the day of their distress?' I must candidly give my opinion that

> there is much of justice in the expectation for, without such aid, numbers of poor creatures, particularly in Monaghan where persecution rages to a great degree, must be ruined and sent to beggary.[45]

Dwyer concluded by proposing that £300–400 of the Old Rent fund be lent immediately 'to support the suffering patriots'. O'Connell strongly resisted. 'The old rent fund', he replied,

> has more than enough of demands on it . . . The interest is applied to the purposes 'as far as it goes' for which that rent was originally collected, and the principal remains a sacred fund to be applied in the same manner when an emergency shall require. Drawing from that fund, even if it were competent to do so, would only relax the efforts of the real friends of the 40s freeholders. Besides, the money drawn could not be replaced without . . . making the new rent illegal.[46]

Not content with this broadside, O'Connell procured a series of unanimous resolutions from the current Munster provincial meeting in favour of maintaining the Old Rent intact. Further, he angled for clerical support by promising that the 'sacred fund' should be entirely devoted to Catholic education once the demands of the Emancipation campaign were over.

But churchmen were not easily led on this special issue. On 30 July, Bishop Coppinger of Cloyne struck the note of boundless clerical sympathy for the freeholders which was to mark the remainder of 1826. 'These poor men', he wrote, 'who generously risked and sacrificed their all, rather than vote against the dictates of their conscience, have an imperious claim upon . . . their catholic fellow-countrymen.'[47] Several priests advanced their own savings to stave off imminent ejectments; others travelled to Dublin to make the case for immediate aid more forcefully before the Association itself. From this it was a short step to priests intervening in debates and even moving resolutions, fierily. One priest from Monaghan, Bogue, supported a proposed raid upon the Old Rent with:

> It was surely very easy for men at a distance from the scene of distress to reason coolly on sufferings which they did not witness; but he who had seen what the forty-shilling freeholders were enduring, must feel more warmly and more acutely. It had been well said, that this fund was created by the forty-shilling freeholders; and they did not come there as beggars to solicit alms; – they did not come there to supplicate a pittance, but to demand a right.[48]

A few days later another Monaghan priest, McCusker, 'commented . . . passage by passage, in the most severe terms' on a defence of

O'Connell's policy by Fr Sheehan, concluding with a motion that 'a letter strongly condemnatory of the principle contained in the letter of Mr Sheehan, should be addressed to that Rev. Gentleman'.[49]

In these circumstances, it was not difficult for the factious opposition to O'Connell, led by Lawless and a contumacious young barrister, Dowell O'Reilly, to challenge his direction at the centre. John Bric, his principal spokesman in Dublin, was ineffectual; and even Sheil, whose efforts to prevent public division in the Association were probably candid, admitted to some disagreement with O'Connell. Even O'Connell's trump card, his professional opinion on legality, was called in question. Some junior counsel dared to proffer a contrary view of the consequences of borrowing from the Old Rent; and on 4 September an editorial in the *Freeman's Journal* ended: 'Experience has proved that his [O'Connell's] opinion is not always infallible, when he mixes politics with law.' O'Connell could do no more than protest when, in his absence, the Association resolved to draw upon the Old Rent – though only when other resources had failed – to save the endangered freeholders.

Undoubtedly he had lost a skirmish; and the movement was temporarily distracted from its ends. Yet all this was comparatively insignificant. It was quite overshadowed – if we take the long view – by three general consequences of the election. First, the Association's power to break the connexion of landlord and tenant had been clearly demonstrated. This had been manifested so far only on a narrow front, but how might it not be expanded and multiplied? Such a consideration was to be ultimately decisive in producing Wellington's 'surrender'. On 12 September 1828, he was to tell Peel privately, 'I confess that what has moved me has been the Monaghan, the Louth, the Waterford and the Clare elections. I see clearly that we have to suffer here all the consequences of a practical democratic reform in Parliament, if we do not . . . remedy the evils.'[50] Secondly, the priests had been engaged far more intimately and vigorously than ever before in the Association's campaigns. The cause of the 40s. freeholders struck the right chord in the clergy, whose political 'education' thenceforth leapt forward, much to O'Connell's later benefit. Finally, the New Rent raised quite respectable amounts, over £6000 by the end of 1826. But more important to O'Connell than money were the opportunities which it afforded to re-assert his national leadership. 'Individual subscriptions', he had written at its launching, 'can never be sufficient. It requires a national effort: it requires the revival of the Catholic Rent. Once before at my voice that fund was created. Once before all Ireland became responsive to the call of patriotism . . . The Catholic people of Ireland are a nation. They should have something in the nature of a national treasury.'[51]

In fact, O'Connell had never been alarmed by the variegated opposition of July–October 1826, which was indeed made possible only by his own protracted absence from the capital. Whatever its occasional disadvantages, an eagerly implicated clergy was of critical importance in the agitation; and the Lawlesses and O'Reillys were soon cut down to their proper size when O'Connell returned to Dublin and resumed regular attendance at the Association's meetings. Moreover, the Old Rent was never needed to rescue the 40s. freeholders; this allowed the division in the Association to remain at the level of polite disagreement. Meanwhile, the drive led by O'Connell to gather in New Rent not only reinvigorated priests and people, but also brought other activities, especially the Catholic Census, back to life. O'Connell was always careful to conjoin the New Rent campaign with Catholic education, Catholic enumeration and similar projects which had been near moribund in the first half of 1826.

Thus the year ended with the movement thoroughly revived, a new electoral strategy and a variety of schemes for maintaining or increasing the momentum of agitation. O'Connell was fortunate that things had fallen out so well at home. For in the parliamentary arena the Catholic cause lost ground in 1826. Although the anti-popery cry and organizations had failed the highest expectations of their supporters in the general election in Great Britain, they had done enough to tilt the balance of votes in the House of Commons. This explains O'Connell's slowness in getting the Catholic question raised again in Parliament, despite his pre-general election threats. At the same time, the surge of new power which he felt in Ireland rendered him impatient with the customary whig counsels of restraint and self-effacement. On 31 December 1826 he replied to the Knight of Kerry's latest appeal, 'I am grown weary of being temperate, moderate and conciliatory to no one useful purpose and without having obtained one single advantage . . . No . . . *temperateness*, *moderation* and *conciliation* are suited only to perpetuate our degradation . . . if we want to succeed, we must call things by their proper names – speak out boldly, let it be called intemperately, and rouse in Ireland a spirit of *action*.'[52] Four years of Irish history had transformed O'Connell's bearing as well as the political temper and nature of his country.

## CHAPTER 11

# The First Hurrah

## 1827–8

### I

Two themes dominated in O'Connell's politics during 1827: the deployment of the New Catholic Association's power within the House of Commons itself and the effort to augment that power throughout the country. The themes were of course interconnected, with the second steadily feeding the first.

The ultra-Protestant party in Great Britain was suddenly weakened by the death of the Duke of York, the heir-presumptive, on 5 January 1827, and the failure of the health of Liverpool, the prime minister, who suffered an incapacitating and ultimately fatal stroke on 15 February. These turns of fortune seemed to O'Connell to present opportunities to apply pressure *within* Parliament itself. The new heir-presumptive, the Duke of Clarence, might prove sympathetic or at least neutral towards the Catholic cause; at any rate, he could scarcely equal his dead brother in virulent ultra-Protestantism. On 15 January 1827 O'Connell asked his friend Bennett, then in London, to make it known to Clarence's entourage that the Irish Catholics

> are disposed to be the most attached people in the world. In plain English the Duke can command Ireland heart, hand and soul if he pleases . . . if possible learn *the wishes* of that party without committing any of them. They *shall* be obeyed. All I want is '*the map of the land*'. I want only the compass, I think I can steer by it.[1]

This was in the best eighteenth-century tradition of an opposition faction attempting to attach itself to the 'reversionary interest', the heir who might bring it to power or influence when he in turn succeeded to the throne. Conversely, O'Connell also sought to use his electoral power to sway Parliament itself, and this anticipated various later British devices whereby the politically deprived exercised leverage upon the politically privileged. Again on 15 January, he practically instructed the Knight of Kerry to join the pro-Catholic whig magnate, the Marquess of Lansdowne, if – as then seemed likely – he entered a reconstructed cabinet. Lansdowne, O'Connell promised, 'would bring with him into office all the support which the Catholics of Ireland . . . could give to any administration'.[2] A week after Liverpool's stroke, he wrote to the Knight excitedly,

> We are here in great affright at the idea of the Duke of Wellington being made Prime Minister. If so, all the horrors of actual massacre threaten us. That villain has neither heart nor head. It is impossible to describe the execration with which his name is received amongst us. Could you suggest any act of the Catholic body which might facilitate the views of the Opposition at this moment? And, in particular, could we do anything to forward or support the Marquis of Lansdowne? . . . We could have Catholic county meetings, addresses to the King, petitions to parliament or anything else that public bodies may do, if you deemed it useful.[3]

O'Connell set out a clear order of preference for a new ministry. The Catholics' first choice would be a purely whig cabinet; their second, a 'mixed' cabinet (including if need be, some of the present 'Protestant' ministers); and their third, the current cabinet headed by Canning. On 23 February, he ordered Eneas MacDonnell in London to communicate these priorities to specified Irish county members, Daly and Martin (Galway), Prittie and Hely-Hutchinson (Tipperary), Bernard and Lord Oxmantown (King's), Lloyd (Limerick), Hare (Kerry) and Vesey Fitzgerald (Clare), and also to every other Irish county member who, like these, had been supporters of Liverpool's administration. As the accredited 'agent to the Catholics of Ireland', MacDonnell was to tell as many of the members as he could find immediately that

> the Catholics will deem every man *an actual enemy* who does not support Canning against Peel, Eldon and Liverpool. You can go farther and pledge yourself that the men who at this crisis decline to support the Catholic against the no-popery part of the cabinet will meet with decided opposition at every ensuing election. In short it strikes me that you should now take a decided part with *all* our Irish members – [one word illegible] to rally them all if you can for a new cabinet, failing that to a partially new cabinet, failing that to a decidedly Canning administration. James Daly and Vesey Fitzgerald are both Peelers. If you can get *at* these gentlemen, assure them that we will organize an immediate opposition to them in their own counties unless they take a decided part with Mr Canning in any ministerial struggle now going forward. *You may pledge yourself* to have these sentiments re-echoed by public meetings and carried into practical effect.[4]

O'Connell also enjoined MacDonnell to demand an early debate in the

Commons upon the Catholic claims. From long experience of the evasions of 'friends', he rehearsed all the deprecatory arguments in favour of delay with which MacDonnell would certainly be greeted, and to which he must close his ears as if to the blandishments of the siren.

> When they tell you what *will be* if you postpone, reply with the old adage, *What will be, shall be*. Use my name if it be of the least value either here or in England as the author of this advice. Terrify *our* ministerial friends into an abandonment of Peel, etc., and *insist on* an immediate discussion.[5]

This was a remarkable attempt to manipulate conduct in the House of Commons from outside the system. O'Connell's menaces were directed solely at Irish county members who seemed likely to support Wellington for the premiership. The reason is obvious. The Association had shown in the general election of the preceding summer that it had the capacity to seat or unseat the great majority of the Irish county members. Unfortunately for O'Connell his threat was far from immediate; the new Parliament was only eight months old. None the less, no erring county member could discount it safely. Thus the ultimatum could conceivably turn about twenty to thirty votes in the House of Commons, a most significant outcome when divisions were often very close. To put it in general terms, O'Connell was working out, in a first, rudimentary and vicarious form, the idea of an independent Irish faction at Westminster, deriving its power from controlled agitation at home and the struggles of British politicians for office. Faintly, the Parnellite decade, the 1880s, was foreshadowed.

As things fell out, both the objects of O'Connell's lobbying were achieved, although it is impossible to decide what part the lobbying itself played in producing this result. An early debate on the Catholic claims took place when Burdett introduced a motion in favour of Emancipation on 5 March 1827, and on 10 April Canning became prime minister at last. O'Connell was furious at the outcome of Burdett's motion, a defeat by 276 votes to 272. In his '*malignity*' (as he himself half-seriously termed it), he called a Catholic meeting in Ennis, where he was on circuit, on 11 March, at which every Irish member who supported the government was declared anathema and plans were drawn up so to organize through a Liberal Club in co. Clare that only obedient candidates would be returned at the next election. The meeting also determined to petition not only for Emancipation once again but also – *in terrorem* – for both Repeal and parliamentary reform. Correspondingly, O'Connell lashed out at the tame reaction of the Association in Dublin to the news of Burdett's defeat. 'There is a want of spirit and of energy, a crouching beneath defeat which both surprise and afflict me', he told the Association's secretary, Dwyer. 'The resolutions of the separate meeting were puling and weeping but suggesting nothing. There was no manly *rebound*.'[6] The chairman of the Dublin meeting, Sir Thomas Esmonde, had even tried to suppress a letter from O'Connell to the Association because of its 'warmth' of tone and advocacy of Repeal, but Lawless had forced his hand by threatening to read the letter himself should the secretary fail to do so. 'Alas', wrote O'Connell, 'how little do the fault-finders know the species of material with which I have to deal, the kind of persons who eternally clog every movement and who would prefer breaking my head to smashing the pates of 500 Orangemen.' Such men were 'sure to be at the side of *power* and *authority*'.[7]

But O'Connell was soon subject to steady counter-pressure from the whigs (the Knight of Kerry being, as usual, the principal conduit) to stay his hand lest Canning lose the premiership through his association with Irish turbulence. Once Canning was appointed, O'Connell fell completely into line. His earlier burst of indignation and renewed defiance, which may have been in part factitious, ceased as abruptly as it had commenced. On 14 April 1827, O'Connell expressed his hope that the new prime minister would form a 'liberal' ministry. Four days later he announced the postponement of an aggregate meeting, which was to launch a fresh agitation for Emancipation, upon the ground that 'discussion might take place that might be disagreeable to some of their sincere [parliamentary] friends'.[8] With good reason, MacDonnell protested from London,

> it was a most grievous error to have stopped your proceedings for a moment in deference to the party manoeuvrings here, and I greatly fear that you will have reason to think so very soon . . . Go on, even now, and determination will mitigate the evil, an evil, be assured of it, that never would have occurred, if you had not evinced vacillation in your Dublin proceedings.[9]

But O'Connell's political tantrum of March was now over; he was back on course, committed to working strictly within the Westminster ambit once again.

Down to Canning's death on 8 August 1827, O'Connell never wavered in supporting the new administration. This may seem strange, for it disappointed him continually. He could scarcely have expected the condition-precedent of the Association's endorsement of

14 April, that Canning form a wholly 'liberal' government, to be honoured. As the Knight pointed out on 23 April, the king's 'voice' alone meant that 'an entirely favourable ministry . . . is *totally impossible*'.[10] O'Connell certainly expected wholesale changes in the membership of the Irish, and to a lesser extent the British, administration. Here he was almost uniformly rebuffed, every specific proposal which he made being summarily rejected. Eldon resigned the British lord chancellorship in pique, and John Doherty (later to become O'Connell's *bête noire* but at this stage apparently a 'liberal') was appointed Irish attorney-general; but otherwise the no-popery phalanxes were undisturbed. Worst of all perhaps, not only did the ultra-Protestants remain entrenched in the executive layer in Dublin Castle, but Lord Manners was retained as Irish chancellor despite a widespread expectation that he would be replaced by Plunket.

Manners continued a rampant Orange partisan: 'He is certainly without disguise', O'Connell told the Knight bitterly, 'and even the shallowness of his own understanding makes him the more dangerous because of the open countenance he gives to every species of "illiberality".'[11] With Manners' encouragement, the Orange party reasserted its dominance of Dublin Corporation. He also barred the way to O'Connell's darling hope that he be granted a patent of precedence by the new government, and cost O'Connell much chancery business because clients believed that Manners would find against him wherever possible. Worst of all, the 'liberals' in the government used Manners to excuse their own inaction. On 9 June 1827 Bennett told O'Connell that Brougham had answered charges of indifference to the Catholic interest with ' "*Oh, Lord Manners is playing the devil.*" He sent me to Lamb [the pro-Catholic Irish chief secretary] who . . . said, "Lord M. is watching every opportunity to embarrass us." "*Tell Mr O'C. I must for a time be worse than Peel* but when we can, we will do all the good we can. Beg of him to have confidence, though we cannot do much, or worse men will come." '[12] O'Connell expounded furiously on the 'exceeding' fortune of the Orange faction. 'They generally have such secretaries as Peel and Goulburn but when they have a more liberal secretary, *his candour* to our enemies makes him a more useful patron to the Orangists than a decided no-popery man could be.'[13] None the less, O'Connell made no move to distance himself from Canning's administration, despite the fact that even such moderates as Bishop Doyle and Sheil were complaining that the Catholic cause fared worse under its false friends than under its open enemies.

How is the constancy of O'Connell's adherence to Canning's regime to be explained? First, in 1827, as always, his antipathy to the tribe of Eldon, Wellington and Peel was so inveterate that reason and calculation simply flew out the window when it was a question of excluding them from office. In a letter of 24 December 1827 O'Connell supplied his more positive strategy. Emancipation was not to be looked for immediately; in appointing Canning, George IV had forbidden him even to raise the question. But O'Connell hoped to prepare for its successful canvass in 1828 by gradually building up liberal Protestant support in Ireland (and to some extent in Britain also). This hope was based upon his expectation that a species of spoils system would operate upon Canning's and Lansdowne's accession to power: a redistribution of places, honours and privileges would be the surest way to attract influential new support for the Catholic claims. O'Connell looked for one specific reward on his own account, the patent of precedence at the bar which would provide some compensation for his being still prohibited from taking silk. He pursued this objective, which would enhance his standing, and doubtless also his income, quite as tenaciously as he had done the Queen's Irish attorney-generalship in 1820. 'I am everyday made to feel more and more', he told Spring Rice on 29 November 1827, 'the injustice which is done to me and my clients by the promotion of my juniors to the inner bar and the neglect to give me what I think my *due* precedency.'[14]

O'Connell was extremely loth to abandon such a congery of hopes, all the more so when the alternative seemed to be more and worse tories in office and another stretch of bawling, brawling, sterile opposition. Throughout the four months of Canning's premiership, he awaited, more or less patiently, the gradual liberalization of both men and measures; and he mourned Canning's death as if he had already shown himself to be Ireland's saviour. 'Mr Canning is dead', he told Mary on 9 August 1827. 'There is another blow to wretched Ireland. No man can become of vital importance to her but he is immediately snatched off.'[15] Nor did O'Connell reject Canning's liberal tory successor, Goderich, out of hand. True, he complained to Bennett on 26 September that the new ministry had shown 'no one symptom' of acting 'honestly by Ireland'. Their conduct 'convince[s] me that they are determined to give us good words as long as these can delude, but their acts, *their acts*, are unequivocal . . . The Orange faction unchecked . . . Gregory in full power at the Castle. The Trenches in full pay and patronage at the Custom House . . . The Hills and the

Blackers and the other *Evening Mail* patrons as strong and influential as ever.'[16] But Gregory and the Trenches, Hills and Blackers had all come through Canning's reign unscathed. In fact, Goderich's accession did not worsen O'Connell's situation materially. On the contrary, not only did he now ask more confidently for minor official favours but also on 24 October Goderich replaced Manners at last by Hart, the English vice-chancellor. Hart proved worth waiting for. He was an able equity lawyer and, as the Knight reported to O'Connell, 'though 74 he is in great mental vigour and, as I saw him picking up a Picci in Regent Street, the other day, I presume also in other vigour, and he is a most agreeable gentleman'.[17] Within five weeks O'Connell exulted, 'The system of favouritism has already disappeared.'[18] His chancery briefs had multiplied, and he was emboldened to ask Spring Rice, obliquely, to bring the question of his precedency before Hart. When however Spring Rice appeared to reply evasively, O'Connell unloosed all the pent-up irritation of the year:

> It is indeed well that the individual character of Sir Anthony Hart serves to mitigate that system of exclusion which is almost as effectually in action now as ever it was. We have a little also of the grace of hypocrisy to mitigate that system but beyond these advantages – such as they are! – the change of administration has not reached this country for any one useful purpose. Our enemies were at all events sincere, and they deserved respect on that account.[19]

Significantly, this quarrel was soon mended, and within a few days Spring Rice had written to Hart pleading O'Connell's case. It is equally significant that O'Connell's ultimate failure to obtain his patent of precedence did not move him from his course of qualified support of the administration. He still placed his hopes in making common cause with Irish Protestant liberals and even with unwary members of 'the Orange party'. After reaffirming his faith that such a strategy would undermine the remaining English resistance to the Catholic claims, he assured Mary on 1 December 1827, 'Darling, I really do expect Emancipation this sessions'.[20]

## II

At no stage during 1827 did O'Connell play the suppliant or the inferior in his dealings with the whigs, nor did he expect them to yield more than he could force them to. The relationship was a liaison of convenience. The whigs needed Irish 'tranquillity' to strengthen their hand in claiming a part of government. O'Connell looked for, and to a nited degree obtained, a mitigation of Orangeism in the Irish lministration and a larger share in the places and douceurs for his olitical clients and friends. In the longer run, he banked upon the formal alliance slowly bringing home to the British public that oncessions to the Catholics, and especially the final concession of mancipation, was the only means of rendering Ireland governable. or such a policy to succeed, he needed to be demonstrably strong at ome; and the Association was the index of his strength. Hence the eaf ear which he turned to the whig pleas of April 1827 that he do anning's new administration the 'infinite service . . . [of] bringing, at ast for the present, the Association to a close'.[21] Hence also his reless efforts, both before and after Canning was appointed, to widen nd deepen the Association's hold upon Irish popular opinion.

On 2 January 1827 O'Connell called upon Doyle (and other mpathetic bishops) for aid in two of the Association's current mpaigns, the 'Education Census' and the collection of the New atholic Rent. Both had especial clerical appeal, the first as that ction of the general Catholic census which would reveal the extent of otestant proselytizing of the young, the second because the priests ival 'proprietors', as it were) always responded fiercely to landlord taliation upon the 40s. freeholders. O'Connell approached Doyle ost gingerly, pleading 'an honest conviction of the paramount utility f these measures to our religion and country', and the certainty 'that e persecution of the 40s. freeholders has recommenced, and that we e much pressed for relief by persons who suffer persecution for not nding their children to proselytizing schools.'[22] But it was also true at the Rent and census were O'Connell's own particular prescrip-ons for vivifying and co-ordinating the Association. O'Connell ppended a list of the priests in Doyle's diocese who had already sent census returns; only six had done so, most with forms incomplete. his shows two points of interest – O'Connell's minute knowledge of nd detailed work upon Catholic organization even in (to him) latively unfamiliar parts of Ireland, and the comparative failure of e census device at this stage, except where, as in Waterford and ismore, the bishop insisted on complete clerical compliance with 'Connell's direction.

The Rent remained O'Connell's foremost organizational concern roughout 1827. Even when on circuit, he regularly returned his own onthly subscription, often with other sums which he had gathered cally and a hortatory address to be read to the Association in Dublin. typical accompanying letter, sent from Cork on 5 April, argued that

> the continuance and permanence of the Catholic Rent can be secured onl by giving the example of unabated perseverance in the payment of sma sums month after month. In fact the people who are both zealous an honest are everywhere ready to pay. If there could be found individuals the more wealthy class to take the trouble of acting as collectors.
>
> There is nothing our enemies dread so much as the extension an permanence of the Catholic Rent.[23]

Dissatisfied with the Rent returns, O'Connell carried a resolution the Association meeting of 17 July calling upon each parish priest establish an effective system of collection in his area. To maximize th appeal, denominational education and voter-protection were agai placed in the forefront of the Rent's objectives. But the 'reform' of Jul proved ineffective – only once did the weekly Rent exceed £100 durin 1827 – and at the close of the year O'Connell devised a ne 'churchwarden' system. Each parish was to appoint two churc wardens, one by the nomination of the priests, the other elected by th parishioners. On the churchwardens was placed all the local work the Association – the selection and oversight of the Rent collectors; th completion of the census returns; the furnishing of reports o proselytizing, evictions, the disposition of the district landlords an the local impositions of the Established Church; and the maintenanc of electoral registers. The plan succeeded immediately, if not (in th nature of things) universally. In its very first week of operation th Rent rose to £604, and the other deficiencies began quickly to b supplied. But this was only half the story. The regular communicatio between the wardens and the central body was of equal importance t O'Connell. As the wardens drew other parishioners of standing int the work, Peel rightly discerned 'some scheme of general organisatio of the Roman Catholic population' in the venture.[24] Moreover, b securing the appointment of his son Maurice as co-ordinatin Secretary of Churchwardens, O'Connell kept the organization unde his direct control.

O'Connell had been careful to leave considerable power in th priests' hands. He agreed with Sheil, 'Our great object should be t bring the priests into efficient and *systematic* action.'[25] Privatel O'Connell was not much disturbed by the successes of Protestar evangelization in the remoter regions. 'They are buying wretches i every direction', he told Mary on 22 March 1827, 'who are a disgrac to them and no loss to the church they desert.'[26] But he appears to hav been truly worried by the Evangelicals' educational drive. At any rat this really touched the clerical nerve and was in consequenc maintained as a leading item in the Association's business. Characteristically, O'Connell was not content with denunciation but moved on to designing a Catholic counter-system. His efforts culminated in the Association's grant of £1500 on 19 December 1827 towards the establishment of a model school in Dublin 'on such a plan as to be capable of extending scientific education to the poorer classes of Ireland as suggested in the late letter of the Rt Rev. Dr Doyle':[27] pleasing Doyle was a useful bonus. *Pari passu*, and in keeping another favourite grievance of the clergy, Catholic burials, on the boil, O'Connell progressed beyond mere abuse (though again he maintained this briskly) during 1827. He welcomed L'Estrange's proposal to the Association on 15 September that Catholics enclose their own burial grounds, reiterated his opinion that there was 'no legal obstacle whatever' to such a course, and on 27 October committed the Association to supporting the purchase of land for cemeteries. Again, ecclesiastical and political interests were being intermeshed.

But service to the Church did not always march in step with forbearance towards Canning's and Goderich's ministries. Here Doyle was O'Connell's most dangerous critic. On 8 June 1827, he complained bitterly that O'Connell's ministerial friends had done nothing to oppose either the renewal of state grants to proselytizing educational societies or two recent bills which rendered more secure the stipends of the ministers of the Church of Ireland at the expense of the Irish Catholic population. He had always doubted, he wrote,

> whether it were not better for the Irish Catholics to see Canning and the Grenvilles forced to join the Whigs in opposition, rather than to see the Whigs playing second fiddle to Canning, and both truckling to the Court and the Bishops; but as all are not as patient as I am in politics, nor all so averse to the building of buttresses to the oligarchy and the Church by accepting of Emancipation on Canning's principles, I have known how to be silent and to hold my own opinions without interfering with those of others but I am confident that the public would expect of you that you should do everything in your power, now that the Catholic Association is silent, to save us from being swallowed alive by a cormorant Church without being able to emit a cry.[28]

Humiliated yet perhaps not altogether displeased to possess such a lever, O'Connell forwarded Doyle's letter to the Knight for communication to 'our friends in the Cabinet', with the comment, 'It is not pleasant to be reproached with all that has not *been done* for this country.'[29] On 30 September Sheil also expressed his disquietude on the effects of O'Connell's policy upon the Church and Association:

> We should not hide from ourselves, the public mind is beginning to cool. The reason is, I think, this: when Peel and Dawson and our decided antagonists were in office, the Catholics were exposed to perpetual affronts which kept their indignation alive. The priests, especially, were held in constant ferment. But now that Lord Lansdowne is in, we say to each other, 'what a pity that our good friends in the Cabinet cannot do us any service!' and, convinced that they cannot, we 'take the will for the deed'.[30]

Sheil urged that the priests be roused by a more vigorous use of the burials issue; earlier he had proposed at the Association that the bishops compose and enjoin the recitation of a prayer 'that God would turn the heart of his Majesty's ministry'.[31] This last may have shown small knowledge of episcopal sensibilities, but it certainly indicated Sheil's alarm at what he saw as the growing political torpor of the clergy. Such sharp words from men of Doyle's and Sheil's standing help to explain O'Connell's greater concentration, during the second half of 1827, upon the work most likely to draw in the Church.

As virtually the solitary advocate of accommodating the 'liberal' administrations of the year, O'Connell had to bestir himself repeatedly to maintain his dominance in the Association. He resisted every proposal put forward by a potential rival. At the start of 1827, he opposed, initially, the first form of Wyse's detailed programmes for a pyramidical national political organization under the title of 'Liberal Clubs'. On 19 January, MacDonnell proposed from London that the Association propagandize overseas and especially on the continent, and also the setting up of a 'statistical committee' to gather data on the income and conduct of the clergy of the Church of Ireland; O'Connell ignored both suggestions. On 12 March James Dwyer, secretary of the newly-founded Hibernian Bank, pressed for a standing committee of the Association to provide continuity of meetings; O'Connell condemned the scheme as at once illegal and tending to introduce 'secret management into Catholic affairs'.[32] At the Association meeting of 21 July Lawless (in O'Connell's absence) pronounced the existing system of Rent collection 'Barren and unproductive'[33] and carried a resolution in favour of a simultaneous Sunday collection in all parishes to provide a defence fund for the 40s. freeholders; three days later O'Connell called an extraordinary meeting which rescinded Lawless's resolution. Sheil's proposal at a Catholic meeting on 22 September to set up a central committee to correspond with all the Irish parochial clergy was never heard of thereafter.

O'Connell was especially ruthless in crushing Lawless's challenge on the Rent. There seems no reason to doubt Lawless's charge that

O'Connell packed the extraordinary meeting of 24 July to ensure a majority. Certainly, in addressing the meeting, he depicted Lawless as coercing the priests and attempting also to use their bishops to coerce them, and he decried the practice of 'collecting at the chapel doors'.[34] When Lawless announced that he would raise the question again at the next ordinary meeting of the Association on 4 August, O'Connell (from circuit) addressed an artful letter to the meeting combining an assertion of his directional authority ('no person *can* know more of the details of the collection of the Catholic Rent than I do'), a 'most earnest entreaty' to his 'friend Mr Lawless' to think better of his proposal, and a shameless playing of the clerical card:

> Besides being, in my humble judgement, quite ungenerous to interfere with the ordinary resources of the clergy and of charity, it would also, in my humble opinion, be very ungrateful.
>
> The Catholic clergy have individually contributed to our funds. Poor as they are they have not only almost universally contributed to these funds but they have actually contributed as much as, if not (and this is my recollection) much more than, the wealthy classes of the Catholic laity. Would it therefore not be cruel of us to obtrude in any way between the Catholic clergy and these, their almost only resources! . . . the more ready they are to make such a sacrifice the more scrupulous should we be not to resort to the indelicate and unfeeling plan of interrupting any part of their small income.[35]

Vainly did Lawless protest that his plan allowed for the priests' withdrawing their normal 'offerings' before transmitting the balance to the Association. O'Connell had beaten him from the field; his motion was abandoned.

In fact, O'Connell later incorporated most of the proposals made by others during 1827 in his own schemes. His 'County Clubs' plan was 'patently imitative'[36] of Wyse's Liberal Clubs. The collection of data on the income and bearing of the Established Church in the various localities was eventually added to the parish returns. The church-warden system was from the start centrally co-ordinated, and the wardens themselves were instructed to attend the masses on the first Sunday of every month (to be named 'Rent Sunday') to collect subscriptions at the chapel doors! All this makes clear O'Connell's absolute determination to maintain his supremacy within the organization. Its power and efficiency as a political weapon were all-important in 1827; but so too was maintaining his grip – and his alone – upon the hilt.

A much larger, subterranean challenge to O'Connell's leadership, and indeed to the very nature of the movement which he had created, may however have been developing during the year. Wyse certainly believed so; and while Sheil may have been the foremost observer and delineator of the immediate in the Association, Wyse was incomparably his superior in discerning the large and gradual movement of events: in the 1820s, at least, he may be spoken of without absurdity as an Irish de Tocqueville. Wyse traced the origin of the change to a New York meeting in 1825 in support of the Association at which separatist, radical and republican resolutions, composed by the former United Irishman, William McNevin, were unanimously adopted. 'The Friends of Ireland', embodied at this meeting, spread gradually through North and South America, often under the lead of old '98 men and generally attracting those who 'had brought with them the burning sense of accumulated injury – the liveliest desire of retaliation – a deep and solid detestation of the very name – of the very thought, of England'.[37] By 1829 a formidable confederation committed to furnishing aid in Ireland's struggle against her 'oppressors' was on the point of being launched in Washington.

Not immediately, but certainly during 1827, Wyse believed, this development began to affect Ireland. Wyse did not mean that a specific party had been formed; but

> an identity of reasoning, and an identity of feeling . . . has been gradually growing up . . . This identity, by an attentive observer, may be traced through many of their public speeches; but a much better proof of its existence may be found in the frankness and fervour of familiar conversation. Amongst the inhabitants of the large commercial towns, particularly amongst the tradesmen, amongst the younger members of the bar, and even of the church, its principles are to be met with in full vigour.[38]

Wyse saw in this the formative stage of a struggle for control of the Association (and thereby of the Catholic 'nation') in which the violent faction would ultimately triumph over O'Connell.

> O'Connell, who had set out with exciting, was in the latter period of the struggle frequently obliged to moderate, and to allay. This moderation was not the effect of a change in the man, but it was the effect of a change in the men around him. The interposition for a time would doubtless have been regarded. Past services, great experience, habitual command, and numerous adherents, bound by personal as well as public ties, would have, for a long period, assured to him the full enjoyment of his ancient supremacy. But it is not to be concealed, that that supremacy would soon have declined, without an entire acquiescence in the more vehement propositions of his competitors . . . The opposition to their measures

would have furnished grounds for impeachment before the multitude, with whom such men, from the very nature of their principles, would soon have become the favourites; or, had he allowed himself to make the base compromise of principle to popularity, they would have gained by the accession of his name and influence the strongest support to their own cause. Any man who has observed the late proceedings of the Catholic Association, with impartiality, cannot have avoided perceiving that such a contest *had actually commenced* . . .[39]

This was of course speculation, and Wyse, like many intelligent contemporaries, tended to read the future in terms of the recent French Revolutionary past. None the less it is true that the Association, even at home, drew in a remarkable number of former United Irishmen, in much the same fashion as the Land League was later to prove a magnet for ex-Fenians. It is also true that Wyse's account prefigured, most arrestingly, many of the features of the Parnellite era, down even to the significance of American money in extending the agitation and the possibility of depositing such funds in Paris in O'Connell's name, to render them inviolable by the British government. Finally, it is true that some among the younger agitators had begun to speak – if only *sotto voce* – of O'Connell, now in his fifties and having lived almost half his life in the preceding century, as *passé*. All in all, Wyse had probably glimpsed a real potentiality – that is, if Emancipation had continued much longer to be the Cheshire cat which always dissolved as one drew near. O'Connell was no historical seer; but as a superb political animal he would have understood instinctively these consequences of hope too long deferred. Perhaps he really was seeing the 'Wolf' he had so often cried when he wrote to Bennett on 26 September 1827, 'If it [Emancipation] is not carried soon, these countries will certainly separate. I see the growing materials of separation . . . the disastrous struggle will be delayed by us who *now* possess influence, but come it will.'[40]

## III

To turn the coin over, and look at 1827 in British political terms, Liverpool's stroke in February had placed the Catholic issue at the centre of the power struggle for the succession. Peel bid on the strength of the anti-Catholic feeling in the Commons, Canning on the pro-Catholic sentiment there. It was soon clear that neither Peel nor Wellington could form a wholly anti-Catholic Ministry. Conversely, the defeat of Burdett's motion in favour of the Catholic claims on 5

March, though smaller than generally expected, was none the less critical in weakening Canning's hand in dealing with George IV. He could not now hope to form a pro-Catholic ministry; so the 'open system', long disastrous for Emancipation, would remain. Although references to his sacrifices for the Catholic cause had been for years part of Canning's stock in trade, his career since 1822 had shown abundantly that office was his overriding aim, provided it came in the face-saving form of the 'open system'. In forming his ministry, he even drew over a large number of the whigs, headed by Lansdowne and Brougham, into support of shelving the Catholic issue *pro tem*; he also bowed to George IV's demand that the Irish Administration remain substantially anti-Catholic. Thus the formation of a government in which three-quarters of ministers were pro-Catholics was in reality of small advantage to O'Connell.

How things would have developed had Canning lived it is difficult to say. Although, immediately, the whigs had been emasculated as a pro-Catholic force by the involvement of many of them in the 'open system', their large number in the coalition might have built up at last irresistible pressure to make some compromise on the Catholic question a government measure. Meanwhile, Dublin Castle might be gradually 'de-Orangeized'. These long-term developments were evidently what O'Connell had in mind when he told the Irish people, on Canning's death, that 'the blessings which under his administration we hoped so soon to enjoy in reality, have now suddenly been hurried from us, and show like a dim and distant vision.'[41] Goderich lacked the master's reputation and charisma, and appeared to accentuate the anti-Catholic bias of the Irish Government by appointing Lord Anglesey (then supposed to be an anti-Catholic) to succeed Wellesley as lord lieutenant. It was not however these deficiencies which finally determined O'Connell to recommence agitation upon the fullest scale, but rather the rapid distintegration of the ministry itself towards the close of 1827.

O'Connell's recommitment to agitation was wholehearted. In January 1828 a massive fourteen-day meeting was held in Dublin to organize petitions for the forthcoming parliamentary session; the churchwarden system was instituted, with immediate effect; Wyse's new *Political Catechism*, designed to politicize the masses systematically, and his Liberal Club proposals were approved; and on Sunday 13 January, simultaneous meetings were held in nearly 1600 of the 2500 parishes in Ireland. Even more than the churchwarden system, Wyse's schemes constituted a most ambitious plan of slow but ever-intensifying political education and development, to relate Irish popular organization upon a national scale to House of Commons politics. But the simultaneous meetings were to act as a sudden blow. This national show of strength had been inspired by the Suppression Act of 1825 and rendered a concrete proposition by Sheil two years later. The actual chain of meetings of 13 January 1828, coinciding as they did with Sunday masses and supplied as they were with ready-made petitions, may have constituted a rudimentary form of concerted action. None the less, a total attendance of one and a half million persons (as calculated by the *Dublin Evening Post*) was an impressive demonstration of both Catholic force and the Association's organizational capacity. O'Connell had rightly discerned the potentialities of massing vast numbers at a single direction when he wrote to Doyle on 29 December 1827, 'The combination of national action – all Catholic Ireland acting as one man – must necessarily have a powerful effect on the minds of the ministry and of the entire British nation. A people who can be thus brought to act together and by one impulse are too powerful to be neglected and too formidable to be long opposed.'[42]

The replacement of Goderich by Wellington on 22 January 1828, and Peel's return to the Home Office four days later, at once enflamed and seemed to justify the new offensive: in angry reaction, the Association, with O'Connell's concurrence, passed the fateful resolution that every pro-ministerial parliamentary candidate for an Irish constituency would henceforth be opposed. O'Connell failed to recognize that the new prime minister was the most likely of all British politicians to bow to the type of pressure demonstrated by the simultaneous meetings of 13 January. As early as 1825, Wellington had come to the conclusion that, sooner or later, the Catholic question would have to be compromised. The capacity to summon forth more than a million persons at will was a powerful argument, to such a mind as his, against allowing such forces to be built up further. It certainly fits this view of the matter that in his first three months of office Wellington should have been exploring, confidentially, possible compromise solutions. Similarly, his agreement in April 1828 to the repeal of the Test and Corporation Acts, which had discriminated against nonconformists, was so clear a precedent for the removal of Catholic disabilities as to suggest a 'dry run' for Emancipation. At the same time, Wellington had been careful to keep on terms with the ultra-tories, as best he might. This became at once more critical and more difficult when the now annual motion for Catholic relief was carried in the Commons on 12 May 1828 by a majority of six.

Meanwhile O'Connell adhered unwaveringly to the whigs in opposition. 'Lord Lansdowne has gone out of office not only with honour unsullied but with character exalted', he told the Knight on 27 February 1828. 'His *whole party* certainly deserve the public confidence and amply justify that confidence.'[43] But he was not so besotted a partisan as to miss the significance of Wellington's decision to repeal the Test and Corporation Acts. Immediately he proposed, at the Association meeting of 1 May, that the January resolution to oppose every ministerial parliamentary candidate be rescinded. For once, O'Connell failed. That this was an index of the growing power of the radicals within the organization is confirmed by O'Connell's letter of 27 May 1828 to his friend Bennett, superscribed '*Most Confidential*'. The nature of O'Connell's secret negotiations through his trusted intermediary may be obscure, but the need to conceal the degree of his 'moderation' is crystal clear.

> See *B*[rougham] as speedily as possible. *I confide* much in your discretion. Should *we* be able here to do anything, which indeed is not now probable, you may take a *pledge* for me but recollect the Catholics must press forward. The manner and matter of the pressure may be regulated . . .
>
> See Blount, the English Catholic Secretary, from me and tell him that the 'Securities' will produce an immediate rupture between the English and Irish Catholics . . . Tell him I *must* lead in that war. Eneas, the pious Eneas, is raving on the subject. Jack Lawless is mad with delight at a good row. [Stephen] Coppinger [a 'progressive' in the Association] grins a ghastly smile at the prospect of a good quarrel with the English Catholics. See Blount privately. Tell him I would not *write this* because I only wish you to speak it.[44]

Although British and Irish politics, and Wellington's and O'Connell's manoeuvrings, were pursuing largely independent courses, they touched electrically now and then. It was the imminent return of the tories to office which had determined O'Connell to return to the path of remorseless agitation, and Wellington's appointment which had led the Association to resolve that every pro-ministerial candidate should be opposed. Conversely, it was Wellington's decision to rid himself of the most 'liberal' members of his cabinet – probably to prepare the way for a Catholic compromise – which forced the hand of the Association. Vesey Fitzgerald, one of the sitting members for co. Clare, succeeded as president of the board of trade, and was thereby compelled to seek re-election. With the public commitment to oppose every ministerialist still intact, O'Connell was most awkwardly placed. Fitzgerald was a consistent pro-Catholic and lavish distributor of official favours about the county, his father a popular landlord and a former Grattanite. Fitzgerald would be backed moreover by the entire weight of the landed property of Clare, now that the nobility and gentry had learnt by the experiences of 1826 that the political 'rights' of their order, as such, might be at stake.

The critical difficulty for the Association when it met on 14 June 1828, only seventeen days before polling, was to find a candidate quickly – or at all. It was however the forward element which dominated at the meeting and, with whatever misgivings, O'Connell acquiesced in the eventual decision to challenge Fitzgerald at the polls. He agreed moreover to draft the address to the Clare Liberal Club and to descend upon the county, with his principal lieutenants, for the actual days of the election. A subsequent emergency meeting of the Association voted £5000, as a first instalment, for electoral expenses. Thus O'Connell found himself, in effect, presiding over machinery, already in motion, to fight a county election *à la* Waterford in 1826 without a contestant to which that machinery could be attached. Yet seven more days passed before two of the Association's Clare members, Thomas Steele, a quixotic (or perhaps Sancho Panza-ish) Protestant squireen, and the Barry Lyndonesque James O'Gorman Mahon arrived in Ennis to invite Major MacNamara to stand. MacNamara, a minor Clare landlord and O'Connell's close friend, was the only practicable candidate; no other proprietor in the county could be supposed even to consider standing against his order.

As feared, the Association's delegates found MacNamara unwilling to stand against Fitzgerald because of family favours received; the young William Smith O'Brien, another though more remote possibility as a candidate, was apparently in the same position. Steele's and Mahon's rapid traverse of the chapels of Cratloe, Sixmilebridge, Newmarket-on-Fergus and Ennis on Sunday 22 June left them in no doubt that the priests and the 40s. freeholders were ready to obey the Association blindly. On the other hand, the tenants would not openly oppose their landlords and risk terrible reprisal unless 'they were certain of a contest'.[45] Mahon posted back to Dublin with these mixed but essentially dismal tidings on the evening of the 23rd. Before the next day was out, however, all was transformed by O'Connell declaring himself a candidate.

## IV

Success has many fathers, and the line of those with some credit for the idea of a Catholic presenting himself as a parliamentary candidate runs from John Keogh, who had pressed its advantages many years before, through a liberal Protestant, Alderman Roose, to P. V. Fitzpatrick (son of the bookseller, Hugh Fitzpatrick), who actually proposed it to O'Connell on 24 June 1828. Fitzpatrick found O'Connell loth to stand; he had neither money nor the wish to throw up his profession – or even to lose the business of the current law term. He may also have been doubtful of success, and conscious of the dreadful consequences of defeat for both his own and the entire movement's public standing. But Fitzpatrick overbore him, promising to gather in all the necessary funds himself – as indeed he did. (Unwittingly, Fitzpatrick had taken the first step towards becoming O'Connell's financial and general 'manager' for life!) That very evening O'Connell concocted his electoral address to meet the next day's newspapers. Significantly he struck out on a strongly sectarian line at once.

> The oath at present required by law is, 'That the sacrifice of the Mass and the Invocation of the blessed Virgin Mary and other Saints, as now practised in the Church of Rome, are impious and idolatrous'. Of course, I never will stain my soul with such an oath; I leave that to my honourable opponent, Mr Vesey Fitzgerald. He has often taken that horrible oath; he is ready to take it again, and asks your votes to enable him so to swear. I would rather be torn limb from limb than take it.

The address went on to present the choice as one 'between the sworn libeller of the Catholic faith and one who has devoted his early life to your cause, who has consumed his manhood in a struggle for your liberties.'[46] Clearly, the classes were despaired of, and all O'Connell's energies directed to prising the peasant vote from the proprietors by the lever of religion.

The contest instantly became a new 'trial by combat'. The lay Catholic commitment may be gauged from Fitzpatrick's gathering £100 from each of sixteen Dublin Catholics within twenty-four hours of O'Connell's announcement as well as from the succession of mass demonstrations as O'Connell travelled from Dublin to Ennis from the afternoon of 28 June to the early morning of the 30th. It was, however, the involvement of the priests which mattered most. Doyle, to whom O'Connell first and most desperately appealed, recognized this instantly, and called for total support for O'Connell (with a tribute to the devotion of 'your time, your talents, your fortune, and your life' to the 'sacred cause') in a public letter.[47] At the other end of the ecclesiastical spectrum, Rev. Thomas Maguire, an ordinary country priest but the best-known religious controversialist of the day, hastened immediately from Leitrim to Clare. The Irish government had fondly hoped that the Church would divide upon the candidature. 'O'Connell', reported Anglesey, the new lord lieutenant, 'finds himself so much opposed by some of the most respectable of the Bishops, and by many of the lower clergy also, that he is quite wild.'[48] This was to misread the situation. O'Connell could count upon a clerical closing of ranks behind him as 'Catholic champion'. Even the cautious primate, Archbishop Patrick Curtis, had told him only a month before that he would trust O'Connell's judgment rather than his own in Catholic politics. In the event, almost the entire priesthood of the constituency campaigned for O'Connell, most of them in Ennis itself, the county town. Only one parish priest (duly execrated and humiliated) worked in Fitzgerald's interest. This was probably the decisive factor in O'Connell's victory. Sheil provided an epitome of the clerical influence in describing his own electioneering in the chapel at Corofin on the Sunday before the poll. The parish priest, John Murphy ('rather a study' for the enthusiast MacBriar in *Old Mortality*, tall, pale, emaciated, his face 'long, sunken and cadaverous, but . . . illuminated by eyes blazing with all the fire of genius') threw off his vestments after mass and called upon his people in Irish to sacrifice themselves for O'Connell, their faith and their fatherland.

> It was a most extraordinary and powerful display of the externals of eloquence . . . his intonations were soft, pathetic, denunciatory, and conjuring, according as his theme varied, and as he had recourse to different expedients to influence the people – shouts of laughter attended his description of a miserable Catholic who should prove recreant to the great cause, by making a sacrifice of his country to his landlord.
>
> The close of his speech was peculiarly effective. He became inflamed by the power of his emotions, and while he raised himself into the loftiest attitude to which he could ascend, he laid one hand on the altar, and shook the other in the spirit of almost prophetic admonition, and as his eyes blazed and seemed to start from his forehead, thick drops fell down his face, and his voice rolled through lips livid with passion and covered with foam. It is almost unnecessary to say that such an appeal was irresistible. The multitude burst into shouts of acclamation, and would have been ready to mount a battery roaring with cannon at his command. Two days after the results were felt at the hustings; and while Sir Edward O'Brien stood aghast, Father Murphy marched into Ennis at the head of his tenantry, and polled them to a man in favour of Daniel O'Connell.[49]

Ennis, wrote Thackerary a little later, 'stands up on the [River]

Fergus, a busy, little, narrow-streeted, foreign-looking town, approached by half a mile of thatched cots'.[50] It comprised a tangle of gloomy thoroughfares and lanes knotted about the marketplace and the cramped courthouse square. The square, with the tops of several tributary streets running into it from crazy angles, constituted the auditorium of the election. But the stage itself shifted, according to scene, from the courthouse steps to the green-bedecked balcony of O'Connell's lodgings, on the right-hand side. Successively, one or other focused the attention of the surging peasantry. Many of these camped on the watermeadows of the Fergus; but when they returned daily to their playhouse, the compression originally signalled by their convergence from all directions along the hilly roads of Clare was powerfully magnified. In its way, this was symbolic of the event: Bonaparte had shown contemporaries that to mass and concentrate one's numbers at the enemy's weakest point was the key to victory. Doubtless the monochromatic 'set', with grey skies and limestone walls and buildings generally prevailing, threw the drama which was being enacted into a higher relief.

O'Connell himself, with endless variety of tone and mood, played the by-election as theatre from the beginning. When preceded on nomination day by Vesey Fitzgerald's tears as he spoke of his father lying close to death, and by an attack from Francis Gore, a Clare proprietor and unsuccessful counsel, for his 'betrayal' of the 40s. freeholders in 1826, he burst out in response,

> And am I now to be subjected to the taunts of a briefless barrister, and a bigot without business? Of what use is my success to me? I have wept over my lot in private – for, unlike some people, I never shed my tears in public – and should I not deplore the cruel fate which places the Gores and other Protestants above me in my native land?

When Edward Hickman, a considerable Clare landlord and notorious duellist, publicly threatened to shoot O'Connell if he canvassed his tenants, O'Connell turned the encounter into profitable ridicule by lauding Hickman but adding,

> but he hasn't told you one thing – sure boys, he's the greatest playactor in the world. And, sure you all know what a playactor can do. He can pretend to be what he isn't at all. Now that is what Mr Ned Hickman is about. He's well aware that every one of you is determined to vote for me, but he wants to keep square with Mr Vesey FitzGerald, and that's what makes him play off the farce.[51]

On 5 July when O'Connell's lead in votes was already overwhelming, he joked with the crowd in proto-Kiltartanese, 'Arrah, bhoys, where's Vasy Vijarld at all, at all? . . . sind the bell about for him. Here's the cry for yez:-

*Stholen or sthrayed,*
*Losht or mishlaid,*
*The President of the Boord of Thrade!*'[52]

The 40s. freeholders and their accompanying crowds often responded as a sort of collective stage personage. When, for example, Mr Vandeleur's tenants, about one hundred strong, marching in from Kilrush behind their landlord's carriage, reached Ennis square, and O'Connell rushed forward on the platform 'and lifted up his arm'[53], the contingent deserted Vandeleur *en bloc*. When a priest announced that a 40s. freeholder who had voted against O'Connell had just dropped dead, the crowded square fell into breathless silence, and the entire body of people knelt in unison.

But popular and participating drama was only one of the theatrical levels at which O'Connell worked. He was also well aware that distant, sophisticated audiences were following the play, at various days' remove, in Dublin, London and even Paris and Vienna. He had himself declared on 21 June that the fate of Emancipation hung upon the Clare election, and this was the general view among the politically educated abroad as well as in Ireland and Great Britain; hence the eagerness and amplitude with which the fortunes of each day's polling in Ennis were reported. For the benefit of this 'export trade', so to speak, O'Connell counteracted his populism by exemplary conduct in his business with the electoral officers – the sheriff was astonished by his invariable courtesy and moderation – and strove to appease, and in effect apologize to, Fitzgerald and the other denigrated Clare gentry whenever he could safely do so. The play however really rested upon its stage management. The 3000 county voters were accompanied by perhaps ten times that number of supporters, friends, relations, wives and children. The mere housing, feeding and ordering of such throngs, and the enforcement of the two 'general orders' of the campaign – no drinking and no physical disturbance – demanded direction and discipline in a very high degree. The county Liberal Club had helped to prepare the way. But it was little more than three months since it had been inaugurated or at least invigorated by O'Connell, so that in Ennis, in contrast to Waterford in 1826, it was the priests (there were about 150 of them in the town) who bore the burden of working out and executing the logistics of polling week. They were of course also crucial in building up and maintaining pressure upon the 40s. freeholders. Murphy of Corofin wrested away the body of voters led by the solitary pro-Fitzgerald priest, Coffey, at the very vestibule of the election booth with the cry, 'Men, are ye going to betray your God and your country?' Fitzgerald's own tenants seemed to hang in the balance until suddenly debauched (except for a handful) by Fr Tom Maguire's stentorian appeal:

> You have heard the tones of the tempter and charmer, whose confederates have through all ages joined the descendants of the Dane, the Norman, and the Saxon, in burning your churches, in levelling your altars, in slaughtering your clergy, in stamping out your religion. Let every renegade to his God and his country follow Vesey FitzGerald, and every true Catholic Irishman follow me.[54]

By the end of the third day of polling, O'Connell was almost 1000 votes ahead. But it was important to him that the margin should be overwhelming, and when the poll closed he led by 2057 to 982. He had secured 67 per cent of the votes cast; it would have been 70 per cent had not 300 of his votes been disallowed upon the technicality of a printer's error in the oath which they had sworn. Fitzgerald's agent moved to have O'Connell's return declared invalid on the ground that he would never subscribe to the parliamentary oaths abjuring Roman Catholicism. But the assessor ruled that all this must await his appearance at the bar of the House of Commons; meanwhile, he had been duly elected 'as knight to represent' co. Clare. O'Connell's response was modest and conciliatory. He beseeched the landlords of the county not to avenge themselves upon the wretched 40s. freeholders, and assured them that he went to Parliament only to support retrenchment and 'the maintenance of every man's civil and religious rights and to prevent revolution'.[55] Similarly, he attempted to conciliate the British government upon his return to Dublin, 'Wellington and Peel, if you be true to old England, for I love and cherish her . . . all shall be forgotten, pardoned and forgiven upon giving us Emancipation, unconditional, unqualified, free, and unshackled.'[56]

Much the best-remembered comment upon the Clare election is Fitzgerald's 'I have polled all the gentry . . . to a man [but] . . . All the great interests broke down and the desertion has been universal. Such a scene as we have had! Such a tremendous prospect as opens before us!'[57] Even Peel, to whom this was written on the night on which the polling closed, was driven to a rare flight of imagination: 'We were watching the movements of tens of thousands of disciplined fanatics, abstaining from every excess and every indulgence, and concentrating every passion and feeling on one single object; with hundreds of police and soldiers, half of whom were Roman Catholics . . . is it consistent with common prudence and common sense to repeat such scenes and to incur such risks of contagion?'[58] Fitzgerald was depicting the ultimate and Peel the immediate consequences of O'Connell's example. The historic link of property and power had suffered a second blow, still heavier than the first in 1826. But O'Connell's election did even more – it put the government into checkmate. As he himself put it at the Association meeting of 10 July 1828, 'What is to be done with Ireland? What is to be done with the Catholics? One of two things. They must either crush us or conciliate us. There is no going on as we are.'[59] This was fundamentally correct, as was O'Connell's implication that the government would have eventually to choose the second course. Even if it banked upon O'Connell being sincere in anathemizing violence – and he was still sufficient of an unknown quantity in British politics for this to appear a very considerable risk – the cabinet could not bank upon the movement remaining under his control, or discount the danger of successive intensifications of hostile pressure such as that produced in Ennis. It would not be easy to coerce George IV and the ultra-tories into conceding the substance of Emancipation. But how much more formidable, and perilous, would it be to attempt to coerce the forces of Catholic Ireland, as now concentrated by and in the Association.

In making his assessment of 10 July, O'Connell counted upon Wellington's extreme reluctance to use armed force in civil crises, although this by no means precluded him from encouraging doubts about the reliability of the military in Ireland. In fact, immediately upon his return from the election, he publicly sent 'this whisper' to Wellington's ear, 'Three hundred soldiers threw up their caps for me since I left Ennis.'[60] O'Connell could also count upon Wellington's extreme reluctance either to resign from office – which would lead almost certainly to a whig-dominated ministry – or to call a general election – which would lead almost certainly to the loss of control of many other Irish county seats by the landed interest. O'Connell did however take one considerable risk. He made no attempt to claim his seat in the House of Commons before the current session ended on 28 July. This had the obvious advantage of maintaining pressure upon the government in Ireland. But it also meant that Wellington and Peel were given at least six months' breathing space before Parliament reassembled. In the interval, O'Connell would have to keep up the highest pitch of agitation without having any immediate or specific objective. He would have to hold back violence despite the rapid development of an Irish Protestant backlash which would in turn provoke Catholic anger. He would have to beat off the radical challenges to his leadership and management which a lengthy period of apparent inaction or regression might invite. Events were to establish the gravity of all these dangers. None the less he gambled upon his own power of domination. After almost two decades of clambering and slithering, he had at last attained the top of the greasy pole. The question was, could he stay there in balance long enough to seize the prize?

But beyond all political courses and calculations, O'Connell had triumphed as a man. He felt it fully: the moment the polls had closed he dashed off letters reporting his return (including, according to the *Limerick Chronicle*, four to Wellington, Peel, Goulburn and Eldon, respectively!) franked by himself as Member of Parliament. 'The cover [franked 'D.O'C.'] of this will announce to you a cheering fact',[61] he wrote to one Dublin supporter. All Catholic Ireland exulted too. Even before the result was announced in the capital, Dwyer, the Association secretary, felicitated him excitedly,

> My dear Sir,
>
> I have no doubt but that I am right in attaching these delightful consonants [M.P.] to your name. What an era? I never expected to have such a pleasure during the natural period of *my* life. You can have no idea of the enthusiastic feeling which prevades every rank in the city on this momentous crisis. Our receipt of rent this week exceeds two thousand pounds.[62]

O'Connell had prudently decreed that the celebration of victory should be as orderly and muted as the contest. But the Association insisted upon at least a welcoming procession of '*chariots* and *infantry*' to escort him into Dublin from four miles outside the city: 'a *proclamation* goes forth tomorrow [6 July] calling upon the people *not* to illuminate but they shall be gratified with a procession.'[63] So it was to be – cavalcades, multitudes, banners, bands, wands, green boughs and leafy wreaths – all along the slow, crowd-broken way from Clare: these were perhaps the sweetest days of all. As he left Ennis on 7 July 1828, O'Connell was enthroned upon a triumphal car. Lettered in gold about its sides, it bore his own cherished epigraph of the quarter-century's struggle,

> *Hereditary bondsmen! know ye not,*
> *Who would be free themselves must strike the blow?*

*CHAPTER 12*

# The Famous Victory,

## *1828–9*

### I

'Hard pounding', Wellington's prescription for Waterloo, was called for once again after the Clare election. If Waterford had convinced him that Emancipation must come, Clare had convinced him that it must come quickly; and on 1 August 1828 he presented a memorandum to George IV proposing the removal of most Catholic disabilities, together with suppression of the Association and the disenfranchisement of the 40s. freeholders. Peel, the king, Lyndhurst (the lord chancellor), the remainder of the cabinet and a sufficient number of reactionary peers and influential ultra-tories had now to be battered into acceptance of the inevitable. Peel needed no persuasion that the substance of the Catholic claims had now to be conceded, but a steady barrage of appeals to his sense of duty was required to induce him to remain a member of the government which would eventually conduct the Protestant surrender. In due course, Peel's submission brought Lyndhurst's in its train, which made it very likely that the other members of the ministry would fall domino-like into concurrence when their time came to look the realities in the face. George IV and the Protestant intransigents however would have to be manoeuvred as well as bullied to their doom, and Wellington's attempts simultaneously to buy time, calm their fears, conceal his own intentions and counter bellicosity all round led him into utterances too opaque for even the appellation 'Delphic'. His labours multiplied when on 14 August 1828 the Brunswick Constitution Club of Ireland was founded, in imitation of the Association's Liberal Clubs but with the purpose of fighting *à outrance* for 'the integrity of our Protestant Constitution'.[1] They spread rapidly throughout the country and across to Britain.

Meanwhile, O'Connell, like the remainder of the public and in fact all except a handful at the centre of government, was wholly ignorant of the ministerial developments of August and remained so for several months; in effect, George IV's refusal to make any commitment whatsoever muzzled Wellington for the remainder of 1828. During September the situation in Ireland grew very dangerous. O'Connell and his executive were faced with the problem of maintaining the momentum of the movement without affording the government an opportunity to institute a prosecution or their followers an opportunity to slip the leash. O'Connell's direct response was twofold. First, the Irish Protestant counter-movement was met with the rhetoric of 'loyal' violence. 'Would to God', he exclaimed at the large provincial meeting at Clonmel on 25 August, 'that our excellent Viceroy Lord Anglesey would but only give me a commission, and *if* those men of blood should attempt to attack the property and persons of his Majesty's loyal subjects, with a hundred thousand of my brave Tipperary boys, I would soon drive them into the sea before me.'[2] Secondly, O'Connell sanctioned a proposal of Lawless's to try to extend the organization and activities of the Association to the Ulster counties – at least to those border counties with large Catholic populations: this had the double advantage of diverting the troublesome 'Honest Jack' and, possibly, tapping new veins of moral force and money. Both devices proved ill-judged, although it is difficult to suggest better alternatives or to accept that the Association could safely have lapsed into masterly inactivity after Ennis. O'Connell's 'brave Tipperary boys' answered his braggadocio by a series of demonstrations and processions which soon reached the point of burning a police barracks. Meanwhile, Lawless's 'invasion' of Ulster at the head of a mass of Catholic peasants was confronted at the first sizeable town beyond the 'border', Ballybay, by several thousand Orangemen determined to repel him by force. He prudently but humiliatingly retreated. As Wyse later wrote, 'Ballybay might have been entered, but a rebellion that very night would have commenced in Ireland'.[3]

O'Connell had left for Derrynane before these moments of danger occurred, and Sheil had to intervene immediately. On 25 September the Association resolved, at Sheil's instigation, against the holding of any further processions or demonstrations (simultaneously blaming the government's inaction for their occurrence) and called upon O'Connell desperately for help. He answered with an authoritative address to the same effect. This was published in the nick of time, on 30 September, a day before the Irish executive proclaimed all political assemblages. The Association had learned its lesson, and devoted the winter of 1828–9 to restraining the actions of their followers. Anglesey had read the situation correctly when he reported on 8 September: 'I calculate upon a quiet winter in acts, but not in language . . . the Catholics are persuaded that the Brunswickers will bring on collision if they can, with the view of committing the government against them. This is what the leaders will endeavour to avoid.'[4] In this they were greatly helped by the fact that Anglesey himself had been completely converted to Emancipation, as both irresistible and the solvent for Irish discontents, by O'Connell's victory at Ennis. 'Lord Anglesey is gone mad', Wellington observed. 'He is bit by a mad Papist; or instigated by the love of popularity.'[5] At any rate, he demonstrated a steady sympathy with O'Connell's cause during the remainder of 1828, most dramatically of all when he refused to prosecute Steele and O'Gorman Mahon for their part in a demonstration in November and even left them intact in their magistracies. This indicated to the Orange faction that the lord lieutenant had gone over to the enemy (and nothing better suited O'Connell's book in calming and cheering his own supporters) and Wellington's failure to remove him (he feared the Irish Catholic reaction) seemed to show a calamitous weakness in the anti-Catholic defences, even at the centre.

At a deeper level of response, O'Connell was governed, in the latter half of 1828, by what he read as the lessons of 1825. He would concede nothing but depend upon the weight of Catholic pressure forcing the issue on its own. In 1825, he told his friend Pierce Mahony (now a parliamentary agent in London), he should have 'kept up that salutary apprehension' of Irish disorder which would have brought Liverpool to his knees,

> but, instead of *that*, I listened in an evil hour to the suggestions of Mr Plunket, etc., who said that if we conceded 'the Wings' by way of security, we should certainly carry the bill . . . I procured for this purpose public tranquillity. The Ministry saw that I had appeased the storm, they considered that the danger was passed and the House of Lords scouted our Emancipation bill. Nay, Peel . . . actually taunted me with having betrayed popular rights in order to attain the objects of my personal ambition.
>
> I was deceived once but I should indeed be more than insane, I should be indeed 'a knave or a fool' if [I] were to be deceived in the same way again.
>
> We shall never be emancipated but as we were relieved in 1778, 1782 and 1793, that is, when it becomes *necessary* for the English Government to do something for Ireland.[6]

O'Connell's first objective was therefore to 'control' (his own word) as many Irish M.P.'s as possible. 'If I had fifty county members obliged to attend constantly and to vote against every ministerial measure', he wrote to Mahony, he would soon be bought off by the grant of Emancipation. In earnest of this, he saw to it that the first Association meeting after the Clare election reaffirmed the policy of opposing all pro-ministerial candidates at the polls. He also approved and adopted an elaborated form of Wyse's Liberal Clubs proposal. During the second half of 1828 clubs were set up (sometimes, as in the case of Sligo, by O'Connell directly) in a dozen Irish counties, and earlier foundations were reorganized and fitted into the rapidly developing confederation. By the beginning of 1829, the majority of Irish counties belonged to the network (there were Liberal Clubs even in two of the Ulster counties, Monaghan and Down, though, strangely, none in Kerry), and several of the cities and larger towns ran clubs separately. This set the scene for national political action upon a most formidable scale. It was also intended to cement middle-class command of the popular movement. The subscription to the county clubs was high, 30s. per annum, and the membership of the constituent parish clubs restricted to 'the principal gentry, clergy, churchwardens, and such of the respectable farmers as can read'.[7] O'Connell tried to ensure that even his rank and file would be free of troublemakers. The only supporters whose assistance he would accept, he told the parish priest of Cashel during the Tipperary disorders of September, 'are the *good, honest, religious* men . . . The men I want to contribute to that sacred fund [the Catholic Rent] and to help me to keep the country quiet and to put down Orange oppression are the steady men who are good sons, good brothers, good husbands.'[8] His summoning of provincial meetings of the Association in three of the four provinces during the autumn of 1828 – hitherto such meetings had been occasional and unconnected – is also explicable in terms of his anxiety to canalize, and keep in mastery, the enthusiasm of the masses. The province was the largest unit into which the Association could be broken. By the same token, the provincial meeting was the loudest crowd-hailer and the best medium of popular pageantry at O'Connell's disposal at this time.

Meanwhile, O'Connell never ceased to foster his regular and basic organizational instrument, the Catholic Rent, and its accompanying apparatus. Here he prospered. In addition to the very large sums subscribed to finance the contest in Clare, the Rent brought in nearly £23,000 during 1828 (mostly from 1 July onwards) as against less than £3000 for 1827. Part cause and part effect of this marvellous success, the churchwarden system grew steadily more settled and expansive.

Of special significance in the long months of suspended crisis was the development, through the wardens' work, of parish Reading Rooms (supplied with free newspapers by the Association) and local arbitration or adjudication of disputes over property or easements and personal or factional conflict. Respectively, these signalled a deeper level of systematic indoctrination and the further spread of both the idea and practice of 'alternative government'. Overall, O'Connell's moves may be categorized as a sort of controlled and contingent alienation of the Catholic body from the state. Their vital purpose however was to keep the agitation both fiery and subject to decisive direction from the top.

O'Connell had however also to look to the day when he might be transformed into a professional politician. This was made clear to him on the morrow of the Clare election; letters appealing for or confidently claiming his countenance began to flood in from British agitators and interest groups. In fact, even before the polling closed, the London radicals, headed by Henry Hunt, announced their determination to 'convey' him to Westminster to take his seat with a procession of '50,000' or '60,000'. On 11 July 1828, the Irish liberal peer, Rossmore, begged him to keep his distance from the radicals. All his friends in London, Rossmore wrote, agreed that the time was inopportune for O'Connell to declare himself even a Reformer: 'they think it injures the cause greatly *here at present* and prevents them from being of the use they otherwise could.'[9] O'Connell rejected Rossmore's specific plea that he make no commitment to Reform at a dinner to be held in his honour by the Louth Liberal Club on 14 July. Instead he declared that 'I am now, I ever shall be, a Radical Reformer.'[10] A few days earlier, O'Connell persuaded the Catholic Association to require pledges in future from all candidates for election not only to oppose Wellington's ministry but also to support the cause of parliamentary reform and the repeal of a recent statute which he regarded as particularly obnoxious: the Subletting Act. Diffidently, even deferentially, another liberal Irish peer, Duncannon (heir to the Marquess of Bessborough), urged the unwisdom of these additional obligations upon O'Connell:

> I think . . . the mixing any other matter with it weakens the first pledge and gives a loophole to those who may be inclined by this means to avoid the whole. It appears to me you have now brought the Catholic question to that point that it must be successful unless it is marred by some unfortunate and unexpected circumstance . . . [Wellington] sees a determination in Ireland to be represented only by those who will oppose him or any other

> minister that does not make the Catholic question a *sine qua non*. No minister can look on such a state of things with indifference, but you will pardon me when I say that in my opinion, if he was called on to name the means of relieving himself from some of the difficulty, he could not devise a more likely one to meet his wishes than raising in his opponents' ranks a question like Parliamentary Reform.[11]

But again O'Connell closed his ears to the moderating advice of his parliamentary 'friends'.

None the less, he dealt cautiously with the radicals. He believed that their influence, though a useful support, was limited; later he came to doubt where even their large numbers or agitating experience were of any value. 'He [Hunt] has got *no following*', he wrote on 11 March 1829,

> I was until now convinced that the Radicals were in some power – they are *not*; they are numerous but they have no leaders, no system, no confidence in either Henry Hunt or William Cobbett – not the least – not the least.
>
> This is the case with the reformers generally; they are powerless by reason of the people who considered themselves leaders but who are despicable both from their characters and their vile jealousies and ill temper.[12]

In any event, apart from parliamentary reform (in which, in or out of the House of Commons, O'Connell would always have a vital interest) the only constituent of the radical programme which, in the autumn of 1828, he looked forward to promoting in Parliament was the rationalization of the law. 'Law Reform is now my grand object', he told Staunton on 22 September,

> Everybody should help to get rid of the present most vexatious, expensive, cabalistic and unintelligible system of law proceedings . . . I do not exaggerate when I say that no man since the days of 'the Sainted Alfred' was ever half as useful as I shall be if I can abolish the present nefarious and abominable system and introduce a code of Common Sense both in its mode of proceeding and in its rules and enactments.[13]

For more than a year, this was to remain the foremost element of O'Connell's radicalism.

Moreover the political alliance dearest to O'Connell's heart was still one with the Irish Protestant liberals. Common nationality had claims even against common radical principle. After the formation of the Brunswick Clubs, such an alliance seemed all the more desirable, as a counterpoise. 'In the meantime, what are *our* friends doing?', he demanded of Lord Cloncurry on 4 September 1828, 'Alas! nothing.

They, the Orangeists, have their peers coming forward with alacrity, openly and with ostentation . . . We have scarcely any symptom of sympathy from the higher order of Protestants.'[14] Three weeks later he again wrote bitterly to Cloncurry of 'the deep conviction the Catholics now entertain that they are either opposed or deserted by the Irish Protestants . . . Protestant assistance will be given us [only] when the difficulties are over.'[15] None the less O'Connell maintained his pressure upon susceptible Irish Protestants throughout the autumn of 1828. He was also careful to avoid sectarian provocation. When for example the Association was asked on 6 November to endorse 'exclusive dealing' (refusing to do business with Orangemen or 'Brunswickers'), he crushed the proposal fiercely, demanding 'an advertisement in the newspapers, calling on all persons who have been persecuted and aggrieved by this heartless practice to come forward.'[16] At last he succeeded. In December the Duke of Leinster was induced to head a specifically Protestant movement to support full Emancipation. A meeting held in Dublin on 20 January 1829, attended by eleven Irish peers and correspondingly larger numbers of baronets, knights and landed gentlemen, resolved that the Duke, supported by a considerable body of Irish noblemen and M.P.s, should proceed to London to present a pro-Emancipation petition personally to the king.

Wyse considered this development to have been critically important in converting a sufficient body of English opinion to the idea that Emancipation might be safely granted. But O'Connell regarded a liberal Protestant auxiliary as useful but in no way essential for the immediate purpose: 'we are doing so well', he calculated on 4 September 1828, 'that we can afford, after all, to go on without being encumbered with other aid.'[17] With the future in sight, however, he was eager to forge whatever links he could with the liberal Ascendancy so that (in Wyse's phrase) the 'quarrel, instead of being Catholic and Protestant, was likely to become Irish and English'.[18] The formation, hard on the heels of the Rotunda meeting, of the Friends of Civil and Religious Liberty and the projection of a supra-confessional Irish Association soon after gave hopes that such links might indeed be forged. There were still too many obstacles in the way of a common political front. Ostensibly, both the Catholic Association and the Friends were bound for self-destruction: the achievement of Emancipation, now very likely, was their *raison d'être*. Organizationally, the bodies worked on very different, in fact often contradictory, principles. The Association's commitment to Repeal and opposition to the Subletting Act and similar land legislation repelled almost all Irish whigs; even the degree of parliamentary reform which O'Connell demanded was abhorrent. None the less O'Connell had produced junctions and collaborations from less promising materials in the past, and there was never a more sanguine or ingenious politician. But whatever his parliamentary prospects or ambitions, he had yet to force an entry into the arena. By now the time had come for him to make the attempt, in accordance with his earlier determination, to win admission to the Commons on the first day of the new parliamentary session. On 6 February 1829 he embarked at Dublin for Holyhead, attended by a train of 'courtiers' like a prince of old.

## II

Since August 1828 Wellington had been immobilized by George IV's refusal even to discuss Emancipation; he had no means of forcing him to terms until a decision would be inescapable, that is, when the speech from the throne was being prepared in January 1829. An attempt to persuade the king, in a memorandum of 18 November 1828, that any further resistance to Catholic Relief was futile, failed utterly. This may explain Wellington's letter of 11 December to the Catholic primate, Curtis, promising (according to one reading) eventual relief, which in turn set off an extraordinary *pas de trois* between these two and the lord lieutenant. By the time the flurry of correspondence and breaches of 'confidentiality' at last died away, Anglesey had been recalled. He had demonstrated a steady sympathy with O'Connell's cause during the last five months of 1828, most dramatically of all when he had refused to prosecute Steele and O'Gorman Mahon. The Steele–O'Gorman Mahon affair was in fact the major charge in Wellington's indictment. But no one doubted that it was the general tenor rather than any particular manifestation of Anglesey's conciliatory treatment of the Catholics which had produced his downfall. The parallel with Fitzwilliam's recall as lord lieutenant in 1795, which had marked a sudden turnabout in British policy and raised the curtain upon decades of rejection, seemed alarmingly close.

O'Connell responded to Anglesey's dismissal not only by presiding over a species of national mourning but also by enlarging his agitatory armoury. On 13 January 1829 (the day of Anglesey's departure) he instituted an inspectoral system in the Association. A national inspector was to visit each county successively and appoint five local county inspectors who would in turn ensure that each parish was 'worked' by churchwardens and that Association policy was enforced there. Significantly, the local inspectors were given the additional duty of monitoring and helping to suppress the agrarian secret societies in their districts. O'Connell followed this up by a circular letter to the Irish Catholic bishops calling on each to support a further drive for the collection of the Rent in his diocese. These additional turns of the screw were never really tested, but O'Connell was clearly aiming at further increases in centralization, political arousal and campaign funds.

When at the beginning of February 1829, however, the news reached Dublin that Emancipation would be substantially ceded, the bar 'party' within the Association began to press for the suspension of agitation lest the king or ministry be given a pretext for withdrawing Catholic relief. 'Nothing can so well become us as "mild behaviour and humility", when the least intimations of national pacification are held out', Sheil told the Association on 3 February.[19] He also set about lobbying the bishops for support for his proposal that the Association be immediately dissolved. Possibly O'Connell was attempting to counter this when he wrote to Doyle on 4 February that 'the blessing you bestowed' upon the Clare contest was now being realized, and when he added, 'If I get into the House, Catholic education will have an unremitting and sincere advocate.'[20] Even after he had had perforce to leave the Irish field of battle, O'Connell continued the struggle against the appeasers. On 8 February he sent forth a public letter from Shrewsbury (on his way to London) urging that the Association remain in being at least until Emancipation had been enacted. But the 'Orange Papists', as L'Estrange called them, proved too powerful when O'Connell was away from Dublin; on 12 February Sheil, claiming the endorsement of 22 of the 26 Catholic bishops, carried his resolution that the Association disband itself forthwith.

Upon reaching London on 9 February O'Connell found that two of his recent commitments were likely to prove embarrassing. First, in an address to the freeholders of Clare on 28 January he had promised to attempt to take his seat in the Commons at the opening of the parliamentary session. But he was persuaded to postpone such a 'provocation'. This exposed him to the radical Hunt's rebuke of 17 March,

> the course of seclusion which you have been advised to adopt since you have arrived in London, together with your not having even attempted to take your seat in the House of Commons as you had promised, and as the public had a right to expect that you would have done, . . . are the most

> powerful causes of the criminal apathy of which you so justly complain, and I am quite sure that the above alluded to want of action on your part, has been, and still is, the sole cause of the torpor and indifference of the London Reformers . . .[21]

Secondly, in his Shrewsbury letter of 8 February 1829 O'Connell had called upon the Association 'to reject any bill of emancipation, no matter how extensive if accompanied by any such interference' with the elective franchise.[22] But on 3 March he came under heavy pressure from Brougham to acquiesce in the expected government bill to disenfranchise the 40s. freeholders. 'He spoke to me a great deal on the freehold wing', O'Connell wrote to Mary that evening,

> He wanted to get some countenance from me for the Whigs supporting that wing. I need not tell you that he totally failed. They *trapped* me before. They cannot possibly succeed in that way a second time. Besides, darling, I really am too much indebted to the 40s freeholders. You do not think I could ever turn my back on the poor fellows in Clare. I argued with Brougham in the strongest terms on the subject and showed him how useless it would be to call it a measure of concession, if they were at the same time to destroy the rights of the people at large. Brougham left me, perhaps dissatisfied but certainly without any encouragement from me, decidely the reverse.[23]

He even suspected foul play. His election for Clare had just been challenged (unsuccessfully, as things turned out) on the ground of undue influence on the part of the Catholic clergy, and Brougham's visit immediately preceded the striking of the parliamentary committee to try the petition. 'It was *curious*', O'Connell told Dwyer, 'that Brougham should come to me the very day – the morning of the day – on which my committee was and is to be formed . . . just the day when it is most likely that I should wish to be in favour with the men who might form that committee.'[24] Although O'Connell rapidly came round to the 'opinion [that] the £10 [franchise] will really give more power to the Catholics',[25] he did not abandon the 40s. freeholders immediately. In a public address issued on 7 March 1829 he still called for 'decided, determined, energetic, but constitutional opposition' to their disenfranchisement;[26] and at a meeting of Irish Catholics held in London on the same day, he beat down the 'trimmers' – among them N. P. O'Gorman, Eneas MacDonnell and Pierce Mahony – on the issue of petitioning in favour of the doomed electors. But though the meeting also called on the whigs 'to resist the Disenfranchisement Bill at all hazards', O'Connell had to report sadly on 11 March that 'Brougham and all the party gave in. The Opposition, to a man, will vote for it.'[27] O'Connell probably expressed his true feelings when he bemoaned the whig tergiversation to Dwyer as 'cruel – very cruel';[28] but from now on he virtually threw up the cause of the 40s. freeholders as hopeless. His pledge to reject Emancipation, if accompanied by their disenfranchisement, dropped out of sight in the euphoria of the larger triumph.

Why did O'Connell, who had stood on the right wing of the Association throughout 1828, stand on the left wing – to the left even of Lawless who had supported the immediate dissolution of the Association – during the early spring of 1829? First, he believed that Emancipation would not be safe until George IV was actually forced to put pen to the paper of a successful bill; therefore, no weapon should be laid down before this happened. Next, the 'betrayal' of 1825 had left an ineffaceable mark upon him; he was determined to be neither gulled nor opened up to charges of self-interested opportunism a second time. Last – and perhaps not least – Mary was intensely interested in the outcome, and his political conscience was 'informed' by her surveillance. The characteristic note of his reports to her from England was struck in the very first with, 'I will not hesitate to take a decided and honest part. That, sweetest, *you* will readily allow.'[29]

But all this lay in the shadow of the coming Emancipation. Though common report had it that the ministry's concessions would be large and unqualified, O'Connell could not be easy until the government had committed itself in public. On the expected eve of the announcement of its intentions he wrote nervously to Mary,

> I cannot write politics this day because, my own darling, there is a tremulous anxiety about me for tomorrow. Tomorrow is the awful day, *big with the fate of Cato and of Rome*. You see, love, how poetic I am grown. The fact is that as the crisis approaches on which we *must* know everything, one cannot bring one's mind to do otherwise than merely wish that the time of certainty were come . . .[30]

But all was well. On 6 March 1829 he wrote again, exultantly, 'Great and glorious triumph as far as the Emancipation bill goes – no Veto – no payment of clergy – no ecclesiastical arrangements.' As to the obnoxious clauses, he would 'drive a coach and six' through that aiming 'to prevent the *extension* of the Jesuits and other monastic orders', while a prohibition upon Catholic bishops using territorial titles for their sees was dismissed as 'absurd and childish'. [31] This was fair judgment. Apart from the reservation of a handful of the chief offices of state, the ministerial bill granted Emancipation unalloyed: 'I always said', O'Connell boasted to Dwyer, 'that when they came to emancipate they would not care a bulrush about those vetoistical arrangements which so many paltry Catholics from time to time pressed on me as being useful to Emancipation.'[32] He proved correct in advising the regular clergy – his 'fee' being 'one moment of recollection of me occasionally at the pure and Holy sacrifice'[33] – that they had nothing to fear from the bill because only the attorney-general could act under it against them, and he could procure no testimony as every potential witness would incriminate himself if he gave evidence. Correspondingly, it was only the bishop himself who could be prosecuted in the matter of ecclesiastical titles.

O'Connell remained both delighted and fearful while the bill wound its way through the Commons and Lords. From Dublin, where he returned briefly towards the end of March, he plied his current parliamentary intermediary, Mahony, with appeasing information and assurances that the Catholics were prepared to 'offer' the people to the government. If in addition to Catholic relief a grant for public works were forthcoming, he wrote on 28 March, 'The people will be taken out of *our* hands by Emancipation as we took them from Capt. Rock by *our* agitation'. He also offered to abandon the attempt to take his seat before the Emancipation bill was enacted – in the event he made none – if such a step might endanger the measure. 'This may be an impeachment to my head', he told Mahony, 'but literally my heart overrules me. Thus the language of silly novels steals into politics. I will be sturdy enough on all other points but on this I have, I own it, a woman's weakness.'[34] But there may have been more to it than 'woman's weakness'. Postponement might not only ease the passage of the bill through Parliament but also so place the ministry in his debt that they would submit quietly to his entering the Commons after the Relief Act had done away with the offensive oaths. Mahony later claimed that members of the government, during the Easter recess of 1829, had assured him that the government as such would not oppose O'Connell's attempt to take his seat under the new legislation.

On 11 April 1829 O'Connell was able to tell Mary from London that the bill had passed the Lords. 'It will receive the Royal assent on Monday [13 April] and thus the ascendancy and proud superiority which your neighbours had over you will be at an end the day you receive this letter', he added significantly. It is touching as well as a measure of his pent-up anxiety that he should have specified for her in advance '*the minute*' of liberation – '*about* 20 minutes after four by the Dublin clocks'.[35] In the same vein, his letter to Dwyer of 14 April was superscribed 'The first day of freedom!' To Dwyer he wrote, 'It [the Relief Act] is one of the greatest triumphs recorded in history – a bloodless revolution more extensive in its operation than any other political change that could take place. I say *political* to contrast it with *social* changes which might break to pieces the framework of society.'[36] To Mary he had already written, 'And it was your husband contributed *most* . . . Was it not, sweetest?'[37] Even cruel posterity could not quarrel with either asseveration.

## III

Some months after the passage of the Catholic Relief Act, O'Connell, in arranging with Isaac Goldsmid to serve as parliamentary spokesman for Jewish Emancipation, set out the lessons he had learned from more that two decades of campaigning. 'Allow me at once to commence my office of your advocate', he wrote on 11 September 1829,

> and to begin by giving you advice. It is: not to postpone your claim of right beyond the second day of the ensuing session. Do not listen to those over cautious persons who may recommend postponement. Believe an agitator of some experience that nothing was ever obtained by delay – at least in politics – you must to a certain extent force your claims on the parliament. You cannot be worse, recollect, even by a failure and you ought to be better by the experiment . . .
>
> You must I repeat *force* your question on the Parliament. You ought not to confide in English liberality. It is a plant not genial to the British soil. It must be *forced*. It requires a *hot-bed*. The English were always persecutors. Before the so styled reformation the English tortured the Jews and strung up in scores the Lollards. After that reformation they still roasted the Jews and hung the Papists. In Mary's day the English with their usual cruelty retaliated the tortures on the Protestants. After her short reign there were near two centuries of the most barbarous and unrelenting cruelty exercised towards the Catholics . . . The Jews too suffered in the same way. I once more repeat. Do not confide in any liberality but that which you will yourself rouse into action and *compel* into operation.[38]

This expressed O'Connell's now-settled conviction that force – albeit moral, agitatory, intimidatory force – was the only father of concession in British politics. Yet it also made clear his wish to work inside, and with the grain of, that system, wherever possible. His belief in the English penchant for persecution was not accompanied by personal rancour or national righteousness; it was simply (as he saw it) a fact of public life.

Perhaps the key to O'Connell's extraordinary political equipoise was this largemindedness. In crushing challenges to his leadership, he might be merciless or unscrupulous. But, after all, his principal political business was to lead; and he never sought more than to force a challenger back to what he regarded as his proper station of subordination. He forgave personal slights freely, quickly and unconditionally. Several followed hard on the heels of Emancipation. He was blackballed when on 12 May 1829 he allowed his name to go forward for election to the Cisalpine Club, the association of the English Catholic elite. Members of that elite raced shamelessly and successfully to beat him to the honour of becoming the first Catholic M.P. since penal days. The Speaker of the Commons, Charles Manners-Sutton, a nephew of his old adversary Lord Manners, malignly (as he believed) refused him admission to the House under the new Relief Act. Peel and other leading tories surreptitiously and treacherously (as he believed) directed ministerial supporters to back the Speaker in the subsequent debate. Bitterest of all, when in October 1829 the first body of Catholic counsel in Ireland was admitted to the inner bar, O'Connell was excluded from the list, which was moreover composed almost entirely of his juniors in years and fame. Even his chief rival Sheil was soon added to the number. No insult could have cut deeper. Since 1808 O'Connell had been driven to exertion by resentment of both the injustice and the financial implications of the prohibition on his taking silk. Yet in reporting his rebuff by the Cisapine Club to Dwyer on 14 May 1829 he 'heartily [forgave] them all', merely adding 'But it was a strange thing of them to do; it was a comical "testimonial" of my services in emancipating them.'[39] Anticipating Manners-Sutton's enmity, he observed 'I am a good deal indifferent on the matter. I know that I have demonstrated my right, and that it will be understood and felt in Ireland.'[40] On the debate upon his claim to admission to the Commons, he observed, with rueful humour, 'I should still have had a chance of success but for the conduct of Sir James Scarlett, who made a very strong and argumentative speech in my favour and concluded by declaring that he would vote against me. This, of course, was a decisive blow. But the Attorney-Generalship is vacant, and poor Sir James is a man.'[41] He never inveigled against Sheil or any other of the newly admitted Catholic silks, but bore the blow to his pride and hopes in silence.

O'Connell's magnanimity was something more than the practised politician's useful phlegm and calculated provisionality of alliances and enmities. It was rooted in the ductility of his character. The defect of this quality, in politics no less than financial dealings, was what Hunting Cap had once condemned as 'the softness and facility of your disposition'.[42] This led O'Connell into over-responsiveness to his company, audience, surroundings or immediate circumstances. On balance however his 'charity' was a political advantage – given of course the northern star-like fixity of his ultimate goals. It rendered him perpetually resilient, flexible, fertile in device and ready for accommodation within the grand circle of the negotiable.

The passage of the Catholic Relief Act provides a classic instance of his elasticity. The Irish 40s. freeholders and his own chance of immediate entry into the House of Commons were finally jettisoned in the name of the greater good, though O'Connell was partly compensated by being released from the dual dangers of dependence on a vulnerable electoral force and of incurring the horrific – literally ruinous – penalties attached to illegal entry into Parliament. He made no attempt to combat the punitive clauses of the Act. The fact that he considered them inoperable was enough. O'Connell used the same philosophy in politics as in law, for him the verdict was *the* thing; and just as Wellington and Peel had added the humiliating provisions to their bill in order to ease the sufferings of the ultra-Protestants, so O'Connell acquiesced in the odious clauses in order to assuage the cabinet's unspent resentment of its defeat. Again, for a variety of prudential reasons, not least among them the conciliation of the government, O'Connell forbade exuberant celebration of the achievement of Emancipation. For this, he was prepared even to anger Mary, although his attempt to mitigate his offence was also characteristic of his method. 'I was sorry we differed about the illumination', he wrote to her from London on 15 April 1829,

> but my great reason for being anxious about the prevention of that measure was least you or my girls should be insulted by an infuriate banditti. I should be glad and yet sorry that Maurice was at home. With these mixed feelings, which to a certain extent were applicable to many other families besides my own, I did strongly recommend them [the Catholics of Dublin] not to illuminate. It would be I thought the mere personal gratification of a triumph which might be considered insulting just at the moment when, having got a real and substantial advantage, we want no feathers but, darling, why do I *now* annoy about my opinions? If I were in Dublin I would probably have given up my opinion to yours. At all events, darling, we would not have quarrelled about it.[43]

Correspondingly, O'Connell greeted the Relief Act as the complete accomplishment of his objectives. Yet it was notorious that the 'relief' was limited to the dismantling of barriers to entering certain public offices and professional ranks. *Ipso facto*, it directly concerned only the bourgeoisie and upper orders. Even for them it merely unlocked doors: forcing entries was quite another matter.

How then are we to explain O'Connell's paeans of triumph in 1829? His own initial responses to the final passage of the bill provide some answers. As we have seen, he wrote at once to Mary that she could now stand as an equal with Irish Protestants, and to Dwyer that he had achieved a political, while avoiding a social, revolution. Soon afterwards, on 1 May 1829, he told James Sugrue that when admitted to the House of Commons (he then expected that this would happen within a week), 'I intend to take an *immediate* active part in the proceedings. I need not say to you how impatient I am to be useful.'[44]

The first answer concerned feelings. O'Connell argued – to use the language of a later analogy – that one must begin by thinking of oneself as a man rather than a coloured man; next, one should try to *behave* as if this assertion were in fact the truth; finally, one strove to force the supremacists into acknowledging its reality – insofar at least as a reforming statute could alter attitudes, or even conduct. To O'Connell the Relief Act signified the formal end not only of the 'Catholic crouch' in Ireland but also of the ethos of deference and quietism in which he had grown up. Even the formidable Hunting Cap had known his place under Protestant domination; even the gallant General Daniel had advised his nephew as late as 1819 to 'Put less effort into Emancipation . . . nothing can advance by even a day the time marked out by Providence.'[45] This was of course partly explicable in terms of difference in generation. But no one had done more than O'Connell to deepen – one might even say, create – that particular generation gap, and his own younger brothers were much closer in outlook to their uncles than to himself. Moreover, the intangible benefits of Emancipation – self-esteem, a sense of power and triumph, and similar psychological satisfactions – were by no means unimportant in O'Connell's eyes, and these could be enjoyed, existentially or vicariously, by hundreds of thousands of Irish Catholics who had gained nothing else. Among these satisfactions we should number the colour and busyness, the dash and spirit, which the new political culture of the 1820s had brought to multitudes of hard, barren lives and wretched places. The fifteen-acre tenant who had marched twenty miles in his contingent to the polls, the Ballybricken butcher who had patrolled Waterford with his white wand of authority during election week, the curate who had preached up the

Rent, the collector at the chapel gate, the shopboy who built a speakers' platform upon barrels, the clerk who broadcast weekly to the illiterates from the columns of the *Morning Register*, would never forget that there had once been heady days.

'We were probably the most conservative-minded revolutionaries that ever put through a successful revolution', Kevin O'Higgins concluded at the end of the Anglo-Irish conflict of 1916–21.[46] He should have excepted O'Connell whose second cause of pride in the achievement of Emancipation – as set out in his letter to Dwyer of 14 April 1829 – was its shoring up of the existing social structure. New Left historians have no need to search about for evidence of O'Connell's adherence to the established class system. Not only did he not disguise, he openly avowed his fear and hatred of social disturbance and disorder. When he spoke of the Relief Act as accomplishing a political revolution, he meant that one great chain of legal discrimination had been struck off the body politic; when he gloried in the event, it was because (in one of his own favourite phrases) not a single drop of human blood had been shed in its accomplishment. In all this, there should be nothing to surprise us. O'Connell belonged to one well-known and well-marked camp in each of the great antitheses of contemporary radicalism. He was a respectable, a rationalistic and a moral-force radical, as against his blackguard, millenarian and violent 'comrades' of the left. All of them however would have shared his view that Emancipation was a political advance, however some might have deplored its social ineffectuality. And all of them would also have shared his basic premise, that the case for Emancipation rested upon indefeasible individual right and the absolute *civil* equality of every person – or at any rate every adult male.

O'Connell's third reason for exultation when the Relief Bill passed was not general but particular – that it opened the way for his self-realization. His letter to Sugrue of 1 May 1829 made clear his eagerness to begin a parliamentary career at once. The painfully successful agitator of fifty-three years of age was no different from the boy of nine or ten who had dreamt of emulating Flood and Grattan, or the youth of seventeen solemnly rehearsing for the day on which he would enter the grand theatre of the world, or the young man of twenty-one who debated methodically with himself as to which faction he would join when he attained at last the Irish House of Commons. If the term 'born politician' has not been debased by over-use, it may surely be applied to him. His manoeuvres of July 1828–

April 1829 show the hand of the master at every twist and turn; but his manoeuvres of 1808–9 had been scarcely less skilful. Though O'Connell was a political auto-didact, he had little to teach himself, and that little was grounded surely in his intelligent analysis of every past experience. The agony of a suppressed natural function (to steal words from Shaw) was almost over. He had spent forty years too long in Cicero's vestibule, but now, finally, the Relief Act had released him for the auditorium. Even joy in the evening was joy.

## IV

We do not know when, or even whether specifically, O'Connell decided to abandon law for membership of the House of Commons. A London counsel might combine the two careers while he awaited judicial office or a solicitor- or attorney-generalship. But this was impracticable for an Irish barrister, let alone one who would also purport to lead a national party; in themselves, parliamentary sessions would have eaten up more than half the law terms. Thus while O'Connell probably still intended to practise in the interstices of politics, he also knew that his future work and income as a lawyer would be both relatively small and intermittent. It may well be that he never chose deliberately to change careers. Once he had been induced to contest co. Clare – and significantly his resistance to doing so was grounded in his straitened circumstances and the temporary interruption of his practice – there was really no turning back. Nor was he called upon to alter the pattern of his life immediately. Because he did not attempt to take his seat during 1828, he could pursue his profession in the ordinary way throughout the remainder of the year.

When however he left Dublin for London on 3 February 1829, he also, practically speaking, left the Irish bar behind him, once for all. It was his clear intention to enter the House of Commons and adopt a parliamentary career as soon as possible. At some time during the preceeding seven months he must have considered how he and his family were to be supported without the great majority of his legal earnings, and with the added burden of several months of residence in London every year. Yet the first surviving indication of a possible solution only comes in a letter of 10 February 1829 from his friend Cornelius MacLoghlin, who wrote, 'Let me know how things will go on as in the event of your taking your seat, I have a proposition to make that will tend to your future ease and comfort and enable you to devote your entire time to your country.'[47] This was evidently the first step towards the setting up of the O'Connell testimonial on 25 March, for MacLoghlin was one of the seven treasurers 'of the very first mercantile rank' (the brewer Arthur Guinness and the banker David La Touche were others) of the subscription fund. O'Connell showed no compunction in becoming, in effect, a national pensioner, although once the testimonial was turned into an annual O'Connell Tribute, this was to expose him to unceasing gibes as 'the big beggarman'. On the contrary, he followed the progress of the testimonial anxiously, reporting news of promised subscriptions in detail to Mary. In turn, Dwyer and others reported news to him. 'In fact', O'Connell wrote to John Primrose in Kerry on 25 April, 'the thing would be splendid if there were persons capable of conducting it. Every parish should be collected by itself. It was the single shillings that swelled the Catholic Rent. But this is not for me to say and therefore you will of course use the strictest silence as to *my* saying so.'[48] O'Connell's fears of mismanagement of the subscription drive were groundless. The testimonial amounted finally to almost £30,000, well over half the total of Rent raised during the years 1824–9. As ever, O'Connell was worried about immediate needs and blithe about the distant future. He had told Primrose on 25 April, when his expectations were still modest,

> Whatever money is collected in Kerry [in fact, £1500 had been collected there already] should be sent up and lodged in the Hibernian Bank to my credit as rapidly as possible. I think it is likely that the subscription will be sufficient to get me quite out of debt and to pay my daughters' fortunes. If it does so much, I shall be quite content.[49]

Correspondingly, he had written to Mary soon after the testimonial was publicly announced, 'Now if the subscription goes on well, darling, I will have you here [London], please God, early in May.'[50]

This makes clear the intermingling (not to say, confusion) of private and public money which was to characterize O'Connell's finances for the remainder of his life, and also his pressing family needs. Six of his children were now adults, and finding careers or husbands for them had become an urgent business. Kate and Betsey were still unmarried and dowries of £5000 would be their expected portions if they were to remain in the higher professional or lower gentry ranks. Part of Ellen's dowry – she had married into this rank in 1825 – was still outstanding. Morgan was proving expensive: neither his careless, happy disposition nor his life as an Austrian cavalry officer made for economy. On 7 July 1829 he acknowledged receipt of £100, as the first instalment of a sum needed to rescue him from some scrape, adding,

> Be assured, my dear father, that this is the last time I will make any such extravagant demand . . . I will however endeavour to prove to you by my future conduct of the change operated in me and of my firm unalterable resolution not again to involve myself in such a predicament. These are not empty words. Time will prove the truth of them.[51]

Ensuring that Maurice (who became twenty-six on 23 June 1829) married well was, however, the O'Connells' most desperate concern. On 6 March 1829 O'Connell reported to Mary a dinner held in his honour by 'rich Jews in the City' with the (perhaps wistfully) jocular comment, 'Perhaps Maurice could pick up a £50,000 amongst them.'[52] A month later he told her that Maurice was 'disposed to make us all happy. It would crown *all* if he were to fix himself *now* well.'[53] The search for a good match for Maurice was however far from a mere matter of general encouragement or unlocated aspiration. O'Connell's letter of 15 April from London makes it clear that Mary was expected to engage in the Dublin marriage mart on her son's behalf: 'Darling heart's love, how I wish to hear about Maurice and Miss Redington or Miss O'Brien! Speak to him yourself about Miss O'Shea. I really think it is to say the least of it *unkind* to bring her to his neighbourhood. Is it a trap?'[54] Did it ever cross O'Connell's or his wife's minds that they were playing a part not unlike that which Hunting Cap had unsuccessfully essayed in 1802? At any rate, their fate as marriage brokers resembled his, just as Maurice's fate as a lover resembled theirs, for he too was to wed secretly and 'unsuitably' in the end.

The warmth of feeling in the family was quite restored. While Maurice was with him in London, O'Connell delighted Mary repeatedly with reports of his social and political success. As he wrote on 5 March 1829,

> Maurice is in perfect good health and spirits and goes to all the parties he is asked to. There are many. A lady told me he was the handsomest man of the deputation. I told her his mother was of the same opinion and I added that he was very like his mother. I was so proud to be able to say so. He will go with me into the City and indeed everywhere else where I am asked to dine.[55]

Similarly, he commented antiphonally on reports of his children's doings at home. After learning, apparently, that his youngest son, Daniel, had recovered from illness, and that Kate and Betsey had been presented at Dublin Castle, he replied, on 13 April,

> Darling love, how my heart is at ease about our sweet Danny. Give him my

> tender love and a sweet kiss for his *fado*. Tell my girls how sorry I am that I did not see them in their Court dresses. I wish I had been present when my Betsey was kissed by the Duke. She must have blushed pretty deeply as much [from] indignation as anything else.[56]

O'Connell seems to have set the tone of family intercourse. Certainly, his daughters wrote to him with equal warmth. Kate, for example, followed his departure from London of 3 February 1829 with a solicitous letter about outside travelling on his coach. 'Many a cold and wet mile', she went on, 'I travelled that way with my dearest father when I used to be obliged to ask if it was still raining, he kept his Catty so covered up from all the rain and wind.'[57]

But Mary remained the heart of all. She was ill during the spring of 1829, possibly the beginning of her long decline in health. Kate wrote to O'Connell on her behalf in February, and Fr L'Estrange said mass for her at home. Whether or not O'Connell's suggestion that she might join him in London for the final weeks of the current parliamentary session was seriously meant, she did not in fact live there for over two years. Possibly O'Connell guessed that this would be so. At any rate, he told her on 10 February, 'Your state of health is my great and foremost source of anxiety.' In the same letter he called her still 'my consolation and my solace'.[58] So she truly was. She remained the sole vent for much of his inner political plans and ambitions, the recipient of his private worries over money, slights or corpulence, the confidant of his Lenten penances. The intimate traffic of almost thirty years continued in its daily course. When in late August 1829 Kate had again to take up her mother's pen, O'Connell answered, 'This day I am *afflicted*, *afflicted* . . . because you were too ill to write yourself. My own, own Mary does not at all understand how I love her.'[59] Perhaps he felt again a premonitory tremor, an early intimation of the death of love.

But nothing – dubious income, exigent children or ailing wife – could now hold O'Connell back from total commitment to a parliamentary career. His first thought was to save as much as possible of his political base at home. The moment 10 Geo.IV c.1, suppressing the Catholic Association, was enacted, on 5 March 1829, he sent word to Ireland that the Liberal Clubs should not be dissolved: they had escaped, in his opinion, the prohibitions of the law. Six days later he set out for Dwyer his scheme for preserving at least the skeleton of the old Irish Catholic organization:

> as the law stands, the Finance Committee of the Association can receive no

> more money [but] . . . the Catholic rooms should be kept up by a subscription of from five to ten shillings by each individual, to pay current expenses of newspapers, coals, candles, clerks, &c.
>
> It will serve as a nucleus for talking over Catholic and Irish affairs. Call it the Catholic Reading-rooms. A few months will enable us to do better, but in the meantime a rallying point of this kind is wanting and a reading-room is just the very best you can have.
>
> Let me press the necessity of having such an establishment and put my name and my sons', Maurice, Morgan, John and Dan, as original subscribers. Let us attempt to keep it on foot for some months at least if we can get but ten subscribers. There is no danger of the Lying Act affecting us.[60]

The new vestigial association took its name, discreetly, from its Dublin meeting place, '12 Burgh Quay'. O'Connell's prime objective however was to enter the Commons immediately. As he told Mary on 11 April, 'I *am determined* to spend this sessions in parliament. It would never *do* for the people to have me out of it. I will fight the battle of Ireland and of Catholicity there better than anywhere else save in a Parliament in College Green.'[61] When on 18 May 1829 the Commons finally rejected O'Connell as member for Clare, he arranged to 'have a borough ready for the rest of the sessions',[62] while awaiting re-election for the county. He told Mary on 21 May that he expected to take his seat within a week. He was careful to guard himself from her reproaches for either abandoning principle or squandering their money.

> Darling, you of course know me too well to suppose that I would barter any one of my principles for the world's wealth. No, love, I go in for the borough, as I did for Clare, perfectly my own master. Of course you have not the least uneasiness on that head. It will give me a station and rank in addressing the people of Clare and give weight and importance to my exertions in that county. I want too to bring before the country my parliamentary capacities. I want to show of what use I could be to Catholic charities and other Catholic purposes. Do not therefore, my darling heart, be in the least degree mortified at my taking advantage of a free borough for the rest of this sessions. Depend upon it that it can serve only to make me more respected by the public. You will I repeat be greatly pleased with my address to the people of Clare. It would have amused you to have heard the paltry squaling [squealing?] of the voices of the other speakers after me in the House of Commons.[63]

It might have been an English pocket borough which O'Connell so confidently expected. Certainly the Irish pocket borough, Tralee, for which he was in negotiation with its owner, Sir Edward Denny, was far from 'free'; the asking price was reported as £3000. In any event, O'Connell failed to secure a temporary seat, and had to await the second Clare by-election which had been set to commence on 30 July. For a time O'Connell had reason to fear a contest. He was unlikely to lose – a careful canvass had shown him to be clearly ahead even under the revised register of voters – but the costs would be heavy and his testimonial fund perhaps correspondingly diminished. Characteristically, however, he was more concerned with the political than with the financial consequences of being unopposed. 'If I succeed in Clare, especially after a contest', he told Mahony on 4 June,

> it will rouse a fresh spirit in all the counties in Ireland. The only danger is that there shall not be a contest for in that case the usual torpidity will follow, recent exertions there being no adequate stimulant to keep up excitement. But a contest in Clare would rouse all the dormant passions and give an energy to opposition which would not be easily appeased.[64]

Yet this was the very moment when O'Connell was seriously tempted to accept an invitation from his old tory enemies, the Beresfords, to act as counsel for Lord George in a forthcoming by-election in co. Waterford; the fee would have been at least £600. O'Connell was careful to condition that 'there is to be no expectation that I will do anything beyond my professional duty; that is, there is to be *no sale* by me nor any purchase by them of my political exertions'.[65] But the world at large would scarcely have drawn this nice distinction, and O'Connell was fortunate that, in the end, he heeded Dublin advice to resist the monetarily attractive but politically dangerous temptation. How strangely divided can a man's courses be! Simultaneously, O'Connell was ready to sacrifice money for political advantage in co. Clare, and to toy for several days with what would surely have turned out to be the sacrifice of political reputation for money in co. Waterford.

Despite various alarms O'Connell was returned unopposed for co. Clare on 30 July 1829. It was too late for him to take his seat before Parliament would reassemble in the following November. But at least it was certain that he had finally won through. Where would he now move politically? An unknown ocean lay ahead: Cortez-like, 'He star'd at the Pacific'. In his address of 25 May to the electors of Clare (mocked as the 'Address of the Hundred Promises'), he pledged himself to work for a host of Irish local government and tax reforms, an increase in Irish parliamentary representation, the restoration of the 40s. freehold franchise, an Irish poor law, the repeal of the

Subletting Act and measures against absentee proprietors. To Mahony he wrote on 4 June, 'I am most thoroughly convinced that nothing but "the Repeal of the Union" can permanently serve her [Ireland's] interests.'[66] Upon his election, he assured Bentham, 'I avowed myself on the hustings this day to be a "Benthamite", and explained the leading principles of your disciples – the "greatest happiness principle" – our sect *will* prosper . . . You have now one Member of Parliament *your own*.'[67] Soon after, in proposing a scheme for Catholic glebes and parochial houses, he told Doyle:

> Since my return for Clare I have begun to write a species of circular to the Catholic prelates tendering my parliamentary services . . . I have long been of opinion that Catholic interests would never be effectually served in parliament until they were represented by a Catholic man of business, sincere at least in his religious professions.
>
> The present state of the Catholic Church in Ireland demands, I humbly conceive, great attention. Things cannot possibly remain as they are. I do not forsee anything of a retrograde nature, and therefore I look solely to her advance . . . you will smile perhaps mournfully at my enthusiasm and look upon it as but a source of barren speculation but recollect that enthusiasm is the *only* parent of great success.[68]

Behind the apparent infinity of the directions which he might take lay the same simple dream that had driven him on since childhood. During the long vacation of 1814 he had held a grand picnic for a group of friends on an island in one of the Killarney lakes. On 22 May 1829 he recalled that day and 'the speech I made on giving the memory of Washington'. His conclusion had been much cheered. 'Did it not convey this idea? "He found his native land a pitiful province of England. He left her – Oh Glorious destiny! – an independent and mighty nation".'[69] Whether we move backwards or forwards in time, the frame was ever the same. What was stamped on the beginning boy of 1783 was still stamped upon the bruised and soiled politician of 1829. The old vision of becoming his country's Washington continued to hold him in its thrall. There would never be escape from his own inherent ardour, or the hereditary bondage of his ancestry, time or place.

# *References*


## *MISE-EN-SCÈNE*

1 4 Oct. 1838, W. J. Fitzpatrick (ed.), *Correspondence of Daniel O'Connell the Liberator* (London, 1888), vol. ii, pp. 151–2.
2 ibid., p. 152.
3 M. F. Cusack, *The Liberator (Daniel O'Connell) his Life and Times, Political, Social and Religious* (London, 1872), p. 31.
4 *Freeman's Journal*, 4 July 1828.

## *CHAPTER 1*
## Growing Up
*1775–93*

1 M. MacDonagh, *The Life of Daniel O'Connell* (London, 1903), pp. 8–9.
2 Mrs M. J. O'Connell, *The Last Colonel of the Irish Brigade. Count O'Connell and Old Irish Life at Home and Abroad 1745–1833* (Cork, 1977), vol. i, p. 305.
3 ibid., p. 122.
4 'The Gaelic Background', in M. Tierney (ed.), *Daniel O'Connell. Nine Centenary Essays* (Dublin, 1949), pp. 7–8.
5 A. Houston, *Daniel O'Connell: His Early Life, and Journal, 1795 to 1802* (London, 1906), pp. 129–30.
6 W. J. O'N. Daunt, *Personal Recollections of the late Daniel O'Connell* (London, 1848), vol. i, pp. 14–15.
7 This was written in 1849 by S. H. O'Grady, *Catalogue of Irish MSS in the British Museum*, vol. i, p. 162, and quoted in G. Murphy, 'The Gaelic Background', in Tierney, *Daniel O'Connell*, op. cit., p. 5.
8 O'Connell to W. S. Landor, 4 Oct. 1838, in Fitzpatrick, *Correspondence of O'Connell*, op. cit., vol. ii, p. 151.
9 W. Phelan, *The History of the Church of Rome in Ireland* (London, 1827), quoted in D. MacCartney, 'The Writing of History in Ireland, 1800–30', *Irish Historical Studies*, vol. x, 1957, p. 361.
10 6 Aug. 1829, M. O'Connell (ed.), *The Correspondence of Daniel O'Connell* (Shannon and Dublin, 1972–80), vol. iv, pp. 87–8.
11 D. Gwynn, *Daniel O'Connell* (revised centenary edn, Oxford, 1947), pp. 21–2.
12 6 Oct. 1794, O'Connell, *The Last Colonel*, op. cit., vol. ii, pp. 152–3.
13 Daunt, *Personal Recollections*, op. cit., vol. i, p. 116.
14 ibid., vol. ii, pp. 77–8.
15 ibid., vol. i, p. 116.
16 *Cork Magazine*, Sept. 1848, p. 643, quoted in T. Wall, 'Louvain, St. Omer and Douai', in Tierney, *Daniel O'Connell*, op. cit., p. 41.
17 16 June 1789, O'Connell, *The Last Colonel*, op. cit., vol. ii, p. 80.
18 14 Jan. 1790, ibid., p. 84.
19 2 Sept. 1790, ibid., p. 90.
20 Daunt, *Personal Recollections*, op. cit., vol. ii, p. 26.
21 *Irish Monthly*, vol. x, 1882, p. 336.
22 3 Feb. 1792, O'Connell, *Correspondence*, vol. i, p. 1.
23 O'Connell to Hunting Cap, 16 April 1792, ibid., p. 2.
24 Wall, 'Louvain, St. Omer and Douai', in Tierney, *Daniel O'Connell*, op. cit., pp. 34–5.

25 16 April 1792, Fitzpatrick, *Correspondence of O'Connell*, op. cit., vol. i, p. 3.
26 30 June 1792, O'Connell, *Correspondence*, vol. i, p. 3.
27 14 Sept. 1792, ibid., p. 5.
28 O'Connell to Hunting Cap, 14 Sept. 1792, Fitzpatrick, *Correspondence of O'Connell*, op. cit., vol. i, p. 5.
29 14 Sept. 1792, O'Connell, *Correspondence*, vol. i, p. 4.
30 Wall, 'Louvain, St. Omer and Douai', in Tierney, *Daniel O'Connell*, op. cit., p. 45.
31 MacDonagh, *Life of O'Connell*, op. cit., p. 17.
32 Gwynn, *Daniel O'Connell*, op. cit., p. 39.
33 K. F. Roche, 'Revolution and Counter-Revolution', in Tierney, *Daniel O'Connell*, op. cit., p. 69.
34 10 Dec. 1795, O'Connell, *Correspondence*, vol. i, pp. 20–1.

*CHAPTER 2*
## London
*1793–5*

1 O'Connell, *Correspondence*, vol. i, p. 6.
2 O'Connell to Hunting Cap, 1 July 1793, ibid., p. 7.
3 O'Connell to Hunting Cap, 21 March 1793, ibid., p. 5.
4 1 July 1793, ibid., p. 6.
5 24 Nov. 1793, ibid., p. 9.
6 ibid.
7 26 Dec. 1793, ibid., pp. 10–12.
8 O'Connell to Hunting Cap, 11 March 1794, ibid., pp. 13–16.
9 O'Connell to Hunting Cap, ibid., pp. 13–14.
10 22 Aug. 1794, ibid., pp. 18–19.
11 O'Connell, *The Last Colonel*, op. cit., vol. ii, p. 151.
12 12 March 1794, ibid., p. 148.
13 14 March 1795, ibid., p. 162.
14 26 Jan. 1794, ibid., p. 145.
15 Houston, *Early Life and Journal*, op. cit., p. 93.
16 ibid., p. 95.
17 O'Connell to Hunting Cap, 26 Oct. 1795, O'Connell, *Correspondence*, vol. i, p. 19.
18 10 Dec. 1795, ibid., p. 20.
19 Houston, *Early Life and Journal*, op. cit., 30 Dec. 1795, p. 95.
20 ibid., 31 Dec. 1795, pp. 97–8.
21 ibid., 18 Jan. 1796, p. 115.
22 ibid., 29 Dec. 1795, p. 91.
23 ibid., 10 Dec. 1795, p. 93.
24 Count O'Connell to Hunting Cap, 26 Feb. 1795, O'Connell, *The Last Colonel*, op. cit., vol. ii, p. 157.
25 Houston, *Early Life and Journal*, op. cit., 11 Dec. 1795, p. 70.
26 ibid., 3 Jan. 1796, p. 101.
27 ibid., 13 Dec. 1795, p. 77.
28 ibid., 30 Dec. 1795, pp. 92–3.
29 ibid., late 1795, p. 64.
30 ibid., 19 Jan. 1796, p. 115.
31 ibid., 12 Dec. 1795, p. 76.
32 ibid., p. 75.
33 Daunt, *Personal Recollections*, op. cit., vol. i, p. 35.
34 Houston, *Early Life and Journal*, op. cit., 5 Dec. 1796, p. 129.
35 ibid., 19 Jan. 1796, pp. 115–16.
36 ibid., 18 Jan. 1796, pp. 113–14.
37 W. Godwin, *Enquiry concerning Political Justice and its Influence on Morals and Happiness* (Toronto, 1946), vol. i, p. 274.
38 ibid., vol. i, pp. 251, 259.
39 Houston, *Early Life and Journal*, op. cit., 30 Jan. 1796, pp. 119–20.
40 ibid., 3 Jan. 1796, p. 102.
41 O'Connell to Hunting Cap, 22 April 1794, O'Connell, *Correspondence*, vol. i, p. 17.
42 Houston, *Early Life and Journal*, op. cit., 13 Jan. 1796, p. 110.
43 ibid., 19 Jan. 1796, p. 116.
44 ibid., 20 Jan. 1796, p. 118.
45 ibid., 19 Jan. 1796, p. 116.
46 ibid., 20 Jan. 1796, p. 118.
47 ibid., p. 125 footnote f.

48 O'Connell, *Correspondence*, vol. i, pp. 23–4.
49 Houston, *Early Life and Journal*, op. cit., 31 Dec. 1796, p. 156.
50 ibid., p. 157.
51 ibid., pp. 156–7.
52 17 Jan. 1796, O'Connell, *Correspondence*, vol. i, pp. 22–3.
53 Houston, *Early Life and Journal*, op. cit., 16 Dec. 1795, p. 85.


*CHAPTER 3*

## Dublin

*1795–1800*


1 O'Connell to Hunting Cap, 17 May 1796, O'Connell, *Correspondence*, vol. i, p. 25.
2 n.d., O'Connell, *The Last Colonel*, op. cit., vol. ii, p. 272.
3 Houston, *Early Life and Journal*, op. cit., p. 166.
4 3 Jan. 1797, O'Connell, *Correspondence*, vol. i, p. 27.
5 Houston, *Early Life and Journal*, op. cit., 18 Jan. 1797, p. 176.
6 ibid., p. 177.
7 ibid., 19 Jan. 1797, p. 178.
8 ibid., 23 Jan. 1797, p. 185.
9 ibid., 24 Jan. 1797, p. 186.
10 O'Connell, *Correspondence*, vol. i, p. 29.
11 Houston, *Early Life and Journal*, op. cit., p. 204.
12 ibid., 29 Dec. 1796, p. 155.
13 ibid., 4 March 1797, p. 206.
14 ibid., 20 Feb. 1797, p. 202.
15 ibid., 22 Jan. 1797, p. 184.
16 ibid., 25 March 1797, p. 213.
17 ibid., 31 March 1797, p. 215.
18 Daunt, *Personal Recollections*, op. cit., vol. ii, pp. 98–9.
19 Houston, *Early Life and Journal*, op. cit., 25 Jan. 1797, p. 190.
20. ibid., 7 Jan. 1797, p. 174.
21 ibid., 25 Jan. 1797, p. 190.
22 ibid., 28 Jan. 1797, p. 193.
23 ibid., 20 Feb. 1797, p. 202.
24 ibid., 28 Jan. 1797, p. 193.
25 ibid., 24 March 1797, p. 211.
26 ibid., 28 Jan. 1797, p. 193.
27 ibid., 13 Jan. 1798, p. 216.
28 ibid., 7 Dec. 1796, p. 129.
29 ibid., 10 Dec. 1796, p. 137.
30 ibid., p. 138.
31 ibid., 5 Jan. 1797, p. 168.
32 ibid., 20 Feb. 1797, p. 202.
33 ibid., 13 Dec. 1796, p. 142.
34 ibid., 10 Feb. 1797, pp. 196–7.
35 ibid., 31 Dec. 1796, p. 159.
36 ibid., 24 Dec. 1796, p. 148.
37 ibid., 7 Jan. 1797, p. 174.
38 ibid., 13 Jan. 1798, p. 229.
39 ibid., 29 Dec. 1796, p. 156.
40 Hunting Cap to O'Connell, 15 Feb. 1798, O'Connell, *Correspondence*, vol. i, p. 31.
41 Houston, *Early Life and Journal*, op. cit., p. 229.
42 O'Connell, *Correspondence*, vol. i, pp. 32–3.
43 W. J. Fitzpatrick, *Secret Service Under Pitt* (London, 1892), p. 357.
44 W. J. Fitzpatrick, *'The Sham Squire' and the Informers of 1798; with Jottings about Ireland a Century Ago,* new edn (Dublin, 1895), pp. 307–8.
45 Hunting Cap to O'Connell, 15 Feb. 1798, O'Connell, *Correspondence*, vol. i, pp. 31–2.
46 Daunt, *Personal Recollections*, op. cit., vol. i, p. 117.
47 Entry in his fee book, *Irish Monthly*, vol. x, 1882 p. 587.
48 Daunt, *Personal Recollections*, op. cit., vol. i, p. 49.
49 Houston, *Early Life and Journal*, op. cit., p. 235.
50 ibid., 4 Jan. 1799, p. 241.
51 'I survived', in J. M. Thompson, *Leaders of the French Revolution* (Oxford, 1948), p. 10.
52 Daunt, *Personal Recollections*, op. cit., vol. i, p. 119.
53 R. L. Sheil, *Sketches, Legal and Political*, (ed.) M. W. Savage (London, 1855), vol. i, p. 205.

54 ibid., pp. 215–16.
55 ibid., p. 208.
56 O'Connell to Mary, 19 Aug. 1806, O'Connell, *Correspondence*, vol. i, p. 155.
57 Daunt, *Personal Recollections*, op. cit., vol. i, pp. 118–19.
58 ibid., p. 202.

*CHAPTER 4*
## Love and Money
*1800–15*

1 Daunt, *Personal Recollections*, op. cit., vol. i, p. 133.
2 O'Connell, *Correspondence*, vol. i, p. 34.
3 O'Connell to Mary, 13 June 1801, ibid., p. 58.
4 28 April 1801, ibid., p. 49.
5 1 Dec. 1801, ibid., p. 65.
6 9 Feb. 1802, ibid., pp. 69–70.
7 25 May 1801, ibid., p. 54.
8 O'Connell to Mary, 3 April 1822, ibid., vol. ii, p. 364.
9 O'Connell to Mary, 9 Feb. 1802, ibid., vol. i, p. 70.
10 28 Nov. 1800, ibid., p. 34.
11 O'Connell to Mary, n.d., ibid., p. 77.
12 30 Dec. 1802, ibid., p. 85.
13 n.d. [probably Jan. 1803], ibid., pp. 87–8.
14 O'Connell to Mary, 5 Feb. 1803, ibid., p. 91.
15 O'Connell to Mary, n.d. [probably 7 April 1803], ibid., p. 96.
16 O'Connell to Mary, 3 Dec. 1803, ibid., p. 108.
17 18 Nov. 1802, ibid., p. 81. In fact Ellen and Splinter married in 1803.
18 25 Nov. 1802, ibid., p. 82.
19 29 Jan. 1803, ibid., p. 87.
20 1 Feb. 1803, ibid., pp. 88–9.
21 3 Feb. 1803, ibid., p. 90.
22 16 Aug. 1805, ibid., p. 143.
23 9 Nov. 1804, ibid., p. 119.
24 16 Nov. 1804, ibid., p. 121.
25 16 April 1805, ibid., p. 137.
26 10 Nov. 1803, ibid., pp. 100–1.
27 25 July 1805, ibid., p. 141.
28 12 Aug. 1805, ibid., pp. 142–3.
29 31 March 1806, ibid., p. 149.
30 11 Oct. 1810, ibid., p. 238.
31 30 March 1808, ibid., p. 171.
32 30 March 1811, ibid., p. 252.
33 1 April 1811, ibid., p. 253.
34 9 April 1803, ibid., p. 97.
35 29 Sept. and 1 Oct. 1812, ibid., p. 309.
36 15 March 1809, ibid., p. 193.
37 29 March 1809, ibid., p. 198.
38 14 Jan. 1809, ibid., p. 188.
39 16 March 1810, ibid., pp. 217–18.
40 O'Connell to Mary, 24 March 1809, ibid., p. 195.
41 C. Dickens, *David Copperfield* (London, 1907), p. 167.
42 M. R. O'Connell, 'Daniel O'Connell: income, expenditure and despair', *Irish Historical Studies*, vol. xvii, Sept. 1970, p. 204.
43 O'Connell to Denis McCarthy, 20 Jan. 1806, O'Connell, *Correspondence*, vol. i, p. 147.
44 15 April 1806, ibid., p. 153.
45 O'Connell to Mary, 27 Aug. [1806?], ibid., pp. 155–6.
46 n.d. [probably 6 Aug. 1806], ibid., p. 154.
47 9 March 1807 and 12 March 1807, ibid., pp. 159–61.
48 26 March 1807, ibid., p. 161.
49 2 April 1806, ibid., p. 150.
50 2 April 1808, ibid., p. 172.
51 31 March 1808, ibid., p. 172.
52 n.d. [probably 18 or 25 Sept. 1809], ibid., p. 205.
53 16 May 1811, ibid., p. 257.
54 13 March 1815, ibid., vol. ii, p. 14.
55 14 March 1815, ibid., p. 16.
56 21 March 1816, ibid., p. 88.

## *CHAPTER 5*
# Public Lives
*1800–13*

1 J. O'Connell (ed.), *The Select Speeches of Daniel O'Connell, M.P.* (Dublin, 1867), vol. i, pp. 8–9.

2 Hunting Cap strongly opposed and condemned O'Connell's line of argument: 'For me I have always disapproved of what I conceived to be an unwise and intemperate conduct in that body for some years back, whether they assumed the character of the Catholic Convention or of the aggregate or select meeting of the Catholics of Dublin . . . They seem to me totally to have lost sight of what in my humble opinion should be the main object for their consideration and that was, whether it was to the benignant interposition of the executive Government or to the generous and spontaneous liberality of their countrymen who composed the two houses of parliament that they were really beholden for the favours they had received and to which it was, upon sober and rational reflection, they were to look up for a farther extension of them . . . is it not peculierly [*sic*] unfortunate that the Catholics of the metropolis would not attend to that consideration, and not deprive themselves and their brethren of the only support and shelter they had – the countenance and kindness of the executive Government . . . [?]' Hunting Cap to O'Connell, 30 Jan. 1800, NLI, MSS 15473.

3 O'Connell to Captain Seaver, O'Connell, *Correspondence*, vol. vii, p. 202.

4 Daunt, *Personal Recollections*, op. cit., vol. i, p. 203.

5 O'Connell to Mary O'Connell, *Correspondence*, vol. i, p. 99.

6 18 Nov. 1803, ibid., p. 102.

7 O'Connell, *Select Speeches*, vol. i, p. 15.

8 O'Connell, *Correspondence*, vol. i, p. 127.

9 19 Dec. 1804, ibid., p. 131.

10 23 Dec. 1804, ibid., p. 132.

11 19 March 1805, ibid., p. 133.

12 Gwynn, *Daniel O'Connell*, op. cit., p. 81.

13 O'Connell, *Select Speeches*, vol. i, p. 14.

14 R. Dunlop, *Daniel O'Connell and the Revival of National Life in Ireland* (London, 1900), p. 29.

15 *Hansard*, 25 May 1808, vol. xi, col. 619.

16 Collection of Milner's letters published by Sir John Coxe Hippisley in 1813, p. 5, quoted in B. Ward, *The Eve of Catholic Emancipation* (London, 1911), vol. i, p. 74.

17 O'Connell, *Select Speeches*, vol. ii, p. 20.

18 O'Connell, *Correspondence*, vol. i, pp. 193–4.

19 O'Connell, *Select Speeches*, vol. i, pp. 20–4.

20 Daunt, *Personal Recollections*, op. cit., vol. i, p. 101.

21 O'Connell, *Select Speeches*, vol. i, p. 24.

22 Gwynn, *Daniel O'Connell*, op. cit., p. 85.

23 Hunting Cap to James O'Connell, quoted in James O'Connell to O'Connell, 17 Jan. 1811, O'Connell, *Correspondence*, vol. i, p. 245.

24 M. F. Cusack (ed.), *The Speeches and Public Letters of the Liberator* (Dublin, 1875), vol. ii, p. 259.

25 Dunlop, *Daniel O'Connell*, op. cit., pp. 37–8.

26 This phrase was used by Sergeant Howley. See Gwynn, *Daniel O'Connell*, op. cit., p. 88.

27 *A Full Report of the Speech of Counsellor O'Connell at the Catholic Meeting at Limerick, July 24, 1812* (Dublin, 1812), pp. 3, 13.
28 *Hansard*, vol. xxiii, col. 56.
29 O'Connell, *Correspondence*, vol. i, p. 292 n. 3.
30 Dunlop, *Daniel O'Connell*, op. cit., p. 43.
31 ibid., p. 47.
32 ibid., p. 53.
33 A Munster Farmer, *Reminiscences of Daniel O'Connell during the Agitations of the Veto, Emancipation and Repeal* (London, 1847), p. 25.
34 ibid., p. 43.
35 Dunlop, *Daniel O'Connell*, op. cit., pp. 55–7.

*CHAPTER 6*

## Championing

*1813–15*

1 Munster Farmer, *Reminiscences of O'Connell*, op. cit., p. 18.
2 *Freeman's Journal*, 8 Feb. 1813.
3 O'Connell, *Select Speeches*, vol. i, pp. 244–5.
4 ibid., p. 248.
5 ibid., p. 261.
6 ibid., p. 258.
7 ibid.
8 ibid., p. 267.
9 ibid., p. 303.
10 ibid., p. 269.
11 ibid., p. 255.
12 ibid., pp. 270–1.
13 ibid., p. 297.
14 ibid., p. 301.
15 ibid., p. 304.
16 Munster Farmer, *Reminiscences of O'Connell*, op. cit., p. 31.
17 C. S. Parker, *Sir Robert Peel from his private papers* (London, 1891), vol. i, p. 117.
18 *Freeman's Journal*, 3 Dec. 1813.
19 O'Connell, *Select Speeches*, vol. i, pp. 341–2.
20 *Dublin Evening Post*, 4 Dec. 1813.
21 O'Connell, *Correspondence*, vol. i, p. 347.
22 O'Connell, *Select Speeches*, vol. i, pp. 366–7.
23 Monsignor Quarantotti to Dr Poynter, C. Butler, *Historical Memoirs of the English, Irish and Scottish Catholics, since The Reformation* (3rd edn, London, 1822), vol. iv, Appendix, Note II, p. 522.
24 *Freeman's Journal*, 9 May 1814.
25 MacDonagh, *Life of O'Connell*, op. cit., p. 92.
26 Parker, *Sir Robert Peel*, op. cit., vol. i, pp. 116–17.
27 14 Dec. 1813, O'Connell, *Correspondence*, vol. i, p. 347.
28 MacDonagh, *Life of O'Connell*, op. cit., p. 65.
29 ibid., p. 66.
30 *Freeman's Journal*, 28 Feb. 1814.
31 O'Connell, *Correspondence*, vol. i, p. 360.
32 MacDonagh, *Life of O'Connell*, op. cit., p. 88.
33 O'Connell, *Correspondence*, vol. i, pp. 370–1.
34 18 Sept. 1814, ibid., p. 380.
35 23 Sept. 1814, ibid., pp. 381–2.
36 O'Connell, *Select Speeches*, vol. i, pp. 447–8.
37 15 May 1815, O'Connell, *Correspondence*, vol. ii, p. 35.
38 [1 June 1815], ibid., p. 41.
39 17 March 1815, ibid., p. 19.
40 25 March 1815, ibid., p. 24.
41 2 April 1815, ibid., p. 26.
42 13 June 1815, ibid., p. 49.
43 12 July 1815, ibid., p. 53.
44 O'Connell, *Select Speeches*, vol. ii, p. 17.
45 ibid., pp. 18–19.
46 ibid., p. 32.
47 Nicholas P. O'Gorman to O'Connell, 19 Aug. 1813, O'Connell, *Correspondence*, vol. i, p. 337; *Dublin Chronicle*, 18 Aug.

1813, quoted in O'Connell, *Correspondence*, vol. i, p. 338 n. 5.
48 Nicholas P. O'Gorman to O'Connell, 19 Aug. 1813, O'Connell, *Correspondence*, vol. i, p. 337.
49 Parker, *Sir Robert Peel*, op. cit., vol. i, p. 186.
50 4 Feb. 1815, O'Connell, *Correspondence*, vol. ii, p. 7.
51 MacDonagh, *Life of O'Connell*, op. cit., p. 69.
52 O'Connell to Richard Newton Bennett, 31 Jan. 1815, O'Connell, *Correspondence*, vol. ii, p. 6.
53 MacDonagh, *Life of O'Connell*, op. cit., p. 75.
54 [probably 3 Feb. 1815], O'Connell, *Correspondence*, vol. ii, p. 7.
55 4 Feb. 1815, ibid., p. 8.
56 MacDonagh, *Life of O'Connell*, op. cit., p. 81.
57 Rickard O'Connell to O'Connell, 4 Feb. 1815, O'Connell, *Correspondence*, vol. ii, pp. 7–8.
58 6 Feb. 1815, ibid., p. 9.
59 [probably 3 Feb. 1815], ibid., p. 7.
60 3 March 1815, ibid., p. 10.
61 Parker, *Sir Robert Peel*, op. cit., vol. i, p. 188.
62 Lord Whitworth to William Gregory, 1 Sept. 1815, ibid., p. 189.
63 William Gregory to Lord Whitworth, 3 Sept. 1815, ibid.
64 [1 Sept. 1815], O'Connell, *Correspondence*, vol. ii, p. 62.
65 Robert Peel to O'Connell, 4 Sept. 1815, ibid., p. 63.
66 O'Connell to Richard Newton Bennett, [4 Sept. 1815], ibid., p. 63.
67 5 Sept. [1815], ibid., p. 65.
68 5 Sept. 1815, Parker, *Sir Robert Peel*, op. cit., vol. i, p. 193.
69 O'Connell to Denys Scully, 13 Sept. 1815, O'Connell, *Correspondence*, vol. ii, p. 66.
70 George Lidwill to O'Connell, [25 Sept. 1815], ibid., p. 70.
71 O'Connell to Denys Scully, 16 Sept. 1815, ibid., p. 67.
72 20 Sept. 1815, ibid., p. 68.
73 O'Connell to Denys Scully, 16 Sept. 1815, ibid., p. 67.
74 Extracts kept by Sir Robert Peel, Parker, *Sir Robert Peel*, op. cit., vol. i, pp. 193–4.
75 Henry Drummond to Sir Robert Peel, 8 Sept. 1815, ibid., p. 197.
76 William Cockburn to Sir Robert Peel, 13 Sept. 1815, ibid., p. 197.
77 O'Connell to Denys Scully, 20 Sept. 1815, O'Connell, *Correspondence*, vol. ii, p. 69.
78 30 Sept. 1815, ibid., p. 70.

## *CHAPTER 7*
## Entr'acte
*1816*

1 7 Jan. 1816, O'Connell, *Correspondence*, vol. ii, p. 78.
2 2 April 1816, ibid., p. 93.
3 *Freeman's Journal*, 11 April 1816.
4 *Dublin University Magazine*, July 1839, p. 113.
5 O'Connell to Mary, 26 March 1816, O'Connell, *Correspondence*, vol. ii, p. 89.
6 O'Connell to Mary, 17 April 1816, ibid., p. 102.
7 O'Connell to Mary, 9 April 1816, ibid., p. 98.
8 11 March 1816, ibid., p. 85.
9 20 March 1816, ibid., p. 88.
10 11 March 1816, ibid., p. 84.
11 13 March 1816, ibid., p. 86.
12 26 March 1816, ibid., p. 89.
13 29 March 1816, ibid., p. 91.
14 1 April 1816, ibid., p. 92.
15 O'Connell to Mary, [24 Aug. 1816], ibid., p. 114.
16 13 March 1816, ibid., p. 86.
17 O'Connell to Mary, 4 Aug. 1816, ibid., p. 104.
18 O'Connell to Mary, 8 Aug. 1816, ibid., p. 107.

19 4 Jan. 1816, ibid., p. 77.
20 17 Feb. 1816, ibid., p. 83.
21 22 Jan. 1816, ibid., p. 80.
22 4 Jan. 1816, ibid., p. 77.
23 O'Connell to Mary, 16 Jan. 1816, ibid., p. 80.
24 22 Jan. 1816, ibid., pp. 80–1.
25 4 Feb. 1816, ibid., p. 81.
26 26 March 1816, ibid., p. 90.
27 17 Feb. 1816, ibid., pp. 83–4.
28 29 Sept. 1816, ibid., p. 121.
29 21 Aug. 1816, ibid., p. 113.
30 8 April 1816, ibid., p. 97.
31 13 April [1816], ibid., p. 100.
32 11 March 1816, ibid., p. 84.
33 18 March 1816, ibid., p. 87.
34 13 April [1816], ibid., pp. 100–1.
35 10 April [1816], ibid., pp. 98–9.
36 4 April 1816, ibid., p. 95.
37 Mary to O'Connell, 8 April 1816, ibid., p. 97.
38 1 March 1817, ibid., p. 135.
39 9 Aug. 1816, ibid., p. 98.
40 11 Aug. 1816, ibid., p. 110.
41 22 Aug. 1816, ibid., pp. 113–14.
42 1 March 1817, ibid., p. 135.
43 22 Jan. 1816, ibid., p. 81.
44 10 Jan. 1816, ibid., p. 78.
45 22 Aug. 1816, ibid., p. 114.
46 13 Jan. 1816, ibid., p. 79.
47 1 April 1816, ibid., p. 93.
48 13 Jan. 1816, ibid., p. 79.
49 18 March 1816, ibid., p. 88.
50 26 March 1816, ibid., p. 90.
51 13 Jan. 1816, ibid., pp. 79–80.
52 3 April 1816, ibid., pp. 94–5.
53 5 Aug. 1816, ibid., p. 105.
54 6 Aug. 1816, ibid., p. 106.
55 17 Oct. 1816, ibid., p. 123.
56 24 Nov. 1816, ibid., p. 123.
57 1 Sept. 1816, ibid., p. 117.
58 3 Sept. 1816, ibid., pp. 117–18.
59 17 Oct. 1816, ibid., p. 123.
60 16 Oct. 1816, ibid., p. 122.
61 26 Sept. 1816, ibid., p. 120.

*CHAPTER 8*

## Ploughing Sands

*1817–22*

1 O'Connell, *Select Speeches*, vol. ii, p. 38.
2 *Dublin Evening Post*, 5 July 1817.
3 ibid., 22 July 1817.
4 O'Connell, *Correspondence*, vol. ii, pp. 159–60.
5 O'Connell to Charles Phillips, 26 Sept. 1817, ibid., p. 165.
6 O'Connell to Owen O'Conor, 21 Dec. 1817, ibid., p. 184.
7 24 Aug. 1818, ibid., pp. 178–9.
8 O'Connell to Mary, 10 June 1817, ibid., p. 147.
9 10 June 1817, ibid., p. 147.
10 O'Connell to Charles Phillips, 26 Sept. 1817, ibid. p. 165.
11 2 Nov. 1818, ibid., p. 183.
12 21 Dec. 1818, ibid., p. 184.
13 11 Feb. 1819, ibid., p. 197.
14 30 Jan. 1819, ibid., p. 195.
15 15 June 1819, ibid., p. 202.
16 21 Oct. 1819, ibid., pp. 225–6.
17 O'Connell to ——, 21 Oct. 1819, ibid., p. 226.
18 O'Connell, *Select Speeches*, vol. ii, p. 68.
19 *Dublin Evening Post*, 30 Oct. 1819.
20 O'Connell, *Select Speeches*, vol. ii, p. 72.
21 1 Jan. 1821, Letter to the Catholics of Ireland, ibid., p. 95.
22 O'Connell to Mary, 19 March 1820, O'Connell, *Correspondence*, vol. ii, p. 246.
23 ibid., p. 208 n.1. (Supplied by Eric T. D. Lambert.)
24 3 Aug. 1819, ibid., p. 207.
25 27 Aug. 1819, ibid., p. 217.
26 O'Connell to John Finlay, 6 March 1820, ibid., pp. 236–7.
27 17 April 1820, ibid., p. 257.
28 15 June 1820, ibid., p. 264.
29 Morgan to O'Connell, 25 Aug. 1820, ibid., p. 274.
30 13 Oct. 1820, ibid., p. 286.
31 O'Connell to Hunting Cap, 5 Jan. 1822, ibid., p. 346.
32 O'Connell to Thomas Spring Rice, 16 Nov. 1820, ibid., p. 288.
33 O'Connell to Lord Cloncurry, 16 Nov. 1820, ibid. p. 288.

34 O'Connell to Thomas Spring Rice, 16 Nov. 1820, ibid., p. 288.
35 17 Nov. 1820, ibid., pp. 290–2.
36 24 Nov. 1820, ibid., p. 292.
37 [probably 26 Nov. 1820], ibid., p. 295.
38 15 Dec. 1820, ibid., p. 298.
39 [11] Nov. 1820, ibid., p. 304.
40 8 May 1821, ibid., p. 322.
41 O'Connell, *Select Speeches*, vol. ii, p. 96.
42 ibid., p. 110.
43 ibid., p. 125.
44 O'Connell, *Correspondence*, vol. ii, p. 314.
45 14 April 1821, ibid., p. 315.
46 23 April 1821, ibid., p. 319.
47 18 June 1821, ibid., p. 326.
48 Dunlop, *Daniel O'Connell*, op. cit., pp. 118–19.
49 MacDonagh, *Life of O'Connell*, op. cit., p. 110.
50 *Freeman's Journal*, 4 Sept. 1821.
51 ibid., 10 Sept. 1821.
52 O'Connell to Mary, 12 Oct. 1821, O'Connell, *Correspondence*, vol. ii, pp. 335–6.
53 MacDonagh, *Life of O'Connell*, op. cit., p. 111.
54 'The Irish Avatar', *The Works of Lord Byron*, (ed.) E. H. Coleridge (London, 1922), vol. iv, pp. 559–60.
55 O'Connell, *Select Speeches*, vol. ii, p. 139.
56 O'Connell, *Correspondence*, vol. ii, p. 366.
57 William Plunket to O'Connell, 10 April 1822, ibid., p. 376.
58 see O'Connell to Marquess of Wellesley, 11 July 1822, in O'Connell, *Select Speeches*, vol. ii, p. 171.
59 O'Connell, *Correspondence*, vol. ii, pp. 404–5.
60 O'Connell, *Select Speeches*, vol. ii, pp. 171–4.
61 20, 21 Dec. 1822, O'Connell, *Correspondence*, vol. ii, pp. 412–13.
62 T. Wyse, *Historical Sketch of the late Catholic Association of Ireland* (London, 1829), vol. i, pp. 194–5.

*CHAPTER 9*
## Reaping Whirlwinds
*1817–27*

1 O'Connell, *Correspondence*, vol. ii, p. 141.
2 ibid., p. 142.
3 15 April 1817, ibid., p. 144.
4 See James to O'Connell, 18 May 1817, ibid., p. 144.
5 10 June 1817, ibid., p. 146.
6 12 June 1817, ibid., p. 149.
7 ibid., p. 150.
8 11 Aug. 1817, ibid., p. 163.
9 O'Connell to Charles Phillips, 26 Sept. 1817, ibid., p. 165.
10 ibid., p. 169.
11 31 May 1817, ibid., p. 145.
12 12 June 1817, ibid., p. 150.
13 24 June 1817, ibid., p. 152.
14 23 June 1817, ibid., p. 151.
15 23 July 1817, ibid., p. 158.
16 10 June 1817, ibid., p. 146.
17 14 July 1817, ibid., p. 155.
18 22 July 1817, ibid., p. 157.
19 O'Connell to Connell O'Connell, 18 May 1818, ibid., pp. 176–7.
20 A. Trollope, *Framley Parsonage* (London, 1961), p. 203.
21 O'Connell, *Correspondence*, vol. ii, p. 205.
22 3 Aug. 1817, ibid., p. 162.
23 30 July 1819, ibid., p. 206.
24 O'Connell to Mary, 4 Dec. 1827, ibid., vol. iii, p. 360.
25 14 May 1822, ibid., vol. ii, p. 388.
26 O'Connell to Kate, 24 May 1822, ibid., vol. ii, p. 392.
27 30 July 1819, ibid., p. 205.
28 28 March 1822, ibid., p. 362.
29 22 Dec. 1820, ibid., p. 299.
30 19 April 1821, ibid., p. 318.
31 15 Jan. 1822, ibid., p. 350.
32 17 Feb. 1822, ibid., p. 357.

33 18 Jan. 1822, ibid., p. 355.
34 James to O'Connell, 17 Feb. 1822, ibid., p. 357.
35 28 March 1822, ibid., p. 363.
36 22 March 1822, ibid., p. 362.
37 1 April 1822, ibid., pp. 363–4.
38 5 April 1822, ibid., pp. 369–70.
39 8 April 1822, ibid., pp. 372–3.
40 4 May 1822, ibid., pp. 382, 389.
41 26 May 1822, ibid., p. 394.
42 O'Connell to Mary, 23 May 1823, ibid., p. 475.
43 26 March 1823, ibid., pp. 456–7.
44 12 March 1823, ibid., p. 447.
45 27 Dec. 1822, ibid., pp. 417–18.
46 O'Connell to James Sugrue, 7 Oct. 1822, ibid., p. 411.
47 O'Connell to Mary, 6 March 1823, ibid., p. 444.
48 ibid.
49 22 and 23 May 1823, ibid., p. 475.
50 20 April 1823, ibid., p. 463.
51 14 June 1823, ibid., p. 486.
52 O'Connell to Mary, 14, 16 and 17 June 1823, ibid., pp. 486–7.
53 O'Connell to Mary, 13 June 1823, ibid., p. 483.
54 O'Connell to Mary, 14, 15 and 17 June 1823, ibid., p. 486.
55 13 July 1823, ibid., p. 501.
56 4 Sept. 1823, ibid., p. 505.
57 8 Sept. 1823, ibid., p. 506.
58 11 Sept. 1823, ibid., pp. 507–8.
59 16 Sept. 1823, ibid., p. 508.
60 17 Sept. 1823, ibid., pp. 509–10.
61 O'Connell to Mary, 27 Jan. 1824, ibid., vol. iii, p. 10.
62 4 Feb. 1824, ibid., pp. 17–18.
63 6 Feb. 1824, ibid., p. 23.
64 12 Feb. 1824, ibid., p. 29.
65 16 Feb. 1824, ibid., p. 33.
66 24 Jan. 1823, ibid., vol. ii, p. 429.
67 O'Connell to Mary, 14 May 1822, ibid., p. 388.
68 O'Connell to Mary, 26 Sept. 1824, ibid., vol. iii, pp. 79–80.
69 O'Connell to John Primrose, Jr, 14 June 1825, ibid., p. 184.
70 1 Nov. 1825, ibid., pp. 196–7.
71 4 Dec. 1825, ibid., p. 211.
72 Mary to O'Connell, 18 Feb. 1825, ibid., p. 114.
73 2 Dec. 1825, ibid., p. 209.
74 *Ireland and its Rulers since 1829* (London, 1844–5), p. 19.
75 *The Irish Bar, comprising anecdotes, bon-mots and biographical sketches of the bench and bar of Ireland* (London, 1879), p. 235.
76 8 May 1822, O'Connell, *Correspondence*, vol. ii, p. 385.
77 18 March 1826, ibid., vol. iii, p. 240.
78 30 Oct. 1827, ibid., p. 353.
79 19 May 1827, ibid., p. 315.
80 4 Dec. 1827, ibid., p. 360.
81 8 Dec. 1827, ibid., p. 362.
82 4 May 1825, ibid., p. 160.
83 7 May 1825, ibid., p. 166.

*CHAPTER 10*

## Four Years of Irish History

*1822–6*

1 Gwynn, *Daniel O'Connell*, op. cit., pp. 143–4.
2 Rules and regulations of the Catholic Association of Ireland, Wyse, *Catholic Association of Ireland*, op. cit., vol. ii, appendix xiv, p. xxxvii.
3 *Freeman's Journal*, 25 Oct. 1824.
4 ibid., 17 May 1824.
5 J. A. Reynolds, *The Catholic Emancipation Crisis in Ireland 1823–1829* (New Haven, 1954), p. 66.
6 *Freeman's Journal*, 2 March 1824.
7 *Dublin Evening Post*, 27 Jan. 1824.
8 G. de Beaumont, *Ireland: social, political and religious*, (ed.) W. C. Taylor (London, 1839), vol. ii, p. 79.
9 *Freeman's Journal*, 17 June 1823.
10 O'Connell to Mary, 9 March

1824, O'Connell, *Correspondence*, vol. iii, p. 50.
11 *Freeman's Journal*, 4 Dec. 1824.
12 ibid., 3 Dec. 1824.
13 ibid., 2 Aug. 1824.
14 B.L. Peel papers 40322, f. 119, quoted in Reynolds, *Catholic Emancipation Crisis*, op. cit., p. 51.
15 Robert Peel to J. L. Foster, 2 Nov. 1824, R.I.A., Peel Letters to J. L. Foster, quoted in Reynolds, *Catholic Emancipation Crisis*, op. cit., p. 58.
16 *Saunder's Newsletter*, 17 Dec. 1824.
17 3 Feb. 1825, *Hansard*, n.s. vol. xii, col. 65.
18 10 Feb. 1825, ibid., cols. 171–2.
19 ibid., col. 260.
20 28 Feb. [1825], O'Connell, *Correspondence*, vol. iii, p. 125.
21 Sheil, *Sketches, Legal and Political*, vol. ii, p. 47.
22 O'Connell to Mary, 28 Feb. [1825], O'Connell, *Correspondence*, vol. iii, p. 125.
23 O'Connell to Mary, [7 March 1825], ibid., pp. 131–2.
24 8 March 1825, ibid., p. 132.
25 17 March 1825, ibid., pp. 141–2.
26 Lord Colchester, *Diary*, 17 March 1825, quoted in Dunlop, *Daniel O'Connell*, op. cit., p. 157.
27 4 March 1825, O'Connell, *Correspondence*, vol. iii, p. 128
28 O'Connell to Edward Dwyer, 15 March 1825, ibid., p. 140.
29 Dunlop, *Daniel O'Connell*, op. cit., p. 158.
30 *Sketches, Legal and Political*, op. cit., vol. ii, pp. 29–30.
31 [7 March 1825], O'Connell, *Correspondence*, vol. iii, p. 131.
32 *Dublin Evening Post*, 18 Aug. 1825.
33 Dunlop, *Daniel O'Connell*, op. cit., p. 169.
34 W. J. Fitzpatrick, *The Life, Times and Correspondence of the Right Rev. Dr. Doyle* (Dublin, 1880), vol. i, p. 451.
35 *Freeman's Journal*, 14 July 1825.
36 O'Connell, *Correspondence*, vol. iii, p. 131.
37 Wyse, *Catholic Association of Ireland*, op. cit., vol. i, pp. 286–9.
38 19 June 1826, O'Connell, *Correspondence*, vol. iii, pp. 248–9.
39 O'Connell to Mary, 21 June 1826, ibid., p. 250.
40 *Freeman's Journal*, 6 July 1826.
41 ibid.
42 John Palliser to —, 24 June 1826, I.S.P.O., Official Papers, second series, 58822/915, quoted in Reynolds, *Catholic Emancipation Crisis*, op. cit., p. 96.
43 *Freeman's Journal*, 8 July 1826.
44 ibid.
45 O'Connell, *Correspondence*, vol. iii, p. 265.
46 O'Connell to Edward Dwyer, 31 Aug. 1826, ibid., p. 268.
47 *Freeman's Journal*, 9 Aug. 1826. Coppinger's letter to O'Dwyer was read at the Catholic Association meeting of 7 August 1826.
48 ibid., 8 Sept. 1826.
49 ibid., 11 Sept. 1826.
50 Parker, *Sir Robert Peel*, op. cit., vol. ii, p. 64
51 *Dublin Evening Post*, 11 July 1826.
52 O'Connell, *Correspondence*, vol. iii, pp. 282–3.

## *CHAPTER 11* The First Hurrah *1827–8*

1 O'Connell, *Correspondence*, vol. iii, p. 288.
2 15 Jan. 1827, ibid., p. 287.
3 22 Feb. 1827, ibid., p. 291.
4 23 Feb. 1827, ibid., pp. 292–3.
5 ibid., p. 293.
6 21 March 1827, ibid., p. 300.

7 ibid., p. 301.
8 *Dublin Evening Post*, 19 April 1827.
9 Eneas MacDonnell to O'Connell, 23 April 1827, O'Connell, *Correspondence*, vol. iii, p. 307.
10 Knight of Kerry to O'Connell, 23 April 1827, ibid., p. 309.
11 28 May 1827, ibid., p. 316.
12 9 June 1827, ibid., p. 322.
13 O'Connell to Richard Newton Bennett, 11 June 1827, ibid., p. 325.
14 29 Nov. 1827, ibid., p. 358.
15 9 Aug. 1827, ibid., p. 340.
16 26 Sept. 1827, ibid., pp. 344–5.
17 24 Oct. 1827, ibid., p. 350.
18 O'Connell to Thomas Spring Rice, 29 Nov. 1827, ibid., p. 358.
19 O'Connell to Thomas Spring Rice, 11 Dec. 1827, ibid., p. 364.
20 1 Dec. 1827, ibid., p. 360.
21 Henry Brougham to O'Connell, [28 April 1827], ibid., p. 310.
22 2 Jan. 1827, ibid., p. 285.
23 O'Connell to Edward Dwyer, 5 April 1827, ibid., p. 303.
24 Robert Peel to Lord Anglesey, 7 April 1828, quoted in Earl Stanhope and Edward Cardwell (eds.), *Memoirs by Sir Robert Peel* (London, 1957–8), vol. i, pp. 36–7.
25 Richard Sheil to O'Connell, 30 Sept. [1827], O'Connell, *Correspondence*, vol. iii, p. 347.
26 22 March 1827, ibid., p. 302.
27 *Dublin Evening Post* 22 Dec. 1827.
28 8 June 1827, O'Connell, *Correspondence*, vol. iii, pp. 319–20.
29 9 June 1827, ibid., p. 322.
30 30 Sept. 1827, ibid., p. 346.
31 Wyse, *Catholic Association of Ireland*, op. cit., vol. i, p. 300.
32 O'Connell to Edward Dwyer, 21 March 1827, O'Connell, *Correspondence*, vol. iii, p. 301.
33 *Dublin Evening Post*, 26 July 1827.
34 ibid.
35 O'Connell to Edward Dwyer, 3 Aug. 1827, O'Connell, *Correspondence*, vol. iii, pp. 336–7.
36 Reynolds, *Catholic Emancipation Crisis*, op. cit., p. 102.
37 Wyse, *Catholic Association of Ireland*, op. cit., vol. i, pp. 310–11.
38 ibid., pp. 317–18.
39 ibid., pp. 320–1.
40 O'Connell, *Correspondence*, vol. iii, p. 345.
41 *Freeman's Journal*, 23 Aug. 1827.
42 O'Connell, *Correspondence*, vol. iii, pp. 372–3.
43 27 Feb. 1828, ibid., p. 377.
44 27 May 1828, ibid., pp. 381–2.
45 Thomas Steele, quoted in Wyse, *Catholic Association of Ireland*, op. cit., vol. i, p. 379n.
46 *Freeman's Journal*, 26 June 1828.
47 Bishop Doyle to O'Connell, 27 June 1828, Fitzpatrick, *Right Rev. Dr Doyle*, op. cit., vol. ii, pp. 75–6, and *Freeman's Journal*, 28 June 1828.
48 Lord Anglesey to Robert Peel, 23 June 1828, Stanhope and Cardwell (eds), *Memoirs of Sir Robert Peel*, op. cit., vol. i, p. 131.
49 Sheil, *Sketches, Legal and Political*, op. cit., vol. ii, pp. 117–18.
50 W. M. Thackeray, *The Irish Sketch Book* (London, 1843), p. 177.
51 MacDonagh, *Life of O'Connell*, op. cit., pp. 157, 161–2.
52 O'Flanagan, *The Irish Bar*, op. cit., p. 249.
53 Sheil, *Sketches Legal and Political*, op. cit., vol. ii, p. 136.
54 MacDonagh, *Life of O'Connell*, op. cit., pp. 161, 162.
55 ibid., p. 164.
56 *Dublin Evening Post*, 12 July 1828.

57 Fitzgerald to Peel, 5 July 1828, Stanhope and Cardwell (eds.), *Memoirs of Sir Robert Peel*, op. cit., vol. i, p. 114.
58 Robert Peel to Sir Walter Scott, 3 April 1829, Parker, *Sir Robert Peel*, op. cit., vol. ii, pp. 99–100.
59 MacDonagh, *Life of O'Connell*, op. cit., p. 165. See also *Dublin Evening Post*, 12 July 1828.
60 *Dublin Evening Post*, 12 July 1828.
61 O'Connell to Cornelius MacLoghlin, 5 July 1828, O'Connell, *Correspondence*, vol. iii, p. 386.
62 Edward Dwyer to O'Connell, 5 July 1828, ibid., p. 387.
63 ibid.

## *CHAPTER 12*
## The Famous Victory
*1828–9*

1 *Dublin Evening Post*, 26 Aug. 1828.
2 Wyse, *Catholic Association of Ireland*, op. cit., vol. i, p. 45.
3 ibid., p. 408.
4 Lord Anglesey to Robert Peel, 8 Sept. 1828, quoted in speech on 4 May 1829 in debate in House of Lords on his recall from Ireland, *Hansard*, n. s., vol. xxi, col. 999.
5 Duke of Wellington to Lord Bathurst, 24 Nov. 1828, A. Wellington (ed.), *Despatches, Correspondence and Memoranda* (London, 1867–80), vol. v, p. 280.
6 17 Sept. 1828, O'Connell, *Correspondence*, vol. iii, pp. 407–8.
7 Wyse, *Catholic Association of Ireland*, op. cit., vol. ii, p. clxx.
8 O'Connell to Rev. Michael Slattery, 2 Sept. 1828, O'Connell, *Correspondence*, vol. iii, pp. 402–3.
9 11 July 1828, ibid., p. 301.
10 *Morning Register*, 17 July 1828.
11 27 Sept. 1828, O'Connell, *Correspondence*, vol. iii, pp. 414–15.
12 O'Connell to Edward Dwyer, ibid., vol. iv, p. 27.
13 22 Sept. 1828, ibid., vol. iii, pp. 411–12.
14 4 Sept. 1828, ibid., p. 404.
15 24 Sept. 1828, ibid., p. 412.
16 *Freeman's Journal*, 15 Nov. 1828.
17 O'Connell to Lord Cloncurry, O'Connell, *Correspondence*, vol. iii, p. 404.
18 Wyse, *Catholic Association of Ireland*, op. cit., vol. ii, p. 48.
19 *Dublin Evening Post*, 5 Feb. 1829.
20 O'Connell, *Correspondence*, vol. iv, p. 6.
21 17 March 1829, ibid. p. 31.
22 *Freeman's Journal*, 11 Feb. 1829.
23 O'Connell, *Correspondence*, vol. iv, p. 16.
24 3 March 1829, ibid., pp. 17–18.
25 O'Connell to Mary, 6 March 1829, ibid., p. 20.
26 O'Connell to the People of Ireland, *Freeman's Journal*, 12 March 1829.
27 O'Connell to Edward Dwyer, 6 March and 11 March 1829, O'Connell, *Correspondence*, vol. iv, pp. 24, 27.
28 12 March 1829, ibid., p. 28.
29 8 Feb. 1829, O'Connell, *Correspondence*, vol. iv, p. 8.
30 4 March 1829, ibid., p. 18.
31 O'Connell to Mary, 6 March 1829, ibid., p. 20.
32 O'Connell to Edward Dwyer, 6 March 1829, ibid., p. 22.
33 O'Connell to Rev. W. A. O'Meara OSF, 18 March 1829, ibid., p. 32.
34 28 March 1829, ibid., pp. 35–6.
35 11 April 1829, ibid., pp. 43–5.
36 14 April 1829, ibid., p. 45.
37 11 April 1829, ibid., p. 43.
38 11 Sept. 1829, ibid., p. 96.
39 14 May 1829, ibid., p. 59.

40 O'Connell to Knight of Kerry, 12 May 1829, ibid., p. 55.
41 O'Connell to Charles Sugrue, 20 May 1829, ibid., p. 63.
42 Hunting Cap to O'Connell, 16 May 1811, ibid., vol. i, p. 257.
43 15 April 1829, ibid., vol. iv, p. 46.
44 1 May 1829, ibid., p. 52.
45 30 July 1819, ibid., vol. ii, p. 205.
46 *Dail Reports*, vol. ii, p. 11.
47 10 Feb. 1829, O'Connell, *Correspondence*, vol. iv, p. 11.
48 25 April 1829, ibid., p. 50.
49 ibid.
50 13 April 1829, ibid., p. 44.
51 7 July 1829, ibid., p. 81.
52 6 March 1829, ibid., p. 21.
53 8 April 1829, ibid., p. 41.
54 15 April 1829, ibid., p. 46.
55 5 March 1829, ibid., p. 19.
56 13 April 1829, ibid., p. 45.
57 8 Feb. 1829, ibid., p. 9
58 10 Feb. 1829, ibid., p. 11.
59 28 Aug. 1829, ibid., p. 94.
60 11 March 1829, ibid., pp. 26–7.
61 11 April 1829, ibid., p. 43.
62 O'Connell to Mary, 21 May 1829, ibid., p. 66.
63 21 May 1829, ibid., p. 66.
64 O'Connell to Pierce Mahony, 4 June 1829, ibid., p. 74.
65 O'Connell to David Mahony, 14 June 1829, ibid., p. 77.
66 O'Connell to Pierce Mahony, 4 June 1829, ibid., p. 73.
67 30 July 1829, J. Bentham, *Works*, (ed.) J. Bowring (Edinburgh, 1843–59), vol. xi, p. 20.
68 6 Aug. 1829, O'Connell, *Correspondence*, vol. iv, pp. 87–8.
69 O'Connell to John Howard Payne, ibid., pp. 70–1.

# Select Bibliography


## I PRIMARY SOURCES

1 MANUSCRIPTS

Diocesan Archives, Kildare and Leighlin, Carlow.
Dublin Diocesan Archives. Drumcondra, Dublin.
O'Connell Papers. University College, Dublin Archives.
O'Connell Papers. National Library of Ireland.
Scully Papers (in the possession of Mr B. MacDermot).

2 PARLIAMENTARY PAPERS

Parliamentary Reports. First report from the Select Committee on the State of Ireland, vol. xxxv, no. 129, 1825.
Parliamentary Reports. Select Committee of the House of Lords, Appointed to inquire into the State of Ireland, vol. xxxvi, no. 181, 1825.

3 PARLIAMENTARY DEBATES

Cobbett's *Parliamentary Debates.*
Hansard, T. C., *Parliamentary Debates*, 1st and 2nd series.

4 PUBLISHED SELECT DOCUMENTS AND LETTERS

Aspinall, A. (ed.), *The Letters of George IV, 1812–30*, 3 vols (Cambridge, 1938).
*A Collection of Speeches by D. O'Connell and Richard Sheil, on subjects connected with the Catholic Question* (Dublin, 1828).
Cusack, M. F. (ed.), *Speeches and Public Letters of the Liberator*, 2 vols (Dublin, 1875).
Fitzpatrick, W. J., *Correspondence of Daniel O'Connell the Liberator*, 2 vols (London, 1888).
Houston, A., *Daniel O'Connell: His Early Life and Journal, 1795–1802* (London, 1906).
O'Connell, J. (ed.), *The Life and Speeches of Daniel O'Connell M.P.*, 2 vols (Dublin, 1846).
O'Connell, J. (ed.), *The Select Speeches of Daniel O'Connell M.P.*, 2 vols (Dublin, 1854–5).
O'Connell, M. R. (ed.), *The Correspondence of Daniel O'Connell*, 8 vols (Shannon and Dublin, 1972–80).
Wellington, A. (ed.), *Despatches, Correspondence and Memoranda of Arthur Duke of Wellington*, 8 vols (London, 1867–80).

5 NEWSPAPERS AND PERIODICALS

*Dublin Evening Post*
*Freeman's Journal* (Dublin)
*The Times*

6 CONTEMPORARY PRINTED SOURCES

Anon., *A Historical Sketch of the Condition of the Irish People before the commencement of Mr O'Connell's career; a History of the Catholic Association; and Memoirs of Mr O'Connell* (2nd edn, Edinburgh, 1835).
Barrington, (Sir) J., *Historical Anecdotes of Ireland*, 2 vols (London, 1833).
Barrington, (Sir) J., *Rise and Fall of the Irish Nation* (Paris, 1833).
Civis (pseud.), *The Important Discovery; or, a reply from Civis, to a letter addressed by Daniel O'Connell, Esq. to the Marquis Wellesley* (Dublin, 1822).
Courtenay, E., *A Narrative by Miss Ellen Courtenay, of most*

extraordinary cruelty, perfidy and depravity, perpetrated against her by Daniel O'Connell, Esq., M.P. for Kerry. ([London], 1832).

Daunt, W. J. O'N., *Eighty-Five Years of Irish History, 1800–1885*, 2 vols (London, 1886).

Daunt, W. J. O'N., *Ireland and her Agitators* (Dublin, 1867).

Daunt, W. J. O'N., *A Life Spent for Ireland. Selections from the Journals of W. J. O'Neill Daunt*, (ed.) A. I. O'N. Daunt (Shannon, 1974).

Daunt, W. J. O'N., *Personal Recollections of the late Daniel O'Connell, M.P.*, 2 vols (London, 1848).

Doyle, J. W., *An Essay on the Catholic Claims* (Dublin, 1826).

Doyle, J. W., *Letters on the State of Ireland* (1825).

Fagan, W., *The Life and Times of Daniel O'Connell*, 2 vols (Cork, 1847–8).

Graeme, J., *O'Connell, His Contemporaries and Career* (Dublin, 1842).

Gregory, (Lady) Isabella Augusta (ed.), *Mr Gregory's Letter-box, 1813–1830* (London, 1898).

Huish, R., *The Memoirs Private and Political of Daniel O'Connell, Esq., M.P., His Times and Contemporaries* (London, 1836).

MacGee, T. D., *Historical Sketches of O'Connell and his Friends* (Boston, 1845).

Madden, D. O., *Ireland and its Rulers since 1829*, 2 vols (London, 1843–4).

A Munster Farmer, *A Letter to Daniel O'Connell . . . occasioned by the petition adopted at the late aggregate meeting of the Catholics of Ireland* (Dublin, 1824).

[O'Connell, D.], *Historical Account of the Laws Against the Roman Catholics of England* (London, 1811).

*Mr. O'Connell's Letter to the Lord Lieutenant* [concerning the sentence passed on the Rev. Mr Houlton] [Dublin, 1823].

*A Letter to the Members of the House of Commons . . . on the Legal Right of Roman Catholics to sit in Parliament, to which is added a reply to E. B. Sugden* (London, 1829).

Pearce, R. R., *Memoirs and Correspondence of the Most Noble Richard Marquess Wellesley*, 3 vols (London, 1846).

Peel, (Sir) R., *Memoirs by Sir Robert Peel*, (eds.) Stanhope, Earl and Cardwell, E., 2 vols (London, 1857–8).

Plowden, F., *History of Ireland from its Union with Great Britain, 1801 to 1810*, 3 vols (Dublin, 1811).

*The Speeches of the Right Honourable Richard Lalor Sheil, M.P.*, with memoir by Thomas MacNevin (Dublin, 1845).

Sheil, R. L., *Sketches, Legal and Political*, (ed.) M. W. Savage, 2 vols (London, 1855).

Taylor, W. F., *A Munster Farmer's reminiscences of Daniel O'Connell* (London, 1847).

Wakefield, E., *An Account of Ireland, Statistical and Political*, 2 vols (London, 1812).

Wyse, T., *Historical Sketch of the late Catholic Association of Ireland*, 2 vols (London, 1829).

Wyse, T., *The Political Catechism, explanatory of the Constitutional Rights and Civil Disabilities of the Catholics of Ireland* (London, 1829).

## II SECONDARY SOURCES

### 1 BOOKS AND ARTICLES

Anglesey, Marquess of, *One Leg:*

*The Life and Letters of Henry William Paget, First Marquess of Anglesey, K. G., 1768–1854* (London, 1961).

Auchmuty, J. J., *Sir Thomas Wyse, 1791–1862. The life and career of an educator and diplomat* (London, 1939).

Best, G. F. A., 'The Protestant Constitution and its Supporters, 1800–1829', *Transactions of the Royal Historical Society*, fifth series, vol. 8, 1958.

Bowen, D., *The Protestant Crusade in Ireland, 1800–70: a study of Protestant-Catholic relations between the Act of Union and Disestablishment* (Dublin, 1978).

Brock, W. R., *Lord Liverpool and Liberal Toryism, 1820 to 1827* (Cambridge, 1941).

Broderick, J. F., *The Holy See and the Irish Repeal Movement, 1829–47* (Rome, 1951).

Bryce, J., *Two Centuries of Irish History, 1691–1870* (London, 1888).

Chart, D. A., *Ireland from the Union to Catholic Emancipation* (London, 1910).

Connolly, S. J., *Priests and People in Pre-Famine Ireland, 1780–1845* (Dublin, 1982).

Corcoran, T., 'O'Connell and Popular Education', *Studies*, vol. 18, June 1929.

Corcoran, T., 'O'Connell and University Education', *Studies*, vol. 18, Sept. 1929.

Curran, Constantine P., 'Religious Aspects of O'Connell's Early Life. I – His Deistic Tendencies', *Studies*, vol. 18, March 1929.

Cusack, M. F., *The Liberator (Daniel O'Connell) his Life and Times, Political, Social and Religious* (London, 1872).

Davis, R. W., 'The Tories, the Whigs, and Catholic Emancipation, 1827–1829', *English Historical Review*, vol. xcvii, no. 382, Jan. 1982.

Dunlop, R., *Daniel O'Connell and the Revival of National Life in Ireland* (London, 1900).

Edwards, R. D., *Daniel O'Connell and his World* (London, 1975).

Fitzpatrick, W. J., *The Life, Times and Correspondence of The Right Rev. Dr. Doyle*, 2 vols (Dublin, 1880).

Gash, N., *Mr. Secretary Peel: the Life of Sir Robert Peel to 1830* (London, 1961).

Gladstone, W. E., 'Daniel O'Connell', *Nineteenth Century*, Jan. 1889.

Gwynn, D., 'Bishop Doyle and Catholic Emancipation', *Studies*, vol. 17, Sept. 1928.

Gwynn, D., 'Religious Aspects of O'Connell's Early Life. II – The Catholic Democrat, 1790–1815', *Studies*, vol. 18, March 1929.

Gwynn, D., 'Daniel O'Connell and his Lieutenants', *Studies*, vol. 18, June 1929.

Gwynn, D., *The Struggle for Catholic Emancipation, 1750–1829* (London, 1928).

Gwynn, D., *Daniel O'Connell and Ellen Courtenay* (Oxford, 1930).

Gwynn, D., *Daniel O'Connell* (revised edn, Oxford, 1947).

Hamilton, J. A., *Life of Daniel O'Connell* (London, 1888).

Hill, J., 'The Politics of Privilege: Dublin Corporation and the Catholic Question, 1792–1823', *The Maynooth Review*, vol. 7, Dec. 1982.

Horgan, J. J., *Great Catholic Laymen* (Dublin, 1907).

Inglis, B., 'O'Connell and The Irish Press 1800–42', *Irish Historical Studies*, vol. viii, March 1952.

Inglis, B., *The Freedom of the Press in Ireland, 1784–1841* (London, 1954).

Kelleher, D. L., *Great Days with O'Connell* (Dublin, 1929).
La Faye, J. de., *O'Connell* (Paris, 1896).
Lecky, W. E. H., *Leaders of Public Opinion in Ireland*, 2 vols (New York, 1912).
Lefevre, G. J. S., *Peel and O'Connell. A Review of the Irish Policy of the Parliament from the Act of Union to the Death of Sir Robert Peel* (London, 1887).
Luby, T. C., *The Life and Times of Daniel O'Connell* (Glasgow, [187?]).
Machin, G. I. T., *The Catholic Question in English Politics 1820 to 1830* (Oxford, 1964).
Macken, U., *The Story of Daniel O'Connell* (Cork, 1975).
Mansergh, P. N. S., *The Irish Question 1840–1921: a commentary on Anglo-Irish relations and on social and political forces in Ireland in the age of reform and revolution* (3rd edn., London, 1975).
Moley, R., *Daniel O'Connell: Nationalism without Violence: an essay* (New York, 1974).
Mulvey, Helen F., 'The Correspondence of Daniel and Mary O'Connell', in M. R. O'Connell (ed.), *The Correspondence of Daniel O'Connell* (Shannon and Dublin, 1972–80), vol. i.
MacCaffrey, L. J. *Daniel O'Connell and the Repeal Year* ([Lexington, 1966]).
MacCartney, D., 'The Writing of History in Ireland 1800–30', *Irish Historical Studies*, vol. x, no. 40, Sept. 1957.
McCartney, D. (ed.), *The World of Daniel O'Connell* (Dublin, 1980).
MacCullagh, W. T., *Pro-Consul and Tribune. Wellesley and O'Connell* (London, 1880).
MacDonagh, M., *Bishop Doyle* (London, 1896).
MacDonagh, M., *Daniel O'Connell and the Story of Catholic Emancipation* (Dublin, 1929).
MacDonagh, M., *The Life of Daniel O'Connell* (London, 1903).
MacDonagh, O., 'The Contribution of O'Connell', in B. Farrell (ed.), *The Irish Parliamentary Tradition* (Dublin, 1973).
MacDonagh, O., 'The Politicization of the Irish Catholic Bishops, 1800–1850', *Historical Journal*, vol. xviii, 1975.
McDowell, R. B., *Public Opinion and Government Policy in Ireland, 1801–1846* (London, 1952).
McDowell, R. B., *The Irish Administration, 1801–1914* (London, 1964).
Macintyre, A., *The Liberator: Daniel O'Connell and the Irish Party, 1830–47* (London, 1965).
Nemours, G., *Daniel O'Connell* (Paris, 1893).
Niebuhr, B. G., *Letter upon Roman Catholic Emancipation and the State of Ireland in 1829* (London, *1887).*
Nowlan, K. B., *The Politics of Repeal. A Study in the Relations between Great Britain and Ireland, 1841–50* (London, 1965).
Nowlan, K. B. and O'Connell, M. R. (eds), *Daniel O'Connell: Portrait of a Radical* (Belfast, 1984).
O'Brien, G., 'O'Connell and the Ireland in which he lived', *Dublin Review*, vol. 184, 1929.
O'Brien, M. C., 'The Gaelic Background', *Irish Times*, 6 Aug. 1975.
O'Brien, R. B., *Fifty Years of Concessions to Ireland*, vol. i (London, n.d.).
O'Connell, B. M., *O'Connell Family Tracts*, nos 1–3 (Dublin, 1947–51).

O'Connell, Mrs M. J., *The Last Colonel of the Irish Brigade, Count O'Connell, and old Irish life at home and abroad, 1745–1833*, 2 vols (London, 1892).

O'Connell, M. R., 'Daniel O'Connell: income, expenditure and despair', *Irish Historical Studies*, vol. xvii, no. 66, Sept. 1970.

O'Connell, M. R., 'Daniel O'Connell and Religious Freedom', *Thought*, vol. 50, no. 197, June 1975.

O'Connell, M. R., 'O'Connell Reconsidered', *Studies*, vol. 64, Summer 1975.

O'Connell, M. R., 'Daniel O'Connell and his Family', *Irish Times*, 6 Aug. 1975.

*O'Connell Centenary Record 1875* (Dublin, 1878).

O'Faoláin, S., *King of the Beggars* (New York, 1938).

O'Ferrall, F., *Daniel O'Connell* (Dublin, 1981).

O'Ferrall, F., 'The Only Lever . . . ? The Catholic Priest in Irish Politics, 1823–29', *Studies*, vol. 70, winter 1981.

O'Ferrall, F., *Catholic Emancipation: Daniel O'Connell and the Birth of Irish Democracy* (Dublin, 1985).

O'Flanagan, J. R., *Bar Life of O'Connell* (London, 1875).

O'Flanagan, J. R., *Life and Times of Daniel O'Connell* (Dublin, 1875).

O'Rourke, J., *The Life of O'Connell* (Dublin, [1875]).

Ó Tuathaigh, G., *Ireland before the Famine, 1798–1848* (Dublin, [1972]).

Ó Tuathaigh, G., 'Gaelic Ireland, Popular Politics and Daniel O'Connell', *Journal of the Galway Archaeological and Historical Society*, vol. xxxv, 1975.

Parker, C. S. (ed.), *Sir Robert Peel from his private papers*, 3 vols (London, 1899).

Plunket, D., *The Life, Letters, and Speeches of Lord Plunket*, 2 vols (London, 1867).

Reynolds, J. A., *The Catholic Emancipation Crisis in Ireland 1823–1829* (New Haven, 1954).

Roberts, M., *The Whig Party, 1807–12* (London, 1939).

Senior, H., *Orangeism in Ireland and Britain 1795–1836* (London, 1966).

Tierney, M. (ed.), *Daniel O'Connell. Nine Centenary Essays* (Dublin, 1949).

Tierney, M., 'Politics and Culture: Daniel O'Connell and the Gaelic Past', *Studies*, vol. 27, Sept. 1938.

Torrens, W. T. MacC., *Memoirs of Sir Richard Lalor Sheil*, 2 vols (London, 1855).

Trench, C. C., *The Great Dan. A Biography of Daniel O'Connell* (London, 1984).

Ward, B., *The Eve of Catholic Emancipation, 1803–1829*, 3 vols (New York, 1911–12).

Whelan, B., 'Behind the Scenes of Catholic Emancipation', *Dublin Review*, vol. 184, 1929.

Whyte, J. H., The Influence of the Catholic Clergy on Elections in Nineteenth Century Ireland', *English Historical Review*, vol. lxxv, 1960.

Wyse, W., *Memoirs of Sir Thomas Wyse* (Waterford, 1901).

2 THESES

O'Ferrall, F., 'The Growth of Political Consciousness in Ireland 1829–1847: a Study of O'Connellite Politics and Political Education', Ph.D. thesis, Trinity College, Dublin.

# *Bibliographical Note*

*MISE-EN-SCÈNE*

M. R. O'Connell's Preface in volume i of his edition of the *Correspondence* includes a brief description of the O'Connell locale and an outline of the O'Connell genealogy; the latter is set out in detail in B. M. O'Connell's *Family Tracts*.

*CHAPTER 1*

'The Gaelic Background' by Gerard Murphy (Tierney, ed., *Daniel O'Connell: Nine Centenary Essays*, pp. 1–24) is a penetrating and imaginative short survey of its subject. An article of the same title by M. C. O'Brien (*Irish Times*, 6 Aug. 1975) and Gearóid Ó Tuathaigh's 'The Folk-hero and Tradition' (McCartney, ed., *World of Daniel O'Connell*, pp. 30–42) and J. A. Murphy's 'O'Connell and the Gaelic World' (Nowlan and O'Connell, eds, *O'Connell: Portrait of a Radical*, pp. 32–52) are also important considerations of O'Connell's place in his native cultural inheritance. For O'Connell's sojourn at Fr Harrington's school, see P. Thompson, 'Reddington's Academy on the Great Island' (*Cork Examiner*, 22 July 1972).

Thomas Wall's 'Louvain, St. Omer and Douai' (Tierney, ed., *Daniel O'Connell: Nine Centenary Essays*, pp. 25–50) is an excellent study of O'Connell's Continental education.

*CHAPTER 2*

For a general account of late-eighteenth-century British radical organization and thought, see S. Maccoby, *English Radicalism 1786–1832* (London, 1955); for the French Revolutionary period, H. T. Dickinson, *British Radicalism and the French Revolution* (London, 1985); and for Godwin, in particular, M. Butler, *Burke, Paine, Godwin and the Revolution Controversy* (Cambridge, 1984). The main source for the life and career of General Count Daniel O'Connell is Mrs M. J. O'Connell's *Last Colonel of the Irish Brigade*.

*CHAPTER 3*

C. Maxwell, *Dublin under the Georges: 1714–1830* (London, 1936) and M. Craig, *Dublin, 1660–1860* (London, 1952) provide useful descriptions of the late-eighteenth-century city.

'The Volunteers and Parliament, 1779–84' by P. D. H. Smyth (T. Bartlett and D. W. Hayton, eds, *Penal Era and Golden Age: Essays in Irish History, 1690–1800*, Belfast, 1979) illuminates the reality of the early Volunteering movement which O'Connell persistently idealized.

W. E. H. Lecky, *A History of Ireland in the Eighteenth Century* (new impression, London, 1913), vols iii and iv, remains the best detailed survey of Irish politics in the 1790s; T. Pakenham, *The Year of Liberty: the Story of the Great Irish Rebellion of 1798* (London, 1969) is the most up-to-date general account of the 1798 rebellion and its aftermath.

*CHAPTER 4*

Mulvey's 'Correspondence of Daniel and Mary O'Connell' (O'Connell, ed., *Correspondence*, vol. i, pp. xix–xxx) is a sensitive and perceptive analysis of

O'Connell's marriage as revealed by the letters between him and his wife, and M. R. O'Connell's 'Daniel O'Connell: income, expenditure and despair' is the authoritative source for O'Connell's personal finances.

The widespread tradition that O'Connell was unfaithful to his wife and fathered many bastards deserves some special consideration. I have found only two pieces of evidence which lend any colour whatever to such assertions. The first is the charge by Ellen Courtenay in her *Narrative*, published in 1832, that O'Connell had violated her in his house in Dublin fifteen years before and that she bore him an illegitimate son in November 1818. Denis Gwynn devoted a monograph, *Daniel O'Connell and Ellen Courtenay*, to an investigation of the case and concluded, convincingly, that the story was baseless. O'Connell himself claimed (in a letter of 14 January 1832) to have ascertained, through inquiries, that Courtenay was acting with a company in Gosport and the Isle of Wight during 1817, the year in which he was meant to have raped her in Dublin, and also that she was in fact childless. Earlier (in a letter of 30 November 1831), he made the point that such a 'calumny . . . would have been worth any money in Ireland at any time during the last twenty years, that is, if it had the least face of probability' (O'Connell, *Correspondence*, vol. iv, p. 367). Furthermore, it is suggestive that her pamphlet was published by Barnard Gregory, editor of the *Satirist* (London). Gregory was notorious as a blackmailer of prominent public men, occasionally obtaining large sums of money for refraining from publishing highly derogatory material: he was fined heavily and gaoled briefly for his part in the attempted blackmail of the Duke of Cumberland in 1839. Courtenay's (or Gregory's) style in the pamphlet is typical of the language used in this blackmailing trade, common in the 1820s and 1830s – 'Vain were all my struggles, all my prayers, all my cries for assistance; he sunk the man in the brutality of the monster, and desisted not from his prey'. (For this subject generally, see I. McCalman, *Radical Underworld: Prophets, Revolutionaries and Pornographers in London, 1795–1840*, Oxford, 1987). Taking the evidence as a whole, I conclude that O'Connell was almost certainly innocent of the charge. Certainly, he paid Courtenay nothing – though payment would not have necessarily implied guilt, as these blackmailers were sometimes bought off merely to avoid trouble.

The second possible shadow on O'Connell's reputation arises from Mary O'Connell's objection in 1823 to his visiting Miss Gaghran, who had been their children's governess up to the preceding year. O'Connell agreed not to visit her in future without Mary's express agreement, adding, 'Surely I said enough on that subject – at least I think I did – to set your mind at ease. But why should it be otherwise, I confess I am at a loss to understand. I never in my life showed the slightest tinge of preference to any being above you' (O'Connell, *Correspondence*, vol. ii, p. 522). Mary had long disliked Miss Gaghran, and perhaps also been jealous of her capabilities; and this is probably the explanation of her objection to O'Connell's calling on her. Mulvey rightly concludes that 'Subsequent letters [in one of which O'Connell was given a commission by Mary to get Miss Gaghran to execute some embroidery for her] . . . strengthen the impression that Mary was accusing her husband of conduct inconsiderate to her feelings but not sexually immoral' (ibid., vol. i, p. xxix).

The question remains: why has O'Connell gone down in Irish popular tradition as a tireless womanizer? Why have innumerable legends of immense virility gathered about him? Diarmiad Ó Muirithe, the leading authority on the folklore of O'Connell, has suggested a plausible answer, that O'Connell acquired legendary status in the countryside even in his own time: 'All these stories are the product of the folk-mind. The heroes of old, on whom the O'Connell of folklore is to a great degree modelled, were ever famous for their sexual energy.' (D. Ó Muirithe, 'O'Connell in Irish Folk Tradition', in Nowlan and O'Connell, eds. *O'Connell: Portrait of a Radical*, pp. 59–60.)

## *CHAPTERS 5 AND 6*

Ward's *Eve of Catholic Emancipation* presents the full background of the Catholic question (especially in its British bearings) in the early nineteenth century; and R. Dudley Edwards' essay 'O'Connell and Rome' in McCartney, ed., *World of Daniel O'Connell* (pp. 125–42), usefully places O'Connell in this general context.

McDowell's *Public Opinion and Government Policy in Ireland* and Ó Tuathaigh's *Ireland before the Famine* are recommended as surveys of Ireland in the first half of the nineteenth century. McDowell's main emphasis is on political and constitutional matters; Ó Tuathaigh's, on social and economic.

Roberts, *The Whig Party, 1807–12*, remains a valuable authority on whig attitudes and ideology, not just for the years dealt with specifically but also for the early nineteenth century as a whole. Gash's *Mr Secretary Peel* is the standard work on Peel's early career.

## *CHAPTER 7*

O'Connell's income from the bar may have been underestimated by earlier scholars, who generally assumed that his fee-books tell the whole story. In fact, the information from this source is not consistent. For instance, *two* fee-books cover the same eight years, 1798–1805: the one which has usually been drawn upon (P/12/5/152, UCD Archives) lists fewer fees and produces smaller annual totals (roughly one-third less in most cases) than the other (NLI MS 130). Secondly, it is unlikely that the fee-books listed all O'Connell's professional income; in particular, returns from election, registry and arbitration work may have been omitted. This would help to account for such discrepancies as his telling his wife on 4 December 1827 that his income (the context suggests that the reference is to his *bar* income) is 'upwards of £7,000' per annum, whereas his fee-books gives annual totals of £3893, £4497 and £4868 for 1825, 1826 and 1827, respectively (Reynolds, *Catholic Emancipation Crisis*, p. 38 n.2) or his claim 'to have earned professional emoluments [which] exceeded £8,000' in 1828 (Cusack, *Speeches and Letters*, vol. ii, pp. 259–69), whereas his fee-book gives a total of £5178 for that year. O'Connell was apparently making a more or less precise calculation when he reported earnings of over £8000 in 1828, for he went on to say that it was 'an amount never before realised in Ireland in the same space of time by an outer barrister'. Wherever there is a clear and specific choice, I have preferred the higher figure.

## *CHAPTER 8*

P. J. Jupp, 'Irish Parliamentary Elections and the Influence of the Catholic Vote, 1801–20' (*Historical Journal*, vol. x, 1967) provides a good description and analysis of the general election of 1818 in Ireland. Brock, *Lord*

*Liverpool and Liberal Toryism, 1820–7* is recommended for an understanding of tory policies and approaches to Irish and Catholic, as well as more general, issues. See also N. Thompson, *Wellington after Waterloo* (London, 1987).

*CHAPTER 9*

For further information on O'Connell's children and landed property, see M. R. O'Connell, 'O'Connell and his family' (McCartney, ed., *World of Daniel O'Connell*, pp. 19–29), 'Daniel O'Connell and his family' (*Irish Times*, 6 August 1975) and 'O'Connell: Lawyer and Landlord' (Nowlan and O'Connell, eds, *O'Connell: Portrait of a Radical*, pp. 107–20).

*CHAPTERS 10–12*

O'Ferrall, *Catholic Emancipation* is an excellent study of contemporary political organization and two other authoritative books, Machin, *Catholic Question in English Politics*, and Reynolds, *Catholic Emancipation Crisis*, provide further information on various aspects of Irish and Anglo-Irish politics, 1823–9. Wyse, *Catholic Association of Ireland*, is the best primary source for the same subjects, and Sheil's essays, 'The Catholic Deputation' and 'The Clare Election', in his *Sketches, Legal and Political* (vol. ii, pp. 19–54 and 121–42), are especially important eye-witness accounts of important happenings in O'Connell's campaign for Emancipation.

# Biographical Notes

Henry William (Paget) first Marquess of ANGLESEY (1768–1854).
Army officer, MP 1790–6, 1802–4, 1806, 1807–10. 1812 became Earl of Uxbridge. 1815 created first Marquess of Anglesey. Master-general of the ordnance 1827–8, 1846–52. Lord lieutenant of Ireland 1828–9, and again 1830–3.

Lord ANNALY (John Gore) (1718–1784).
1764 he became chief justice of the King's Bench. 1766 he was made an Irish peer.

Dr Herbert BALDWIN.
First cousin of O'Connell. From a landowning family, Clohina, co. Cork. 1832–7 MP for Cork City.

Nicholas BALL (1791–1865).
1836 admitted as a bencher of the King's Inns; 1836 MP for Clonmel; 1837 attorney general; 1838 privy councillor of Ireland; 1839 till his death judge of the common pleas. He was the second Catholic promoted to a judgeship after the Relief Act.

Sir Edward BELLEW (d. 1827).
Sixth baronet, Barmeath, co. Louth.

Richard Newton BENNETT (1769–1836).
Called to the Irish bar in 1796. Married Sophia Hart. 1832 appointed chief justice of Tobago. 1833 suspended from his post because of alcoholism.

Lord George Thomas BERESFORD (1781–1839).
Third son of the Marquess of Waterford. 1830–1 MP for co. Waterford.

Rev. Thomas BETAGH, SJ (1739–1811).
With other members of the Society of Jesus (after its suppression) he carried on a school in Dublin where he became a curate. He was subsequently appointed parish priest in Dublin and vicar-general of that archdiocese.

Maxwell BLACKER (born c. 1774).
Called to the bar 1795. He was appointed chairman of the Dublin quarter sessions in 1826.

Anthony BLAKE (1786–1849).
Though a Catholic he was a member of the Irish Administration of Marquess Wellesley who appointed him chief remembrancer in 1823. His *Thoughts upon the Catholic Question* was published in 1828.

Edward BLOUNT (1769–1843).
Secretary of the English Catholic Board from 1822 and later of the British Catholic Association. 1830–2 MP for Steyning.

Simon BOLIVAR (1783–1830).
Leader of revolutionary armies which gained independence for most of South America from Spanish rule.

John BRIC (1793–1826).
Clerk to O'Connell in 1815; admitted to King's Inns in 1816 and to Middle Temple, London, in 1819. He was called to the bar in Dublin in 1824 and killed in a duel in Dublin in December 1826.

Admiral Pedro Luis BRION (1782–1821).
A wealthy Jewish merchant from Curacao. Admiral of Bolivar's naval forces 1816–19.

Henry Peter BROUGHAM (1778–1868).
Barrister and whig-radical MP. In 1830–4 while lord chancellor he carried through significant law reform. In 1830 he was created

Baron Brougham and Vaux. He was also an advocate of the abolition of slavery and of educational and parliamentary reform.

Col. Samuel BROWNE.
Colonel of York Light Infantry and deputy quarter-master general, c. 1814.

Major George BRYAN (1770–1843).
1837–43 MP for co. Kilkenny.

Sir Francis BURDETT (1770–1844).
Fifth baronet. Entered Parliament in 1796 and was MP for most of the period until 1844. Political and radical reformer.

Charles BUTLER (1750–1832).
Secretary to the English Catholics 1782–91; member of the English Catholic Board from 1808. He was called to the English bar in 1791, the first Catholic to qualify since 1688, but he scarcely ever appeared in court. In 1831 he was made a bencher of Lincoln's Inn.

James BUTLER (1780–1863) of Waterville, co. Kerry.

Captain Whitwell BUTLER of the Irish Revenue Force. Formerly a naval officer.

George CANNING (1770–1827).
Canning's toryism was founded on the maintenance of the royal prerogative, but he also advocated the repeal of Catholic disabilities and the gradual removal of restrictions on trade and commerce. He held a number of cabinet posts including the foreign office in 1807 and 1822. In April 1827 he became prime minister in an alliance with the whigs.

John CARTWRIGHT (1740–1824).
English radical. From 1775 he advocated universal suffrage, annual parliaments and the ballot.

Robert Stewart, Viscount CASTLEREAGH (1769–1822).
1797–8 acting chief secretary in Ireland. 1798–1801 chief secretary. He was in favour of the Union and repeal of Catholic disabilities. He resigned in 1801 following the king's refusal to grant Emancipation. In 1802 he became president of the (East India) board of control. 1805–6, 1807–9 secretary of state for war. 1812–22 foreign secretary.

James Caulfield, fourth viscount and first earl of CHARLEMONT (1728–1799).
He was involved with the Octennial Bill of 1768, the Volunteer movement and measures for Irish independence in 1782. He was in favour of a regency during the king's indisposition, but opposed both Catholic Emancipation and the Union.

Valentine Browne (Lawless), second Baron CLONCURRY (1773–1853).
United Irishman 1795–8. He was imprisoned 1798, 1799–1801 on suspicion of treason. He wrote many pamphlets against the Union and was a warm advocate of Catholic Emancipation, but differed from O'Connell in the early 1830s because he did not want to hamper Lord Anglesey's second administration (1830–3). He was created Baron Cloncurry (UK) 1831.

William COBBETT (1762–1835).
Journalist and political radical. 1802–35 proprietor and editor of the weekly *Political Register*. 1803–12 he produced the *Parliamentary Debates*.

Rev. William COCKBURN.
He married Robert Peel's sister, Elizabeth, in December 1805. In 1822 he became Dean of York.

Rev. Patrick COLEMAN (d. 1838).
Curate of Townshend Street Catholic chapel for many years. P.P. of St Paul's, Dublin 1825–8; St Michan's, Dublin, 1828–38. Sometime vicar-general of the Dublin archdiocese.

Sir Nathaniel CONANT (1745–1822).
Chief magistrate at Bow Street 1810–20.

Elizabeth (Betsey) CONNOR (1777–1815).
Sister of Mary O'Connell and wife of James Connor of Tralee.

James CONNOR (c. 1763–1819).
Clerk of the peace for co. Kerry. Husband of Mary O'Connell's sister Betsey. He conformed to the Church of Ireland in order to qualify as an attorney but reverted to Catholicism before his death.

Frederick William CONWAY (1782–1853).
1806–12 he edited the *Freeman's Journal*, and from autumn 1808 the new Dublin weekly, the *Messenger*. 1814–53 he was editor and proprietor of the *Dublin Evening Post*. A Protestant.

Sir John Singleton COPLEY (1772–1863).
Attorney-general 1824–6; master of the rolls 1826–7; in 1827 he was created Baron Lyndhurst; lord chancellor 1827–30, 1834–5 and 1841–6; chief baron of the exchequer 1831–4.

Stephen COPPINGER (1795–1858).
Called to the Irish bar in 1818.

Rev. William COPPINGER (1753–1830).
Catholic Bishop of Cloyne and Ross 1791–1830.

Walter ('Watty') COX.
Editor of a Dublin monthly periodical, the *Irish Magazine* (1807–15).

John Philpot CURRAN (1750–1817).
In 1782 he became a king's counsel, and was elected to the Irish House of Commons in the following year. 1806–14 master of the rolls. A strong supporter of Catholic Emancipation. On retirement in 1814 he received an address from the Catholic Board.

Rev. Patrick CURTIS (1740–1832).
Catholic Archbishop of Armagh and primate of all Ireland 1819–32.

James DALY (d. 1847).
1805–11 MP for Galway borough, 1812–30, 1832–5 for Galway county. In 1845 he was created Baron Dunsandle.

John (Bligh), fourth earl of DARNLEY (1767–1831).
Succeeded in 1781. He took his seat in the Irish House of Lords in 1789. A whig.

George Robert DAWSON (1790–1856).
1815–30 MP co. Londonderry, 1830–2, Harwich. Under-secretary of home department 1822–7. In 1816 he married Mary Peel, Robert Peel's sister.

Robert DAY.
In 1798 he became an Irish judge.

Thomas DENMAN (1779–1854).
MP 1818–26, 1830–2; chief justice of the king's bench 1832–50; knighted 1830; created Baron Denman of Dovedale 1834.

Sir Edward DENNY (d. 1831).
Third baronet. High sheriff of Tralee 1794. Commanding officer of the Yeomanry Corps 1802–3. 1828–9 MP for Tralee.

John Norcot D'ESTERRE (d. 1815).
Provision merchant to Dublin Castle. Member of the Trinity guild of the common council. Captain on half-pay in the Royal Marines since 1810.

John DEVEREUX (1778–1860).
He took part in the 1798 rebellion, was hidden by Fr William L'Estrange and then went into voluntary exile in the USA. Bolivar accepted his offer to raise a volunteer force in Ireland for service in Venezuela. His legion reached there in the second half of 1819, but he did not arrive until June 1820 by which time the legion had mutinied and the greater part had been sent to Jamaica. In 1824 he returned to England having, on his own admission, made a considerable fortune.

William George Spencer (Cavendish), sixth duke of DEVONSHIRE (1790–1858).

Succeeded in 1811. A whig.

John DOHERTY (1783–1850).
Solicitor-general 1827–30. Lord chief justice of the common pleas 1830–50.

William DOWNES, first Baron Downes (1752–1826).
He became an MP in 1790 and two years later a justice of the king's bench; 1803–22 lord chief justice of the king's bench; 1806–18 vice chancellor of the University of Dublin; 1822 an Irish peer.

Rev. James Warren DOYLE O.S.A. (1786–1834).
Catholic Bishop of Kildare and Leighlin 1819–34. Author of numerous works under his episcopal initials J.K.L. He gave evidence to parliamentary committees in 1825, 1830 and 1832.

William DRENNAN (1754–1820).
Belfast physician, United Irishman, poet. In 1791 he wrote the original prospectus of the Society of United Irishmen. He was tried for sedition and acquitted in 1794. In 1808 he founded the *Belfast Magazine*.

John Scott, first baron ELDON (1751–1838).
In 1788 he became solicitor-general; created Baron Eldon in 1799. 1799–1801 lord chief justice of the common pleas, and in 1801–6 and 1807–27 lord chancellor. Created earl of Eldon in 1821. He was strongly opposed to the Catholic claims throughout his career.

J. ELLIOTT.
Merchant, proprietor of London and Dublin Parcel Office.

Robert EMMET (1778–1803).
A United Irishman who organized a rising in July 1803. The rioters were easily dispersed. He was tried and hanged.

Thomas ERSKINE (1750–1823).
A whig, a very successful barrister, first Baron Erskine. In 1792 he defended Paine when he was prosecuted for *The Rights of Man*. Paine was found guilty and Erskine was dismissed as the Prince's attorney-general. In 1802 he became chancellor of the duchy of Cornwall.

Sir Thomas ESMONDE (1786–1868).
Ninth baronet, succeeded in 1803.

Chevalier Christopher FAGAN (1733–1816).
A kinsman and friend of the O'Connell family. Formerly a captain in the French army. He ran a school from his house in London.

Hugh FALVEY.
Still a Catholic in 1768 when he tried to save his own lands through the intervention of a Protestant friend. Conformed later to the established church, saved his land and was called to the Irish bar. He frequently acted as trustee for Hunting Cap and Morgan O'Connell, as nominal purchaser of their property, and for other purposes.

Lord Thomas FFRENCH (1765–1814).
A Catholic and strenuous supporter of complete Emancipation. Succeeded in the baronetcy in 1784.

John FINLAY (1780–1856).
Called to the bar in 1809.

William Vesey FITZGERALD (1783–1843).
Chancellor of the exchequer (Ire.) 1812–16, lord of the treasury (UK) 1812–17, envoy to the court of Sweden 1820–3. 1808–12, 1813–18 and 1831–2 MP for Ennis; 1818–28 MP for Clare; 1829 MP for Newport; 1830 MP for Lostwithiel. He was made an Irish peer in 1832, and an English peer in 1835. Lord president of the board of control 1841–3.

John FITZGIBBON (1749–1802).
Earl of Clare, lord chancellor of Ireland from 1789. He consistently used his influence to resist reform

and was totally opposed to Catholic Emancipation.

Hugh FITZPATRICK (d. 1818).
Bookseller. He published Denys Scully's *Statement of the Penal Laws* in 1812 and was prosecuted for libel for so doing. He was fined £200 with eighteen months' imprisonment.

Patrick Vincent FITZPATRICK (1792–1865).
Educated at St Patrick's College, Maynooth, and called to the Irish bar. He became O'Connell's close friend, confidant and political 'manager' and was largely responsible for the collection of the 'O'Connell Rent' from 1830. He was assistant-registrar of deeds from 1847 to 1865.

Christopher FITZ-SIMON (1793–1856).
Landowner and barrister (1821). Married O'Connell's daughter, Ellen. 1832–7 MP for co. Dublin; clerk of the crown and hanaper 1837–56.

William (Wentworth Fitzwilliam), second Earl FITZWILLIAM (1748–1833).
1794, 1806 president of the council, Dec. 1794–March 1795 lord lieutenant of Ireland.

Henry FLOOD (1732–1791).
A prominent leader of the popular party. It was through him that a powerful opposition was organized in the Irish House of Commons. His main objects were to shorten the duration of parliament, reduce pensions, create a constitutional militia, and secure the independence of the Irish legislature. 1775–81 vice-treasurer of Ireland, but removed from office because of his hostility to the government. In 1783 he entered the English House of Commons. He opposed the extension of the franchise to Catholics.

Charles James FOX (1749–1806).
Foreign secretary in 1782, 1783 and 1806, and leader of the opposition for many years. An advanced liberal.

Sir Philip FRANCIS (1740–1818).
Reputed author of *Junius' Letters*.

Matthew FRANKS.
Deputy guardian and keeper of the rolls. O'Connell's memorial for admission as a student of King's Inns was signed by a Mr Franks, barrister, and a Mr Franks, attorney.

Mary Jane GAGHRAN (c.1787–1854).
Sister of John Gaghran, physician. She married William Ford, town clerk of Dublin city. Governess for O'Connell's children.

Frederick John Robinson, Viscount GODERICH (1782–1859).
MP from 1806. He held a variety of cabinet posts 1810–13. 1823–7 chancellor of the exchequer. 1827 he was created Viscount Goderich and appointed secretary of state for war and the colonies and leader in the House of Lords. Aug. 1827–Jan. 1828 prime minister. He held office again in the 1830s. In 1833 he was created Earl of Ripon. He was opposed to Catholic Emancipation early in his career but supported Grattan's motion for a committee on Catholic claims in March 1813. He denounced the Catholic Association in 1825 but did support the Roman Catholic Relief Bill in 1829.

William GODWIN (1756–1836).
At first a Nonconformist minister. *Political Justice* published in 1793. In 1833 he was made Yeoman of the Usher of the Exchequer, and was allowed to retain this sinecure for life, though it was abolished soon after his appointment. He married Mary Wollstonecraft.

Isaac GOLDSMID (1778–1859).
A wealthy financier and philanthropist, and the political leader of the British Jews at this time. He was active in the foundation of

University College, London. Created a baronet in 1841.

Thomas GOOLD (1766?–1846).
Called to the Irish bar in 1791. MP in the last session of the Irish Parliament. In 1823 third serjeant; 1830 king's serjeant; 1832 master in chancery.

Henry GOULBURN (1784–1856).
Chief secretary for Ireland 1821–7; chancellor of the exchequer 1828–30, 1841–6; home secretary 1834–5. Resisted the Catholic Emancipation bill in 1821.

Henry GRATTAN (1746–1820).
He espoused free trade, Irish parliamentary independence (for which the House of Commons voted him £50,000 for land to show the nation's gratitude), the disbanding of the volunteers in 1783, tithe commutation, and Catholic Emancipation. Founded the Whig Club. He entered the UK House of Commons in 1805.

Charles (Grey), second Earl GREY (1764–1845).
He opposed the Union in 1800, and supported the Catholic claims 1800–29. Prime minister 1830–4.

Arthur GUINNESS J.P. (1768–1855).
He became the head of Guinness' brewing firm in 1803. Director of the Bank of Ireland 1808–39; governor 1820–2. Supporter of Catholic Emancipation.

Thomas HARDY (1752–1832).
In January 1792, Hardy, with a few friends, founded 'The London Corresponding Society' with the object of promoting parliamentary reform. On 12 May 1794 he was arrested on a charge of high treason, but in November found 'not guilty'.

William HARE (1801–56).
1826–30 MP for co. Kerry; 1841–6 for St Albans. He was styled Viscount Ennismore 1827–37, succeeding to the earldom of Listowel in 1837.

Rev. James HARRINGTON S. J.
He ran an 'academy' at Reddington, near Cove, co. Cork, which was said to have been the first school opened in Ireland by a Catholic priest after the relaxation of the penal laws.

Sir Anthony HART (c.1754–1831).
In 1816 he was appointed solicitor-general to Queen Charlotte. He was vice-chancellor of England April–Nov. 1827; lord chancellor of Ireland from 1827 to 1830; knighted in 1827.

Edward HAY (1761?–1826).
He acted as secretary to various associations for the Emancipation of Irish Catholics, but was superseded as secretary to the Catholic Board in 1819, supposedly for having opened communications with a cabinet minister without authority. He died in penury.

Rev. Richard HAYES O.F.M. (d. 1824) of the Franciscan College, Wexford. Expelled from the papal states, 1816.

John HELY-HUTCHINSON.
1826–30 and 1831–2 MP for co. Tipperary.

Richard HELY-HUTCHINSON (1756–1825).
MP from 1777; from 1788 in the Irish upper house as Baron Donoughmore. He voted for the Union, hoping thereby to secure Catholic Emancipation. In 1800 he was created Earl of Donoughmore and elected as one of the twenty-eight representative peers of England.

Robert HICKSON (d. 1816) 36 College Green, Dublin.

Robin HICKSON of the Square, Tralee.
In 1809 or 1810 he became a Roman Catholic 'publicly'.

Francis HIGGINS (1746–1802).
When he owned the *Freeman's Journal* he placed it, and his own services, at the disposal of the government in Dublin. In 1788 he

was appointed a magistrate, but was dismissed by Fitzgibbon three years later. In 1794 he was struck off the roll of attorneys. In 1795 he warned the government of the projected attack on the lord lieutenant, Lord Camden, and acted as informer on the revolutionary movement before and during 1798.

Prince Alexander Leopold Franz Emerich von HOHENLOHE Waldenburg Schillingfurst (1794–1850).
Ordained a Catholic priest in 1815. He was renowned for the miraculous cures attributed to him.

Henry HUNT (1773–1835).
Radical, reformer and orator who spoke at St Peter's Fields (Peterloo) in 1819; imprisoned 1820–2; 1830–3 MP for Preston.

Peter Bodkin HUSSEY (1778–1838) of Farrinakilla, co. Kerry. Barrister.

Charles KEMBLE (1775–1854).
His early performances on the stage were unsuccessful mainly because of his ungainly figure, but he was said to have improved steadily over thirty years. His 'affectations of speech were the subject of much satire'. He managed Convent Garden from 1822–3.

John Philip KEMBLE (1757–1823).
1788–96, 1800–2 manager of Drury Lane Theatre. In 1802 he bought a sixth share of Convent Garden.

Valentine Browne, second Earl KENMARE (1788–1835).
1801–12 styled Viscount Castlerosse; succeeded to the title in 1812.

Rev. Peter KENNEY S.J. (1779–1841).
In 1812 he was appointed vice-president of Maynooth College, where he stayed for about a year. He was the Superior of the Jesuit mission in Ireland for many years, and later its vice-provincial. Opened Clongowes Wood College, co. Kildare, in May 1814, and later helped in the establishment of St Stanislaus College, Tullabeg, and of the Jesuit residence of St Francis Xavier in Dublin.

John KEOGH (1740–1817).
Dublin merchant. Led the Irish Catholics 1791–1808. He had sympathy with the objects of the United Irishmen but refused to allow Catholic claims to be compromised by connection with them.

Maurice Fitzgerald, Knight of KERRY (1774–1849).
Hereditary Knight of Kerry. He represented Kerry for thirty-six years. 1799–1801 commissioner of customs in Ireland. He was in favour of the Union. 1801–7 at the board of the Irish treasury. 1827 lord of the English treasury. 1830 vice-treasurer of Ireland. Dec. 1834–Mar. 1835 lord of the admiralty.

Abraham Bradley KING (1773–1838).
Alderman and king's stationer. Lord mayor of Dublin in 1813 and in 1821. Former deputy grand master of the Orange order. 1821 created a baronet.

John KIRWAN.
A London merchant.

Thomas KIRWAN.
Merchant, Abbey Street, Dublin.

Henry Petty (-Fitzmaurice), third marquess of LANSDOWNE (1780–1863).
Chancellor of the exchequer 1806–7. In 1809 he succeeded as third marquess of Lansdowne. In 1818 he became the earl of Kerry, viscount Clanmaurice and the twenty-third baron Kerry and Lixnaw, and in the same year reverted to the family name of Petty-Fitzmaurice. 1827–8 home secretary; 1830–4, 1835–41, 1846–52 lord president of the council; 1852–8 in cabinet but without office. He was lord lieutenant of Wiltshire from 1829 till his death. Above all else Catholic Emancipation caught his attention.

David LA TOUCHE (1772–1838).
Banker. Third son of Rt Hon. David La Touche MP, Marlay, Co. Dublin.

John LAWLESS (1773–1837).
He was refused admission to the bar by Lord Clare because of his closeness to leaders of the United Irish movement. From 1817 to 1819 he was the editor of the *Ulster Register*, and subsequently of the *Belfast Magazine*. In 1831 he was briefly under arrest.

Nicholas Philpot LEADER (c.1773–1836).
1830–2 MP for Kilkenny City.

Sir Harcourt LEES (1776–1852).
A clergyman 1800–6. He published several pamphlets, chiefly in support of the Protestant Ascendancy.

Augustus Frederick (Fitzgerald), third duke of LEINSTER (1791–1874).
Succeeded to the title in 1804. A whig. Lord lieutenant of co. Kildare from 1831 till his death. Commissioner of National Education in Ireland 1836–41.

Rev. William L'ESTRANGE O.D.C. (d. 1833).
Educated and ordained on the Continent. He was provincial of the Irish Carmelites and prior of St Teresa's, Clarendon St, Dublin.

George LIDWILL (Lidwell) (d. 1839).
Landlord and litterateur. High sheriff of co. Tipperary 1807.

Robert Banks Jenkinson, second earl of LIVERPOOL (1770–1828).
1812–27 prime minister. Though opposed to Catholic Emancipation himself, he had to treat the question as open in order to include pro-Catholic tories in his administration. He was prepared to confer the elective franchise on *English* Roman Catholics and to open the magistracy to Catholic gentlemen.

John MAGEE.
Proprietor and editor of the *Dublin Evening Post*, which he inherited from his father, also a journalist. In 1813 he was prosecuted by the government for publishing an alleged libel on the duke of Richmond's administration. A Protestant.

Maurice (Mark) MAGRATH (born c. 1765).
Educated Trinity College, Dublin 1784–8. 1796 called to the bar. Assistant barrister for co. Wicklow from 1815.

Rev. Thomas MAGUIRE D.D. (1792–1847).
Parish priest of various parishes in the diocese of Kilmore from 1818 until his death. Also dean of Kilmore.

James Patrick O'Gorman MAHON (1800/1803–1891).
1830–1, 1879–85 MP for co. Clare; 1847–52 for Ennis; 1887–91 for co. Carlow.

Nicholas MAHON (c. 1746–1841).
Wealthy woollen merchant, in business in Dublin for over seventy years. A delegate to the Catholic convention of 1792.

Pierce MAHONY (1792–1853).
Attorney, Woodlawn, Killarney. Parliamentary agent to the Catholic Association 1828–9. 1837–8 MP for Kinsale.

James Mountain MAHONY.
Lieutenant, Kerry Militia, 1796–c.1811.

Charles MANNERS-SUTTON, first viscount Canterbury (1780–1845).
Speaker of the House of Commons 1817–35; judge advocate general 1809–17. He was created Baron Bottesford and Viscount Canterbury in 1835.

Thomas MANNERS-SUTTON (1756–1842).
Created Baron Manners of Foston in 1807. 1807–27 he was lord chancellor of Ireland. He voted against the second reading of the Catholic Relief Bill in 1829.

Ralph MARSHALL (1773–1809) of

Callinapfercy, Milltown, co. Kerry. He helped to keep Kerry free of turmoil in 1798 and was concerned about the welfare of his tenants. He was high sheriff in 1799. He joined the Spanish Army in 1808, and was killed at the seige of Gerona.

Richard MARTIN (1754–1834).
In 1782 he was high sheriff for co. Galway. A member of the Irish Parliament 1776–83, 1798–1800, and represented co. Galway in the UK Parliament 1801–26. A firm supporter of Catholic Emancipation.

Edward MAYNE (c.1756–1829).
Justice of the Common Pleas 1806–17; justice of the King's Bench 1817–20.

William Lamb, second viscount MELBOURNE (1779–1848).
Succeeded as the second Viscount Melbourne in 1828. He was chief secretary for Ireland 1827–8, home secretary 1830–4, prime minister July–Nov. 1834, 1835–41.

BISHOP JOHN MILNER D.D. (1752–1826).
Vicar apostolic of midland district, England, from 1803. At first he accepted the royal veto but later became an uncompromising opponent. This led to his expulsion from the English Catholic Board and his exclusion from the meeting of vicars-apostolic in Durham in October 1813. In 1814 the Irish bishops sent him with Dr Murray to act as their agent in Rome to secure the recall of the Quarantotti rescript.

Thomas MOORE (1779–1852).
Both his parents were Catholics. Through his 'Irish Melodies' he became known as the 'national lyrist' of Ireland. He wrote biographies of Lord Byron and Lord Edward Fitzgerald and 'The History of Ireland' for Lardner's *Cabinet Cyclopedia*. His 'Lalla Rookh' was published in 1817.

Rev. Dr Francis MOYLAN (1735–1815).
In 1775 he became Catholic bishop of Kerry; was translated to Cork in 1786. He was in favour of the Union, but eventually opposed the veto.

Rev. Daniel MURRAY (1768–1852).
President of St Patrick's College, Maynooth; archbishop of Dublin from 1823. He opposed the veto.

Eneas MACDONNELL (1783–1858).
Called to the Irish bar 1810. Editor and proprietor of *Dublin Chronicle* 1815–17; editor of *Cork Mercantile Chronicle*. Fined £100 and sentenced to six months' imprisonment in 1816 for publishing a 'libel' written by Denys Scully.

Thomas MCKENNY (1770–1849).
Alderman from 1811, lord mayor of Dublin 1819, created baronet 1831.

Cornelius MACLOGHLIN (1761–1851).
Catholic merchant. A member of the United Irishmen. He was a trustee and treasurer of the O'Connell testimonial in 1829 and of the O'Connell Tribute in succeeding years.

Major William Nugent MACNAMARA (1775–1856).
1830–52 MP for co. Clare. Landowner. High Sheriff, Clare, in 1798.

William James MCNEVIN (1763–1841).
A United Irishman, who was imprisoned 1798–1803. Active in Irish-American politics thereafter.

Myles MCSWINEY.
c.1804 he married O'Connell's sister, Bridget. He acted as land agent to O'Connell from about 1812 to 1822.

John Toler, first earl of NORBURY (1745–1831).
In 1776 he became an MP, in 1789 solicitor general; in 1798 attorney general. He supported the Union and in 1800 became chief justice of the court of common pleas in Ireland and

was created Baron Norbury. In 1825 O'Connell drew up a petition to Parliament calling for his removal on the ground that he had fallen asleep during a trial for murder and was unable to give any account of the evidence. Peel said it would be enquired into but Norbury was not induced to resign until 1827.

Bernard Edward (Howard), twelfth duke of NORFOLK (1765–1842).
He was empowered by an Act of Parliament in 1824 to exercise the office of Earl Marshal notwithstanding his adhesion to Catholicism. He was admitted to the House of Lords in 1829.

Catherine O'CONNELL (*née* O'Mullane) (1752–1817).
O'Connell's mother. She had ten children.

Catherine (Kate) O'CONNELL (1807–1891).
O'Connell's second daughter. In 1832 she married her distant cousin Charles O'Connell.

Daniel O'CONNELL (1816–1897).
Youngest son of O'Connell. 1846–7 MP for Dundalk; 1847–8 for Waterford city; 1853–63 for Tralee. In 1863 he was appointed commissioner of income tax. In 1866 he married Ellen Mary Foster.

General (Count) Daniel O'CONNELL (1745–1833).
Son of Donal Mór and Máire O'Connell, Derrynane. In 1783 he was created count of France. He was Commander of the Order of St Louis, lieutenant-general in the French army, colonel in the British army.

Daniel O'CONNELL (Splinter) (d. 1814).
Son of Edward O'Connell, first cousin of Mary O'Connell. Married in 1803 to Ellen, O'Connell's sister.

Daniel Stephen O'CONNELL (29 Dec. 1812–c.10 Feb. 1814).
Son of O'Connell.

Donal Mór (Big Daniel) O'CONNELL (d. 1770).
Father of Maurice (Hunting Cap), Daniel (General), and Morgan (O'Connell's father). Married Máire Duibh (Mary) O'Donoghue.

Elizabeth Mary (Betsey) O'CONNELL (1810–1893).
O'Connell's youngest daughter. In 1831 married Nicholas Joseph Ffrench.

Ellen O'CONNELL (born 1777).
Sister of O'Connell. In 1803 she married Daniel O'Connell (Splinter).

Ellen O'CONNELL (1805–1883).
O'Connell's eldest daughter. In 1825 she married Christopher Fitz-Simon.

James O'CONNELL (1786–1872).
Youngest brother of O'Connell. Married 1818 Jane O'Donoghue. He lived in Killarney. He was created a baronet in 1869.

John O'CONNELL (1778–1853).
Second brother of O'Connell. In 1806 married Elizabeth (Bess) Coppinger. Lived at Grenagh, near Killarney. High sheriff of Kerry 1838.

Lieutenant John O'CONNELL (d. 1826).
He was referred to as Captain O'Connell in a letter from Mary O'Connell. He was in the 67th Regiment, going on half pay in 1816. He joined the 7th Veteran Battalion in 1820.

John O'CONNELL (1810–1858).
O'Connell's third surviving son. Barrister. 1832–7 MP for Youghal; 1837–41 Athlone; 1841–7 Kilkenny City; 1847–51 Limerick City; 1853–7 Clonmel; clerk of the crown and hanaper, 1857–8. Married Elizabeth Ryan in 1838.

Máire Duibh (Mary) O'CONNELL (*née* O'Donoghue).
Her soubriquet indicated her branch of the O'Donoghue family. She had 22 children, one of whom was Morgan, Daniel O'Connell's father.

Mary O'CONNELL (1778–1836).

Daughter of Thomas O'Connell, a Tralee physician. She married O'Connell on 24 July 1802.

Maurice O'CONNELL (Hunting Cap) (1728–1825).
Eldest surviving son of Donal Mór and Máire O'Connell, Derrynane. Married in 1758. No children. Known as Hunting Cap because he wore a cap to avoid paying the tax on a conventional gentleman's hat. He was a landowner, grazier, merchant and smuggler.

Maurice Daniel O'CONNELL (1803–1853).
O'Connell's eldest child. Called to the bar 1827. 1831–2 MP for Clare; 1832–7, 1838–53 for Tralee. In 1832 he married Mary Frances Scott. Director of National Bank.

Maurice Morgan O'CONNELL (1776–97).
O'Connell's eldest brother. Lieutenant in Count Walshe de Serranti's regiment in British army as part of 'Pitt's Irish Brigade'. He died on active service in San Domingo.

Morgan O'CONNELL (1739–1809).
O'Connell's father.

Morgan O'CONNELL (1804–1885).
O'Connell's second son. In June 1819 he purchased a commission in the Irish South American Legion under Devereux. He served in the Austrian army and returned to Ireland c. 1830. In 1840 he married Kate Balfe. 1832–40 MP for Meath. 1840–6 assistant registrar of deeds; 1846–69 registrar. He fought one duel and was challenged to another on his father's behalf.

Peter O'CONNELL (d. 1824) of Clare.
A considerable scholar in literary Irish and a master of the spoken tongue.

Rickard (Rick) O'CONNELL (d. 1832).
Married Betsey Tuohy of Tralee in 1801. Brother of Mary O'Connell. Lieutenant, 89th Regiment, 1796–1804. Adjutant, Kerry Militia.

Thomas O'CONNELL (c.1735–1785).
Physician, Tralee. Third cousin of O'Connell. They had a common ancestor in Geoffrey O'Connell (c.1569–1635).

Hugh O'CONNOR, merchant, Mountjoy Square, Dublin.

Owen O'CONOR (1763–1831).
Succeeded to the title of The O'Conor Don in 1820. 1830–1 MP for co. Roscommon.

Eugene O'CURRY (1796–1862).
A pioneering Gaelic scholar of distinction. In 1849 and 1855 he examined the Irish manuscripts in the British Museum and wrote the catalogue. He became the first professor of Irish history and archaeology in the Catholic University of Ireland.

Nicholas Purcell O'GORMAN (1778–1857).
Imprisoned in Ennis in 1798. Called to the bar 1803. Member of the Catholic Board. c.1815 became secretary to the Catholics of Ireland and was the first secretary of the Catholic Association. In 1834 appointed assistant barrister.

Richard O'GORMAN (d.1867).
Junior partner in his uncle's woollen business.

Arthur (Art) O'LEARY.
Served in the Austrian Army. O'Leary challenged and struck Mr Morris, a rich Protestant, for offering him only £5 for a famous race mare (no Papist was allowed by law to own a horse of greater value than £5). Morris refused to fight a Papist and got O'Leary outlawed. O'Leary was shot by soldiers on 4 May 1773.

Eileen Dubh O'LEARY (*née* O'Connell).
'Dark Eileen', sister of Hunting Cap. She married Mr O'Connor of Fines at fourteen. He died within six months. She married Arthur O'Leary, later outlawed, in 1768.

James O'LEARY.

Woollen merchant and shopkeeper, Killarney.

Dowell O'REILLY (1795–1855).
Called to the bar about 1824. Attorney-general of Jamaica 1831–55.

Lord OXMANTOWN (Williams Parsons) (1800–1867).
1821–35 MP for King's County. A moderate whig – he voted for Catholic Emancipation and the Reform Bill. He was styled Lord Oxmantown 1807–41; in 1841 he became the Earl of Rosse. He was lord lieutenant of King's county 1831–67 and a representative peer from Ireland 1845–67.

Wray PALLISER (1789–1862).
Kilcomragh Lodge, near Kilmacthomas, co. Waterford. Lieutenant-colonel in the Waterford Militia, 1810–62. Son of John Palliser, Derrylusken, co. Tipperary.

Sir Henry PARNELL (1776–1842).
He held a number of ministerial appointments. He voted against the Union and consistently supported claims for Catholic Emancipation. He had a high reputation as a political economist and writer on finance. In 1812 he succeeded to the baronetcy, and was created Baron Congleton in 1841.

Rev. Robert PARSONS S.J. (1546–1610).
The aim of his public life was to restore England, by persuasion or force, to the Roman church. He was a zealous promoter of the Spanish invasion of England. In 1581–2 he founded a grammar school for English boys at Eu. He later established a similar one on a more solid basis at St Omer with an annual pension from King Philip of Spain in 1592–3. He also established St Alban's and St Gregory's in Spain.

Sir Robert PEEL (1788–1850).
1812–18 chief secretary for Ireland; 1822–7 home secretary. In April 1827 he resigned from the cabinet because he was opposed to Canning on Catholic Emancipation. 1828–30 home secretary again, he now agreed on the need for Catholic Emancipation, and prepared the three bills relating to it. 1834–5, 1841–6, prime minister.

Spencer PERCEVAL (1762–1812).
He successively held the posts of solicitor to the board of ordnance and solicitor general to the queen, solicitor general, attorney general. Under Pitt he insisted on his freedom to oppose Catholic Emancipation. In 1807 he became the chancellor of the exchequer. 1809–12 prime minister. In May 1812 he was assassinated.

William PITT (1759–1806).
Prime minister 1783–1801, 1804–6. During the 1790s he supported Catholic relief bills. When he brought forward the proposals for Union he held out the prospect that the recognition of Catholic claims would follow. In 1801 he resigned because of the king's opposition to measures for Catholic relief.

Arthur James PLUNKETT (1759–1836).
Lord Killeen until 1793, then eighth earl of Fingall. One of the leaders of the Catholics in their agitation for relief. At the head of a corps of yeomen, mainly Catholics, he took an active part in suppressing the 1798 rebellion. He was one of the six extraordinary knights made at the coronation of George IV, becoming a knight in ordinary in 1829. In 1831 he was created a baron (UK).

William Conyngham PLUNKET (1764–1854).
Attorney-general 1805–7, 1822–7; chief justice of the common pleas, 1827–30; created Baron Plunket in 1827; lord chancellor of Ireland 1830–4, 1835–41. He opposed the Union as an Irish MP. In 1807 he

entered the English House of Commons briefly, then again in 1812. He was in favour of Catholic Emancipation but supported the bill for suppression of the Catholic Association, 1825.

George PONSONBY (1755–1817).
MP in Ireland from 1776 until the Union, in England 1801–17. He supported the Catholic claims. He acted as counsel for Henry Sheares and Oliver Bond and led the opposition to the Union in the Irish House of Commons. 1806–7 lord chancellor of Ireland. 1808–17 the official leader of the opposition.

John William PONSONBY, fourth earl of Bessborough (1781–1847).
Lord Duncannon until 1844. Member of Commons 1805–34 almost continuously. 1834 Baron Duncannon of Bessborough. In 1844 succeeded to earldom of Bessborough. 1831–4, 1835–9 first commissioner of woods and forest; 1834–5 home office; 1846–7 lord lieutenant of Ireland. Supporter of Catholic Emancipation and parliamentary reform. He acted as chief whip of the whig party.

William Francis Spencer PONSONBY (1787–1855).
Son of the third earl of Bessborough. He was married to Lady Barbara Ashley-Cooper.

John PRIMROSE (d. 1840) of Hillgrove, Cahirciveen, co. Kerry.
Married Honoria O'Connell, cousin of O'Connell.

John PRIMROSE jr J.P. (c. 1796–1865).
Cousin of O'Connell and land agent to him from 1822. He married Rickarda Connor, daughter of James Connor, niece of Mary O'Connell, in 1830.

Francis Aldborough PRITTIE (1779–1853).
1801 MP for Carlow; 1806–18, 1819–31 for co. Tipperary.

Dominick RICE (1785–1864) of Bushmount, co. Kerry.

Stephen Henry RICE of Day Place, Tralee.
Called to the Irish bar in 1792.

Charles (Lennox) fourth Duke of RICHMOND (1764–1819).
1790–1806 MP for Sussex; lord lieutenant of Ireland 1807–13; governor general of British North America 1818–19.

James ROCHE (1770–1853).
A wine merchant in Bordeaux, who favoured the revolutionary movement originally. In 1793 he was arrested as a British subject and imprisoned for six months. In 1800 he established a bank in Cork with his brother Stephen. It flourished till 1819. He spent the next seven years in London as parliamentary and commerical agent for Youghal and the counties of Cork and Limerick. From 1833 he was local director of the Bank of Ireland in Cork.

David C. ROOSE (d. 1836).
Stockbroker and state lottery office keeper. Knighted in 1830.

Werner William (Westenra) second baron ROSSMORE (1765–1842).
1800–1 MP for co. Monaghan; created Baron Rossmore in Ireland in 1801, Baron Rossmore of Monaghan (UK) in 1838; lord lieutenant of co. Monaghan 1831 until his death.

Thomas RUSSELL (1767–1803).
A United Irishman. A soldier. In gaol 1796–9. In exile in Scotland 1799–1802. When freed, he went to Europe. In 1803 he returned to Ireland and was involved in Emmet's plans. He was arrested in September 1803 and executed in October.

William SAURIN (1757?–1839).
In 1796 the Irish bar elected him captain commandant of their corps of yeomanry. In 1798 he was granted a patent of precedence after the prime

serjeant, attorney general and solicitor general. He served the government in some of the trials arising out of the rebellion. His opposition to the Union was based on professional interest and hostility to the Roman Catholics. From 1807–22 he was attorney general for Ireland and at the centre of opposition to the Catholic claims. In 1828 he was an active promoter of the formation of the Brunswick Club.

Sir Charles SAXTON, second baronet (1773–1838).
Under secretary for Ireland 1808–12. 1812–18 MP for Cashel.

Sir James SCARLETT (1769–1844).
Knighted in 1827. Attorney general 1827–Jan. 1828, 1829–30, chief baron of the exchequer 1834–44. He was created Baron Abinger in 1835.

Denys SCULLY (1773–1830).
Barrister. In 1803 he published a pamphlet against the Union – 'An Irish Catholic's Advice to his Brethren, how to estimate their Present Situation, and repel French Invasion, Civil Wars and Slavery'. In 1812 his *Statement on the Penal Laws* appeared. It resulted in the prosecution of the printer, Hugh Fitzpatrick.

Alice SEGERSON (*née* O'Connell).
One of Hunting Cap's older sisters. Married John Segerson/Sigerson, Ballinskelligs Manor, about 1750.

John SEGERSON (Sigerson) (d.1825) of Westcove, Caherdaniel, co. Kerry.

John SHEARES (1766–1798) and Henry SHEARES (1753–1798).
They became imbued with the political principles of the Revolution when visiting France in 1792. Both were lawyers. The younger brother John governed their political actions. In 1798 they were elected to the directory of the United Irishmen. After the 1798 uprising, they were charged with high treason and publicly executed.

Rev. John SHEEHAN (d. 1854).
P.P. St Patrick's Waterford 1828–54.

Richard Lalor SHEIL (1791–1851).
Barrister and dramatist. Favoured the veto but joined O'Connell in forming the Catholic Association. In 1827 he was indicted for seditious libel but a change of prime minister led to the dropping of the prosecution. In 1830 admitted to the inner bar. In 1831 MP for Milborne Port, 1831–2 co. Louth, 1832–41 co. Tipperary, 1841–51 Dungarvan. He reluctantly took the pledge to support Repeal. In 1838–9 Commissioner of Greenwich Hospital; 1839–41 vice-president of board of trade; 1841 judge advocate-general. At the trials of the 'traversers' in 1844 he acted for John O'Connell. From 1846–50 master of the mint. 1850–1 minister at the court of Tuscany.

Dr Edward SHERIDAN, Dominick St and 39 Usher's Quay.

Richard Brinsley SHERIDAN (1751–1816).
Statesman and dramatist. He opposed the war with America 1782. Under-secretary for foreign affairs. 1783 secretary to the treasury. He was conspicuous in the proceedings against Warren Hastings. He opposed the Union between Great Britain and Ireland.

John (Talbot) earl of SHREWSBURY, also earl of Waterford (1791–1852).
Admitted to take his seat in the House of Lords under the Roman Catholic Relief Act in 1829. 1841 Commissioner for inquiring into the best mode of promoting the Fine Arts in the UK. Hon. Member of the Pontifical Academy of St Luke's, Rome.

Mrs Sarah SIDDONS (1755–1831).
Very highly regarded as an actress after her first few years. Married in 1773. Had five children.

Henry Addington, first viscount SIDMOUTH (1757–1844).

In favour of the Union. Opposed Catholic Emancipation. From 1789–1801 speaker of the House of Commons; 1801–4 first lord of the treasury and chancellor of the exchequer; president of the council several times; 1806–9 lord privy council; 1812–21 secretary of the home department.

Major Henry Charles SIRR (1764–1841).
1778–91 in army. From 1791 onwards he was a wine merchant. In 1796 on the formation of the yeomanry in Dublin he was appointed town-major or head of police. He retired in 1826. In 1808 he was appointed a police magistrate for the city of Dublin.

Charles SMYTH (1715?–1762).
Apothecary. Irish county historian – published histories of counties Down, Waterford, Cork and Kerry.

Thomas SPRING RICE (1790–1866).
MP 1820–39; under-secretary to the home office 1827–8; secretary to the treasury 1830–4; chancellor of the exchequer 1835–9; created Baron Monteagle in 1839.

Charles STANHOPE, third earl (1753–1816).
Politician and man of science. He supported the French Revolution and opposed the Union in 1800.

Sir Edward STANLEY (d.c. 1852).
Deputy barrack master to the city of Dublin, sheriff's peer. Wine and provision supplier to Dublin Castle.

Rev. Dr Gregory STAPYLTON (1748–1802).
He was Procurator of the English college at Douai for twelve years. In 1787 he was appointed President of the English College at St Omer. For a time he and his students were imprisoned. He later converted a school at Old Hall Green in Hertfordshire into a Catholic college. In 1800 he accompanied Rev. John Nassau to Rome on an important secret mission, and was raised to the episcopate and made vicar apostolic of the Midland district.

Michael STAUNTON (1788–1870).
Editor of *Freeman's Journal* 1813–24; proprietor of the *Dublin Evening Herald* 1821–3; editor and proprietor of the *Morning Register* 1824–43; lord mayor of Dublin 1847.

Thomas STEELE (1788–1848).
He raised money for and joined the revolt against Ferdinand VII of Spain 1823–4. A Protestant but one of the earliest members of the Catholic Association. An enthusiastic supporter of O'Connell.

Henry Villiers STUART (1803–1874).
1826–30 MP for co. Waterford; 1830–1 for Banbury. In 1839 he was created Baron Stuart de Decies of Dromana.

Thomas (Howard) earl of SUFFOLK (1776–1851).
1802–6 MP for Arundel. Colonel of the Wilts. Regiment of the Militia. He succeeded to the earldom in 1820.

James SUGRUE.
Cousin and friend of O'Connell, for whom he acted as informal financial agent before 1830.

Napper TANDY (1740–1803).
He was elected as the first secretary of the United Irish society in late 1791. In 1792 he tried to revive the Volunteer movement. In 1793 he left Ireland before his trial related to a pamphlet he wrote called 'Common Sense'. In 1799 he was returned to England and convicted for the part he played in the invasion of Rutland Island.

Arthur THISTLEWOOD (1770–1820).
He planned a number of risings and assassinations. His final plan, which was to be launched from a loft in Cato St, was to assassinate cabinet ministers, attack Coutt's or Child's Bank, set fire to public buildings and

seize the Tower and Mansion House where a provisional government was to be set up. After its failure Thistlewood was hanged.

Sir John Courtenay THROCKMORTON (1753–1819).
Fifth baronet; member of the English Catholic Board from 1808.

Theobald Wolfe TONE (1763–1798).
In 1792 he became assistant secretary to the general committee of Catholics. Before ending its existence the Catholic convention voted him £1500 and a gold medal as thanks. Founder of the United Irish Society. In 1798 he was captured with a French expedition to Ireland. He cut his throat the night before he was to be executed.

Dominic TRANT (d. 1790).
KC. Member for Dingle in the Irish parliament.

William Le Poer TRENCH (1771–1846).
Third son of the first earl of Clancarty. Member of the Board of customs (Ire.).

John Thomas (Barnewall), baron TRIMLESTON (1773–1839).
He succeeded in 1813.

Rev. Dr John Thomas TROY (1739–1823).
1776–84 Catholic bishop of Ossory. From 1784 archbishop of Dublin. He was on terms of friendly cooperation with Dublin Castle. He believed that Catholic Emancipation would never be granted by the Irish Parliament so supported the proposal for Union in 1799.

John Ormsby VANDELEUR (c. 1766–1828) of Kilrush, co. Clare.
Commissioner of customs for Ireland 1799–1801, 1809–10, 1814–22.

Richard Colley (Marquess) WELLESLEY (1760–1842).
1797–1805 governor general of India. 1820–8 lord lieutenant of Ireland. He was in favour of removing the disabilities of Catholics and resigned when Wellington (his brother) became prime minister pledged to the Protestant Ascendancy. from 1832–4 again lord lieutenant of Ireland.

William WELLESLEY-POLE (1763–1845).
Chief secretary for Ireland 1809–12; created Baron Maryborough in UK in 1821; succeeded as third earl of Mornington in peerage of Ireland in 1842. He was Perceval's chief supporter in his resistance to the concession of the Catholic claims, but in May 1812 he formally acquiesced in his brother's (Marquess Wellesley) more liberal views on the Catholic question.

Arthur (Wellesley) duke of WELLINGTON (1769–1852).
Chief secretary for Ireland 1807–9. Commander-in-chief of the army 1809–27. Prime minister 1828–30, Nov.–Dec. 1834. Foreign secretary Dec. 1834–April 1835. 1842 reappointed commander-in-chief by patent for life.

WILLIAM IV (1765–1837).
In 1779 he joined the navy. In 1789 he was created Earl of Munster and Duke of Clarence and St Andrew's. In 1811 he became admiral of the fleet, in 1827 lord high admiral. In 1830 he succeeded as William IV.

Mary WOLLSTONECRAFT (1759–1797).
Writer and feminist. Married William Godwin.

Alexander WOOD.
Irish journalist for the *Traveller* in London.

Sir Matthew WOOD (1768–1843).
In 1807 he became alderman of the ward of Cripplegate Without and in 1809 was appointed sheriff of London and Middlesex. Lord mayor 1815–17. 1817–43 MP for city of London. A consistent radical and

supporter of all the whig ministries. He was one of the chief friends and advisers of Queen Caroline.

Stephen WOULFE (1787–1840).
1830 crown counsel for Munster; May 1835 third serjeant; 1835–8 MP for Cashel; 1836 solicitor general for Ireland; 1837 attorney general for Ireland; 1838 chief baron of Irish exchequer, first Catholic so appointed.

Sir Thomas WYSE (1791–1862).
Chairman of the co. Waterford election committee in 1826. In 1829 he recommended dissolution of the Catholic Association and published *A Historical Sketch of the Catholic Association*. At the 1830 election he withdrew from co. Waterford in favour of O'Connell but he was elected for co. Tipperary. He retired from Tipperary in 1832 and was MP for Waterford city from 1835 to 1847. Lord of the treasury 1839–41. He favoured a subordinate parliament for Ireland but declined to join the Repeal Association. In 1847 he was defeated at Waterford because of Young Ireland opposition. 1846–9 Secretary for board of control for India. 1849 British minister at Athens.

Frederick Augustus, duke of YORK and Albany (1763–1827).
Second son of George III and close companion of George IV.

Apart from using such conventional sources as the *Dictionary of National Biography*, the *Handbook of British Chronology* and *The Complete Peerage of England, Scotland, Ireland, Great Britain and the United Kingdom* (ed. Hon. Vicary Gibbs, London, 1910), I have drawn largely on the annotations in M. R. O'Connell, ed., *Correspondence,* as well as those in Macintyre, *The Liberator*, and *Parliamentary Results in Ireland, 1801–1922* (ed. B. M. Walker, Dublin, 1978), in compiling these Notes.

# Index

Details of O'Connell's relationships are indexed under the names of the people involved: e.g. his relationship with his uncle, Hunting Cap, is indexed under O'Connell, Maurice (Hunting Cap).
Noblemen appear under their titles.
Titles of books are listed under the name of the author.
The method of alphabetical arrangement is letter-by-letter.
Sub-headings are arranged in chronological order when possible.

INDEX